Contents

Acknowledgements

Thanks must go to:The Worshipful Company of London Goldsmiths for the Travel Fellowship; Karl and Doris for advice, tent and riffle-pan; Bill Anderson of Butte County, founding editor of *California Territorial Quarterly,* for the Macnamara challenge and a friendship. The late R.R. Miller, Emeritus Professor, UC at Hayward, the late 7th Marquess and the present 8th Marquess of Hertford, Admiral Seymour's descendants, encouraged me. HE The Mexican Ambassador in London, and Marcella of his staff supported my first narrative, and Carlos Enrique Abreu and Erendira Penez of Archivo General de Mexico found the Macnamara dossier for me. Martin Roberts and fellow teachers put up with my Sierra tales. Dan Fox 'polished' my maps.

So many archivists contributed: Rachel Naughton of the Goold Centre, Melbourne; staff at Honolulu archdiocese, Hawaii State Archive, Bishop Museum, and Bronwen Solyom of Manoa Library, University of Hawaii. Patrick Connors SJ trawled Georgetown cathedral crypt between stints upriver in Macnamara's wake. The Archivist of All Souls College, Oxford was helpful; thanks to Oxford's Dominicans for use of their library. Jesuit archivists helped in London, New York and Fordham, Franciscans at Santa Bárbara and Les Péres Picpus in Rome. Mark Price, Manager at Ragley Hall arranged new illustrations and Paul Maher of the Gardai Archive, Dublin, invoked common sense! *Coordinardora* Emma de Ramon Acevedo and Anna Bravo Jura ('head buried in papers like an ostrich') of the Chilean National Archive, Adriana Luna-Fabritius, of Mexican Visual History website, were key helpers. Amanda Martin of the Scillies Museum and Tresco Figureheads, Richard Hunter of *Figurehead.com*, Andy Peters, figurehead carver at Waterperry for their interest, and Jim and Wendy Reilly for literature on *Palinurus* figurehead: Macnamara crossed much water. Bodleian staff, Oxford University, particularly Jane and Johanna at Vere Harmsworth US Library and Joanne Edwards, Latin American specialist Warwickshire Record Office, Warwick, offered a warm welcome on cold days. Helen Sims, IBM Librarian, Hursley, UK, helped access all William Parrott's 1845 messages. Maria Orchard, our kind neighbour, helped with Spanish correspondence and Greg Harkin, of All Hallows archive, found valuable material. The Archbishop of Mexico allowed publication of his predecessor's portrait.

Thanks go to The Bancroft and Huntington Libraries in California, UT at Austin Latin American Collection, and in London, to the Royal Horticultural Society, Royal Geographical Society, the London Geological Society, National Archive, British Library, British Newspaper Library and National Maritime Museum; to staff of the city public libraries in Oxford, Monterey and Los Angeles; in Ireland to priests of Killaloe diocese, the Presentation Order Archivist; the late Hugh Fenning OP, Dr Liam Chambers, Edward Whelan of Limerick Archive, Michael McMahon of Corofin, and especially Peter Beirne of Ennis Archive. Dr Ciarán O Murchadha kindly read my slant on Irish events in his busy schedule. I am also indebted to Kerby Miller, Curators' Professor of History at the University of Missouri-Columbia, for his advice and accompanying comment.

The late Michael Costeloe shared a life's research and new leads. Roy Foster, Oxford Carroll Professor of Irish History, believed 'Macnamara deserves to be taken seriously.' Macnamara's will vanished, but Joseph Murphy of Limerick still showed a solicitor's interest. New Royal Navy diaries and US naval papers have been used here but no archive survives the Bondholders, Barron and Forbes Company or ruling Cabinets in Mexico, Washington and London, only fragments. 'Macnamara' and 'MacKintosh' are spelled here as they signed themselves. Glen, my wife, has put up with Macnamara and Seymour for fifteen years, and with me for forty. I thank her for that and so much more.

List of Abbreviations

CHSQ & CHQ: *California Historical Society Quarterly* (now *California History*)

CO: Colonial Office (London)

CTQ: *California Territorial Quarterly*, B & P Anderson, Paradise, Butte Co., CA

FO: Foreign Office (London)

HBMG: Her Britannic Majesty's Government (now HMG)

HBMS: Her Britannic Majesty's Ship (now HMS)

ILN: *Illustrated London News*

LHS/RHS: London Horticultural Society (now Royal Horticultural Society)

NMM: National Maritime Museum (London)

ODNB: *Oxford Dictionary of National Biography* (new online edition, ongoing from 2004)

RGS: Royal Geographical Society (London)

RN: Royal Navy

SCHSQ & SCQ: *The Quarterly:Southern California Historical Society* is (now)*Southern California Quarterly*

TNA: The National Archive (London) (formerly PRO (Public Record Office))

UP: University Press

USM & USN:US Marine and US Navy

USS: US Ship

WRO: Warwickshire Record Office, Warwick, UK, repository of the Seymour Papers

List of Plates

1. Mid-morning, 7 July 1846, (L-R) USS *Cyane*, flagship *Savannah* and *Levant* salute US flag raised at Monterey. In Los Angeles, Macnamara was being awarded his land; at sea Admiral Seymour was becalmed, heading for Monterey. *W.A Coulter, 1902. Monterey Public Library, California History Room Archives.*

2. £600,000 in Californian gold and Mexican *pesos* entering the Bank of England, 1849, 'securely transported' by HMS Calypso for British merchants to avoid Mexican dues. Official smuggling damaged Royal Navy discipline and Mexico's ability to repay debt. *Illustrated London News, 20 September 1849, Oxford City Public Library.*

3. Eighteenth century Royal Arms of Ireland over the door of the Irish College, with the tricolour of the modern Irish Republic. The former college is now the Irish Cultural Centre, Paris. *Author*

4. Bishop John Hynes O.P., Apostolic Administrator, British Guiana, 1843-6, Apostolic Vicar, 1846–56. *M. Gardignani, Rome, 1860. Melbourne Diocese Historical Commission.*

5. Fort Ross[iya], California. A colony around Bodega Bay claimed the area as Tsarist Russian territory in 1812. President Monroe worried about a Russian base in North America. Russia abandoned it in 1842. *Author.*

6. Plaza Mayor, Mexico City. The Archbishop's former palace lies near the top of the side street behind the parked bus between his Cathedral (L) and Presidential Palace (R). *Dan Fox.*

7. Texas Legation, London, 1842-5, down 'No 3' passage, entrance in side of wine shop. The outstanding wine account was settled with the shop by Texas patriots in 1995. Ashbel Smith, ambassador, and Luis Cuevas, former Mexican ambassador, failed to reconcile

Texas and Mexico. An independent California would have had a London embassy too. *Author.*

8. Posada y Garduno, Archbishop of Mexico, 1840–46, licensed Macnamara to preach in English and French in Mexico and Alta California. He supported his Project. *Cardinal Rivera Cerrera, Archbishop of Mexico, and Visual Library, E.U.I., Mexico History.*

9. HMS *Collingwood,* 80 guns, flagship RN Pacific Station under Admiral Seymour, 1844-48.
Illustrated London News, 22 March 1845, Oxford City Public Library.

10. Admiral Sir George Francis Seymour, RN, Pacific Station 1844–48, with HMS *Collingwood* in background. *F. Lucas, 1852. Marquess of Hertford, Ragley Hall.*

11. Wardroom table, HMS *Collingwood* used by Macnamara, Frémont, Somerville, Walpole, Kit Carson, Hertweg, Seymour, consuls and merchants. Side-stays held it in floor hooks in heavy weather. *Marquess of Hertford, Ragley Hall.*

12. Figurehead of former HMT *Palinurus,* wrecked off Scilly Isles while making for London from British Guiana, 1848. Under Navy requisition, it conveyed Macnamara from Honolulu to Mexico in 1846. *Scilly and Tresco Museum: Amanda Martin, Curator Isles of Scilly Museum.*

13. Tullig, an 'unhoused' (evicted) village, near Macnamara's first parish of Kilkee-Killard. Landlords demolished 20% of Clare peninsula inhabitants' homes. *Illustrated London News, 15 December, 1849, Courtesy Oxford City Public Library.*

14. Chilean government agreement to Macnamara's Osorno colony, registered [no date] October 1848. *Archivo Nacional de Chile.*

15. Sluicing for gold on Gold Mines River, Co. Wicklow. Over 800 lbs of gold was found 1796-1802. *Aquatint, J. Bluck after T.S. Roberts 1804. Reproduced by Permission of The Geological Society of London.*

16. Nineteenth century Irish settler graveyard, Great Central Valley, California, *Mike Hornick, Salinas.*

17. John Charles Frémont, c. 1857, *Brooklyn Museum.*

Maps

IRELAND
(From 1801 – 1922, part of
United Kingdom of Great Britain and Ireland)

A. Ireland, 1801-1922, part of the United Kingdom of
Great Britain and Ireland. *Dan Fox*

BRITISH GUIANA, 1841

B. British Guiana 1841. *Dan Fox*

MEXICO AND TEXAS, 1845

C. Mexico and Texas
1836-45. *Dan Fox*

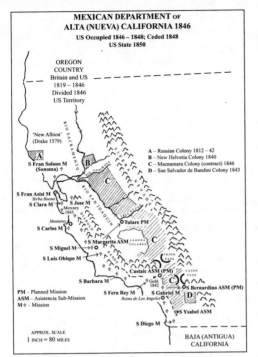

MEXICAN DEPARTMENT OF ALTA (NUEVA) CALIFORNIA 1846
US Occupied 1846 – 1848; Ceded 1848
US State 1850

OREGON COUNTRY
Britain and US
1819 – 1846
Divided 1846
US Territory

'New Albion'
(Drake 1579)

S Fran Solano M (Sonoma)

A – Russian Colony 1812 – 42
B – New Helvetia Colony 1840
C – Macnamara Colony (contract) 1846
D – San Salvador de Bandini Colony 1843

S Fran Asisi M
Yerba Buena
S Clara M
S Jose M
Mercury 1845
Monterey
S Carlos M
Tulare PM
S Margarita ASM
LAGUNA TULARES
S Miguel M
S Luis Obispo M
TEJON PASS
Castaic ASM (PM)
CAJON PASS
Gold 1842
S Barbara M
S Fern Rey M
S Gabriel M
S Bernardino ASM (PM)
Reina de Los Angeles

PM – Planned Mission
ASM – Asistencia Sub-Mission
M – Mission

S Ysabel ASM

S Diego M

APPROX. SCALE
1 INCH = 80 MILES

BAJA (ANTIGUA) CALIFORNIA

D. Mexican Department of Alta (Nueva) California 1846, US-occupied 1846–48, ceded to the US 1848 and a US State in 1850. *Dan Fox*

PERU
BOLIVIA
PACIFIC OCEAN
PARAGUAY

Arica
Valdivia
Corral
15 M
25 KM
Coquimbo
Trumao
La Union
Valparaiso
SANTIAGO
Osorno
Concepcion
Macnamara's Irish Grant
COLONISING ZONE 1845
Valdivia
Osorno
Ancud
Chiloe Island
ARGENTINA
Ancud
Chiloe Island
ATLANTIC OCEAN

CHILE, 1848

F. Chile 1848. *Dan Fox*

REINA DE LOS ANGELES CENTRE, 1846

Reina de Los Angeles
Church
N

CALLE PRINCIPAL

Carillo
Moreno Botello

Gov's HQ
'el Palacio' Stearns
PLAZA
Pico

Coronel
Olvera

'el Palacio' Stearns
Governor's HQ

CALLE PRINCIPAL

E. Reina de Los Angeles, California Departmental Capital, 1846. *Dan Fox*

Maps   xi

Introduction

That Queen Victoria's subjects, let alone her government, ever contemplated 'British California' surprises most people. Sir Francis Drake claimed it as 'New Albion' for Queen Elizabeth I in 1579, but it may as well have been the dark side of the moon. She kept it a state secret lest Spain be upset. 'New Albion' was still on Royal Navy charts in 1846 and Drake's Bay is a magnet for British visitors to California. In 1769, Spain sided with American colonists in their fight for independence, but had to send soldiers, missioners and settlers to Alta California, fearing Britain would invade. It was Spain's first and only serious display of interest in its northern wasteland.

I dipped in and out of the valleys of the Sierra Nevada in 1995, between Mariposa and The Cascades, with tent and gold pan, in a banger from *Rent-a-Relic*, and with a field mouse family in my glove locker. My field research was the Irish goldminer and patterns of immigration. The Worshipful Company of Goldsmiths gave me the opportunity and Bill Anderson, founder of *California Territorial Quarterly* in Butte County, offered me the challenge: 'Macnamara is a British and Irish story. The evidence *must* be over there, because it's not here!'[1]

In early summer 1845, the British ambassador in Mexico informed London that Eugene Macnamara, a recently arrived Irish priest, wanted to bring Irish settlers to the empty Mexican department of Alta California. The Irish were British subjects and the British embassy in Mexico was an Irish enclave. In August, the London *Times* reported this 'effective aid to British policy', but did not name Macnamara. *The Times* was read by the US ambassador, and usually reached Washington about three weeks after publication. Several Irish provincial newspapers carried the story. President Polk's new confidential agent in Mexico City also confirmed it personally. Ten weeks of secret, intense activity followed his report, all centred on the British threat to colonise California. In December, the President issued a public ultimatum against new European settlement anywhere in North America; privately he confirmed that he meant California. In May 1846, a state of war with Mexico was declared to have been created by Mexico and the US took Alta California as its first prize of war, to pre-empt Britain.[2]

Publicly, British politicians disclaimed interest in California. Privately they played with temptation, sending ambiguous signals to Mexico, to British individuals, institutions and their own agents and bailiffs on the ground, the ambassador, the admiral of the Pacific Station and several consuls. In 1837, British private holders of Mexican Loan Bonds were offered a 50 per cent discount on the purchase of 1.25 million Mexican frontier acres, including 250,000 in Alta California, unspecified but exclusively for colonising. Land purchase would help offset Mexico's impossible mounting debt. Admiralty Lords also wanted San Francisco Bay as a naval base for the Pacific, as Australia and New Zealand were being colonised; merchants in Britain and the US wanted it as terminal for the China trade. Britain had taken Hong Kong in 1841 as its China terminal and 'Port Francisco' would be the perfect complement. British merchants in Mexico already traded mercury from China; China had adopted the Spanish, then the Mexican *peso*, as the early 'trade dollar'; Cantonese business partners were known as *compradores*. Washington claimed a mystical US destiny to expand territory, and had been offering to buy the ports of Alta California (and more) since 1835. California gold was publicised in London and Washington in 1843, and significant mercury was signalled in 1845. Mexican and *californio* leaders wanted Britain to purchase, settle and protect Alta California from the US, but the department was isolated by distance and time-lapse communication.

Macnamara travelled half the globe, at least 30,000 miles, by sail, saddle and occasionally steam. He left clues as overlanders left wagon scours on Sierra passes. He was granted land for two colonies in the extremes of hispanic America, one in 'Hell with Blankets' Central Valley, Alta California; the second in the temperate rainforest of Valdivia Province, Chile. Both regions were usurped Indian homelands and old Spanish mission territory. The Royal Navy carried Macnamara, the *californio* Governor gave him 20,000 square miles, Mexico offered warships to ferry his settlers, and Chile confirmed to him a further 100 square miles.

THE DOSSIERS

His files have their own story. I retrieved the dossier *El Proyecto Macnamara* from the Mexican National Archive in 1997.[3] Its contents help authenticate a second file, confiscated by US soldiers from the California Governor in 1846, then published by the Senate Military Affairs Committee in 1848 to 'prove' British conspiracy. The originals can no longer be located.

Macnamara had a third file, his own, on which Mexican Supreme Congress based its final approval in 1847, acknowledging it held his contract copies only, and that the originals were in enemy hands. In 1852, Macnamara's copies, title deeds to land 'in Mexico and elsewhere', were found among his effects in Paris. They too have disappeared.

The London *Times* reported nothing about Macnamara after 1845. The Catholic weekly, *The Tablet*, lost him in 1844, after chronicling his misadventures in British Guiana. An anonymous, malicious letter to Archdeacon Hamilton of Dublin in 1845 claimed he had 'apostasised', a form of ecclesiastical self-erasure. Later, nineteenth-century Irish immigrants to the US dismissed his story as malicious fiction. Mexico's last, faint hope of saving California from the US was garbled into a morality tale of British bungling and conspiracy. Historians, to use USN Chaplain Colton's metaphor, 'made the most of the blubber and the bones' of California history, but never unravelled the Macnamara story.

THE COORDINATES

In 1886, Hubert H. Bancroft, the iconic historian of California, accepted that Macnamara, a 'patriotic dreamer', did visit California, but Bancroft suspended further judgement as he had no access to British archives. He was sure that Macnamara had been used as a 'bugbear' (bogeyman, alibi, smokescreen) by US expansionists, but despite his expertise, he did not know that a Mexican colony contract was not the same as a private personal land grant, which was limited to eleven square leagues. He concluded that the Governor's 'grant' of 3000 square leagues was *ultra vires* and therefore fraudulent. He did not know that a Governor could 'convey' unlimited land for colonising, as long as he submitted it to the approval of Supreme Congress in Mexico. As Bancroft wrote, Macnamara was suddenly, surprisingly and generously eulogised by John 'Pathfinder' Frémont, his self-proclaimed nemesis of 1846.[4]

In 1967, Mary Karam, a scholarly nun, traced Macnamara to Killaloe diocese, County Clare, western Ireland, in the years 1837-41.[5] Ignatius Murphy, Vicar General and historian of Killaloe, added that the curate had been suspended for misconduct and had 'volunteered' for the mission in Guiana, Britain's sole south American colony.[6]

The British Guiana mission suffered a stormy schism. Macnamara went to Rome in protest, Pope Gregory XVI deposed his bishop, and later, Pope Pius IX sent in Jesuits 'to grub out the weeds'. A 'Secret Journal' of events in Macnamara's time was withheld from Jesuit novices. The Pope admitted his shame, and his church won the respect of the Guiana colony for its response to the scandal.

I searched the British archives (and many more) closed to Bancroft. The personal papers of Admiral Sir George Seymour, British Pacific Station, allegedly Macnamara's co-conspirator, survive intact. He carried Macnamara as a stranded British subject, enabling the priest to complete the project. Contrary winds prevented Seymour from reaching Monterey before the US Navy occupied it. He could not raise Britain's flag nor 'make the bite' he had wished.[7]

No known portrait exists of Eugene ('Owen') Macnamara, who was thirty-one years old when he arrived in Mexico City in 1844. His character remains shadowy. Admiral Seymour judged him 'intelligent and straightforward'. US Consul Larkin told President Polk of his 'very good appearance' and 'citizen [non-clerical] clothes'. Lt Somerville, *Collingwood*'s Acting Commander, found his fellow Irishman a boon travelling companion, while Nathan Proctor, Seymour's Protestant Irish chaplain, appreciated Macnamara's 'clever and pleasant' company, if not his politics or his church.

Macnamara was a maverick in the Texas sense, the unbranded, unclaimed steer in mid-herd. To be expelled from college and to be suspended three times by three bishops in three years was at very least 'misunderstanding' on a grand scale. He travelled half the globe and routinely bounced back after adversity. Uniquely, he was accused of being Protestant Britain's Jesuit Papal agent. He impressed Rome, the Archbishop of Mexico, the admiral veteran of Trafalgar, naval officers of his own age, *californio* officials, and British and US diplomats. In the end he secured his land and presumably some sense of purpose with it.

LAST 'EXEAT'

New evidence accumulated after my first published version of the Macnamara story in 1999. The late Professor Michael Costeloe of Bristol University sent fresh leads. (I understood the accolade 'generous with his scholarship' in *The Times* obituary after his death in August 2011). Many other leads came my way, from Michael, from naval papers, institutions I had overlooked, and digitised archives and newspaper collections of every kind, unimaginable in the 1990s. *The Tablet* has the most efficient online archival access I have encountered. When Macnamara died in 1852, his colonists were due in US California, in Chilean Valdivia, and he had suddenly become eligible to submit his Mexican contract to be judged by a new US Land Commission.

Professor Costeloe's published work on British Mexican bondholders and on Britain's commercial grip on Mexico has now bridged a gap in understanding the Mexican debt and discounted land offer to bondholders in lieu of cash. Newspapers, the US Senate, the British House of Commons called it 'sale or mortgage of California by secret treaty', as if between governments, as if the land could somehow be forfeit were Mexico to default on cash payments, and as if the land offered was exclusive to Alta California. It was never a security, but an offer to repay in kind, one which was never taken up.

The bondholders were constant background noise to Project Macnamara. The 1837 land deal stimulated British interest in colonising California to a peak: it was feasible and tempting. Macnamara was also close to the bondholders' agent in Mexico, a powerful player.

The unfathomable British game of cricket was played in nineteenth-century Ireland, in schools, seminaries and military compounds. Mexico City saw an expatriate cricket club (the MCC) founded in 1827, which even US ambassador Poinsett joined to socialise and glean intelligence. Members spent Sunday morning in civilised company, while devout wives attended church. Admiral Seymour's men played cricket in the cool of the evening on Mexican beaches and international Test Cricket matches still electrify Guyana politics. The game offers Olympian metaphors for life, where 'success' is not about 'winning', but 'playing the game', even 'losing grandly'. John Frémont, Macnamara's and Britain's self-styled opponent, and no cricketer, saluted Macnamara's failure and 'a mind which had conceived a project so far reaching, [facing] overthrow in the moment of complete success'.[8]

ANOTHER AGE, ANOTHER LANGUAGE

A church exeat was a bishop's permit (or order) for a priest to leave his diocese: 'let him exit'. A nation's representative was (and is) a 'Minister (Plenipotentiary)', but 'ambassador' is employed here; 'Legation' interchanges with 'Embassy'. Alta California was occupied by the US in 1846, and became a US State in 1850. Baja (Lower) California remains Mexican. Monterrey is near the Gulf of Mexico; Monterey is in Alta California. Mercury and quicksilver are classical and medieval terms for the liquid metal we played with as children in the dentist's waiting room, before Health and Safety found out.

Californio describes 7000 mainly Mexican and Indo-hispanic settlers in Alta California; alongside them lived perhaps 800 *anglos* and around 20,000 coastal Indians, former tenants of the dissolved missions; 100,000 Indians lived in the eastern Central Valley. I have adopted David J. Weber's population estimates.[9] In Texas, the majority of the 140,000 settlers in 1845 were *anglos*. *Tejanos*, fewer in proportion than *californios*, defended The Alamo and one became first Vice-President of the Texas Republic. *Texan* superseded *Texian* after US Statehood.

Los Angeles, '[City of the Queen of] the Angels', was a *pueblo* founded from San Gabriel Mission eight miles away. It was a *ciudad* (city) like Monterey, as it had been capital *pueblo*, 1836 and 1845–46. Breathtakingly styled *El Pueblo de Nuestra Senora La Reina de Los Angeles de Porziuncula* from the early name of its river and for its church, it had about 1500 inhabitants in 1845. Its contemporary abbreviation, *Reina de Los Angeles*, is used here to remind of another era. Catholic angels always played service roles, never leading parts.

In Macnamara's day, rival Christian denominations enjoyed their folk-memories like comfort rags, each confident of its own monopoly of truth, yet in Britain, Ireland and on frontier missions they could also be – indeed had to be – reasonable neighbours. Mixed-faith marriage and education were part of Irish life in the eighteenth and early nineteenth century, although statistically, opportunities for both were limited, and after 1850 both were increasingly condemned. Curate Macnamara's first parish priests worked routinely with Protestant clergy and continued to do so during the Famine. Friar Mathew, the temperance crusader who recruited Macnamara, administered the Pledge to Protestant ministers and was voted Floor Privilege by the US Senate, but was shunned by some Irish bishops for collaborating with Protestants. In the heat of the British Guiana schism, Bishop Hynes stayed at an Anglican mission while his parishioners recaptured his church in town. 'What wonder,' he reflected, 'that we Catholics are so disrespected by Protestants.'

The nineteenth-century Irish were British subjects. In 1801, after a failed rebellion, the ancient Kingdom of Ireland lost its Dublin Parliament to Westminster. However inadequate, it had at least been Irish and had initiated its own reform. 'Home Rule', or 'Repeal' of this forced Union, became an Irish aspiration for 120 years. In 1922 Ireland gained virtual independence as Free State *Eire*, but six of the nine Ulster Province counties remained in the UK, 'Partitioned' as the UK Province of Northern Ireland. The present Irish Republic was declared by Dublin in 1948. Macnamara's ethnic Irish were fellow-subjects with the ethnic English, Welsh and Scots, but Ireland was 80 per cent Catholic. Latin American republics, whose laws tolerated only Catholic worship in public, preferred Victoria's Irish as settlers whom they had long known as mercenaries, refugees and exiles.

Mexico held more territory in North America than the other two landlords, Britain and the US. Former landlords, France and Spain, evicted or bought out, watched closely. The Republic of Mexico's Departments (formerly States until 1836, except The Californias which had been 'Territories') stretched from Yucatán to the Oregon Country frontier, and from former French Louisiana (New France) to the Pacific, embracing today's Texas, New Mexico, Utah, Nevada and both Californias. It held this poison chalice legacy for just twenty-five years. The Tsar of Russia planted a trading colony in Spanish Alta California around 1812 as Russia spread south, but it did not expand inland and was forced to evacuate in 1842 due to declining trade. Texas proclaimed independence in 1836. British North America, formerly part of 'New France', became the nucleus of 'the Canadas' and Oregon Country, shared by the US and Britain, was divided in 1846 to create the present northwestern US-Canadian border states.

The United States of The North, as Mexico called the US, stretched not 'from Sea to shining Sea', but west only to The Rockies. It bought much of New France (Louisiana and more) from Napoleon; it bid to buy Alta California from Mexico on several occasions between 1835 to 1847, then took it; it bid Spain unsuccessfully for Cuba, but bought Alaska from Russia. Texas ploughed its republican furrow for nine years before joining its 'sister republic' in 1845.

Oregon Country was not colonised by Britain, but left to the rule of Hudson's Bay Company after 1818, which excluded all colonising. US settlers began to head there in the 'Great Migration' of the 1830s, and finally asked Washington for US 'Territory' status. A few British colonists were introduced by HBC, but too late. 'Not worth a barren Scottish acre' Captain John Gordon, RN, rated it, but in 1846 the US gave a year's notice to end the 1818 treaty. After twelve months of posturing, a frontier was agreed: it wasn't worth a war. Alta California, however, was.

Between losing Texas in 1836 and its own defeat in 1848, Mexico lost 1.3 million square miles or some 55 per cent of its land; US territory expanded by a third. Mexico fought a US army of over 100,000, but US domestic feeling was strong against 'Mr Polk's War'. In defeat, Mexico was relieved of a burdensome frontier and even before peace was concluded in 1848, *El Siglo IX* asked, on 4 April, for a clean start – education, policing, toleration and immigrants, preferably German or Irish.

The journey overland from Mexico to California could take a month, on trails vulnerable to Indian attack; to sail from the eastern US to California took two months, and to Oregon Country another month. Newspapers and mail from Britain to the US east coast and to Mexico took about three weeks. The delay in communication would shape events.

The churches of the California missions have been restored, but like sixteenth-century British and Irish monasteries, the missions themselves were dissolved and their assets sold to enrich others. By the end, morale was low. Macnamara met the last friars, numerically and spiritually in decline. Mission success and failure are not the subject of this book, but they feature. A Jesuit missioner in Guyana reminded me that mission realities are grey, not black and white. Despite papal and Spanish demands for respect, the mission Indians were abused as well as protected. Naval officers on the Pacific noted that Protestant missioners preoccupied with hula dancing were equally upset by the European waltz. Education, labour and religion in Europe employed coercion and missionaries exported it, yet the last California missioners banned corporal punishment 160 years before British schools ended it; California mission Indians were studying in Europe when young Macnamara was sent to Paris. US and British naval officers in 1846, generally churchgoers, expressed variously concern and admiration for missioners across the denominational divides. Anglican Governor Light, Pope Pius IX and Methodist-cum-Presbyterian President Polk were better placed than modern readers are to discern washers of feet from those they called 'fanatics' and 'wolves' and they made such judgements forcefully.

The race to take Alta California took place seventy years and one war after US independence from Britain. American mistrust of imperial Britain ran deep, just as a folk memory of 'Yankee colonial trickery' persisted in Britain. Serving commanders on the Pacific in 1846, Seymour, Biddle and Sloat, former enemies ageing in uniform, remembered the burning of The President's Mansion and the capture of HMS *Macedonian*; London ambassador MacLane's grandfather had fought alongside Washington. History is threads, not slices. Ghosts haunted Anglo-American relations, as the Armada haunted the Pilgrim Fathers. A Royal Navy light frigate had Nelson's aura, greater than the sum of its twenty-six cannon. Seymour had served on HMS *Donegal* at the tail-end of Trafalgar at the age of sixteen, and in 1843 they cleared a London square for Nelson's statue to monitor France from a giant column. In spirited rivalry, France watched California and the Pacific islands. The atmosphere in the theatre was electric before Eugene Macnamara emerged onto the California stage in front of an international audience.

When California Indians discovered mercury, they called it 'white water which you cannot keep in your hand'. This story is mercurial and any clumsiness in its handling is mine.

John Fox
Oxford 2013

Chapter 1

Colonisers, Missioners, Traders and Cannon

Mexican Alta California fell to the US Navy on 7 July 1846. Of the two warring landlords of North America that day, Mexico had no flag to strike and the US did not fire an angry shot. The admiral acting for Britain, the third major landlord, arrived a week too late to make a difference. He had been becalmed, then met contrary winds. The US took Monterey, California's port of entry, described by a US officer as 'a miserable village'. Weeks before, the British and US commanders had commiserated about their landlords' failure to brief them.

At 10.20 a.m., 225 US marines and sailors landed below the Monterey Customs House.[1] A Navy captain proclaimed US rule in Spanish and English; arms were presented for the rising US flag, and 21-gun salutes roared out from two of the three US warships anchored in Monterey Bay. As the Commodore's ADC raised the flag, the halyard snagged, and a younger fellow-midshipman shinned up the pole to release it. Many of the landing force were back on their ships before 11.00 a.m. In 1842, at 15, the same Spanish-speaking ADC, assistant to the previous Commodore, had composed a similar proclamation and had raised the US flag on the same flagpole, after negotiations with the same elderly Mexican *capitán* of militia. Ashore, he discovered communications in Spanish showing

1

that his commander had overreached himself. The US flag was struck, the Mexican flag raised, saluted, and apologies were made for the international *gaffe*.

In 1846, there was no apology. By 11 a.m, US-controlled territory stretched from the Atlantic to the Pacific. Mexico lost its most neglected possession and many Americans believed that Britain had been prevented from taking it. Above Monterey, the *castillo* redoubt rebuilt in 1842 to deter a repeat attack had no cannon or powder, nor did the *presidio* billet Mexican soldiers. The militia *capitán*, pleading lack of authority, flag, munitions and men, left town early with a strong feeling of *déjà vu*. Monterey's sole tricolour had been taken north by the departmental *Comandante* with the sole cannon and a threadbare company to face down rebel US settlers (see Plate 1).

At the capital *Ciudad* Reina de Los Angeles, the Departmental Assembly approved *El Proyecto Macnamara* that morning; 13,500 square miles (the Governor made it 20,280 a week later) were conveyed to Eugene Macnamara, an Irish priest, to settle 10,000 British subjects from Ireland (the Governor made it 15,000). The Assemblymen rose, aware of the day's rising heat, but unaware that they had just lost Alta California altogether.

A hundred miles north of Monterey 50 US settlers had protested in mid-June against the *Comandante*, requisitioned his horses and raised a Star-and-Bear flag modelled on Texas and California Lone Star flags of 1836.[2] Offshore, US warships monitored Monterey and San Francisco Bays; inland, US army topographers put away survey instruments to become soldiers again supporting the settlers. Their officer, Lt John Frémont, was uniquely privy to the secret intentions of President and Cabinet over Alta California and since November 1845, a personal courier from the President had followed him to California with confidential instructions.

The telegraph was in its infancy and news still crawled. Fifty-four days after Monterey fell, word that the US held Alta California reached the President. He was 'indebted to the courtesy of the British Legations' in Mexico and Washington, for kindly informing him he had it.

THE PRIZE

Mexican Alta California was unsurveyed by its own landlord. US surveyor Frémont called it a 'shadowy land'. It returned a fiscal pittance to Mexico City, which returned nothing in exchange. Jasper O'Farrell from Wexford, its first and only surveyor, had yard-chained only 1450 square miles by 1846. Europeans saw just another wasteland left by Spain, a 'Mexican Siberia', distant and barely populated. It had arable valleys and indications of mineral wealth, but it had not been prospected. The mission friars heard Indian talk of gold before 1800, and significant gold was found near ex-mission San Fernando in 1842; samples went to the Foreign Secretary in London and the Secretary of State in Washington, the bulk to the US Mint.

Britain, Spain, France and the US sent consuls to Monterey, with no commercial justification on a coast trading in tallow and hides; Prussia monitored from Mexico City. They reported home on each other and on the intrigues of the *californios* whom they nudged towards independence. Most knew that one day America would take it, but consuls for Spain and Britain favoured a British protectorate, the French consul hoped loudly for French intervention and US consul Larkin was appointed President Polk's confidential agent there in 1845. Prussia fantasised. Hudson's Bay Company came from the Oregon Country looking for new beaver colonies and it was mooted that they or the East India Company might run Alta California as a commercial fiefdom.

The most notable mineral find of all was mercury ore (cinnabar) of notably high yield. Mercury was essential for extracting silver and gold by amalgamation. Silver was Mexico's great export, and its *peso* an international currency, from Nanking to London. Mercury allowed Mexico to meet Europe's need for silver and gold currency, which Europe lacked the mines to produce.

Much of western North America, former New Spain, was empty and undefined. Alta California was explored seriously by Spain only in 1769, when threatened by Russia and Britain. Fifty years later, Spain was expelled from all the Americas. Independent but bankrupt, Mexico inherited a neglected frontier and serious Indian liabilities in Texas, New Mexico and The Californias, which a Mexican population of seven million could not afford to defend or develop. *Pobladores*, settlers, *colonos*, immigrants were vital. In Mexico City liberal federalists and conservative centralists fought over whether to rule territories as Federated States (the Constitution 1823–36), or as centralised Departments (the Constitution 1836–46). Marginalised *californios* saw centralist *mexicanos* as a threat. North of Alta California lay cold Oregon Country; it was not worth a war. Britain and the US held it in common on a year's notice, which the US presented in 1846.

Mexico lost Texas when *anglo* colonists, Americans, Europeans, and a *tejano* minority, declared independence in 1836. A *tejano* settler from Yucatán signed the declaration as vice-President and Britain accredited a Texas Legation in London.[3] Coahuila, part of the Mexican *State* of Texas until 1836, was left behind in the *melée*, separated as a new Department; it declared itself 'Rio Grande Republic' in 1840. The ethnic gravity of *anglo* settlers – 20,000 in 1836, 140,000 in 1845 – drew Texas towards the US. Successive Mexican governments failed to swallow pride, cut losses and recognise Texan independence. They lacked the continuity for coherent policy. Lopez de Santa Anna, defeated and captured in the Texas independence war, was President eleven times and exiled three times. (Nine of ten Mexican presidents between 1835 and 1846 were ejected from office.)

In April 1845, Mexican troops were ordered north to the strip of territory between the Rios Nueces and Bravo (US Rio Grande), claimed by the US as Texas territory in Spanish times. A year later, Mexican soldiers crossed it to attack an American patrol similarly ordered there. In May President Polk declared not war, but 'that a state of war exists by act of Mexico'. He was accused at home, abroad and even by his own naval officers, of provoking 'Mr Polk's War', without consulting Congress. Mexico fought back, proud and poor, as war spilled into its homeland, but Polk was determined to have California. His confidential agent and the London *Times* reported from Mexico, August 1845, that a colony of British subjects from Ireland was being planned for Alta California; it galvanised Polk into ten weeks of secret activity. He allocated $40 million to buy Alta California, sent a secret envoy to Mexico, appointed more agents, and sent a confidential courier to California. His first Message to Congress in December was an ultimatum to Britain to stay away. Slow news – weeks from Mexico to Washington, months from the Pacific to London – shaped events. At Monterey, in July 1846, Commodore Sloat, USN Pacific Squadron commander, knew of the Nueces strip incident in April, but not of Polk's 'statement of war' in May, or of the compromise agreement with Britain over Oregon in June. A private express courier told Sloat enough in mid-May to send him hastening to California, where he felt war was inevitable.

Sloat learned that Captain Frémont had supported a local US settler uprising after the President's courier contacted him, presumably with instructions. One of Sloat's own ships had conveyed the courier to California. Frémont's attitude and even brutality towards *californios* and Indians disturbed rebels and US officers alike. Settler leaders claimed he had made more of their insurrection than they had intended. His role since 1842 had been to reconnoitre the West, still the property of another landlord, but coveted by the US. Frémont's father-in-law was Senator Thomas Benton, Democrat expansionist and Chairman of the Senate Military Affairs Committee which oversaw his expeditions.

The clash of landlords was dress-rehearsed in 1842. Like Commodore Sloat, USN Commodore Ap Catesby Jones believed the US was at war with Mexico and that a British admiral's flagship, HMS *Dublin*, was racing north to take Monterey, the then capital and port of entry. After a three-day reign, Jones retreated and visited Reina de Los Angeles where, after his apology to the Governor, a ball was held with characteristic Mexican *gusto* for celebration. The Governor, grateful for the rare spotlight on his Department, treated Jones as an honoured guest who had also clarified US policy.

Months later, an aristocratic British captain declared the Hawaiian (Sandwich) Islands British, to protect the private claims of a British consul and others. The US and France missed their moment and Captain Lord Paulet ruled Honolulu for four months before a British admiral arrived to apologise and strike the flag. In 1846, under the same standing order as Jones, to take the California ports in the event of war with Mexico, John Sloat's overreach paid off. The war he had predicted really had broken out, although orders arrived only after he left the Pacific theatre for home. The British Admiral really was heading for Monterey and a British coloniser was in Reina de Los Angeles securing land on the morning Sloat struck.

BRITISH DESIGNS ON ALTA CALIFORNIA

The US had grounds to be concerned about Alta California, always prey to the wildest rumour. British diplomats, traders and newspapers had pressed for a decade to colonise it; the French and Prussians had made noises. San Francisco Bay was its key facility: shelter for a fleet, a policing base for the Pacific, and a trade terminal one months' steam from China. In 1836 Britain and France offered to arbitrate between Mexico, the US and the new Texas Republic. Private British holders of Mexican bonds asked London for 'steps' and 'appropriations' to help them recover the money they had loaned Mexico in 1824 and 1825. US and British naval squadrons circled each other on the Pacific with friendly caution, but long memories. The Royal Navy played policeman worldwide, exercising a constable's traditional discretion about 'reasonable force' on a far-flung beat. It cleared pirates, arrested slavers, hunted smugglers and restored expelled missioners (regardless of religious denomination), while fathoming Pacific island politics. Bombarding a non-compliant port for commercial or retaliatory reasons was part of a policeman's day.

After Britain abolished slavery empire-wide in 1834, the Royal Navy claimed the right to 'visit' all (including US) vessels, to search for slave cargoes, while onshore, fugitive US slaves could find asylum in British North America (Canada). In 1838 a British squadron at Vera Cruz escorted British diplomats ashore to end a French blockade and bombardment damaging British commerce; it also forced Mexico to meet French claims in part. China ceded Hong Kong island to Britain as a naval and trading base when the Royal Navy re-imposed the British Indian opium trade. (The US also signed a trade agreement in 1844, but without securing any base on either side of the Pacific.) Off Nicaragua, in 1842, the British blockaded San Juan to enforce a repayment to Central American bondholders in London. In 1845 an Anglo-French flotilla forced La Plata river to help British merchants trade inland without paying Argentine Federation customs, and to protect settlers already there. (Admiral Seymour told Admiral Inglefield on La Plata how he envied him his clarity of mission.) In 1845, Captain Gordon, the British Foreign Secretary's brother, shelled Arica, (then in Peru) when it refused him water, destroying the British consul's roof in the process.

San Francisco Bay and Chiloé Island, Chile, were potential British bases, but Britain had key footholds elsewhere, like Gibraltar in Spain, Aden in Arabia and Hong Kong in China. In 1844 *californio* leaders asked Britain for the protection it had long afforded Corfu and the Ionian Isles. In 1846, Foreign Minister Lord Aberdeen threatened to send thirty capital ships to Admiral Seymour's Pacific Station to face down the US over Oregon, but with a peacetime Royal Navy pared to a quarter of its wartime strength, long-distance defeat was a distinct possibility. It was brinkmanship and brag, not threat.

General Paredes y Arrillago, Mexican dictator-President in 1846, was anti-American and set on installing a Mexican royal dynasty. He admired royal Britain, but suspected its cultural closeness to the US; France's 'citizen monarchy' was a hybrid, Spain was too recent a bad memory. British merchant-diplomats, mine engineers and speculators already ran the Mexican economy, and some of them financed Paredes. President Polk plotted to slip him $2 million to pay his soldiers, if it could be hidden from the US Congress. Polk needed stability in which to negotiate buying California. Instead, Paredes sent Eugene Macnamara to California to secure land.

In 1837, 1,250,000 non-specified acres in five northern Mexican departments were offered at discount to bondholding creditors in Britain for colonising – of these, 250,000 lay in Alta California. A raft of schemes followed, trumpeting the advantage of colonising Alta California, with Australia, New Zealand and China in mind. Nine years later, Parliament discussed California, but briefly, and when America and Mexico were already at war. British pride had been dented in 1812–14, an earlier landlord war. In 1846 Britain refused to be drawn into another loser's war, even for a Pacific port.

The Royal Navy patrolled the Mexican and Oregon coasts, as well as the Tahitian, Hawaiian and other islands. Dispersed from Russian Alaska to the Falkland Islands (colonised in 1840), Seymour's 350 guns on the Pacific Station seemed adequate for policing, but not for the annexing or defending of territory: 'England deceives herself by the consciousness of her naval superiority,' wrote US Navy Secretary Bancroft in August 1845. 'If Oregon were ceded today, England could not keep it … Her ships would be powerless. They could enter a harbour, but how could they occupy it?'[4] Seymour knew that better than Bancroft, but he had no instructions from London, could not rely on the captain of his only other major warship, and his only troops were shipboard marine detachments. He could not occupy the hinterland of a California port or defend Oregon.

Of Britain's vessels on Station in 1846 (the US had 330 guns in the region, while Mexico's entire navy totalled 63 guns), only two were capital battleships. The 50-gun HMS *America* was commanded by John Gordon, brother of Lord Aberdeen, Foreign Secretary. He conveyed Lt William Peel, the Prime Minister's son, on an intelligence mission to Oregon, 'his observations worth many pages of reports', Seymour believed. HMS

Collingwood, 80 guns, dominated everything afloat. Smaller vessels – frigates, sloops and a steamer – performed ostensibly non-political tasks like hydrography and exploration. Seymour, a veritable renaissance man, sent observations to Admiral Beaufort (of the Wind Scale) Captain Fitzroy (of HMS *Beagle* and Darwin), and to *Collingwood*'s architects at Deptford. The Royal Navy, like its masters, threatened a heavier punch than it could land, but it had spirit.

The 'brag' game between the US and Britain over Oregon Country could have tipped into war. Unexpectedly to the public, if not to their rulers, Britain agreed a compromise frontier at 49 degrees in June 1846. President Polk, worried about opposition at home and his war with Mexico, was as relieved as Britain to have avoided another front; both countries saved face and averted possible defeat. In the UK, Ireland slipped into famine.

Admiral Seymour had no recent orders from London about Oregon, let alone about California. Eugene Macnamara brought him instructions to land diplomats; they were a year old and useless to a proud admiral facing US hostilities. Orders to Commodore Sloat from the US Navy Secretary also went astray. Events outpaced communications and Seymour, in the absence of any alliance with Mexico, fell back on neutrality as his compass. He would defend Alta California only if it declared itself free of Mexico, just as had the Texas Republic. Unknown to Seymour, in December 1845 the British government put aside any thought of California, leaving him permanently off-side. Deck-fighter at 16 under Nelson, ever ready to 'make a bite', Seymour recognised he was too far from home to hold even an independent and willing Alta California for his ambivalent government. He was drawing a blank ticket, he complained, 'in a lottery of blanks'.

Rumour was potent in Alta California and shaped politics: it had the British vice-consul offering the Governor a Royal Navy landing party at Santa Bárbara during a General Council called to discuss independence. Governor Pío de Jesús Pico regularly confided in the vice-consul. HMS *Juno*'s landing Macnamara at Santa Bárbara days later gave the rumour credence. Mexico's land option for bondholders was also garbled everywhere into a 'British mortgage treaty on California'. *Californios* and Americans read conspiracy into every coincidence. Admiral Seymour was a wise diplomat, especially chosen for Pacific lotteries, but his transporting of Eugene Macnamara on four British naval vessels in seven months, was the great mistake of his tour. It 'proved' Britain's sinister intent.

ST PATRICK'S ON THE JUMNA

Eugene Macnamara rode a missionary wave following European migrations and empires. After the humiliating of church authority by the French Revolution, the prospect of newly discovered, unbaptised millions was re-invigorating. The resulting zeal also helped distract from concerns in society and in churches at home. Protestants and Catholics competed for souls and notched up spiritual 'results' in fields more receptive than Europe. Mission colleges sprouted in Paris, Rome allowed the Jesuits to re-group, Spanish and Portugese kings could no longer exclude other Europeans, and the Pope's writ now ran, in curbed form, in Latin America. Conversions and church attendance were simplistic but visible measures of 'success'; non-statistical success was less easily recorded, and often eclipsed by the misdeeds of soldiers, settlers and inevitably of bad missioners. Many sought common ground, to serve and learn in a dialogue; others came to purge difference. Some educated, protected from famine, defended against settlers and treated Indians and Polynesians humanely; others treated them poorly. Britain's church census of 1850 showed that while religion was still a social bond, only half the population attended church or chapel. Missioners reflected the culture which bred them and education, religion and labour in Europe had their dark sides.

Old Europe exported old quarrels, as early Spanish missioners brought to the Americas the fervour of domestic crusades against Jew and Muslim. Tahiti was bounced like a ball from Captain Cook and pioneering British Protestant missioners to French protection and Catholic missioners. USN Lt 'Paddy' Rowan criticised missioners for trying to 'cram religion down throats, with no preparation to receive it', and the obsession of some with perceived 'deviance', in dance or polygamy. Nineteenth-century communitarians, like Owen and Lancaster, founded schools and communities in Latin America free of religious influence. *El Mercurio de Valparaiso* reported on 19 December 1845, that the Bolivian consul in Chile had advised his government to recruit Irish colonists and their '*honrado y liberal*' clergy, especially Jesuits, and ignore Europe's prejudice, since the Jesuits had been the most credible missioners of all.

As Protestant and Catholic British, US and French missioners evangelised a 'third world' beyond the hispanic 'new world', Pope Gregory XVI (1831–46) looked to re-evangelise old Spanish America. Compensating for his predecessor, Leo XII, who in 1826 ordered Latin

America to submit again to Spain, he also made up for two hundred years in which the authority of Rome's missionary watchdog, The Office for Propaganda Fide, and the papal appointment of bishops had been banned in the colonial Americas.

In the 1830s young European priests and nuns volunteered for the missions in droves. Protestant ministers and lay missioners with families formed societies comparable to Catholic religious orders. Pope Pius IX told Macnamara's former bishop, John Hynes, in 1852, that the 'missionary migration spirit of modern nuns' turns them into *girandole* '[spinning fireworks]'; he also warned that the 'refuse of the clergy' was being sent to the West Indies with exeats given 'to bad priests to get rid of them, wolves to other missions'.

Britain's and France's empires and the expanding United States provided the new mission arenas. Of Britain's non-conforming churches, outside the established state church, the Methodists expanded their membership across the Atlantic until they were the largest denomination in the US. President Polk attended his wife's Presbyterian church, but was 'Methodist-inclined'. Baptists, Congregationalists and Presbyterians flourished, and looked to their respective countries' new territories. The London Missionary Society worked in the Pacific and Caribbean islands, and Guiana; American branches of the Presbyterian, Congregational, Methodist and Baptist churches followed US interests to Hawaii. Where Protestant and Catholic met in the islands or Oregon, their feuding was better recorded than their sharing. The Jesuit de Smet and a Methodist missioner made firm friends as they travelled Oregon Country together in the 1830s. US Protestant missioners in Hawaii protested, however clumsily, at the ruler's cruel treatment of rival Catholic missioners. 'Methodist' and 'Jesuit' insults exchanged between rival missioners (usually neither) were backhanded compliments; damning a rival's 'converts' as 'perverts' could co-exist with good manners, where frontiersmen needed community to survive. David Douglas and Thomas Coulter, Scots and Irish Protestants and botanists in Alta California in the 1830s, thought the Spanish missioners 'a most upright and honourable class of men'[5]

Pope Gregory created over seventy flexible mission zones (Apostolic Vicariates), an old device by which mission bishops (Apostolic Vicars) and priests (Apostolic Missioners) answered directly to Rome. Spanish missioners in the Americas were *misioneros Apostólicos*', as was Eugene

Macnamara in Guiana. Vicariates gave a temporary, neutral designation to politically disputed territories. They also allowed the Pope to evade the old Spanish and Portuguese right to appoint bishops which they still claimed in the new American republics. Slowly, Rome retrieved authority from Catholic kings of another era.

Sometimes Popes miscalculated. Gregory based the new diocese of Both (*Ambas*) Californias at San Diego in 1840, severing it from the Mexican diocese of Sonora, but its first and only bishop lived and died at Santa Bárbara. Pope Pius IX recognised the dividing of The Californias by peace treaty in 1848 through creating separate US and Mexican dioceses. The uncertain Texas Republic became a Vicariate in 1840. Oregon, shared by Britain and America for nearly thirty years, was a single Vicariate, but within weeks of the frontier agreement, Rome divided it into one British and two US dioceses. In 1840 Gregory gave Mexico City its first native Archbishop since independence, after its absentee Spanish incumbent died in self-imposed exile. The California missions were reduced by Mexican confiscation in 1834 to parish churches with gardens, their Spanish friars replaced by Mexican, the land sold to *californio* ranchers. Robbed and enfeebled, lacking diocesan priests, teachers and doctors, and the oldest mission no older than 65 years, the California missions disappeared before their prime.

Aware of colonial abuses, Pope Gregory demanded that slavery be opposed and the native-born ('aboriginal') be respected, yet the Spanish governor of Cuba refused to publish his condemnation of slavery and the Irish bishop of Charleston declared southern US 'domestic service' exempt. Spanish Imperial law protected Indians in theory, but cheap labour came with cheap land, and Madrid was far away. In later California, under Mexican 'liberation', 20,000 Indians were turned off their mission tenancies. The independence of the Americas from Spain and Portugal came at a cost, which the Indians paid.

Jesuit missioners in Baja California and Sonora, before their expulsion by Spain in 1767 and suppression by Rome, 'brought a high opinion of the Mexican Indian' – culturally barbarian, but not an amoral savage. It contrasted with the pessimism of some Catholic missioners and the Protestant Calvinist view that without Christ everyone was depraved. Coercion was commonplace in European religion and society, and its object was often 'original sin'. The 'saved', endowed with the grace of 'restraint', would help curb chaos and excess, particularly in matters of decorum and sexual relations. The ending of human sacrifice and infanticide were more easily recognisable achievements.

Education was a memorable Jesuit legacy to the Mapuche Indians on Chiloé island, Chile. Agriculture and new crops taught by the Jesuits in the Sonora desert ended annual famine and migration. Famously Paraguay Jesuit missioners defended the Indians against fellow colonials. California Franciscan talk of 'savages' came with spiritual and educational decline as Mexican friars replaced Spanish-born missioners in 1834. When Eugene Macnamara trained in Paris, two young Californian Indians from San Luis Rey Mission went to Spain and to Rome. The giant convent in Mexico City where Macnamara preached for a year housed a school for Indians. Had the missions not been killed off, and had California not been reduced by neglect and unrest, its short-lived church would have Indianised, as inevitably as its Spanish personnel Mexicanised.[6] Despite Rome's narrow restriction, notably in India and Japan, early missioners believed in respectful assimilation; the dusky Aztec Virgin of Guadalupe was Tonantzin, Mother of the Aztec gods, re-depicted by an Indian painter as Palestine Mary.

The line of twenty-one missions founded in Alta California, 1769–1823, followed the coast northwards from the twenty former Jesuit and nine Dominican missions already in Baja California. From San Diego of Alcalá to San Francisco of Solano, the California dedications are now dwarfed by the towns and cities which were once their *pueblos* and outposts. Spain intended them to secure the coast against foreign intruders, but never extended them east into Indian country, the San Joaquin [Central] Valley, where 'new souls to be saved' actually lived. In 1840, six years after the missions were dissolved, the new Californias diocese and President Herrera's promise to return mission funds signalled a tenuous revival, but more through foreign colonisers like Macnamara and their promised chaplains, than the familiar pattern.

Post-Reformation Catholic England, underground and furtive, was an early Apostolic Vicariate. By 1840, it was subdivided into eight. Of these, the London Vicariate covered the capital of Protestant Britain and its Empire in which Catholics won civil rights in 1829. To a church empire of new vicariates from The Cape to Calcutta, British Guiana was added in 1837. To straddle the Pacific islands, Pope Gregory created 'Oceanic Vicariates',

Occidental and Oriental, in which French missioners competed with US and British Protestants for the ears of island rulers.

Breaking with old 'entrenched traditional allegiances', like Spain's claim to church authority, the Pope regulated Catholic missions through the Office for the Propagation of The Faith (*Propaganda Fide*). An Association for The Propagation of The Faith (APF), with branches in Dublin and throughout Europe, disseminated funds, contacts and news, which kept missions in touch. The Austrian Hapsburgs, self-appointed Holy Roman Emperors – Napoleon abolished the originals – financed Vicariates. Missionary excitement ran so high that rumour spread to and from California in 1836 that Pope Gregory was to set an example by visiting Ireland.

Eugene Macnamara joined the mission trail from a Paris seminary packed with Irish recruits in a city where at least four major mission colleges opened from 1814. After serving on the 'home mission', he made a fresh start in the Vicariate of British Guiana.

Catholic Emancipation in 1829 restored to British (and Irish) Catholics most rights and freedoms lost after the Reformation. Liberated Irish clergy were freed to answer the Pope's call that 'British [catholic] subjects be missionaries within the British Imperial ambience'. Macnamara's clerical contemporaries were 'tough' and welcomed a challenge, although seminary confinement came to distance them from their roots. Priests, nuns and religious orders became Ireland's export to the English-speaking world, a 'transnational Irish spiritual empire' of vicariates and dioceses from Great Britain to Australia. Royal St Patrick's College, Maynooth, taking clerical and lay students, funded and inspected by the British government in exchange for an oath of loyalty, fittingly supplied priests to world missions where God's and Victoria's Kingdoms similarly overlapped.

Idealism and fervour however, sometimes outran sensitivity. The Italian Vicar Apostolic of Tibet and Hindustan, titular Bishop of biblical Bethsaida under Ottoman rule, wrote to Rome and Dublin from Agra in 1840 of the latest 'glory for religion', his plan to build 'a magnificent church opposite the famous Taj Mahal on the bank of the Jumna River'. He asked for Irish priests to make it happen. He defended his mission against local Protestant opposition with help from the commander of the King of Scind's army. In 1844 French priests arrived secretly at Lhasa to tell the

Dalai Lama, 'the object of our journey is to substitute our prayer[book] for yours in your *lamaseries*'. His knowing smile – 'fiendlike?' or 'most amiable?' – threw them, but they did remark on Buddhism's 'external resemblances to Catholicism'.

Macnamara's contracts for Celtic colonies under the Sierra Nevada and in Chilean Patagonia made more sense to a missionary Pope or local bishop than to a British government hoping for San Francisco Bay or Chiloé. Britain held Gibraltar and Hong Kong, but not hinterland Spain or China. Washington, too, wanted San Francisco Bay and, like London, knew of California's mineral wealth, but the Irishman's final contract for a colony on the Rio San Joaquin (he had requested coastal settlements), brought no obvious strategic advantage. Armchair bondholders in Britain, despite Mexico's land discounts, wanted short-term gains from silver mines, not long-term agricultural risks on hostile Indian terrain.[7]

FOOTSTEPS INTO LATIN AMERICA

European Protestants, the English, Scots and Dutch, were banned from settling or trading within the Spanish Empire. In the seventeenth century, with the French, they took much of the Caribbean by force or trespass. Prisoners, exiles, slaves and adventurers settled the islands: Monserrat was nicknamed 'The Emerald Isle', and Honduras and Belize beyond were settled unofficially. Up to 2800 Scots settlers sailed in convoy to Darien on the Isthmus of Panama, 1698–1700, to carve a trade corridor between Europe and the Far East across the isthmus of Spain's empire. Most died in the swamps and jungle, or at Spanish hands. 'New Caledonia' and 'New Edinburgh' were jungle fantasies.

Irish veterans of the Napoleonic war migrated as 'wild geese' to Latin America to fight Spain and raise new republics out of *Las Indias*. Previous generations of British and particularly Irish Catholic refugees from penal laws at home had long been welcome on Spanish territory, and had defended Spanish interests with Irish brigades and regiments. The Irish also understood the colonial desire in the Americas for independence and Irish mercenaries volunteered. Daniel O'Connell's son served with the Irish Legion under Bolivar, with whom O'Connell corresponded. Overthrowing Spain had ready parallels with overthrowing Britain, although Bolivar used force and O'Connell abhorred it. Bolivar's title, *El Libertador*, translated smoothly after his death into *Liberator*, O'Connell's accolade for freeing Catholics, helping to free slaves, and trying to free Ireland.

Bernardo O'Higgins, Supreme Director of Chile and son of an Irish-born Viceroy of Peru, pressed in 1825 for the Irish to colonise Mexican Alta California 'against Russians and North Americans, [their] first colony to be in San Francisco Bay'. He envisaged a colony chain, like the missions, lining the coast from Valparaiso to San Francisco Bay. Ireland's population was expanding on limited land; the new republics, including their sister republic 'The United States of The North', understood the Irish and wider European need for land and freedom. It complemented their own need for settlers to fill empty wastes. O'Higgins also asked General Sir John Doyle to bring Irish settlers to Chile.[8]

Most Irish emigrant ships, however, made for the US, where a million Irish landed between 1814 and 1845. In they had trickled, then flowed, ever since *Ark* and *Dove* landed Catholic and Protestant emigrants from England and Ireland together in Maryland, ten years after *Mayflower*. Latin America competed with the US to attract, but inherited Spanish law restricting religious practice did not help. Those Irish who came to California in and after the 1848/9 Gold Rush came largely from families which had already emigrated to the east coast or Canada. Admiral Seymour, returning to England from a private visit to New York in 1840, recorded in his shipboard diary Irish seasonal workers bringing home quantities of gold coin to their families.[9]

Paper investment in South America's legendary mineral wealth was one alternative to emigrating. During Spain's slow retreat from Latin-America, independence fighters, from Thomas Cochrane to Simon Bolivar, were much feted in London, the new financial centre of Europe. The lure of El Dorado was so strong that even a non-existent republic attracted investors. Between 1821 and 1825 Gregor Macgregor, a veteran of Wellington's army, launched a bond issue for fevered punters. He raised thousands of pounds on twenty-year bonds carrying 6 per cent interest, underwritten by gold, silver, salt and tobacco from his new settlement of Poyais on the Meskito Coast of Honduras and Nicaragua, an old, if questionable, British protectorate. All it needed was settlers. In 1822 hundreds sailed to Poyais, landing into nowhere, stranded on its jungle coastline. Utopia was rarely so literal. When news of the fraud came to London a year later, it did not deter speculators from investing in Gran

Colombia, Chile and Mexico – and, incredibly, in a second issue of bonds for Poyais.[10] Schemes to buy the Philippines and Chinese Turnpike Bonds said everything about the gambling fever of the day.

BOND FEVER

'New Spain' became 'Mexico' in 1821, with its Aztec resonance, Spain's most derelict former territory, the size of the (then) United States. British diplomats and merchants moved in, converted, intermarried and traded, the Catholic Irish particularly welcome. Mexico had bullion to offer and a population ready to buy British goods. Limerick-born Pedro ÓCrouley y ÓDonnell had explored California in a survey of New Spain in the 1770s;[11] Hugo Óconnór had been Spanish governor of Texas, then Yucatán; Juan Dumfi O'Donojú was the last and diplomatically successful Viceroy of New Spain; Dr Thomas Coulter, Dublin botanist, explored California in the 1830s, bringing the sequoia tree back to Glasnevin Gardens; in the prelude to the US–Mexican War, 1845–6, Tomás Murphy was Mexican ambassador in London, Francisco Morfi was President Santa Anna's personal aide, while Justo Sierra O'Reilly represented rebel Yucatán in Washington, with Tomaso O'Horan its congressman in Mexico City.

In 1824 Britain accredited diplomats to Mexico, and in 1826 agreed a treaty of friendship, but this did not amount to a defensive alliance. Britain disliked the Mexican ban on public Protestant worship; Mexico objected to Britain's refusing of civil rights to Catholics. The Catholic Emancipation Bill of 1829 was Britain's step forward, but Mexico rejected religious toleration until 1862. At least both countries outlawed slavery long before the United States, where the pro-slavery lobby muddied all debate about 'destiny' and western territorial expansion. In 1829, Mexico banned US settlers from importing and owning slaves ('domestic labour') in Mexican Texas.

Mexico needed money as well as identity. Loan bonds of £6.4 million (with interest) were sold, not to government or banks, but to thousands of individuals in Britain and Ireland unidentifiable today because the certificates were unnamed bearer-bonds. After a major financial collapse in 1826, bonds revived briefly, occasionally, and with poor returns. It was renegotiated in 1830, 1837 and 1846. Hope, at least, kept a value as interest inflated the debt to £9.2 million by 1837 and £11.5 million by 1845.

Mexico lacked banks. For all its silver mines, some inefficient or worked out, it lacked cash currency. British merchants held mints as collateral on loans to Mexico and shipped coin and bullion by the ton, by mailship and naval vessel, duty-free, to the Bank of England, with government approval. Britain needed silver and gold for currency and commerce, but Europe lacked the mines. 'Security depositing' they called it in London, but Mexico called it 'smuggling', since it evaded duty. The merchants' in-bound smuggling of raw materials and manufactured goods similarly depleted the very customs dues earmarked to repay bondholders. As official smuggling peaked in the 1840s, British and US naval officers expressed shame and contempt at colleagues' involvement. Admiral Seymour, who received a percentage of the silver fee paid to his captains, was angry, yet hoist by his own petard when HMS *America* disobeyed orders by leaving the Pacific with $2 million *pesos* of British merchants' bullion. It was his only other capital ship, vital for facing down any crisis in Oregon or California (see Plate 2).

Mexico, unworthy of credit and overspending on the military, was unable to pay bondholders or compensate individuals. Investing in Latin America in times of 'Mexicomania' was an 'incalculable risk' in an atmosphere of 'radical uncertainty'. When Bondholders approached London in 1836 for 'more active intervention' the British ambassador in Mexico was supportive: '[the British] Government cannot be indifferent', but Westminster preferred a visible hands-off policy. If Foreign Secretary Palmerston asked his ambassador to help an individual bondholder, he would stipulate 'as far as may be proper', but refuse requests if it were 'not a matter for authoritative intervention by HM Government'.[12]

In 1837 a liberal Mexican government re-structured with an offer to bondholders of hundreds of thousands of acres at 50 per cent discount for colonising, in lieu of half the cash debt. The bondholders were not impressed. Bond purchasers, 1824–5, from parsons to generals in London, Liverpool and Dublin, invested, fluttered and gambled in a fantasy world of treasure galleons, with which dull, steady long-term land investment could not compete. Mexico could declare bankruptcy at any time, yet creditors could not confiscate and tow away the land. 'They will offer us Yorkshire next' warned one weary bondholder. If, against the odds, the gamble succeeded, colonies on discounted land *and* cash repayments would provide immense rewards. The restructure was agreed only in 1839.

Investors were gamblers, addicted to hope, land was not offered again after 1847 and the 1824/25 debt was only repaid in 1888.

Macnamara was close to one of the most powerful British merchants in Mexico in 1845, consul Ewen MacKintosh, who that year became bondholder's agent. MacKintosh and Macnamara published California colonising schemes simultaneously and Macnamara lived in MacKintosh's consulate or at the neighbouring embassy. The canny consul may have envisaged the priest's land as an entry vehicle for his own proposed bondholder colony. Once conveyed, the priest's 13 million acres dwarfed the 250,000 in Alta California hypothecated for bondholders, which MacKintosh and partners proposed that the British government should exploit through a bondholder–government partnership. Bondholder finance, underwritten by the British government, would have allowed Macnamara money to pay for the land Mexico was allowing him.

BRITAIN'S COMMERCIAL GRIP

A dozen British companies came to operate in Mexico City after independence; by 1850 twenty more traded and manufactured between the Gulf and the Pacific. They imported 70 per cent of British imports, acted as bankers to the Mexican government, and their advantageous location made them successful. They reinvested little in Mexican industry or on its roads. Mining was the exception, short term and risky, yet they still smuggled their silver out and their merchandise in. Long term, Mexican development was set back by British private enterprise and 'the beggar on the golden throne' became the poorer for it.[13]

The wealth of half-Spanish, half-Irish Eustace (*Don Eustaquio*) Barron was legendary. His 'elegant mansion' at Tepic was fortified and his company employed many locally. He had been British consul there since 1827, and in 1831 London permitted consuls to engage in private commerce. Barron dominated the economy of the eastern Pacific, positively benefitting from his conflict of interests. In 1846, after HMS *America* deserted the Station with silver at Barron's request, Admiral Seymour demanded that the Foreign Office sever all link between consuls and commerce at Mazatlán, San Blas and Tepic. Barron's trading partner, Alexander Forbes, acting-consul after January 1846 when Barron retired to England, had been first to advocate publicly that Britain must colonise Alta California.

In Mexico City, consul MacKintosh (*Don Eugenio*), active partner in Manning and MacKintosh, had a rich man's clout and stability as bankrupt governments rolled over. Like Barron at Tepic, and the Irish banker, Patrick Milmo, at Monterrey, MacKintosh married into a leading Mexican family, joining money to land and connections.[14] 'No government could ignore MacKintosh and his money' or 'his close relations with government figures'. He speculated and diversified like a man possessed and pressed the British government, only weeks after Macnamara's initiative, to underwrite his own proposal to use bondholder land in Alta California. Crucially, MacKintosh was a major bondholder as well as the bondholders' agent.

Leading Mexican families admired Anglo-European style and fashion, and British merchants livened their tastes with porcelain, fabrics, and loans to buy them. Mexico, already mortgaged to British lenders, grew reliant on cheap, untaxed British consumer goods flowing out of Britain's industrial revolution. Presiding over expatriate and social life in Mexico City were the British Legation (embassy) and MacKintosh's Consulate (*el Palacio*) with its grand entrance, royal arms and luxury furnishings. They were neighbours on Calle de Capuchinas near the President's palace.

To Mexican minds the British Crown and British commerce were a hand in a glove. Coincidence, rumour and shrewd merchants nurtured the confusion. Different British governments blew hotter or colder depending on the stakes. Entrepreneur-consuls like MacKintosh, Barron and Forbes financed Mexico, represented Great Britain, and needed only to hint of their influence. 'Access to the corridors of power, notably the Foreign Office, was if not instant, always rapid.'[15] Identifying Britain with private business was dangerously muddling. 'British firms used the Mexican government's condition and the power conveyed by the name of the British Crown to prosper in a countryside where the overall economic situation was desolate.'[16] As British interest shifted in the 1830s from Latin America to the US, so Mexico and Texas, bridging the former Spanish empire with the new US, became the stage where British and US interests clashed, in Texas behind the scenes, and openly and crucially in Alta California, where all three landlords competed for one plot.

It was no wonder that when an Irish priest was reported to President Polk as bringing British subjects to Alta California, just before the bondholders' land option expired, he was assumed to be acting for Britain. He hinted at it, and circumstances suggested it, but no Bondholder archive survives. Mexico's identifying British private with British government interests was sometimes built on pure coincidence. Macnamara spent a year in Mexico City before going to California; he and MacKintosh virtually co-published their schemes. He also brokered a bogus 'British protection' to persuade Mexican shareholders to lease the new California mercury mine to Forbes. Doors opened to the *anglo* preacher at the giant San Francisco Convent; he carried diplomatic letters from the embassy to the Flag Officer Pacific and the Royal Navy conveyed him. Eugene Macnamara meant something to everyone who met him; his eloquence confirmed fears and buoyed hopes. 'We considered him to be an influential person' remembered ex-*Comandante* Castro years later.[17]

Britain followed trade with missioners, colonies and 'protective' annexation – in the old Thirteen Colonies, in Canada with Hudson's Bay Company, in New Zealand and Australia. The East India Company state-within-a-state was doing likewise in India and the opium trade allowed passage into China. Alta California, the US believed, would be the same.

MONROE'S DOCTRINE, POLK'S ULTIMATUM

In 1823, as Spain evacuated from the Americas, President Monroe warned Europeans not to intrude there again. He was targeting Spain and a conservative Holy Alliance – Austria, Prussia and Russia – formed in 1815 to uphold Christianity; they identified with a monarch's God-given right to rule unquestioned. Republics still reeked of the godless French Revolution. Spain was spent, but tried briefly to reclaim Latin America. Hapsburg Austria helped finance the Pope's new missionaries, including Guiana. Russia (with Protestant Britain and republican France) threatened the eastern Pacific, where apart from a Russian colony and some coastal missions, Alta California was ripe for picking.

British diplomats in Mexico and leading bondholders began to advocate British settlement in Alta California, but Mexico itself was first to attempt a colony. U.S explorers Dana, Hastings and Frémont publicised Eden-in-waiting. Russian imperial trade companies established 'New Archangel' and Fort Ross[iya] at Bodega, to which Mexico responded with a last, northernmost mission and garrison at Sonoma. Johann Sutter established 'Nueva Helvetia' on the lower Sacramento in 1839 and bought the land and contents of the departing Russian colony in 1841. Sutter's was not a mass settlement, but a strand in Mexico's weak land defence of California. 'San Salvador de Bandini', a tiny colony of New Mexicans was founded in 1842 near San Bernardino by a Peruvian *californio* to protect his cattle from Indian rustlers. Prussian diplomats in 1842 proposed that Berlin purchase Alta California, to which the Danish Navy would transport German settlers.[18] Consul de Lizardi in London, then bondholder agent, asked Mexico in 1842 'to encourage [British] colonies on 15 million acres near San Francisco'. France toyed with a tract in the San Joaquin Valley, and its consul in Monterey was imprisoned for resisting US occupation in 1846. Theodor Cordua, a German immigrant, renamed his ranch land on the Sacramento, 'Neue Mecklenburg' in 1844, but 'New' names did not last in California, swamped and outmoded by the Gold Rush after 1848. Sacramento, later trading post for the northern Sierra gold rivers, engulfed 'New Helvetia' and the footings of 'Sutterville'. 'Nations within a nation' made no more sense in the large, swarming population of the 'smelting pot', than covered wagons in defensive circles.

Of all the British schemes, threats, designs and ambiguities concerning California, only *El Proyecto Macnamara* was set in motion, conveyed by *californios* and confirmed by Supreme Congress. Mexico welcomed it: 'Without colonists, the richest country in the world is like the driest desert of Africa.'[19] London turned a deaf, embarrassed ear to its diplomats and merchants, leaving them and its bailiff, the Flag Officer Pacific, bereft of guidance.

The US administration offered repeatedly to buy Alta California's harbours, encouraged by the gold and mercury found in 1842 and 1845. Washington's belief in its 'manifest destiny' to a Pacific coastline ordained by Fate, Progress, Providence, Predestination, Race, Superiority or Natural Selection, intensified in 1845. President Polk came to The Mansion believing that the US right to a Pacific frontier was as self-evident ('manifest') as it was that Mexico could not defend it and that Britain wanted it. Agents, newspapers and prospectuses advertised a California offering more than hides and tallow. Even the Mormons envisaged (and tried) Central Valley as an alternative 'promised land', between their petition to Queen Victoria for Vancouver Island and their final homing in Utah.

For all the US warnings against 'colonisation by foreign monarchies', Washington called *American* migrants to Mexican territory emigrants,

9/2237500

settlers, hunters and trappers, but never colonists. Admiral Seymour called them 'interlopers' and Polk 'a vagabond President [with] an insolent pen' for his final ultimatum to Europe (*de facto* to Britain) in December 1845, to stay away from settling any part of North America (*de facto*, Mexican Alta California). A decade before, Edward Wakefield, the British reforming advocate of colonies, challenged the US directly: 'What is a new state founded in the western desert of America, if it is not a new colony?'[20]

'PAPER EMPIRES', 'PALACES IN THE DESERT', 'TABLES IN THE WILDERNESS'

Hundreds of place names across the Americas and the Pacific perpetuate European settlers, names prefixed with 'New', 'Novo', 'Nova', 'Nueva', or 'Neu' to lessen the distance, salve homesickness and disguise the finality of emigration. New Zions and New Jerusalems came easily to visionaries, but no notable New Ireland exists, in spite of Ireland's record migration. An early US plan to separate East Maine as New Ireland in 1779 was aborted; the Irish colony of Hibernia in Texas was small beer; the lava island in Papua New Guinea dubbed New Ireland in the eighteenth century was even smaller, becoming Neue Mecklenburg under German rule, then New Ireland again after the 1919 Versailles Treaty. Eugene Macnamara gave no name to his 20,000 California square miles, although Mexican Supreme Congress called it *Los Tulares* – The Tule, or Cane Rush Marshes – on his behalf. It was located between Sutter's New Switzerland and Bandini's San Salvador, and the lack of premeditated name suggests honest priorities and intent. 'Macgregor, Prince of Poyais' began his fraudulent colony scheme with a fantasy name, a green St George's flag and ornate jewelled insignia, to dazzle and defraud from the start.

Young Latin American republics like Mexico or Gran Colombia (Ecuador and Venezuela after 1830) offered land to colonists. Robert Owen, the Welsh communitarian, accepted 300 square miles in Texas for a colony of common ownership in 1828 and shortly afterwards visited the Ralahine commune in Macnamara's County Clare. Landowners in Ireland and Scotland were anxious to clear surplus populations, but in such a way as to be able to face themselves and their God in church on Sunday. Rural poor migrating into towns created unrest. France had exploded in 1789 when rural Jacobins joined the malcontents of Paris;

Ireland had witnessed it in 1798, although the rebel rural poor had fewer towns to incite. Both upheavals were vivid living memories.

Wakefield described colonising as 'an *art* of vast importance to mankind'. He urged an end to free land in New South Wales, Australia, and contributions instead to a fund financing passages. He had condemned convict transportation and with Wellington's support founded the chartered National Colonisation Society and the South Australian Association. A New Zealand Association, Colonisation Company and Land Company followed, sending settlers to New Zealand in 1839: Britain annexed the islands to pre-empt France. One eleventh of the 20 million acres Wakefield obtained there was reserved for Maori use, the rest bought at substantial value cost lest the Maori feel cheated. By 1850 250,000 settlers populated New Zealand, their settlements named Canterbury and Christchurch for the Anglican clergy who led them. Waddy Thompson, US ambassador to Mexico, admired the 'wonderful adeptness of the [British] to colonise'.[21] The British islands themselves are colonised by Romans, Saxons, Normans, and modern migrants from old Empire and new Europe. In turn, anglo-Normans, Scots and English colonised Ireland.

Wakefield watched the US head west, and the emigrant Irish poor go east for lack of passage money, 'underselling English workmen for a hovel, rags and potatoes, content with wretchedness'. Vacant land in America, he noted was 'open to individuals with a title to possess it'. Fix the land price in the colonies, he urged the Colonial Office, limit the size of plots to preserve land value, and create communities of neighbours, not isolated vast ranches. Young, newly married couples without children were his ideal colonists and villages his ideal community.

Observers predicted that sheer weight of numbers would see the US take Alta California by 1847, but the deep-rooted US fear in 1845 was that Britain, Europe's most powerful, ruthless and navy-borne coloniser and traditional enemy of the US, would secure Alta California before that. A war pitting the US against Britain, Mexico and possibly France in alliance could go either way. The eventual US seizure of Alta California in 1846 and the second major gold discovery there in 1848, turned a settler trickle into a 'Rush', ending all uncertainty.

An ocean away, with a reputation but a depleted fleet, Britain had little State-organised or subsidised emigration. Commonly a minister of religion, or a trusted community leader, would approach or be approached by estate owners, philanthropists or entrepreneurs. In 1842, the Apostolic Vicar of London informed the Archbishop of Dublin that Rome wanted an Irish Apostolic Prefect to accompany Irish and English emigrants to Bolivia. In 1843, Anthony Fahy, an Irish Dominican friar, was sent as chaplain to a small Irish colony on La Plata river, Argentina: five years later, 1,500 settlers were in place. Bishop John Hynes' diary records a senior Jesuit seeking an Irish settlement in Guiana and a proposal for Irish settlers in New Granada from the Cullen brothers, doctor and missioner, in 1851. Hynes' nephew, Bishop Goold of Melbourne, later thanked Queen Victoria for her government's brief Irish Orphan Emigration scheme.

Projects could veer on the wild side: the Milk and Butter Churning Company carried Scots milkmaids to La Plata where they churned a butter mountain before discovering it would not keep and the locals preferred oil. Projects could be fraudulent, as was 'Sir' Gregor McGregor's Poyais. Projects launched in good faith could fail through poor judgement, as happened with the Topo river colony, in Gran Colombia.[22] John Diston Powles, the promoter, published newspapers to press British fashion and taste in Gran Colombia, and imported furniture and fabrics to meet the demand which followed. He also advocated Lancasterian schools, as well-known in Latin America as they were in County Clare. In 1823 Gran Colombia turned to London for money, like Mexico and Chile, and to Powles for colonists. In a poorly assessed but well-organised operation, Powles placed 450 Scots and Irish settlers on the Rio Topo in two locations, 'Gibraltar' and 'Topo', but none made it to 'Gibraltar' and the 200 who reached 'Topo' found the soil toxic, with fresh water some five miles distant.

In 1826 the London Stock Exchange and banks collapsed, taking Powles' Topo company with them. Simon Bolivar made a personal donation to help the colonists and a Parliamentary Committee questioned Powles for fraud. The British ambassador in Caracas provided them with passage money for Canada, while Powles emerged unscathed and undaunted, to join Ewen MacKintosh in pressing to colonise California in 1845 and for more schemes in Venezuela later.

EL PROYECTO MACNAMARA

In 1846 Eugene Macnamara was the first and last British coloniser to secure land in Alta California; Governor Simpson of the Hudson's Bay Company was the only other advocate of colonising even to visit the department. British government policy had been to hope for a strategic windfall, without blowing, shaking or being seen to make the apple fall. Britain had no state tradition of exporting colonists beyond its own colonies, but once private colonies were planted, it had a reputation for protecting and governing them. Cranks, fraudsters, zealots, the vagaries of the Stock Market and the wilderness itself made colonising risky, chaotic, even melodramatic, but Macnamara had a priest's advantage in Latin America and was in the tradition of clergy leading emigrants. Parish and chapel were not yet displaced as the building blocks of British society.

Before President Polk reasserted Monroe's policy in 1845, warning Europe (this time Britain) against new colonising, Macnamara had already challenged the 'American Methodist wolves'. His timing and language were unfortunate, just as the great landlords braced for a war which his project helped accelerate. He was identified with two of the three landlords and through them, with the private bondholder 'mortgage on California'. His timing could not have been worse, in the most sensitive part of North America, just as the British government resisted its last temptation to acquire California. 'Impressive – but too late,' Admiral Seymour decided when he welcomed Macnamara onto his flagship, yet the Irish communitarian still stole a march on commercial giants like MacKintosh and on the US, however late. The California church was also ripe for revival, and *misionero Apostólico* Macnamara had more than one string.

As the Mexican Council of Government debated *El Proyecto Macnamara* in September 1845, the first nationwide potato blight of a five-year run was reported from Ireland. The Famine made the *Proyecto* even more urgent, and its lengthening made Macnamara turn elsewhere.

Later, in England, Admiral Seymour browsed through an old Pacific notebook and paused on the flyleaf. On route to Honolulu in 1846 Macnamara had shared with him a memorandum from Juan Bandini, *californio* coloniser and prospector. Typically, Seymour had taken notes. Bandini had highlighted California's mineral wealth as possible finance for Macnamara's colony. 'Bandini's anticipations', Seymour added in

1851 with gold rush hindsight, 'were realised to an extent no one, Bandini included, could have imagined. It has become a rich and populous country in consequence.'[23] Macnamara, however, faced unbelievably serious obstacles from the hour he obtained his land contract: the US–Mexican war, Mexico's loss of Alta California and the transformation of California by gold, immigrants and US Statehood. John Frémont, who claimed to have foiled Macnamara, spoke years later of the Irish project's 'overthrow in the moment of complete success'.

Chapter 2

Expulsion and Exeat: 1814—41

In December 1844, Eugene Macnamara told the British ambassador in Mexico City that he came from Ennis, County Clare. Daniel 'Liberator' O'Connell had made Ennis famous for electing him as the first Catholic to be admitted to sit in a modern British Parliament. The Ulster-born ambassador would recognise it more readily than nearby Corofin, the priest's home town. 'Macnamara' is a Clare name; 'Eugene' is the latinised or romance Irish 'Eoain/Eoghan', the Scots 'Ewen' and Welsh 'Owain', all of which anglicise as 'Owen'.[1]

COUNTY CLARE

Ennis was a medieval settlement centred on a friary, the gentler face of the medieval colonising of Ireland by the English. English soldiers in the seventeenth century, by then Protestant, stripped Irish friaries, monasteries and convents open to the elements, by which time the colonisers' church had come to identify with the native population, as happened in many mission territories (see Map A).

Eugene was born in 1814, after Ireland's failed rebellion of 1798, and just before Waterloo. Corofin rents remained at wartime levels even after the wartime boom ended. Crop failure and unprotected tenancies turned hardship into arrears, eviction and flight. Agrarian violence increased and sectarianism keened the djstress. In the 1820s West Clare felt the 'Second Reformation', after the Protestant Archbishop of Dublin called on the established Church of Ireland to convert the 80 per cent Catholic majority in a growing population. The rural west, including Clare and its vulnerable poor, was one target area. Mission societies sprouted, scripture readers and open-air 'methody' preachers criss-crossed Ireland and landlords generally welcomed them. Food and schooling were offered as incentives to convert, but moderate Protestants, who had long learned to live with Catholics, expressed dismay at 'Bible wars' and 'Souperism'. Respect between Parson Frederick Blood of the local landowner family in Corofin and Parish Priest John Murphy survived this 'decline in sensitivity'. Catholics reacted and the campaign loomed large in their collective folk memory. Edward Synge, land agent and fundamentalist fanatic, made Corofin his personal crusade, founding a new school which taught mainly Scripture. Murphy condemned it, and later it caught fire.

The law demanded payment of 10 per cent tax (tithe) on farmed land to the established Church, however small the holding. Catholic dead had to be buried in Church of Ireland graveyards, and prayers aloud had to be licensed separately. Burial within religious ruins was forbidden, but widely customary. Daniel O'Connell's campaign for Catholic rights to hold office (he also demanded voting rights for Jews) was near the goal of total Emancipation when he chose Clare for the final act. Despite his condemning political violence, gangs threatened Clare landlords: they ambushed Synge in Corofin (his coachman was killed), and they murdered landlord William Blood in his home.

The Catholic majority in Ennis and Corofin were permitted chapels (no bell, spire or tower), not churches. They were banned from public office, from magistracy to Parliamentary seat. Other legal disabilities had gone – owning arms, property, a horse worth over £5, living in a walled town – an 'overlapping snarl of statutes' which had accumulated since the seventeenth century, but the stigma of 'disloyal papist' remained highlighted in law.

In 1801, after the shock of the failed '98 rebellion, the Kingdom of Ireland was absorbed into and united with those of Britain and Scotland. Dublin's Parliament was subsumed, but into a punitive and inefficient compromise at Westminster. Repeal of this forced marriage was supported by Irish Catholics and Protestants alike. Mixed marriages, shared schooling, and common humanity were acknowleged in daily Irish life as much as were bigotry, absentee landlords and unreformed land legislation. Protestants perjured themselves to hold land for Catholic neighbours; wise rectors turned a Nelson-eye to smallholder Catholics not paying tithe, or praying *alta voce* at funerals. The anglo-Irish landowner could be ethical and caring in spite of wilful neglect by absentee owners and unreformed laws loaded against tenants. Wellington's war had proved the loyalty of Irish and Catholic soldiers. In Ennis, after Catholic civic rights were restored in 1829, a leading Protestant landowner chaired the committee planning the new Catholic church, for which another Protestant had donated the prime site.

A Catholic middle class of lawyers, teachers, merchants and minor property owners had prospered in Clare towns, among them descendants of those expelled from walled Limerick. With Emancipation, Main Street churches replaced Back Lane chapels, although new building took money from other, social priorities. Before the religiously neutral National Schools were instituted in 1831, Joseph Lancaster, the English Quaker educationalist, set up schools in Ennis and Corofin in 1812, on his way to do the same in Latin America, most notably in Mexico. Despite Rome's fear of 'Indifferentism' to religious truth, better-off Catholics and Protestants shared private schools and the RC bishops of Killaloe welcomed and defended the fairness of the National School compromise. Nothing further is known about the Corofin Lancasterian School, but Stephen Halloran's private Classical School in Ennis was said, in 1829, to have educated most of the Catholic clergy of Clare before their seminary training.[2]

The ban on holding public office was the last great disability of those not belonging to the state church, including Catholics, Jews and atheists. Even the best of neighbours could not resolve it. An anti-Catholic oath of Protestant allegiance and the taking of a Protestant sacrament kept gatecrashers out of Westminster, as it had kept them out of Leinster House for twenty years. A Trinity College degree could be conferred on a Catholic after 1794 (Macnamara claimed to have been awarded one), but not one by Oxford or Cambridge until the 1870s. In its day, Catholic Emancipation was a cause-in-parallel with Slave Emancipation (1834) and with Irish Emancipation (1922–3) when the Irish Parliament was restored and a version of independence achieved.

'LIBERATOR' O'CONNELL

For some years O'Connell had worked the Clare legal circuit, holding Emancipation rallies and meetings. Protestant landowners paid his Catholic Association 'rent' of one penny for the campaign. When rumour warned of armed insurrection and the Association was outlawed, O'Connell fought legalism with legalism, founding a *New* Catholic Association. He stood for Clare County in 1828, winning the seat from a sitting member, but was barred from Westminster when he refused the Test Oath. The Duke of Wellington advised the government to emancipate Catholics to head off unrest, and a rumour circulated that John England, bishop of Charleston, Carolina, was raising an Irish force 'for the invasion of Ireland should Emancipation be withheld'.[3]

When O'Connell stood again, for Ennis, 60,000 people cheered and chaired him through town and he sat at Westminster unimpeded. Corofin was abuzz and Eugene Macnamara experienced the elation at an impressionable age. Out on the Atlantic at Baltard Point, an extrovert parish priest, Michael Comyn, notorious for political bluntness and revered for championing his people, hugged voters and threw whiskey punch parties for fellow clergy. He called his peninsular folk 'gentry' and warned English visitors who called them 'peasants' that 'they will be wearing good clothes when you are in the poorhouse'. He probably poured them a whiskey or offered them snuff too – it was Comyn's way.

With Emancipation, Catholic priests no longer needed permits. They led parish communities with new confidence, on laurels handed down from those persecuted in previous centuries. Educated to a point, and from the majority population, their new public voice gradually displaced squire, established church minister, politician and sometimes the constable, although in Ireland even the strongest voice may be devoutly ignored. As community *factotums*, priests made good emigrant chaplains and frontier missioners. Emancipation boosted the authority of bishops, increasingly 'Roman', authoritarian and openly hostile to Protestantism and Britain, generally conflating the two. 'Small differences' between majority Catholic and minority ruling Protestant came to loom larger. Rome and its bishops looked severely on mixed marriage and on integrated ('neutral') education. The 'Second Reformation', the land laws and the later Famine understandably exacerbated mistrust of Protestants. The wider Catholic church in Europe, facing down republicans, democrats and anti-clericals, clung tighter to defending Absolute Truth against 'non-commissioned Apostles' of error, and the spectre of the French Revolution haunted all institutional authority. Irish priests had operated with considerable independence and discretion before Emancipation; by 1850, they found themselves disciplined and scrutinised by bishops, themselves scrutinised and even dazzled by Rome. Macnamara's first bishop in Guiana was so clerically moulded that he spoke of 'mere laymen', 'lay interference' and 'the Hydra of lay democracy'. Pope Pius IX warned Bishop Hynes, Macnamara's second Guiana bishop, that mixed marriage was 'an unmitigated evil, as a bad pear corrupts a sound one', and that Indifferentism was the 'British religion'.[4]

With Emancipation, the number of candidates volunteering for the secular (diocesan) priesthood increased across Ireland, but failed to keep pace overall with the rapid rise in population. Numbers of parishioners rose accordingly, but the uneven distribution of clergy - the bulk in the east and a minority in the west - meant that the west felt the rising ratio of people-to-priests more keenly. Priests were unmarried, as western Catholic rules required, but secular or diocesan priests without vows were allowed property, money and ambition. Curates had rights to board, lodging and a small allowance, the hidden base of a clerical pyramid where bishops, increasingly occupied with the Dublin–Rome circuit, left parish priests effectively in charge. Emigration to the missions tempted some clergy, others were ordered there. Irish clerical influence came to extend beyond Ireland wherever chaplains accompanied emigrants, wherever Apostolic Vicariates became dioceses, and particularly on British imperial frontiers where Hyderabad shared the Irish church and accent with Guiana, Nova Scotia and Australia. 'The nineteenth century Irish were the most internationally dispersed of European national cultures.'[5]

After Emancipation, the Irish bishops reasserted the church's public authority, ending an older 'wilder' Irish church shaped underground, in persecution and in remote countryside. A less regulated Irish religion was ousted: confession and weddings in homes, mixed marriages, parish tenure for life, relaxed Sunday requirement, 'citizen' dress and titles for priests. A popular culture tugged, sometimes fiercely, with a growing clerical church culture. Congregations still had one way left of choosing a priest, or at least of disapproving: they could lock him out from his chapel. Florid devotions from France and Italy were introduced, and a sexual puritanism, variously attributed to Jansenist heresy or to Victorian prudery. Long term, a sense of community, of service (and of sporadic 'wildness') has characterised the Irish in missions, medicine, education, international development, and in peacekeeping for decades in central Africa, given its small population.

Brian Merriman, a hedge teacher of Feakle, east of Corofin, had composed a bawdy Gaelic poem in 1787, before overpopulation was a problem. His *Midnight Court* heard women complain about unromantic males, and advised 'Go to Mass to find a man, pray to lure a man, and fast to appear attractive to a man.' The Court warned against the clergy's 'handsome fee' for the 'fuss and racket' of marrying. Merriman advocated free love: even Jesus was respectably illegitimate. The clergy, warned his *Court*, 'well dressed, well treated and well fed', should re-read St Paul: 'Lust, not a wife, was what a man should shun for life.' Red-blooded, educated young men in Clare had heard or knew of the subversive *Midnight Court* long before it appeared in print in the 1850s.[6]

Other unorthodoxies flourished beyond town. South of Newmarket-on-Fergus in 1831, an agricultural 'common wealth' was founded, inspired by Paraguayan Jesuit missions and Robert Owen's socialist villages. The shortlived Ralahine cooperative on a 1000-acre Vandeleur estate had eighty members, holding all in common. Gambling, alcohol, tobacco, nicknames and corporal punishment were banned. Everyone did field work and Gaelic was spoken. A committee ruled and religious argument was forbidden. Robert Owen visited and praised it, just after taking land in Mexican Texas for a similar settlement. *The Times* of London called it 'a city on a hill'. It collapsed in 1833 when its Vandeleur patron was bankrupted: he had hoped it might help counter rural violence.[7]

Everyone in Clare knew of the Crottyite schism at Birr, King's County (Co. Offaly), on the edge of Killaloe diocese. Priest cousins, Michael and William Crotty, both trained in Paris, took congregations with them in protest about financial irregularity, then about appointments, and finally about Catholic practice and beliefs. Heady personalities, manic fervour and group hysteria spiced real concerns. They stressed the need to work ecumenically, but when one priest became Presbyterian and the other joined the Church of Ireland, their following dwindled. It sobered newly emancipated Catholics trying to make a fresh start and live up to a new image. Clare county and Killaloe diocese were remote yet thought-provoking introductions to life.

RUE DES IRLANDAIS

On 1 March 1832, as a major cholera epidemic broke out, 'Eugene Macnamara from Clare' registered into the sixty-strong Irish College on the Rue des Irlandais, Paris. Numbers in Irish seminaries leapt after 1829, doubling in Rome and quadrupling in Paris.[8] The Paris college lay in the (then) 12th Arrondissement, the old University quarter between St Geneviève church, secularised during the Revolution, and the Luxembourg Gardens. Students were taught by four professors in-house, not at the Sorbonne as before the Revolution. For five years of Philosophy and Theology they needed Latin, French – and motivation. Paris was where nostalgia for the *ancien régime* of unquestioned church authority met optimistic, challenging *modernisme* head-on (see Plate 3).

The Irish College survived from some thirty Irish academies between Prague and Lisbon. In the sixteenth, seventeenth and eighteenth centuries Catholic men went abroad for professional training and careers barred to them at home. The penalty for one trained as a priest returning to Great Britain could be execution. For over two centuries France and particularly Spain hosted thousands of Irish exiles, religious and political, but after 1789 France ceased to be a monarchy, its church was humiliated, and its exiles fled to Britain, welcomed by George III for their monarchist views, if not their church. Symbolic of the change, two Irish College priests, Edgeworth and Kearney, were present at the guillotining of their patron, Louis XVI. The College was closed by the revolutionaries, but reopened by Napoleon exclusively for training priests. Killaloe diocese sent about 30 per cent of its trainee priests there during the nineteenth century, of whom twelve trained in Macnamara's time. On their return to Irish parishes they were teasingly styled, *'M'sieu l'Abbé'*.

Paris was no cloister. In the relatively salubrious 12th Arrondisement, 300 died of the cholera in 1832, including one on Rue des Irlandais; 19,000 died across the city. In June, at the height of the outbreak, a short-lived republican and student insurrection north of the river was put down by cannon and bayonet. Irish seminarians would have heard about it through their close contacts with missioner students on Rue Picpus, even if they missed hearing the gunfire.

A new Rector had been appointed in 1828. Patrick McSweeney, in the heat of Catholic anger at the 'Second Reformation' and the continued denial of civil rights to Catholics, challenged six evangelical Protestant clergy to public dispute, taunting them as 'non-commissioned Apostles'. The debate, chaired by O'Connell, lasted six days, after which McSweeney was appointed to oversee the Paris college as a new broom.[9] He believed that student priests needed discipline and that a Church Belligerent needed hard-trained men to defend Truth under siege. A new generation of clergy was being moulded to man an increasingly assertive church.

France was unsettled and in economic crisis. A 'citizen' King, Louis Philippe, had been installed in 1830 with general, if uneasy support. On the Isle de la Cité, the scars on Notre Dame reminded of the archetypal Revolution which had demolished throne and altar together forty years before. When Victor Hugo's novel *Notre-Dame de Paris* put the battered cathedral back on the map in 1831, tourists flocked. Hugo also witnessed the 1832 uprising, and later expressed its pathos in *Les Miserables*.

Paris clergy polarised between conservatives nostalgic for Kings, Popes and bishops, and modernisers who wanted the church to listen and learn, closer to the people. Student priests felt the tensions. In May 1833, a visiting priest reported 'deplorable indiscipline' and the students' questioning of McSweeney's authority to Paul Cullen, Irish church agent in Rome. William Crotty of the Birr schism had trained on Rue des Irlandais and disapproved of the devotionalism at St Sulpice nearby; he recruited another Irish College student for his schism, and his cousin, Michael, had also trained briefly at St Sulpice. They questioned authority and their followers were so hostile to bishops that the genial Protestant, Lord Rosse of Birr Castle, felt French anti-clericals had invaded his quiet town.

In the wider Paris church, Lammenais, Montalembert and Lacordaire, respected priests and preachers, argued that the 'liberal', 'republican' and 'democratic' might enrich the 'Catholic'. They published *L'Avenir* [*The Future*]. Government and church, they insisted, should be independent, not a power-embrace, although optimism wavered when a Paris mob burned down the archbishop's house in 1830. In August 1832, the new missionary Pope, Gregory XVI, condemned 'Indifferentism': government and church had a joint obligation to uphold Absolute Truth; democracy and free speech bred disorder.[10] That year, Britain refused yet again to forward French reparation money to the Irish College for damage sustained in the Revolution, adding to the general mistrust of London.

Macnamara was in an unsettled community. McSweeney ruled strictly for over two decades, but apparently ineffectively. Students used the 1848 city uprising to strike back at him with street demonstrations, republican cockades on cassocks and graffiti across College walls, reading *Á bas le tyrant McSweeney!* Paul Cullen, by then an archbishop, visited in 1850: 'rough old fellows: poor Ireland has much to fear from its future ministers … this college is in a bad way'. He contrasted them with the orthodox, docile students of his own Irish College in Rome.

On 27 August 1834, after five semesters, Eugene Macnamara was dismissed, '*Renvoyé*'. College registers never recorded grounds for being sent down. He may have gone to the mission college on Rue Picpus, where three 'young Irish presented themselves in November 1834 to complete their theology course'. Three days after Macnamara left, the Administrator-Registrar accused McSweeney of maladministration and was himself dismissed. Four students were *renvoyés* that month, and a fifth in December; four had been sent down in 1833, but only one was dismissed between 1835 and 1838. Three of those expelled in August 1834, including Macnamara, owed fees, but his dismissal was not about finance; others in the red stayed on, others in the black were dismissed.[11]

Students were sometimes advanced early to ordination to fill pastoral gaps or to relieve diocesan finances, sometimes only halfway through training. Others left college unordained (*partis*) for home, or moved (*sortis en ville*) into surrounding Paris. The missionary college of the Picpus Fathers north of the Seine, had long trained French and Irish students 'out of pity' when other colleges ran out of funds during and after the Revolution. McSweeney disapproved of Picpus as too easy-going and beyond his control.

Between 1814 and 1830 a '*grand nombre*' of Irish students, up to 60, passed through the college on the Rue Picpus in the then 8th Arrondisement. The street name was less daunting than *Missioners of the Order of the Sacred Hearts of Jesus and Mary*. They served the Pacific, including the Sandwich Islands (Hawaii), and their Eastern Oceania Vicariate was based on Valparaiso, Chile. In 1831, they were expelled from Honolulu after Protestant missioners gained the Hawaiian ruler's ear. Patrick Short, ex-Irish College and Rue Picpus, fled with Louis Bachelot to Alta California, from where Bachelot returned to Paris in 1832, leaving

Short to staff William Hartnell's ranch school, El Alisal, near Monterey. It is likely that Bachelot was an attraction in Paris, much discussed by seminarists and in evidence. He and Short were returned to Honolulu in 1837 under Royal and French Navy protective escort. Short then spent years in Valparaiso. Such front-line missioners were role models. John England, Bishop of Charleston, USA, who had reputedly threatened an Irish brigade to force Emancipation, visited the Irish College in 1832, to invite students to serve Charleston, New Orleans, Boston or New York: one volunteered immediately.

Macnamara completed training for Killaloe in 1837, perhaps at Picpus, but he did claim later to be a Trinity, Dublin graduate in front of a Protestant naval chaplain who had graduated there in 1837.[12] A decade later, he was still sufficiently fluent in French to preach and hear confessions throughout Mexico and Alta California. In 1837, however, neither street-French nor book-Latin was much use among the Gaelic-speaking parishioners of Kilkee-Killard parish on the Clare Atlantic coast.

KILKEE-KILLARD AND MICHAEL COMYN

'Owen' Macnamara joined two other curates assisting Michael Comyn, larger-than-life parish priest. Whatever Pope Gregory and Rector McSweeney said about Absolute Truth, the Clare peninsula was a world away. Michael Comyn was tolerant and pragmatic, nicknamed *Taoiseach* for his open door and his role as 'priest, ruler and judge' to a 'turf digging, seaweed eating, fish catching, amphibious population, as bad fishermen as farmers, content on the lowest scale of existence'. Charles Lever, a Protestant doctor posted there during a cholera epidemic in 1832, worked with Comyn and returned to lodge with him. His later novel was a tribute.[13] Comyn pledged money in 1830 towards a new Church of Ireland church at Kilkee, and local Protestants reciprocated for his own chapel. A decade later Comyn and the Church of Ireland Rector manned a Famine soup kitchen and campaigned for government relief and local development together. Tact, however, was rarely Comyn's way. When he hosted Friar Mathew, Ireland's Temperance campaigner, after a successful drive in 1841, he laid on dinner with alcohol in abundance.

The parish straddled the peninsula between the Shannon and the Atlantic, along seven miles of Atlantic coast, between Dunmore Bay, Killard, and genteel Kilkee resort. Comyn lived in a large family house at

Baltard Point, known for its books, parties and view of the Arran islands; his mother was his housekeeper. For nearly thirty years he exchanged a feudal loyalty with thousands of peasant parishioners, possibly half of whom spoke English. He spent his energy on them, demanding support for their coracle fishing, confiscation of absentee landlords' land, the development of clayfields into brickyards, a railway line and a mole to make Dunmore Bay a harbour. He supported the Poor Law Commission enquiry into poverty, but opposed the giant parish-Union 'poorhouses' built at Ennis and later at Kilrush, after the government ignored commissioners' recommendations for regeneration and land reform. 'Houses of industry', prominent warnings like the ruined friaries, added to the fear of bad times. The landowner, Col. Vandeleur – who paid for Kilrush workhouse, fever hospital and a site for Comyn's church at Kilkee – also evicted tenants at the height of the Famine.

Between a fifth and third of Comyn's parishioners came to mass on Sunday. Lack of Sunday clothes, seating, distance from church, and the cold and wet of being left outside in winter made worship an ordeal. Children were virtually exempt from attending. As poverty declined and Emancipation was achieved, church-building increased and attendance with it. Irish Catholicism was still a Christianity closer to nature (mistaken by outsiders for superstition), than to church law, centring as much on wells and rites of passage as on priests. The continental devotions, the puritanism, the excessive deference to Popes and clerical authority, known as 'beyond-the-Alps-ism' (*ultramontanismo*), did not take hold immediately after Emancipation. Eugene Macnamara, as a diocesan or secular priest, was 'Mr', not 'Father'. Most priests wore plain 'citizen dress' (as Macnamara wore in Mexico and Friar Mathew on temperance tours) without the mandatory 'Roman' collar. Titles and dress came to matter as public marks of equal status with clergy of the established church; they were also the culture of polarised ecclesiastical centres like Paris and Rome.

Kilkee-Killard parish had older chapels at Lisdeen and Doonbeg which Comyn rebuilt at his own expense in 1829 as if to mark Emancipation. Kilkee chapel was almost complete when Macnamara arrived. To the outsider it was all the back of beyond and Kilkee resort was further away culturally than its six miles from beachcombing Doonbeg. Newspapers told of America beyond, but 3,000 miles was hard for coracle people to visualise. Ships had died on the Clare coast; to emigrate was to tempt fate, but the bards had told of youth, gold and even afterlife below the western horizon. Anywhere had to be more fertile than coastal Clare.

Macnamara saw real poverty in two years at Kilkee-Killard. Occasional distress collections were held in chapel, but food, crops and clothing were the rural currency, not cash. Enthusiastic church-building after Emancipation was blamed for undermining aid to the poor.[14] In summer 1839, potatoes were sent across the Shannon to Kilrush, free of freight, to relieve hunger after a crop rotted. Comyn also asked for a National School at Kilrush, and Macnamara heard him attack the workhouse system during the first Poor Law Guardian elections, insisting his 'peasantry were gentry'. Prosecuted for threatening a magistrate in his indignation, Comyn shared snuff in court with his accuser.

Curates served apprenticeships under parish priests who could inspire or infuriate, some of them *The Midnight Court*'s 'tough old terrors and frozen fogeys'. Michael Comyn must have impressed. 'A master of Irish' he preached in Gaelic after the curates, educated far from the *Gaeltacht*, had preached in English during a Latin mass. A Protestant Gaelic Bible appeared in 1640, a Catholic version in 1981. Comyn would have teased curates about the relevance of Paris to the bogs of West Clare and for their Gaelic howlers, but his hospitality to fellow priests was legendary. Religious orders had their communities, secular clergy did not; a celibate life could weigh, and curates had few rights, save to a room, a horse and an arbitrary £10-£15 p.a. Authority and finance were issues of the day in the newly emancipated Irish Catholic church.

Clare was a backwater, but not isolated. The British empire, the missionary network and emigration to Australia, Canada and USA saw to that. There were alternatives to being a long-toothed curate or an ageing parish priest. A gold-embossed blue handbook, *The [Complete Irish] Catholic Directory*, appeared in Dublin in 1836, allowing priests to see their team positions in a wider world. William Battersby published it to help the missions. Macnamara (now Eugene, not Owen), featured in the 1839 edition with the previous year's news and recruiting calls from every mission.

BORRISOKANE

The Catholic Directory depended on accurate returns by a November deadline. Macnamara did not feature in the 1840 edition, but early in 1840 he was curate at Borrisokane, Tipperary, sixty miles inland and ten miles from Birr. Curates had no stability and bishops could move them to punish, promote, or fill a gap. Being sent to a less wealthy parish could indicate disapproval, but Macnamara succeeded a curate sent to assist his uncle, and Comyn never had three curates again.

Borrisokane, noted Samuel Lewis in 1837, had 'many new houses, 2635 inhabitants, and much improvement'. Its new 'commodious and handsome RC chapel' suggested boomtown. The parish was more arable and better timbered than Kilkee, and to the south, speculators were turning their attention again to the gold, silver and copper under Silvermines Mountain. Doonbeg, in contrast, had 213 people who harvested seaweed, quarried flagstones, and made flannel and frieze.

Macnamara's new parish priest, James Birmingham, recorded his and Macnamara's taking the Temperance Pledge in March 1840, as Friar Theobald Mathew began his crusade. Birmingham, pragmatic and tolerant like Comyn, wrote a book about Mathew, working throughout March and April for publishers in London and New York, while his new curate looked after the parish.[15]

Twenty years among the Cork poor had convinced Mathew that alcohol caused poverty. He began to work with the non-denominational Cork Temperance Association, but was barred from rallying in Tuam and Armagh archdioceses as he represented a non-Catholic organisation. The bishop of Cork, of Murphys' brewing family, was also critical, and Mathew was eventually reported to Rome. Like most other dioceses, however, Killaloe welcomed him and hosted a dozen of his rallies in northern Tipperary.

In two days at Birr at the end of February 1840, soldiers and police had to restrain the 'immense influx from adjacent parishes and remote counties' coming to pledge. 'Mild, assuming, but extraordinary', Mathew arrived at Birmingham's door afterwards, unannounced, 'in plain dress, nothing *a la mode* and nothing ultra-clerical'. He asked to stay overnight and word spread. On 1 March, in Borrisokane town centre, he administered the teetotal pledge to 8,000 people. Like Comyn and Birmingham, he had the respect and affection of many Protestants. It was a far cry from Rector

McSweeney's 'non-commissioned Apostles', and Archbishop Cullen's boast that he had never shared a meal with a Protestant. Good will quickly found common ground, but Mathew, Comyn and Birmingham still guarded against zealots and soupers who might proselytise the poor.[16]

Friar Mathew, an aristocrat from a family of mixed-religion, conferred medals on pledgers, silver to priests and gold to bishops. Twenty priests, including Macnamara, received them at Borrisokane on 1 March. The following day, at Nenagh, 20,000 people pledged, and in January 1841 Mathew visited Comyn at Kilkee-Killard. The 'foul stigma' of 'habitual intemperance' marked out the Irish and to some extent their clergy, but alcohol was an issue throughout nineteenth-century Great Britain. The Temperance movement had the consensus of denominations, governments and even the army and navy, which awarded Temperance medals, too. It coincided with O'Connell's mass meetings for Repeal of the Union, and Mathew's timely crusade – he issued over 5 million medals – literally sobered Irish political crowds. Lay and clerical complaints reached Rome, but the pledge meant less in Italy where wine was integral to diet. The Pope chuckled and remained neutral.

A new Catholic periodical appeared in London in 1840. *The Tablet* concentrated on the Irish, English and colonial Catholic world, Papal Rome, Latin America and the USA. Its editor, Frederick Lucas, a former Quaker with an eye for fair play, was plain speaking. *The Tablet* was unequivocally lay, its copy supplied by overseas correspondents and Lucas' own broad circle. It aired church disputes, polemic, complaints and news; Protestant writers contributed in earlier years, before the church around it hardened. It helped join up the dotted outlines of Battersby's *Directory*. English 'drawing room Catholics' had little in common with Irish immigrant 'cellar dwellers', or with boat-rockers like O'Connell. His stand to free Catholics, Ireland and slaves disturbed those who feared the resurgence of the anti-Catholic mob. Successive American, French and Irish revolutions to overthrow crowns, aristocrats and churches, haunted the genteel of all persuasions. In the colonies and the USA, *The Tablet* reported, Irish *émigrés* were not universally welcome, but Lucas championed their grievances and trumpeted their achievements.[17]

He published O'Connell's rebuke to the Manchester Methodists for bigotry towards Irish Catholics. He also printed Bishop William Clancy's reports from South Carolina and British Guiana, on recruiting priests and making converts. Clancy had been John England's assistant bishop briefly in Charleston, Carolina, before Rome moved him to Guiana in 1837. Battersby's *Directory* took instruction on Clancy's preferred title: 'Titular Bishop of Oriense, Vicar Apostolic of British Guiana, Count of the Holy Roman Empire and Parish Priest of Georgetown', which was a complex heraldic achievement for a Cork farmer's son.

Bishop Clancy reported his 'laying before the Sovereign Pontiff an account of his past mission in Charleston and his new vigour to plant the standard of the cross in British Guiana'. Missioners were trailblazers like colonisers and warrior-explorers. Esoteric place names coloured their reports from an expanding list of British possessions. Clancy made numerous appeals in Europe for funds and recruits. He graced platforms with O'Connell and answered to donors in Rome, Vienna, London and Dublin.

BISHOP CLANCY'S MISSION

William Clancy was ordained at 21 years of age, halfway through the six-year course at Royal Maynooth College: the Irish church exercised a discretion over early advancement. After a country curacy and teaching at Carlow College, Rome made him assistant bishop of Charleston to allow Bishop John England, also from Cork, to go to Haiti in 1834 to negotiate a *concordat*. Clancy would cover his absence.

In December 1834 Clancy was consecrated at Carlow College as a titular bishop. Three months later he requested travel expenses before travelling and permission to advance sixteen students early to ordination for Charleston. They could earn stole fees and customary offerings, saving the diocese their stipend and their college fees. Money preoccupied Clancy. Writing in Latin to Rome he lamented, 'Everyone in Ireland knows that my going out to the American region is an exchange mostly for the worse.' He complained Bishop England had rebuked him for delaying his journey, 'me, now his equal and formerly his friend. If, however, the Holy Father insists, I shall go with a heavy heart [after] the great sacrifice I have made for God, the Roman Curia and the Bishop of Charleston in exchanging my homeland, tranquillity, family and sufficient means of support, for a foreign country, hardships, long journeys and poverty.'

Clancy pulled out every stop to delay going – short sight, lack of money, and a pending 'future transfer request'. John England's brother loaned him money, but England vetoed the student-curates. Clancy delayed until late 1835, scuppering England's negotations in Haiti, but when he did arrive, England explained tactfully in public that the delay was 'due to duties and protracted sickness'. Clancy was ungracious: 'I did not come seeking gold or power – there is less of either in this wilderness of a diocese than in all Christendom.'

Four months later, Clancy asked Rome for release: he had too little to do. Ignoring the inevitable reprimand, he persisted: 'I would prefer any diocese in America or Great Britain to my present connection with Charleston. It is too bad that I should be sent on a voyage of discovery through the old and the new world.' To his credit, he rose to a cholera epidemic, begging unity, tolerance and courage from all denominations as 'all part of one social family'. Bishop England told Pope Gregory, 'Clancy is the best of men ... but unhappy ... distinguished for character, zeal and piety, but in one year he has wrecked church government which has taken years to perfect.' In desperation, England sent him to Haiti in his own role (to prevent his doing further damage), but recalled him.

In 1837 Rome redirected Clancy to British Guiana as its first Apostolic Vicar. John Hynes, Dominican friar and Guiana's first Catholic missioner until 1834, was promoted bishop to replace Clancy at Charleston. Clancy stayed at the Dominican house in Cork, searched Hynes' room, copied a confidential report on Guiana and opened the Papal Brief for Hynes' Carolina appointment. Months later, Bishop England received the Brief, saw the broken seal and refused Hynes' appointment, at which Clancy asked Rome to appoint Hynes as *his* assistant in Guiana. In founding the Guiana Catholic mission Hynes had generated immense goodwill. Rome refused Clancy's request, but left Hynes high and dry there, a bishop with no portfolio.

Clancy lecture-toured Ireland and Europe before sailing to Guiana. He attacked the USA so vehemently for its intolerance of Catholics that the Bishop of Cincinnati came to Ireland to rebut him. Clancy fought back: 'From the altars of Ireland I will continue to dissuade Catholic Irishmen from emigrating to the USA until the Protestant Republican mind changes.' Charleston had its problems, but Clancy inflated them. Finally, in November 1838, he sailed for British Guiana with six priests and four seminarians. Once disembarked at Georgetown, he compiled mission reports from Hynes' old letters and statistics, inflated the number of Catholics, and surfed with aplomb on his own publicity.

The Tablet covered his return trip to Europe for another funding and recruiting drive in Rome, Vienna, London and Dublin. Sharing a platform with O'Connell, he introduced himself, 'called from the swamps of Guiana and Charleston to address the good and respectable in Great Britain'. At Ware College, he thanked student priests for their welcome, 'accustomed [as] I am to congratulatory addresses in the USA, Ireland, Haiti and other countries'. At formal dinner in London he claimed 'to represent the Colonial department', travelling thousands of miles in South America and the Caribbean, to bring to the guests, 'gratitude from the lips of the red man in the primal forests of Guiana, and from the prisons of the sable sons and daughters of Africa'.[18]

THE PRESSED VOLUNTEER

Early in 1841 Eugene Macnamara left Borrisokane parish, home-posted to Corofin. *The Limerick Reporter* announced, 'Removed from Borrisokane, Tipperary, to Corofin, Clare, the Rev. Eugene Macnamara, a most truly Christian minister.' On 13 March the unsympathetic *Limerick Chronicle* reported (in the same column as the suicide of a seminarian at Maynooth, and near the text of an anti-Catholic lecture by a Protestant cleric): 'Rev. E. Macnamara is removed from Borrisokane to Corofin.'

Macnamara remembered Corofin's 'fire eating' parish priest, Stephen Walsh, a 'provincial Boanerges' who preached on Hell, but who continued to fight Edward Synge, as John Murphy had done. Macnamara's posting there was a fiction to conceal that Bishop Kennedy had suspended him and had informed Rome of an offence.[19] Scandal was particularly feared in a newly emancipated church. Kennedy gave Macnamara an *Exeat*, with the reason for his suspension entered on it.

Later that month, Bishop Clancy passed from Rome through London to Ireland, and met Macnamara. He was recruiting priests to force the Colonial Office to subsidise double the four Catholic clergy already funded by the Crown. The Colonial Secretary recognised Clancy as parish priest of Georgetown and a paid civil servant, but not as a Rome-appointed bishop. Britain had no legal mechanism for recognising the Pope or his appointees outside the confines of the Papal States. The priests in Guiana were Clancy's curates, without status and dependent on the parish priest's goodwill. Clancy hoped that by importing more clergy to Guiana as a *fait accompli,* he could exact a larger lump sum from the Colonial Office which he would then apportion. Ominously, of the six clerics he took to Guiana in 1838, two had left by 1841.

Macnamara needed a fresh start and Clancy recruited indiscriminately to save Guiana Catholics 'from paganism, heresy, and those ravening wolves in sheep's clothing', the Protestant missioners. He read Macnamara's *exeat* and kept it. On 26 May, Eugene Macnamara and two other recruits boarded a vessel in the Thames. Clancy saw them off, then informed *The Tablet*:

> Rev. William Nightingale, formerly of London District, Rev. Eugene Macnamara of the Diocese of Killaloe, and a Capuchin friar of Spain, Juan Baptista Esquinigo, have sailed *per* the ship *Rambler* direct from London to Georgetown, on Tuesday 25 May, 1841. Bishop Clancy will ordain two priests for the same Vicariate during Pentecost week in Carlow College, who will sail from Dublin. The Bishop hopes to be accompanied by nuns.[20]

The nuns were to found schools, and included Clancy's cousin, Abigail Cantillon, of the Presentation Order in Cork city, who had helped found a new convent at Midleton. She was recalled in 1840 by her superior, Mary England, who felt she was unsettled and unsettling. Mrs England was sister to John England, bishop of Charleston, who happened to be visiting Ireland at the same time as Dr Clancy.

Clancy had Rome's permission to recruit nuns, conditional on bishops' and superiors' agreement. On 10 June 1841, Clancy visited the Cork convent, but Mary England would not release Cantillon. Privately she thought her 'liable to an infringement of her vows and rules' in Guiana, but told Clancy she could not be spared. He accepted 'God's will', yet a week later 'came to our convent between eight and nine in the morning and called for his cousin. Rev. Mother England prayed him to breakfast with her brother, Dr England [then visiting], but Clancy declined. Immediately afterwards he conducted Sister Cantillon out of the convent without permission or knowledge of her Superior or Bishop, and handed her into a covered vehicle ready at the convent gate.'[21] John Hynes and Mary England called it 'elopement'. Cantillon recruited other nuns from Port Laoise and Carlow, telling them to rendezvous in Dublin, for Guiana in early autumn.

The gorse was colouring the limestone fields in Clare as Eugene Macnamara left Britain for South America. James Macmahon, one of his parishioners at Kilkee, told the Poor Law Enquiry in 1835, 'we are worse than the slaves in the colonies and we give up the ghost at 58 or 60'. Possibly, Macnamara did not see Clare again, but he had a memory of refugees, deprivation, and emigrant ships. He was now making that fresh start himself and his next parish priest was no Michael Comyn.

Chapter 3
Mission and Mayhem: 1841–44

On 3 July, 1841, the brig *Rambler*, thirty-six days out from London, crossed the Demerara estuary bar and crabbed east to the wharves. A customary welcome cheer rose from dozens of European and American merchant ships cabled along the eastern bank. Behind the wharves lay old Georgetown, below the high tide marker. Effluent on mudflats and a tidal build-up of rubbish under new, masonry wharves, well-intentioned, but too dense for the tide to flush, bred 'yellow jack' typhus and malaria for which Guiana was notorious. The nose picked up yard cooking and undrained ditches before the eyes distinguished town, 'veiled in dense tropical vegetation' (see Map B).

UNEASE

Eugene Macnamara and his colleagues disembarked to a waiting crowd for whom a ship brought work. British Guiana was in recession, and long-term unemployment had been most slaves' experience of freedom after 1834: an apprenticeship to pace the emancipation of 85,000 collapsed. 'Commercial and agricultural distress is unprecedented', wrote the US consul in 1841. Cotton exports, badly dented by US competition, and coffee, were down by half, sugar, rum and molasses by a third, and on average three quarters of the workforce had fled from over 300 plantations. Joseph Booker's sugar wharf was empty: he had emancipated his slaves in 1826, eight years before the law required, and his idealism had cost him.[1]

Beyond the wharves, white painted villas and gardens of bougainvillea showed where compensation of £50 per slave to owners had been spent, £4 million to Guiana alone. At Christ Church and its house on Brickdam causeway, Friar William Bates greeted the arrivals in Clancy's absence. 'Our salute was a hearty welcome, [but] we became incredulous as to the Bishop's residence … what we took for a wooden outbuilding was our abode … His Lordship's residence is rough and plain, secured above by a slated roof, but its walls not proof against wind or rain.'[2]

The apprehensive curates were also stoic and experienced. They slipped quickly into a routine of visiting and services at prisons, hospital and the outlying plantations. Coping with humidity and airless mosquito netting took longer. Macnamara baptised his first Guiana child on 11 July at the Essequibo mission, 30 miles from Georgetown; Nightingale was despatched to a fifty-mile stretch of the 'Arabian' [Caribbean] Coast 100 miles away. Most ex-slaves ('labourers') were Baptist or Catholic, and the 2,000 European Guiana Catholics were reinforced by Portuguese migrants, crowding plantation dispensaries, town hospitals and the prisons. Most never reached the fields, preferring the streets where they boosted urban trade. Settler Catholics did not welcome them, and they did not make up the labour shortfall.

As soon as Bishop Clancy arrived from Dublin with six nuns on 5 October, he informed *The Tablet*, 'Nuns of the Presentation Order took possession of a large and commodious building.' In November he told *The Catholic Directory* and *The Madras Catholic Expositor* that the nuns were 'the first of the Order ever established on the continent of America', running six schools already. Governor Sir Henry Light was unimpressed: 'Dr Clancy and the nuns lived in the same house; the nuns and novices quarrelled with the Superior and with each other, and most quitted the establishment.'[3]

Even with Nightingale's transfer to the coast, Macnamara and Bates could not share an outbuilding for long, nor could the bishop and six nuns accommodate them. In December, Clancy sent Bates back to New Amsterdam, where another curate, John McDonnell, had been coping alone. Most of Guiana's 98,000 population lived on the coastal belt where plantations flourished on a rich silt.

Elsewhere, the Spanish friar, Juan Esquinigo, joined John Cullen at Santa Rosa, a Spanish-Indian settlement on the Meruca river. In

Georgetown, Clancy and Macnamara were joined in November by Joseph Kelly from Ireland, but Thomas Morgan worked alone at an Indian settlement and penal colony on the Essequibo, as did Nightingale on the coast. Clancy hoped that employing eight curates as a *fait accompli* would force the Legislature to double the lump-sum stipend.

Britain recognised Catholics, but not the Pope. To the Colonial Office Clancy was no bishop, but a parish priest. Clancy apportioned the lump sum stipend (for four curates) between himself and the current eight curates and like a parish priest in Ireland, decided on the portions. He exaggerated the numbers of Portuguese Catholics to justify his new clergy quota, omitting deaths and repatriations. The ebb and flow of the Portuguese was confusing, but when Clancy asked Rome to add Grenada and Barbados to his 'thinly populated forest' to make it financially viable, Rome also turned him down.[4]

Nightingale was weary on the 'Arabian' coast with heavy-drinking planters for company; he and Morgan were vulnerable alone. Nightingale told his London contact in October of starting a ministry from scratch. He had neither house nor church, but the views and light were beautiful and a prowling tiger kept him alert. 'I was ordered immediately to this coast [although] the Bishop still calls me his chaplain. I must look difficulties in the face and not droop'. He lamented his dependence on 'hospitable and profligate' planters whose workers he was trying to help stabilise. In January 1842, new legislation for working conditions was introduced to tackle unrest and desertion on the plantations, but it did not help Nightingale. 'Here nothing is done without the bottle. It is an insult not to partake [but I produce my Friar Mathew] silver medal. I am [now] not expected at the constant parties where the bottle is the bond. A man knows himself best when he is alone.' He found company in the sea and the view during fever bouts in his hammock, 'my books and my snuffbox my constant solace'.[5]

Medical Officer Hancock attributed much to 'alcohol debauchery', but polluted water and mosquitoes did not help. 'The intemperance to which Europeans in the tropics seem particularly tempted [produces] three fifths of deaths' wrote one Protestant missioner; the London Mission Society blamed the planters' own behaviour for colony unrest. Even Anthony Trollope, who saw the best in Guiana, claimed 'the yellow fever is not half as bad as a fellow with a brandy bottle'. One planter recorded that 'drinking, fighting and rioting are indulged … to an extent known nowhere in Europe, outside of Ireland'. Four of Macnamara's eight colleagues, including Bishop Clancy, became alcohol addicts; Nightingale and Macnamara held Friar Mathew's medal, and sarsparilla was advertised in the Guiana papers, but only the Methodists took temperance seriously.[6]

BISHOP CLANCY'S REGIME

Bishop Clancy and Mr Macnamara took Sunday services in Georgetown, at local plantations and on the estuary islands. The Colonial Jail and five garrison stations (Irish Catholic soldiers, 'a wild set, but pious when befuddled') also required priests during the week. Catholicism required a priest's physical presence to bring mass and confession to all, with no auxiliary or lay ministry to spread the impossible ancient load.

Early each Wednesday, Macnamara visited the Jail, which housed 1,200 male prisoners in eighty cells. Church services brought some respite from the overcrowding and the treadmill, but security was threatened when so many took advantage of the worship break. Unrest and economic depression had expanded the populations of the Colonial and Female jails and the Debtors' Clink, making it a tense year in Guiana cells.

On 15 December, 1841, Eugene Macnamara wrote from his out-house to Bishop Clancy next door:

> My Lord, I attended the Jail this morning to celebrate mass for the Catholic prisoners. The jailer in a loud and blustering manner, with anger in his face, told me I should not celebrate mass … the sheriff had ordered not to admit me. The jailer delivered his message ungraciously and derived pleasure from it publicly in the presence of all the prisoners. I anxiously await your Lordship's will to know what I am to do.

Clancy, sick with fever, gout and drink, forwarded the letter to Governor Light, 'as a painful duty'. He emphasised that the weekly chaplain was *unpaid*, but his pitch rose and his pen wandered off-sheet:

> I need scarcely inform your Excellency that in England … so far from sheriff or jailer *daring to obstruct a priest*

[Clancy's emphasis] … facilities are afforded by every high and subordinate functionary. May I beg as a favour [but] perhaps … in the stronger language of a Christian Bishop, demand as a right, redress for this wanton and unprovoked act of intolerance or incipient persecution, [before I make] complaint to the Colonial Office.[7]

Bishop Clancy enjoyed the sound of office. He once sent a note to the Colony Secretary 'as from a recognised Catholic prelate and a Nobleman, which I am by creation of a European King, to [you] a mere layman, not my equal in spiritual or temporal rank'. On 2 January 1842, after investing two nuns at High Mass, he informed *The Tablet* in London that 'the cathedral [*sic*] was crowded with colonists of the highest respectability'.[8]

Nightingale reached his limit in December and left for New York. His correspondent in London, a *Tablet* trustee, handed his letters to the editor who published them; Bishop Clancy also puffed in the 5 March issue: 'Judge Firebrace's conversion in my presence more than amply compensates for all I have endured during eight years in the swamps and forests of Charleston and Guiana.'[9] He had, in total, spent six of those eight years in Europe. As he wrote, Thomas Morgan on the Essequibo and a lay sister from the Georgetown convent also quit, independently, with $150 of the sister's wages still outstanding.

After reading the latest *Tablet* editions, Clancy sailed on an 1800-mile round trip visit to Nevis, 'ordered by my physician [brother, Francis] to sail among the healthy islands and bathe in the salt waters after recent fevers'. He returned fit to fight back. Nightingale was on £100 salary with passage paid: if so destitute, how did he buy his 'fashionable pony'? If he had a temperance medal from Friar Mathew, 'my co-worker in the apostolate', why was his house full of 'bottles as candleholders? Had he drunk them all?' He cited Bates, McDonnell and Cullen as agreeing with him, but significantly not Macnamara.[10]

After four years in New Amsterdam, John McDonnell requested six months' sick leave from 31 July 1842, later extended to 1 April 1843. Clancy requested sick leave from 30 August, but Sir Henry Light knew this was about more than health and ordered his return by the end of February 1843.[11] Macnamara and Kelly covered Georgetown in his absence, Macnamara receiving twenty-six adult converts up to February

1843, baptising 108 children up to April and enduring the heat, the insects and the nightly frogs' chorus. In March 1843, Joseph Kelly signed off the Georgetown register with *'Deo Gratias!'*, before he too quit Guiana. Half the mission's eight curates departed in the eighteen months after Macnamara landed, and he was now alone in Georgetown.

Governor Light, a devout Anglican, needed Solomon's wisdom to govern rival missions. Next door lay Venezuela, from where Indians had fled down the Meruca river to British asylum when their Franciscan missioners were massacred in Venezuela's independence war of 1823. John Hynes had answered their distress call and John Cullen took over the new 'Santa Rosa' mission on the Meruca from a surviving Venezuelan friar in 1840. Governor Light saluted the mission: 'its worth may be estimated when it is known that upwards of 30,000 Indians had been brought into quasi-civilisation by the Spanish missionaries.' When a Methodist approached Light for permission to demolish a Spanish wayside cross, Light refused him. When a freelance missioner requested 'a licence to teach the Doctrine of the New Jerusalem and to catechise the Indians', Light called it 'religious delusion'.[12] The Governor reported sectarian bad feeling between Presbyterians and Anglicans, but generally the free churches served emancipated slaves well, particularly the London Missionary Society and the Methodists, self-financed with no Government stipend. British nonconformists had led the anti-slavery campaign and incurred the anger of slave-owners, but Methodists also related well to the Church of England from which they stemmed.

The same could not be said of Clancy. In May of 1842, he wrote to Lord Stanley, Colonial Secretary in London, asking tartly whether his stipend for extra priests was being denied 'by a few bigoted Tory planters'. Stanley endorsed it 'intemperate'.[13] Light insisted that as Portuguese immigrants had stopped coming and were in fact leaving, no more Catholic clergy were needed. Clancy complained to Stanley of 'parsimony' and of a 'promise' broken, threatening that he would *order* the Portuguese to leave and would 'advise the governments of Malta, France and Madeira that all Catholic emigrants are likely to have their religious rights eroded or destroyed', signing himself Bishop, Apostolic Vicar, and Count of the Holy Roman Empire.[14]

IMMIGRATION[15]

Immigration was to Guiana what emigration was to Ireland. Emancipation had freed around 85,000 slaves to a four-year 'apprenticeship' before paid labour, but most dug their own allotments and the coffee, cotton and sugar plantations suffered. By 1841, an estimated 5,000 new labourers a year were needed to make up for the drift from plantations, but they did not materialise. Alcohol consumption and the prison population were the colony's only growth areas, and it was hard to attract and finance immigrants.

A small Maltese colony came in 1839, led by a priest, but health and morale were poor. Town and city workers were imported from India, but disliked plantation work. A proposed transplant of Sierra Leoneans in 1843 ended with ships arriving empty. Governor Light complained to the Colonial Land and Emigration Committee (CLEC) about malicious rumours of snow and ice in Guiana and of immigrants being branded and auctioned on landing. Talk of Guiana's being 'Europe's graveyard' was less exaggerated than one planter's description, 'as healthy as Rutland county'. Of 8,000 Portuguese arrivals, many died; many were also repatriated, after a Yellow Fever epidemic in 1842. Their temperament and religion fuelled prejudice: Port Medical Officer Dalton called them 'the refuse of Funchal which has three times emptied its jails to fill British Guiana'. Immigration was topic of the year in 1842 – as in every year since 1834, but the explorer Richard Schomburgck was clear: 'only an egoist without conscience can ask a European to emigrate there'.

In September 1842 one Correa de Costa advertised an intention to bring 500 British socialists to found 'Coburg' (after Prince Albert). They would cultivate grapes, tobacco and coffee, assisted by 'millions' of native Indians. Nothing happened. In 1845, Bernhardt Ries, who had earlier brought in 100 Germans, proposed a German colony at Cartabo Point, on the Essequibo estuary, but only the advance party arrived, speaking no English. Clancy supported it briefly for his claim to a larger stipend. That year the Tropical Emigration Society of London asked to settle 1,500 on the Essequibo: they believed in creating Eden through technology, but their estimate of four years to break in a third of the land paled against their concern that 'the RC priesthood would be jealous of such a large body of Protestants on the river'. The Venezuelan government had already turned them down for their exaggerated publicity and subsidy demands:

by 1847, they were bankrupt. Behind both applications lurked John Diston Powles, instigator of the Topo River fiasco in 1828, Mexican bondholder, and enthusiast for colonising Mexican California.

Bishop Clancy devised his own immigration model. His doctor brother, Francis, came to Guiana in 1838, his nun cousin, Abigail Cantillon, in 1841, and priest cousin, William J. Clancy, left Alabama amid controversy in 1842 to cover for McDonnell in New Amsterdam. The bishop claimed to have seen Irish navvies and cotton workers survive the Southern Carolina climate, worse than Guiana. Forty Irishmen landed at Georgetown in 1836, with others from Britain, to work on coffee estates, but a proposed mixed colony of British juveniles sentenced to transportation and Bulgarian peasants from Constantinople did not arrive. Once employed, Irish workers could turn Irish planter goodwill into resentment. Plantation Donneybrook 'imported 30 Irishmen from Connaught [1839–40] and would pay anyone handsomely to take them. They never miss their evening grog and such wild ruffians are enough to scare the Indians from the settlement altogether'.

Irish migrants were trickling into neighbouring Venezuela 'to lay their bones' at remote mines. John Cullen, Macnamara's colleague on the Berbice, was in touch with the Archbishop of Caracas, the Venezuelan ambassador in London, and his own brother, Edward, a doctor. A Cullen ancestor had served with Bolivar, and Edward stayed with John in Guiana several times, on his way to becoming an eccentric expert on Central America. At the peak of the Irish Famine in 1847, both Cullens asked Britain to send paupers from the west of Ireland to Venezuela; a year later, a senior Jesuit asked Hynes about bringing an Irish colony to the interior. In 1851, after two years surveying in the Panama jungle, Edward Cullen claimed to have found the perfect place for a canal. A reconnaissance party followed, but concluded he had followed a heat mirage and had surveyed in circles.

BISHOP CLANCY TO ROME

Clancy's visit in May–June 1842 to the sulphur springs of Nevis, near St Kitts, had been a disaster. Bath Village was spa to the ailing wealthy; St Kitts welcomed his effusions about their island church, and his promised donation, but he left for Nevis so hastily that he failed to meet the Lieutenant Governor. News came back along the vine to Guiana, and

Governor Light duly told London. 'Dr Clancy and Mrs O'Regan went on plea of ill-health and resided at the same house for some weeks on Nevis. On return, Clancy found his flock scandalised at the intimacy and a petition was signed and addressed to Rome for his removal.'

The Governor had consistent reservations about Clancy. 'He came with great pretensions. He refused to produce to me his credentials, but read them out in his Chapel. I objected to the innovation of Midnight Mass, fearing that Papal ceremonies in the streets might become policy. His correspondence with me was in the tone of supremacy over all civil authority.'[16] At a government dinner in 1839 when the toast 'to the Church' was proposed, Clancy and the Anglican archdeacon rose simultaneously to reply. Clancy stood on his episcopal rank, causing guests to leave. Light continued: 'he refused to account for his spending, his priests received what he chose to give them out of the grants. There were constant quarrels, dismissals, intrigues and mutual recriminations which have ended in appeal to Rome and still greater scandal.'

Before taking sick leave in August 1842, Clancy enlisted *The Tablet* against his critics, 'schismatical, lower class, nominal Catholics', the sort who would steal church plate. He also recalled Friar Bates to Georgetown as Vicar General, working with Macnamara. According to Light, Bates 'associated [in New Amsterdam] with a lady of some attraction, pleading instruction to convert her to the RC faith'. Clancy also asked the Archbishop of Dublin for five priests from All Hallows College to train for Guiana, 'academics who might pray and teach. I have seven priests, four or five more could be usefully employed'. Establishing a college would allow him to import ordained staff for whom he could claim as curates, but a year later when the Dean of All Hallows asked Bishop Hynes for the first fees owed, Hynes referred him to Clancy who still held the funds.[17]

Bishop Clancy put into Ford's Hotel, London. Governor Light had assumed he was going to Rome to rebut complaints, but Clancy was still at Ford's in Manchester Square on 28 February 1843. He approached the Colonial Secretary (and acting-Secretary for War) Lord Stanley, for a subsidised chaplaincy to the Irish Catholic soldiers of the Guiana garrison. Stanley refused him chaplaincy and a chapel, and worse, styled him as 'Reverend'. Clancy, peeved that 'no such person in London' existed, demanding his title of 'Bishop' or 'Right Reverend Doctor'. Stanley apologised in writing, but Clancy would not forgive 'the strange identification of the high title of a bishop with that of a mere deacon'.[18] From Ford's he wrote regularly to *The Tablet*.

Eventually *The Tablet* reported his being in Rome for Easter 1843. He preached at the Jesuit church and attended the Pope at the Easter Mass. He also appealed to have Abigail Cantillon's property forwarded from her Cork convent to Demerara.[19] His six-month leave had lingered to eight by the time he wrote to Lord Stanley in April, explaining that his *nine-month* leave would expire on 1 June, and requesting six months more, 'apprehensive that Vicariate business will detain me in Rome, [and I am] seriously attacked by local fevers'. Stanley was not fooled, 'some mistake has arisen', and allowed the six months, but backdated to 28 February. The regulation half-salary for leave would be paid 'only on return of the absent functionary to the Colony'. Bishop Clancy had no income until he reappeared in Guiana at the end of August.

MR MACNAMARA TO THE POPE

On sick leave in Ireland, John McDonnell probably talked. 'Reports are contradictory' mused Battersby's *Directory*. When he returned in May 1843, he did not continue to New Amsterdam. Macnamara had turned on Friar Bates and demanded that he leave Georgetown to rejoin William J. Clancy at New Amsterdam where the Bishop's cousin was already under a cloud. Bates, Macnamara's superior in Clancy's absence, retaliated by suspending Macnamara, Georgetown curate for nearly two years on what Governor Light called 'a pittance', living in a shanty and covering the bishop's total absence of fifteen months. As Bates and cousin Clancy kicked over the traces on the Berbice, Macnamara acted:

> Last Sunday after Mass, the Rev Mr Macnamara, Catholic pastor of Georgetown, and the Rev Mr McDonnell of Berbice, announced to the congregation from the altar their intention of immediately proceeding to Rome to lay before His Holiness the Pope the degraded and unhappy state of this Vicariate.[20]

The congregation raised a petition, signed by what Light called 'a large and respectable body' of doctors, judges and planters: John Taggart was consul for Portugal and an old friend of John Hynes, the mission founder, now in Rome; Colonel Goodman, former Militia commander, was Colony Secretary for Berbice; Elector Dr Clifton was a lifetime colony Councillor, and Captain Hammill a planter and sea captain. Their complaints included Clancy's drinking, embezzlement, and the lifestyles of Bates and cousin Clancy. Governor Light told London, 'The priests' payment was limited by Dr Clancy to mere subsistence; he refused audits and is charged with misappropriation.'[21]

On 3 June 1843, Macnamara and McDonnell boarded the barque *Mary* for a five-week journey to Liverpool with barrels of sugar, molasses and rum. They used the time to produce a financial account for the Pope. From Liverpool they made for Ford's, London. Conspicuously, *The Tablet* stopped publishing Ford's guest list as well as its own *Roman News* column.

In Rome, Cardinal Fransoni, Prefect of the missions directorate, Propaganda Fide, had already ordered Clancy to resign and the papal gendarmerie to confine him to Rome. Ecclesiastical Rome had its national subcultures, the intelligence hub of the clerical world. Transient Irish officials and missioners were there with reason, but around them circled eccentrics, scholars, those out to dry, those on private means and those who lived for being near the hub with its companionable gossip. Hynes, isolated in Rome since Bishop England rejected him for Charleston in 1838, found it claustrophobic. In later years he denounced it: 'Rome requires a purifying and her dignitaries a humbling.'[22] (See Plate 4.)

Clancy lodged at a city centre convent and was the talk of the Rome Irish, 'running about with [two dismissed professors] without his episcopals'. The three drank, worked their contacts and misinformed *The Tablet*, 'having the world believe that the greatest men in Rome are the Pope, Cardinal Acton and Dr Clancy'. Irish expatriates savouring cool evenings after humid Roman days, frequently spotted them 'disguised in lay costume'.[23]

On 16 July, Hynes heard from consul Taggart that Macnamara was on route to Rome. Immediately he forwarded Taggart's letter to Fransoni, and wrote to Macnamara and McDonnell at Ford's, advising that they delay; he could not order it, but he feared their presence might jeopardise key decisions. On 9 August the Pope confirmed him as Apostolic Administrator to Guiana, with wide authority. Clancy pleaded a sudden need to see Lord Stanley in London, evaded the gendarmes and once in

England took the Demerara mailboat from Southampton. Hynes then regretted stalling Macnamara: 'Clancy has hoaxed Propaganda Fide. His object was not to go to Lord Stanley, but to hasten off with papers connected with [Guiana] to screen himself or turn them to his account.'[24] Clancy also needed his salary.

In 1843 a man could tell one story in Rome, another in London, a third in Guiana and not be found out for months. Clancy stopped briefly at the Irish College, Paris, but told Rector McSweeney nothing. He informed *The Tablet* of his sailing, 'because of the death of several priests, the abandonment of their mission by others, and to reclaim property from schismatics'. He told his doctor brother, Francis, back from Guiana, that he had to 'protect the [nuns] against future aggression from Hynes and his miscreant agents Macnamara and McDonnell'. He told Thomas Griffiths, Apostolic Vicar of London, he had resigned 'on health and eyesight grounds' and was returning to prepare for his successor 'if such be appointed'. Friar Bates, he lamented, had died 'of a broken heart after lay persecution and the flight of Macnamara and McDonnell'. With unconscious irony, he told *The Tablet* that he was preparing for 'a supply of clergymen from Rome'. When his ship watered at Barbados, Clancy invited William Rogers to accompany him to Guiana: Rogers, dismissed by Clancy from Guiana in 1839, agreed to be his Vicar General and secretary, without informing his own bishop.[25]

Messrs Macnamara and McDonnell reached Rome in early September. Hynes read their 'deplorable account' while they rested and made an appointment with Fransoni for the next morning at Propaganda Fide *palazzo*. Fransoni listened to Macnamara and examined the audit which showed 59 per cent of the mission funds unreconciled.[26] The Cardinal told them of Hynes' new authority in Guiana, ordering, 'it must now be made public'. Accordingly, Macnamara wrote to inform Judge Firebrace, and McDonnell wrote to Dr Clifton.

Three days later, Hynes wrote letters authorising Macnamara as Vicar Administrator (Hynes' deputy) and pastor of Georgetown, and McDonnell as pastor of New Amsterdam to replace cousin Clancy. He also wrote to Bishop Griffiths, Vicar Apostolic of London, Governor Light, consul Taggart, Clancy and Abigail Cantillon. Lucas at *The Tablet* had promised a news blackout of at least three months on Guiana. That evening, after a week in Rome, the priests left by stagecoach, but Hynes fretted about the tone of his letters to Clancy and Cantillon. He wrote to Macnamara care of Ford's on 14 September, ordering him not to use them (they were unsealed), but to use two replacement (sealed) letters he enclosed. He would follow to Guiana soon.[27]

On 1 October, they left Southampton by *City of Glasgow*, 'a princely mansion' of 1600 tons, which landed them at Georgetown early in November. John Cullen greeted them, ready for 'any commands from Dr Hynes'. Governor Light had summoned him from Santa Rosa to cover Georgetown when the two left for Rome, but Clancy ejected him from the presbytery and church in September, reasserting himself as Vicar Apostolic.[28]

Throughout September and October Clancy advertised 'a free church' open to all denominations. On his first Sunday back, he accused Dr Clifton of 'lay usurpation', for having read a lesson from inside the altar sanctuary, at Cullen's 'illicit' request. As Clifton, of 'Protestant Cambridge', rose in his pew, Clancy strode down from the altar, collared him and called the police to arrest him for disturbance. The case was dismissed in court, but Clifton counter-charged Clancy, who was summonsed, at which Clifton dropped charges. On the next Sunday, Clancy read out a litany of accusations and justifications. From far away, Pope Gregory ordered him out of Guiana.

John Taggart denounced Clancy in *The Royal Demerara Gazette* for his lies, his 'mephitic family' and as 'the calamity of this Vicariate'. Captive Catholics had endured enough, and most 'including the ladies' wanted nothing to do with Clancy, whose actions were 'no credit to you as a man, nor lustre to your mitre'. A Clancy supporter took a horsewhip to Taggart in the street and was arrested. In October, Dr Clifton finally received McDonnell's letter from Rome confirming Clancy's dismissal, but when he published it in *The Royal Gazette*, Clancy counter-published a denial.

CONFRONTATION

Macnamara and McDonnell disembarked on 10 November, and delivered Hynes' letter to Governor Light immediately. Delivering to Clancy was another matter: 'Dr Clancy laughed at the letters. When the priests, with witnesses, delivered them, Dr Clancy, a burly big-fisted Irishman, walked out with a shillelagh to drive them away. The letters, however, appeared in the newspapers. Both letters were undignified, offensive, impolitic and premature.'[29]

Macnamara delivered the sealed, revised letters to Clancy and Cantillon as ordered, and was left with the originals. Fransoni and Hynes had also ordered him to 'publish' their instructions, but Clancy held the revised letters, controlled the Georgetown pulpit, and cousin William J. controlled New Amsterdam (Bates had died). Macnamara turned to the press as the Saturday editions were being typeset. He handed to the editors of *The Royal Gazette* and *The Guiana Herald* the withdrawn letters to Clancy and Cantillon as 'authentic copies' of those in Clancy's hands. He was tired, angry and both letter versions made the same points. He had orders in person from Fransoni and in writing from Hynes, to 'announce to our congregations that the jurisdiction of Dr Clancy has ceased'. The heralds were barred from the churches, and newspapers broadcast better than pulpits.

Macnamara admitted in print that it was 'unusual for pastors to adopt the press to communicate with their flocks'. He described his Rome interviews, and Clancy's 'two attempts to escape secretly from Rome'. After attacking Clancy's behaviour as 'sinful, sacrilege, illicit and contumaceous', he regretted the spectacle, by which 'scoffers are amused and the serious grieved'. Hynes' withdrawn letters were certainly strong copy:

> Your presence can only be productive of mischief, without surrendering the documents and monies of the Vicariate, leaving me without a shilling to [run] a ruined mission. $25,000 or upwards of funds, grants and contributions are still in your hands. You may hand them to the Rev. Eugene Macnamara who is authorised to demand and receive them. One point more, of great delicacy. You have been residing within the precincts of a convent, causing great scandal and bringing grievous reproach upon the Presentation Order. As guardian of the desolate and scandalised church of Guiana, I forbid your lordship's entering, living and sleeping in that establishment on any pretext. I insist on your retiring without delay. I cannot permit you to exercise any function of Catholic ministry.

Abigail Cantillon and her nuns earned little shrift: 'For the little edification which you have hitherto given to the people of Guiana, you are all to depart.' She went to Rome later to clear her name and spent the rest of her days in Midleton Presentation Convent which she had helped found. The Cork convent from which Clancy had persuaded her to 'elope' would not have her back.

On 11 November Macnamara wrote to Bishop Griffiths of the London Vicariate, begging him 'check this horrid scandal, daily increasing in violence' which put him 'in a cruel dilemma'. He faced Clancy alone, was barred from church property and Hynes was unlikely to arrive soon, let alone be recognised by Clancy or even the Government.

Clancy exchanged his shillelagh for a pen in *The Royal Gazette*:

> I never authorised the publication of a document so manifestly illegal, ungentlemanly and uncanonical. A priest named Eugene Macnamara threw two sealed letters into my house. I could not permit him to enter owing to a recent knowledge of his character. He had been publicly [suspended] by my late Vicar General [Bates] and was [previously] suspended in Ireland by Bishop Kennedy of Killaloe for a transgression. On the arrival of Bishop Hynes in this colony I shall prove his allegations, and those of the clerical traitors who call themselves his friends, to be baseless and wicked fabrications of depraved men.

He also wrote that day to Bishop McDonnell of Trinidad, his nearest fellow bishop. Cullen had contacted McDonnell for advice in Clancy's absence, and Macnamara might do the same. Hynes was 'unjust, ungrateful, ambitious and avaricious [and] Macnamara a rebellious priest of Killaloe formerly suspended for seduction, whose *exeat* I possess'. Clancy then asked ominously what really lay behind Hynes' leaving Guiana in 1835.[30]

IMPLOSION

John Hynes sent further letters on 1 November ordering Macnamara to suspend Rogers and William J. Clancy. Friar Bates was dead, but his mistress still had vestments, church plate and a carriage. Hynes' Roman papers of appointment were delayed, but Lord Stanley could not recognise them as they were Papal instruments. Griffiths found him 'polite, but disinclined to interfere without proof', and asked Paul Cullen, Irish agent in Rome, for some informal evidence. Stanley agreed that a face-saver was needed, given 'the enormous practical inconvenience of a Protestant Government maintaining a Catholic Church establishment without any Concordat with the Pope'.[31] Clancy, meanwhile, wrote to Dr Coyne, Vicar General of Dublin, who shared the letter with Hynes in December, 'breathing direful vengeance against me. He called Macnamara, McDonnell and Cullen "Judases", Taggart "an unbaptised pagan" and threatens that if I approach the colony with the scoundrel priests … he will give us such a reception <u>as we should remember to the end of time</u>.'

In London *The Tablet* broke its embargo briefly. 'We have refrained from publishing. Dr Clancy resigned earlier this year and had no jurisdiction in British Guiana since February [1843]. We are shocked by his letter of September proclaiming his authority' and his threat to 'defend his rights by the sword'. Only on 19 October 1844, three months after Hynes landed in Guiana, did *Tablet* editor Lucas report and document fully Clancy's return to Georgetown in 1843, 'to augment scandal, a turbulent and unscrupulous enemy' affording 'our iniquitous government' pretext to interfere in church affairs. Lord Stanley had to be either 'madman or knave' to have continued paying Clancy. Unhelpfully, Lucas added that Stanley's treatment of Hynes was only to be expected from a former Secretary for Ireland.

Macnamara informed Hynes, 4 December, of Dr Clancy's 'daily increasing violence'. When he and Cullen confronted Clancy at the Post Office, Clancy shouted 'Suspended!' to which they retorted 'Usurper!' Macnamara had to celebrate mass in a private house for his minority congregation. He complained of the Clancy 'family clique' and how cousin Clancy in Berbice 'has pawned the chalice for brandy in a grog shop'. Clancy ridiculed Macnamara's Sunday service as a 'ballroom conventicle'.

Clancy 'interdicted' Macnamara and McDonnell, both already suspended by Bates for going to Rome, but 'a large and respectable body of Catholics' supported them. McDonnell and New Amsterdam parishioners took direct action, breaking down the church door on Christmas Eve, seizing William J. and placing him in a police cell to save him from the unseasonal revenge of other parishioners. A Governor's enquiry followed, since cousin Clancy was a paid civil servant. Bishop Clancy counterattacked the December 'burglars' in court, sued Macnamara for his £30 passage money from 1841, and Macnamara counter-sued for defamation.

When Bishop Hynes finally heard in December that his withdrawn letters had been published, he suspended Macnamara as priest and as Vicar Administrator: 'he acted dishonourably'. The edict did not arrive until February 1844, after Macnamara and McDonnell had already secured from Light the stipend taken off the Clancys. Suspension to Macnamara, as John Cullen arrived yet again from Santa Rosa to take his place, must have lost all meaning. Hynes did admit to Irish agent Cullen, in Rome, that his 'cancelled letters to Clancy were written hurriedly an hour or two before the departure of Mr Macnamara ... they should never have been written,' and that he, Hynes, had been 'sharply rebuked' by Cardinal Fransoni.

As the Catholic mission imploded, Clancy's failing eyesight brought some relief. In April 1844, he fired a gun and threw stones at passing Catholics from the presbytery verandah: all missed. Both Clancys called the Governor's enquiry 'lay interference'. Berbice parishioners petitioned for cousin Clancy's removal, but Bishop Clancy had never seen him drunk and denied a civil court's competence to judge a parish priest. Governor Light, weary of the 'coarseness, rancour and virulence making religion a mockery and our Redeemer a by-word', suggested that 'all be removed, or at least not paid'. When he withheld the Clancy stipends the bishop condemned it as civil interference. Light cut through the pathos and bathos to ask Clancy was he, or was he not 'authorised to perform the rites of the Catholic Church ?' By return, Clancy sent two words: 'I am'. He even returned letters from Rome unopened if they did not style him 'Vicar Apostolic'.

Hynes reached London and sent Rome copies of his second, more conciliatory letter to Clancy. He was angry with himself, but in the nineteenth century, communications lagged so far behind events that the time lag itself shaped those events. Bishop Griffiths in London saw Lord Stanley on 23 January 1844, to be told that as a 'salaried British officer' Clancy had a right to be heard. An apology from John Cullen and a letter from Macnamara about Clancy's court proceedings followed in January, before Macnamara received Hynes' letter of suspension in February.

BISHOP HYNES ARRIVES

Rival supporters grouped as the Apostolic Administrator stepped onto the Georgetown wharf in July, 1844. The Colonial Office saw that Hynes was patently sent by Rome, whereas Clancy had fled Rome, but Clancy was in possession. Clancy even petitioned Light for the return of his salary, accusing Hynes of being pro-slavery. Light was a fair man: 'the convent has given rise to scandal, but in a country like this scandal may be without foundation'. Clancy, without stipend or office, still had the house, church, and 'a numerous congregation'. A mere forty or fifty attended Hynes' public meeting on 18 July, 'planters, stock keepers, clerks, master mechanics, Dr Clifton, Judges Firebrace and Norton'.

On 23 August 1844, the Court of Policy, which ruled Guiana under the Governor, listened to Hynes' case, inspected the documentation and, after adjournment, formally recognised Hynes. *The Royal Gazette* of 24 August made the most of the 'ludicrous scene' and overdue humour. Hynes' messenger brought to the assembly the Papal letter *(bulla)* of appointment, but neither Governor nor Colony Secretary would receive it, lest they be seen to acknowledge the Pope. Two councillors, one a Presbyterian friend of the Catholic community, 'took the Bull by the horns', read it out, proposed a vote to recognise Hynes and 'reconsigned the terrible animal' to its keepers. In September 1844, Hynes petitioned the Governor for troops to repossess the church and house. Light adjudicated with humour: 'public order is not so imperilled, even by so bold and cunning an enemy as Clancy, to warrant my using bayonet and artillery'.

A private stratagem was agreed. Hynes left town to visit Cullen's river mission. On 15 November, lookouts watched Clancy leave the house for the church, then asked for him at the house door. The servant recalled Clancy, who left the church door open behind him. Hynes' supporters dashed in, but in the scuffle which followed Clancy struck Taggart 'with a massive bludgeon' and had to be disarmed. A judge ordered Clancy to hand over the church and the house keys, and Governor Light on London's instruction ordered Clancy to resign. Hynes held his first mass in the church on 8 December, while Clancy maintained a separate congregation at the house for another eighteen months. Hynes renamed Christ Church as Church of The Resurrection, to exorcise, but Light found him nearly as objectionable as Clancy, pretending to 'little less than the Pope might assume were he in British Guiana'.[32]

The schism wasted time and energy, and cut bridges. Like the Crottys of Birr it divided communities; some of its battles arose from outdated *ancien régime* notions of church authority. It had a corrosive effect on Hynes, as shown in his diary entries. In 1847, after accusing the Colonial Office of having supported Clancy through anti-Catholic malice, he was forced to apologise on pain of expulsion from Guiana. The lives of 85,000 freed slaves in an economic depression, and those of planter employers on dwindling revenue were no better for the feud and it took years to repair the damage.

THE POISON POSTSCRIPT

How Macnamara spent the months of suspension before Hynes' return, is not known, but Hynes informed the Court of Policy in August, in person, that 'Mr Macnamara [is] now in actual receipt of the [colony] stipend and acting under my commission.' Evidently all parties were looking forwards. In July, Clancy lost his cases for Macnamara's £30 passage money and for libel, from which Macnamara received £300 damages. Hynes was recognised by the Court of Policy, a procedure published in its entirety by *The Tablet*, 19 October. In mid-November, the church building was secured.

Hynes had punished Macnamara's disobedience, but acknowledged his own share of blame and had evidently reinstated him. An *Exeat* might have been a well-deserved release when Hynes commended Macnamara to the Archbishop of Mexico whom he knew from Rome. Some errant priests received an *Exeat* without recommendation: Hynes stated of John McDonnell in 1845, 'No loss'. Macnamara had not disgraced himself with alcohol, embezzlement or an illicit relationship, or even defied authority in principle. 'Many other' leading Demerara Catholics – Hammill, Goodman and Taggart among them – provided testimonials for him 'to the British residents' in Mexico, as they had to Papal officials in 1843. When the Clancys libelled Macnamara, Hynes supported him in the Court of Policy as 'cruelly assailed', and appealed in *The Royal Gazette* for information about their 'wicked conspiracy to defame'.

Francis Clancy MD, 'late physician to the convent of Guiana', had gone to Rome in November 1843 to lobby for his brother, but Irish agent Cullen refused to see him. In January 1844, Francis sent a diatribe to Hynes about 'monster' Macnamara:

> banished his native diocese for flagitious conduct ... employed his demoniacal arts to induce one of the nuns of Georgetown to elope ... for seven months they abstained from the sacraments rather than be contaminated by his ministry ... This wolf in sheep's clothing, furious at the loss of his prey, shrunk from the contact of virginal purity ... this ostracised priest of [County] Clare ... unparalleled in the annals of human turpitude.

The doctor attacked 'lay democracy' and Hynes' 'conspiracy' with Taggart, contrasting them with Bishop Clancy and the nuns, 'exiles, braving the terrors of the tropics, its swamps, morasses, and yellow fever to diffuse the blessing of religion and education'. The nuns were often cited during the schism, but their actual voices were not heard.

Francis Clancy forwarded his diatribe to Lord Stanley, describing "Rev. ?' [sic] Macnamara as a reckless, abandoned ecclesiastic who fled his diocese for proven seduction'. It was printed in France, distributed September 1844 to the Irish clergy and to Cullen in Rome by James Clancy, a priest brother of the bishop, and in Guiana by Bishop Clancy. Maynooth professors condemned it; Theobald Mathew was shocked by it; Hynes forwarded it to Rome with Macnamara's testimonials from Hammill and Goodman, and asked the Paris Prefect of Police to suppress it. In November 1845, after Macnamara had been a year in Mexico, an anonymously vengeful 'Christianus' wrote to Archdeacon Hamilton of Dublin that Macnamara had 'apostasised'.

Little rancour can have attended Macnamara's departure for Mexico. He passed the church and presbytery, both still in Clancy's hands, on his way to the wharves where he boarded a French ship. He had learned from the wild and the wise about colonies, immigration and Irish failings. He had taken the lead in a crisis and gone to the top. He had seen mission rivalry, and the success of the Methodists. He had heard anti-American sentiment, inflated notions of clerical authority, and had encountered the Colonial Land and Emigration Commission (CLEC) first-hand.

He would have been glad to leave Georgetown, a curate's graveyard where normality had lost its meaning and which had broken lesser men. As the Demerara estuary receded on a lengthening yellow wake, he may have muttered what Joseph Kelly added to his last register entry before leaving in 1843: '*Deo Gratias!*'

Chapter 4

Proyecto: 1844—45

Eugene Macnamara, *pasajero inglés*, disembarked at Vera Cruz on 29 November 1844, three weeks out from Guiana. Mexico City lay four days inland, and the winter traveller from Georgetown, humid and lying below the high tide marker, would feel the air thinning as his road climbed to the capital (see Map C).[1]

Macnamara arrived as President Antonio Lopez de Santa Anna was deposed, his statue-bust toppled and his amputated leg exhumed. A canny, headstrong figure, he personified the misfortunes of his country, most notably the loss of Texas. The Zócalo or plinth of a column planned for La Plaza Mayor in 1843 to mark the Independence victory over Spain, then cancelled, only added to his humiliation by the Texas Republicans. General Mariano Paredes y Arrillaga, his former supporter, installed José Joaquin de Herrera, chairman of the Council of Government, as interim-president pending election. Herrera was a federalist, ready to allow more home rule to Departments like The Californias and Yucatán. Santa Anna, a 'centralist', had reduced States down to Departments in 1836. Texas was poised to join the US. External humiliation, internal unrest over tax and debt, and growing Indian ferment made talk of Federalism or Centralism irrelevant. Mexico could not defend her territories, whatever she called them, and others coveted her Pacific coast. Alta California would follow Texas, weighted towards the US (or Britain) by trespassing settlers, resentful *californios*, and hostile Indians. Without an alliance treaty, British Foreign Secretary Lord Aberdeen dismissed any suggestion of British military support for Mexico as 'Quixotic'.

Citizens mock-paraded Santa Anna's leg, imprisoned its former owner and exiled him four months later. On 2 January 1845, Macnamara took out a visa from the British Consulate, where Ewen MacKintosh of Manning and MacKintosh, 'the biggest speculator in Mexico', fused merchant and consular roles for profit and occasionally to benefit his country. Mexicans so identified British national and private interests, that Lord Palmerston had to warn consuls against addressing 'Counting House letters' from their Consulates. Admiral Seymour on the Pacific advised the Foreign Office to bar them altogether from trade after their demands superseded his own naval authority.

Forty-four people queued for visas that first working day of 1845. Paper, chronically short since the break with Spain, was never wasted. When Santa Anna turned the federalist 'United States of Mexico' into the centralist 'Republic of Mexico' in 1836, the old was quilled out on printed visa blanks and the new penned in.[2] Six months later, Macnamara and consul MacKintosh virtually synchronised colonising proposals for Alta California.

Church protocol demanded that Macnamara call next on the 'portly, benevolent and jovial' Primate, Archbishop Manuel Posada y Garduno, with Bishop Hynes' introduction. The new wasteland diocese of Las Californias, no longer part of the Mexican diocese of Sonora, replaced missions dismantled in 1834, but it was a ghost diocese, without people, priests or money. Even liberal, critical rulers like Herrera, to whom church property was a fiscal resource, re-appraised the missions' role in California security. The Archbishop sat uneasily with any liberal government as Mexico distanced itself from traditional church and state power-sharing. The rundown condition of his palace was symbolic of a political shift since Spain left. He licensed Macnamara to work in Mexico and by February the Irishman was English-language preacher at the giant convent of San Francisco, south of La Plaza Mayor.[3]

WHY MEXICO?

Years later, John Frémont concluded that Macnamara's title 'Apostolic Missioner' was a papal warrant to 'select California for his labours'; he had accused him also of being Britain's colonising agent. Foreign consuls, US agents and Mexican politicians called him a 'Jesuit', European shorthand for a conspirator. It is not known whether he told anyone of his dash to Rome in 1843, but 'Apostolic Missioner' was the courtesy style accorded any Catholic missioner, worldwide, in an Apostolic Vicariate.

Great Britain accorded diplomats to and from Mexico in 1824 and a treaty of friendship (but not of alliance) was subsequently agreed. The London *Times* and *The Tablet* reported over the years on Texas, the Mexican bondholder saga and the vulnerability of California. The US press suspected all Britain's dealings with Mexico and saw it as a rival bidder for independent Texas and restive Alta California, but in 1845 Tory rivals, Peel and Palmerston, united in Parliament to refute *Times* and Paris *Presse* claims that Santa Anna, in 1844, had been 'on the eve of ceding California absolutely to Great Britain for 25 million piastres [*pesos*]', in talks with the British embassy.[4] Lord Aberdeen, Palmerston's successor, consistently supported Texan sovereignty, accorded it diplomatic recognition and a trade agreement, but excluded lending money and any interfering with the Republic's internal slavery policy.

Macnamara would remember the Picpus missioners expelled from Hawaii to Alta California during his time in Paris, and Bachelot's return to France as a mission hero. Bishop Hynes met the Archbishop of Mexico in Rome, and John Urquhart, a fellow Dominican friar, just in from Mexico City, in London in 1844. British investors had bought up giant Mexican loan bond issues to become Mexico's biggest creditors. Of all the Latin-American borrowers, Mexico owed most. The 1.25 million acres across Mexico offered to bondholders at discount in 1837 were common knowledge, but garbled by diplomats, politicians and journalists everywhere as a 'sale or mortgage' of California to Britain as if by government treaty. The land offered had never been a security, to be forfeited were Mexico to fail to repay its debt in cash.

Macnamara carried 'many other letters' from Guiana to 'leading figures', in a cats-cradle of contacts which spanned the Gulf of Mexico: they also marked his good standing. Royal Mail ships linked the Caribbean, Gulf and Guiana. Manning and MacKintosh carried goods to Guiana churches on ships for Mexico. Merchants and missioners shared public vessels and made lasting contacts on five-week voyages between Europe and Guiana. Murphy of Baltimore and New York provided Mexico City and Georgetown with books and general goods, and advertised in Guiana and Mexico newspapers. Dr Joseph Bankhead of the Colonial Hospital, Georgetown, where Macnamara joined the Board in 1843, was first cousin to Charles Bankhead, British ambassador, to whom Macnamara first reported in Mexico.

Mexico was always Gulf news, because of Texas and Yucatán. Beyond them, Oregon and Alta California waited in line like dominoes. Macnamara's Ireland of the 1830s had seen handbills in market towns seeking colonists for Texas. O'Connell opposed it, certain that Texas would be a US slave state. Mexico maintained the old Spanish ban on slavery, prohibiting US settlers in Texas in 1829 from importing 'domestic labour'. O'Connell advocated asking Mexico for land 'near its northern boundary' for an 'asylum of free persons of colour, Her Majesty's subjects' as a buffer to stop Texas slavers expanding into three or four more Texases.[5] The Pope condemned slavery outright in 1839, as Popes had stumblingly, but regularly pronounced for centuries. In 1844 Macnamara entered Mexico knowing something of the complexities of his new mission.

CLEAN START

In May 1845, Charles Bankhead, British Minister Plenipotentiary (ambassador) to Mexico, reported to Lord Aberdeen, Foreign Secretary:

> About six months ago a Roman Catholic priest arrived here from Demerara furnished with letters of introduction to the Archbishop of Mexico from the Bishop of that colony, and [from] many others to the British residents here. Mr Macnamara called upon me. I have had every reason to be pleased with his acquaintance. He is a native of County Clare, Ennis, I believe.
>
> Mr Macnamara mentioned to me some time since that he intended to present a Petition to the President for permission to bring two or three hundred Irish families from Ireland to California and to ask of [the Mexican] Congress a grant of Land on the Bay of San Francisco. He feels sure he could procure a large number of married small farmers to become useful Colonists and gradually strengthen the country. He has received support from the Archbishop [of Mexico], and Senor Cuevas [Foreign Minister, responsible for colonising]

is likewise favourable. He can, however, entertain no hope of an advance of money from Mexico, but he seems to think that if an additional grant of land was given in lieu thereof, he could raise money upon that portion in London sufficient, with aid from the Emigration Committee [*sic* see Chapter 5], to bring over his colonists to California.

I of course could offer him no assistance officially, but upon Senor Cuevas asking me my opinion of Mr Macnamara personally, I had no hesitation in speaking of him as I thought he deserved. I shall receive further information on the subject which I shall submit by the next Packet.[6]

Whatever ideas he brought with him, sixteen months in Mexico City with diplomats, merchants and politicians schooled Macnamara in Mexican reality. The US invited Texas to join the Union, March 1845, which allowed the incoming US President, James Polk, to concentrate on the Oregon dispute with Britain from the start of his tenure, but Mexican President Herrera denounced the invitation. A belated draft agreement of recognition negotiated between Mexican and Texan delegates in May was not ratified in Mexico. By December 1845 Texas was a US State. Waves of illegal settlers would similarly secure California, even if US dollars tabled for its coast and harbours did not, but a war about fences was not the preferred option of any North American landlord. Lord Aberdeen ordered diplomats not to offer Mexico hope of British intervention, although some MPs, including young Disraeli in 1846 on the floor of the Commons, demanded that Britain create 'a California protectorate [to give] ten years tranquillity' to British merchants.[7]

Macnamara was close to Britain's bailiffs and agents in the field and was himself taken for a British agent, but his relationship with the British government was largely coincidental, spiced by his own exaggeration and opportunism. Lord Aberdeen had, however, paused for thought in September 1845 when the Mexican ambassador pressed him to colonise California. As they talked they shared the most recent despatch from the British embassy about Macnamara and consul MacKintosh. British (and US) diplomats, merchants on the ground, and naval personnel knew of California's commercial and mineral potential. San Francisco Bay begged to be someone's Pacific base. They also knew of the bondholders' promised land: the London *Times* correspondent in Mexico City enthused about all such initiatives. Since 1843, four consulates had opened in California, but with so little commercial work that the British consul lived forty miles inland. Sufficient gold had been found in 1842 to export, and a rich mercury find was confirmed late in 1845. California congressman Castañares had pressed central government publicly through *El Siglo IX* to work its gold, to colonise, to send a defence force and to restore its missions, but his advice even in 1844, was too much, too obvious and too late.

Routinely, Bankhead highlighted colonising proposals to Aberdeen, undeterred by Aberdeen's equally routine lack of response. Within weeks of Bankhead's May despatch outlining Macnamara's scheme, consul MacKintosh produced a colonising proposal for California, which Bankhead submitted in full on 30 July, along with further news of Macnamara. The priest was close to the diplomats and in 1847 lived at the embassy or consulate, 5 or 10 Calle de Capuchinas. His colony scheme was in line with other British proposals since 1839, and in Mexico City he had many to advise him, including MacKintosh. They may have collaborated, the communitarian's land and colonists complementing the finance and experience of the speculator consul and his bondholders. US observers believed they worked together, but the evidence is circumstantial.

The support of Mexican Foreign Minister Luis Cuevas was crucial to any would-be coloniser. US observers accused Cuevas, ex-ambassador to London, of being Britain's pawn, despite or perhaps because of his efforts to make his own country recognise Texas. Colonising was his secondary brief, and after he and Ashbel Smith, Texas ambassador in London, failed to normalise relations with Mexico in 1845, he refocused onto Alta California. Crowds and newspapers still bayed for futile 'patriotic' action against the US. In June, Cuevas received Macnamara's petition from President Herrera. It was no longer politic, after Texas, to invite foreigners to settle Mexican territory, perhaps why the Macnamara plan did not appear in the Mexican press. The British had proposed colonies in California ever since the bondholders' land option, to the point where it was exaggerated into an 'alliance' between Britain and Mexico. The British 'glitterati' of Mexico City were the first foreign enclave to have a book club, supplied monthly from London with the ambassador's support.[8] Alexander Forbes' pioneering *History of California* and Robert Wyllie's

Report for Mexican Bondholders were well thumbed before Macnamara landed.

ALEXANDER FORBES' PROPOSAL, 1839

'Old Mr Forbes' (1778–1862) of Barron and Forbes, lived at Tepic, east of the backwater Pacific port of San Blas. Eustace Barron owned cotton and bleaching mills there, two estates and a sugar plantation. The company monopolised Pacific trade and Barron, its Irish senior partner, was British consul with an agent at Mazatlán, four days sail from San Blas. Like Manning and MacKintosh, the company mixed legitimately the consular and the commercial, trading with northern Mexico, the Pacific islands and China. Little happened without their knowing. Forbes visited Alta California for the first time in 1847, during US occupation, but for years he had questioned sailors, traders, botanists and missioners passing through Tepic. Abel Stearns, wealthy US merchant at Reina de Los Angeles, commercial partner and son-in-law of Juan Bandini, doyen of Alta California, was one of Forbes' sources. With Barron and Forbes, Bandini and Stearns had exploited the San Feliciano gold find of 1842. Eugene Macnamara stayed twice at Forbes' Tepic house in 1846 and helped him pull off a business *coup* in California.

A History of Upper and Lower California by Forbes in 1839 was the first English account of The Californias. A column of 300 Mexican colonists had stopped at Tepic in 1834 to await a ship at San Blas for Alta California. They stayed a month (some for life) prompting Forbes to consider inviting British colonists. A publisher's delay allowed him to revise his book after the 1837 bondholders' land option appeared. By then Texas was a free Republic inclining towards the US, which Forbes feared would soon be California's inclination: both had flown the Lone Star in 1836, but only Texas carried its independence through.

Forbes advocated that Europeans colonise Alta California, 'devoid of inhabitants', acknowledging it would also improve his company's books. Little was known about either California, save that Baja was arid and the Alta coastland was fertile. Until the late 1600s they had been thought to be an island or peninsula, and on British charts part of northern Alta remained Drake's 'New Albion' from 1579.[9] Spain and Mexico had not surveyed or prospected Alta California, nor had the missioners yet extended east from the coast into the Central Valley of the Rio San Joaquin. San Francisco Bay was 'discovered' in 1769, only when the first Spanish expedition arrived with the friars. A single Russian settlement was founded around 1812 north of San Francisco Bay with a harbour at Bodega and a stockade Fort 'Ross' some miles further north. Spain and Mexico allowed it and the Tsar gave it some naval support. It lasted thirty years until trade collapsed.

Forbes advocated a west coast steamer line between Panama and the Columbia River to carry trade and immigrants, with a permanent Royal Navy presence. If one British subject had a right to protection, all the more a colony:

> In Great Britain and Ireland millions of human beings of superior intellects and varied acquirements [cannot] find employment or food. No country can excel [Alta] California, but while the population retain their present indolence, it must stand still. [Under an enlightened government promoting colonisation] it could become known and selected as a refuge by the innumerable starving populations of the old world. I know of no place better for receiving the surplus population of Great Britain [despite] antiquated prohibitions and absurd clauses, such as the emigrant must profess the Catholic religion.

The London *Times* Mexico correspondent advised that Parliament take Forbes and the 'rolling tide' of US settlers seriously. Forbes lamented the 'miserably ineffective' missions, dissolved after 'intentions so good', but enthused about the Eden-like Valley which John Frémont confirmed in 1845: 'fresh and vacant, floral and sylvan, and alive with birds and bounteously watered, [no valley in the world compares with] the San Joaquin'. In contrast, the US press saw merchant-consuls like Barron and Forbes as British government scouts, just as Frémont scouted for Washington. Forbes' book was clear, well timed and attracted attention in the three landlords' capitals. He pressed bondholders to use their land discounts, as they would never see cash. The ceding of Alta California, he proposed, could resolve Mexico's $50 million debt to Britain. *El Siglo IX*, called it 'a vehement incitement to a powerful nation to occupy the Californias' and positively urged British bondholders on 13 May 1845 to form a company 'to exercise sovereignty over the land, similar to the East

India Company [given] Europe's mania for procuring colonies.' (See Plate 5.)

In 1840, Forbes sent his book to William Hartnell, English settler in Monterey, but Hartnell did not enthuse; Picpus and ex-Irish College missioner, Patrick Short in Valparaiso, in touch with Hartnell and others in Alta California, complained that Forbes had never seen California; Hartnell's cousin Richard, of the London Foreign Office, advised after visiting in 1839 that no colonists should go there. The bondholders were largely silent, but Forbes did inspire a proposal from Berlin that Prussia displace Mexico's 'paper sovereignty' over California.[10]

THE BONDHOLDERS' LAND OPTION, 1837–47

Mexican Consul Francesco de Lizardi in London was Mexican government agent for handling loan bonds for a decade until his death in 1842. In April 1845, Manuel de Lizardi, his brother and successor, accused of corruption, lost the agency to John Schneider's company, also in London. Financial power in Latin America was concentrated on Austin Friars Street, nicknamed 'Little Mexico', which hosted Robert Crichton Wyllie at No 11, Barclay Brothers at 12, John Diston Powles at 13, and consul de Lizardi at 26.[11] Schneider also acted for Manning and MacKintosh in Britain, and was related by marriage to consul MacKintosh and to John Powles. That same month, MacKintosh became bondholder representative in Mexico and persuaded the government there to a third major restructure of the debt, 1845–46. By then, British bondholders were owed £12 million on the £6.4 million they had loaned twenty years before.

The radical restructure of 1837, ratified in 1839, allowed bondholders to buy colonising land at $1 *peso* an acre, half the standard Mexican tariff and below the US price of $1.25, in five Mexican departments, including Alta California. Half the bonds would carry deferred interest and the option to buy discounted land until 1 October 1847. It was an option for Mexico to repay something in kind, rather than cash. No bondholder consortium was formed to take up the offer and it was not renewed in the 1845–46 restructure. All debt restructures won delay for Mexico and commission for MacKintosh, while bondholders won promises. MacKintosh also overreached himself, typically in purchasing land for colonising in Tamaulipas, which stuck to his hands once war broke out between the US and Mexico.[12]

British bond buyers had subscribed £6.4 ($25.6) million in 1824–5, of which Mexico received between a quarter and a half after 'deductions' and commission, while still remaining liable for the whole. Political instability, military overspending, the milking of Mexico by British companies and a bare seven million population tax-base meant that little at all was repaid. By 1837, with £9.2 ($46) million owed to British bondholders, plus individual legal compensation owed to French and US claimants, debt was paralysing Mexico.[13]

A quarter of a million acres were hypothecated in each frontier department, and the new bond certificate-land warrant stated the land value of the bond alongside its monetary value. It was not department-specific, nor was any certificate named to its owner, or even numbered, which allowed the de Lizardis to print and sell a surplus corruptly. It made straight exchange of old for new impossible in the proposed restructure.

Colonies would have created a buffer against the US: land purchase has been compared to a fire damage sale, a self-inflicted loss to stave off total loss. It was never a 'sale or mortgage of California to England', or 'secret', or a 'treaty' between governments. Admittedly, the language of the agreement, 'valid until the total debt is repaid' was overblown, especially given a proclaimed expiry date of 1847. Debt, by definition, could always be restructured.

Forbes insisted that bondholders use the land offer, colonise Alta California and administer it on the East India Company model. Mexico could admit British settlers to protect it *and* pay off its debt in one move. It might declare independence, like Texas, but with a weighting of British settlers (as US settlers had weighted Texas) it would gravitate naturally to being a British protectorate.

John Diston Powles, promoter of the Topo River failure, 1828, and the Tropical Emigration fiasco in Guiana, 1844, was vice-Chair of the Mexican Bondholders Committee, a sub-committee of the Spanish American Bondholders after 1836. He was also a director of Manning and MacKintosh. He, Forbes, and MacKintosh urged bondholders to set up a colonising company, but the Pacific was not a small speculator's comfort zone. Silence greeted Powles in 1837, Forbes in 1839 and MacKintosh in 1845 when they urged bondholders to buy to colonise.[14] Speculators were hooked on silver mines and hope, and in 1845, the land option was nearing expiry. A Mexican war with the US could cost bondholders everything. The Yucatán declared independence briefly in 1841 and again in 1846; Texas joined the US in 1845; California, in disarray, broke away from Mexico in 1836, and came close to doing it again in 1845.

SOVEREIGN BASES

Richard Pakenham, British ambassador to Mexico, supported Forbes' plan. Mexico, he warned, would soon lose control of its frontiers: US surveyors were mapping and US settlers squatting. A 'Company of Adventurers' should colonise it and seek British protection, but Lord Aberdeen, Foreign Secretary, felt that Britain did not need 'new and distant colonies … multiplying the liabilities of misunderstandings and collisions with foreign Powers'. He believed that a British warship still made for a powerful deterrent, and he was a peacemaker by instinct.

James Forbes (not related to Alexander Forbes of Tepic) became British vice-consul at Monterey, 1843. US Commodore Catesby-Jones' brief invasion of Monterey had revealed American intent. James Forbes' superior, consul Barron at Tepic, sent gold to Lord Aberdeen from San Feliciano in 1843. Vice-consul Forbes was approached secretly by leading *californios* in 1844 plotting to overthrow the Mexican governor, Micheltorena: they wanted British protection afterwards. In March 1845 before Lord Aberdeen's refusal reached Mexico, the *californios* had expelled Micheltorena, installed Pío Pico as first *californio* Mexican governor and *californio* José Castro as *Comandante*. Despite Aberdeen's rebuff, Pico continued to confide in James Forbes. His exaggerated belief in Britain's will and ability to take territory, however far-flung, was common in Mexico and the US.

The taking of sovereign bases, fortified trade bridgeheads on foreign soil, had long been British policy. Gibraltar the most famous, taken by force in 1704 and formalised by treaty in 1713, commanded the southernmost tip of Spain. The East India Company took treaty bases in India in the 1760s. The Cape and the Ionian Islands came in 1815, Singapore in 1819, Aden in 1839, and Hong Kong in 1842, but Britain had no base on the eastern Pacific in either north or south America. A US consul warned in 1837 that Britain would take Gran Chiloé island from Chile in lieu of an overdue bond repayment. The US first offered money for San Francisco Bay in 1835, and British merchants, bondholder officials and admirals lobbied London to make 'Port Francisco' its own. In 1842 consul de Lizardi proposed to the Mexican Finance Minister that bondholders with land warrants settle fifteen million acres near the Bay with colonists, the terminus of a trade corridor through Alta California which would avoid a pointless occupation of the entire department.[15] The *californio* rebels in 1844 had specified help from Britain on the model of the Ionian Islands, including Corfu. Lord Ellenborough, feisty First Lord of the Admiralty, told Admiral Seymour on the Pacific in 1846 that Port Francisco was more vital to Britain and its navy than even Malta or Corfu.

Admiral Elliot, British consul to the Texas Republic straight from taking and governing Britain's new Hong Kong base, promised Mexico a British alliance against the US, but Aberdeen censured him; later he censured Bankhead for a similar assurance. President Polk, however, believed Britain's indignation over both Texas and Oregon masked its real priority, California. As late as March 1845 Britain and France urged Texas to delay joining the US Union and Mexico to recognise Texas. Elliot visited President Herrera in June, but his secrecy and disguise only fed US suspicion. (It was the month Macnamara petitioned.) Elliot proposed a *quid pro quo*: if Mexico recognised Texas, if the US purchased Alta California and if Mexico paid bondholders from the proceeds, Britain would cede Oregon up to the Columbia River and Texas would remain independent from both Mexico and the US. What the well-read British ambassador Bankhead called Mexican 'pride and prejudice', boosted by believing Britain was its formal ally, prevented compromise with Texas.

Sir George Simpson, 'Little Emperor' of the Hudson's Bay Company, private rulers of British North West America, visited Alta California in 1841, as his company came to San Francisco Bay to seek new beaver trapping grounds. HBC had hunted the animal half to extinction in Oregon Country and faced competition from US immigrant trappers. The company prospered on furs (beaver fur hairs add a sheen to felt) brought to its stations or ports to sell in London and on to the furriers and hatters of Europe. HBC kept settlers out, even its own retired employees, but the flow of US migrants into the Columbia and Willamette River valleys grew so great it undermined company authority and drew London and Washington into standoff over the future of the Oregon Country. Simpson considered that were the *californios* to declare independence, HBC might secure a major role in a California-handed *gratis* to British protection.

Abruptly, however, HBC quit Alta California in 1845, concerned about its insecurity. Sir George's observations on its British destiny were shelf curiosities on publication in 1847.[16]

ROBERT WYLLIE'S PROPOSAL, 1843

No Pacific drama was complete without the fastidious, meticulous and verbose Scots busybody, Robert Crichton Wyllie. Co-opted by the Spanish American Bondholders and Mexican sub-committee to visit Mexico and advise, he published *Mexico, A Report for Merchants, Emigrants and Mexican Bondholders* in 1843. He had already advocated colonising Alta California in 1840, pressing George Robinson, Committee chairman, to form a company to recruit and finance. Mexico, he vouched, would take 'the surplus Catholic population of Ireland [and elsewhere] under a wise colonising society', and Mexico's offer of land in 1837 displayed the honour and honesty of a debtor which had borrowed more than any other Latin American state. After touring Mexico to report on it in 1844, Wyllie urged Robinson: 'overrule the Bondholders [at AGM] and *compel* them to go for land'.

From Mexico he corresponded at characteristic length with Alexander Forbes at Tepic, with cousin William Hartnell at Monterey, with agent de Lizardi, and chairman Robinson, both in London. He stayed with Forbes at Tepic in the summer of 1843 to finalise his *Report*. As a silent partner in Barron and Forbes and as a bondholder, Wyllie had his own vested interest in a 'British California'. From Tepic, and later from Honolulu, he continued to ply cousin Hartnell with questions.

Hartnell advised of the gold at San Feliciano, of a need for thirty Jesuits, and of the land then on offer (he had eleven square leagues in November 1844 when Governor Micheltorena, distributed grants ahead of a feared US invasion). Hartnell, however, opposed colonising, and neither Wyllie's rhetoric or assurance could tempt the bondholders. Joseph Tasker of Middleton Hall, Brentford, spoke for a weary, mistrustful majority: 'Notwithstanding vast resources, Mexico's national debt is quite out of all proportion to its boasted wealth and means.'[17]

In Mexico City, Wyllie's conclusion, 'Upper California is the best site for the English bondholders', interested the Foreign Minister responsible for colonising, and intrigued British merchants and diplomats. In

December 1843 Wyllie stayed again with Alexander Forbes, en route to Honolulu. He hoped the bondholders would invite him to reconnoitre California in person, and begged Hartnell to secure land for them both. 'Nothing could justify Britain's interference so much as previous grants of land under the Mexican government to British subjects. Grab all you can for us, if a crisis threatens.'[18] The bondholders' call did not come, but an illusion grew that Britain would protect property in distress as stoutly as it protected its subjects in distress.

Wyllie's long, imaginative *Report* condemned Mexico's taxation, corruption and smuggling. *Mañana* irked him: agent Manuel de Lizardi (Francesco died in 1842) had still not printed the land warrants. He urged Mexico to grow consumables – tobacco, cotton, cocoa and sugar – and avoid mining as immoral. Coastal California was as productive as the USA or India, 'fit for cultivation of their richest tropical products, with labour cheaper than the slave labour of the USA'. The climate suited Europeans better than Texas. His 'Colonising Company' would not be a government agency, and he reassured all that Aberdeen 'would not accept sovereignty [over California] even if it be offered by this [Mexican] government and petitioned by the bondholders'.

He looked at Swiss settler Johann Sutter whose 200 square miles of 'New Switzerland [Nueva Helvetia]' on the Rio Sacramento was under the Mexican flag. A test-purchase in the same valley would be a good start for bondholder warrants. He looked at a Swiss-German colony in Tamaulipas where 1,000 families had eleven square leagues each, but warned that huge *ranchos* isolated people, reiterating Wakefield's principle of community and cooperation. As a devout churchman, Wyllie also reminded bondholders: 'The support of the clergy's respectability as gentlemen is of the highest consequence to the existence of religion here.' Catholic clergy, in particular, identified with the poor, and he stressed that he acknowledged this 'as a Protestant'.

Forbes added a postscript to Wyllie's manuscript draft in July 1843. He asked that 'the old drones of the hive', the *californios*, be taxed to cover colonists' expenses, and that mineral rights be conceded to his proposed 'Colonising Company of Mexico City'. It would need $25m (£6.2m) capital and two years to recruit. Mexico, he argued, must survey its territories and advertise land in European kingdoms, like Britain. 'Speedy colonisation is most important, to protect Mexico and California from foreign aggression

… industrious inhabitants' would increase exports over imports with cotton, silk, sugar, cocoa, vanilla, indigo, coffee and rice, a list familiar to anyone from plantation Guiana'.[19]

Forbes argued that California mattered so little to Mexico, it was virtually on offer and bondholder warrants went halfway to securing it. From Liverpool, home to several bondholders, the US consul reported in August 1845 to President Polk, talk of 'England's mortgage on California', advising him to stand firm on Oregon Country 'to prevent the loss [of California]'.[20] The land warrants and influence on government of the bondholders was overstated; the belief that warrants were specific to California (or any other department) was plain wrong, yet in Parliament in 1846, Disraeli insisted 'California was mortgaged as security on the [bond] loan', and pressed Palmerston to defend it.[21] The land was no more than an alternative form of repayment; forfeit was impracticable and never envisaged (see Map D).

In December 1843, Wyllie presented Forbes with his published *Report*, before sailing for Honolulu. Twelve months later Eugene Macnamara, Catholic priest and subject of a monarch, came to Mexico City and proposed bringing Irish farmer families to Alta California. It was as if Wyllie and Forbes had rehearsed him. He visited Alta California, which Wyllie had not, and which Forbes did only in October 1847. Macnamara spent six weeks there, was ferried everywhere by the Royal Navy and fronted a mining deal for Forbes. In a year in Mexico City, he had learned from previous proposals, been supported by diplomats, and learned about bondholders keen to colonise. The Irishman took on the diplomats' and consuls' baggage too, that persistent suspicion that they (and now he) fronted for the British government.

Isolated Alta California was represented in Supreme Congress. Andrés Castillero, soldier-geologist, was appointed Special Commissioner to California, and Manuel Castañares of the Monterey customs house succeeded him as congressman. He advised President Herrera to send a defence expedition, colonise, and restore the missions to extend them east into Indian territory as had always been intended. After the defence force mobilised in April 1845, William Parrott, US confidential agent in Mexico reported to President Polk that the revolutionary authorities in California would accept Mexico's arms, but not its soldiers, with Micheltorena fresh in their minds. Years later, Castañares claimed to have thwarted 'Jesuit'

Macnamara's *si dit* purchase of the missions for the Jesuit order. In September 1845, as the Council of State debated Macnamara's scheme, Castañares published his correspondence with Herrera, warning that California could easily be lost. He called it a rough diamond ready for polishing.[22]

MACNAMARA'S PETITION, JUNE 1845

Macnamara signed his Spanish petition *Eugenio Macnamara, Misionero Apostólico* in June 1845. Archbishop Posada y Garduno, Foreign Secretary Cuevas and ambassador Bankhead had been sounded, London knew, and Macnamara addressed Herrera with understandable confidence:

> I, Eugene Macnamara, Catholic priest and Apostolic Missionary, submit reflections on Calfornia which is attracting much public attention. It does not require prophecy to foresee this fertile country will soon cease to be part of Mexico [unless it] restrains foreign rapacity. The unanimous voice of the country requests *colonisation* [Macnamara's emphasis] as the speediest, most secure means. Europe has an excess of population and the Irish are the best adapted to the religion, character and temperament of Mexicans – devout catholics, moral, industrious, sober and brave.
>
> I propose, with your Excellency's aid and approval, to place in Alta California a colony of Irish Catholics. I have a triple purpose ... I wish firstly to advance the cause of Catholicism. Secondly to contribute to the happiness of my countrymen, thirdly to [help block] usurpations by an irreligious and anti-Catholic nation. I therefore propose there be conceded to me territory on the coast of Upper California for colonisation. I would prefer to place the first colonists on San Francisco Bay [near] the American [settlers] at Bodega, a little north of San Francisco, abandoned by the Russians. I should first bring 1,000 families [5,000 people]. Afterwards I would establish a second colony near Monterey, and a third at Santa Bárbara. By this means the entire coast, on which most danger is expected, would be secured completely

against invasion ... by foreigners.

For each family I bring, I will require a square league [*sitio*] free of cost; likewise that the children of all colonists when they marry shall receive half a *sitio* as a national gift. I should likewise require exemption from paying taxes ... that colonists be protected by the Government on settling, and shall enjoy all rights. Other lesser issues can be discussed later. These proposals have the fullest approval of the Archbishop. [If my ideas are effected] they may bring happiness to many and in the end consolidate the integrity of this great republic.[23]

His bid for coastal colonies ignored the threat from overland settlers. Despite Commodore Jones' attack, the long-term danger from the US was through the Sierra Nevada passes. Bodega on the coast, abandoned by Russia in 1842 after thirty years, was bought and stripped by Sutter of New Helvetia at bargain price. Due to ignorance about Alta California in Mexico City, neither Macnamara nor Wyllie before him realised that the coastal land they sought (Wyllie 51,891 sq miles, Macnamara, 20,480 sq. miles) was not available, even allowing for confiscated mission land.

Foreign Minister Cuevas asked Bankhead discreetly about the Irish *empresario*. The ambassador was positive and let London know, but Aberdeen still would not commit. Bankhead probably told Macnamara of Cuevas' enquiry, and explained Herrera's dilemma over foreign settlers, necessary, but unwelcome guests. Mexican ways were also slow, California was intact, why the haste? The republican *La Voz del Pueblo*, supporting congressman Castañares, accused Herrera of relegating California to *mañana*. What was needed, the editor warned, with Castañares and Sutter in mind, was 'good colonisation law to protect the immigration of industrious populations, like the Swiss and the Germans'.[24] In July, consul MacKintosh proposed the next and last British scheme.

CONSUL MACKINTOSH'S PROPOSAL, JULY 1845[25]

Charles Bankhead repeatedly warned London that in a war with the US over Oregon:

the United States would without delay take possession of California. The Mexicans look to England as the power most likely to help them and notwithstanding their pride and prejudices, they have not scrupled of late to discuss the disposing of The Californias to Great Britain [were] she willing to purchase them. These discussions are carried on by Persons outside the government. The government themselves dare not publicly entertain such a proposal. I shall be a properly silent listener.

He returned to Macnamara, to nudge a reaction from Aberdeen.

Mr Macnamara's scheme, which I had the honour to mention to your Lordship in Despatch No 52 [May], is still in embryo. Although the Government sees the advantages to be derived from a colony of Irish in San Francisco Bay, still they cannot be brought to give Mr Macnamara any positive assistance. I do not feel myself authorised to offer him any official support, but indirectly I have endeavoured to aid his plans.

He tightened the cuff. 'Mr Consul MacKintosh has placed in my hands for confidential communication to your Lordship a plan of colonisation upon a very large scale. I transmit a copy of his letter and enclose the proposition.' Unlike Macnamara, MacKintosh was a public figure with commercial flare, his company (effectively himself) holding the bondholder agency since April, and with a commercial interest in exploiting the land warrants. He had calculated how to finance a colony and John Schneider, his company agent on the spot in London, now filling Manuel de Lizardi's role, actively lobbied bondholders as well as Aberdeen.

MacKintosh proposed that colonists be enticed. Instead of outright purchase, his 'California Commercial and Colonising Company of Mexico' wanted twenty years mineral rights, and his portfolio of profitable silver mines in Mexico merited him a hearing. After twenty years' tenancy, he proposed, land ownership should revert to the colonists, under British protection, with a 'force of 2,000 men to repel any foreign invasion'.

Long term, Mexico should 'introduce into The Californias half a million European colonists', administered by 'a tribunal, half Mexican, half European'. He recognised the fear of, but need for foreign settlers, yet his speculation lacked urgency.

MacKintosh's scheme went to the Foreign Office and the Mexican Bondholders sub-committee, which promptly sent John Diston Powles and John Schneider, (whose role as Powles' friend, business partner and in-law, MacKintosh's representative, and Mexico's bondholder agent, was positively incestuous) to negotiate with Lord Aberdeen in October. Macnamara, with no London network, went to the Mexican President, as he had once gone to the Pope. MacKintosh's hard-nosed business proposition projecting 500,000 colonists, would cost, but ultimately benefit Mexico, MacKintosh and the bondholders. The trader conditioned his offer with British protection, perhaps seeing Macnamara's project as complement to his own.

Project Macnamara was proposed by an unknown without money and was conceded. 15,000 (3,000 families) were to settle 20,000 square miles, 13 per cent of the present US State, in an Alta California several times greater. Aberdeen did not respond to Bankhead's May or July prompts, having warned his diplomats that bondholders' concerns were not his, whereas the acquiring of territory was. For all that, he shared Bankhead's despatches with the Mexican ambassador at the Foreign Office in September. The US invitation to Texas to draft a State constitution warned him off California.

As long as California remained Mexican (or was taken as an American prize in formal war), England had to remain neutral in the absence of any alliance with Mexico and to save the Oregon talks. British diplomats, consuls and admiral, the landlord's bailiffs, were not to take action, but to 'watch' and to 'see that' no one else benefitted. 'Watch' and 'see that' were hardly briefs.

URGENT

Of the paper colonisers, 'old Mr Forbes' wanted immediate business openings, not long-term schemes; Pakenham was posted from Mexico to Washington, where Oregon consumed him; Simpson's Hudson's Bay Company abandoned California in 1845; Wyllie became a big fish in small Hawaii; bondholders whistled into the wind for cash returns and government intervention, while rejecting land; MacKintosh, when the Mexican War neutered his California scheme, moved to other projects with little regret, and to his eventual ruin. Macnamara's project alone was conveyed and confirmed, dwarfing Johann Sutter's 'New Helvetia' and Bandini's 'San Salvador' on its flanks.

By July 1845, a month after presenting, Macnamara had heard nothing from Herrera, due for a September election to confirm his office. It was speculated that Macnamara's request for land 'free of cost' was the problem, not just his foreign settlers. MacKintosh, too, wanted it free, but proposed alternative funding through mineral rights. Had Macnamara combined dove and serpent, his idealism and clerical ease in opening doors, with the financial shrewdness of other potential colonisers, a response might have been quicker.

He wrote again, upbraiding Herrera for his silence, just when the Mexican press and opposition demanded a show of strength against the US. Herrera, like Aberdeen, was against declaring a futile war for a futile cause. Macnamara offered finance:

> By the hesitation of the Supreme Government [in] establishing an Irish colony in California, it appears the principal and only objection is the expense of transport … easy to overcome without the Government expending a single dollar. Many fathers of [Irish] families in my country, after selling the little land they possess, their cattle, furniture etc, would command [up to £60] … enough to cover their families' voyages. But, it will be necessary to convey many other persons ['*families*' deleted], who lack the means to pay … such as priests, doctors, artisans, young women etc, [and] to obtain money for the purpose. If the Supreme Government should assign me land in California to mortgage, I would be able to obtain money in my own country upon this land.
>
> The Supreme Government should agree to concede [to me] the import duties of the port of San Francisco. The Government does not receive much from that port … No time ought to be lost. We are surrounded by an artful and base enemy [bent on] possessing the best territory of this country and which hates to death its race and religion.

Before another year, The Californias will form part of the American nation [underlined by Macnamara]. Their Catholic institutions will be the prey of the Methodist wolves [*lobos Metodistas*] and the whole country will be inundated with cruel invaders. Whilst I propose repelling them, my propositions ought to be the more admissible as I have no personal interest in the affair save the progress of [religion] and the happiness of my countrymen.

As for the fidelity and affection of these [Irishmen] to the Mexican Government, I answer with my life and [if] a sufficient number [at least 10,000] is brought over, I assure you that this will be sufficient for you to repel at the same time the secret intrigues and the open attacks of the American usurpers.[26]

His forecast of US occupation 'before another year' was accurate: it came in July 1846, just short of a year later. A creeping infallibility pervaded the rest. Missioners, like naval commanders, had to be versatile and make spot decisions, but Macnamara pronounced here on social dislocation, defence, the economics of a territory he had not yet seen, and the duties of a national president. Bishop Clancy, too, had championed the church's right to direct the civil power, and another arch-conservative, Archbishop Posada y Garduno, had given the Irishman every support.

Macnamara's financial calculation was realistic for Irish 'moderate farmer' emigrants, with assets to sell, but not for the needy. In 1846, the poor on the Crown Estates of Ballykilcline, Co. Roscommon, had an average capital of £3 a head. The Crown paid them that to cover their smallholdings, cabins and the twelve shilling [£0.6] journey to Dublin. They had no livestock to sell, which embodied wealth on an Irish farm. The voyage to the USA cost £3 and to Canada, about £2.5. The farmers envisaged by Macnamara were not the poor of Ballykilcline or the smallholders of Kilkee-Killard, but nearer to the prosperous smallholders of Borrisokane and perhaps to his own family at Corofin.[27]

His defence calculation was equally unrealistic, even more when he trimmed his numbers from 15,000 to 10,000, of which 6,000 would be children. Fighting-age Irish males in 1845 were not veterans of Napoleon's war, and rural Irishmen had no military expertise. More reasonable was his expectation of an *empresario's* land bonus. Settlement law allowed some 23,000 acres bonus per hundred families (500 colonists) recruited, but it was hard-earned: an *empresario* and colonising company had to cover surveying, recruiting, transporting and initial supplies.

Macnamara's most credible assertion probably won his hearing on 18 September, immediately after Herrera's permanent swearing-in: '*I have no personal interest* in the affair save the progress of religion and the happiness of my countrymen.' Forbes, Wyllie, MacKintosh and the others would gain cash returns on bonds, fees, profits on settling and processing the land warrants, and on trade with the expanding population. The Irish missioner's hands were clean, unless it were shown that he acted as agent for Britain, its bondholders or its merchants.

AMERICAN 'METHODIST WOLVES'

A US attorney in 1852 described Macnamara as the most anti-American visitor ever to enter California. A California Franciscan judged his hatred of the US so extreme that his story had to be a smear, and his petition a forgery.[28] Mexico, however, did not permit religious toleration until 1862, after years of domestic political pressure. Macnamara's attack on US Protestants would have resonated in the Mexico of 1845.

'Methodist wolves' was probably for local effect, Catholic shorthand for the 'evangelical threat', just as 'Jesuit' on Protestant lips warned of the 'papal conspiracy'. Both were backhanded tributes to the committed in each other's tradition. In the Hawaiian Islands, early Protestant missioners were 'Methodists' to the Catholic Picpus Fathers, although no Methodists served there. To the Protestant missioners the Picpus Fathers were 'Jesuits', although no Jesuits served in Eastern Oceania. When Mexican congressman Castañares and French consul Gasquet called Macnamara a 'Jesuit', it was more warning flare than description. St Matthew's *Gospel* and St Luke's *Acts of The Apostles* recorded Jesus' warning of bogus prophets, 'in sheep's clothing, but ravening wolves', and 'wolves invading the flock'. Feuding Christians quarried such phrases, and Patrick McSweeney had used similar calibre ammunition in 1827 to attack 'non-commissioned Apostles'.

The Methodist revival in eighteenth century England took 'methodical' spirituality to dark corners of Britain, Ireland and America. It touched the English industrial poor, the Irish cabin poor, the mountain Welsh, colonial slaves and wherever formal ministry failed people. A century later the Mormons recruited many Methodists, and by 1846 nearly 5,000 British Mormons had gone to the US; two Mormon groups headed for US-occupied California to test the Rio San Joaquin valley for a New Zion. The Methodists, by then, had become the largest denomination in the US, exceeding Baptists by a million. President Polk attended his wife's Presbyterian church, but told his diary, 'my predilections and opinions are in favour of the Methodists'.[29] On the other side of the hill, the Jesuit Society, an élite order of priests, had spearheaded reform and re-firing of the Catholic church after the Reformation, but the order was temporarily abolished (1773–1814). In Spanish territories they were enlightened missioners, as in China and Japan, respectful and keen to assimilate, but they made enemies of Catholic kings and prelates in Rome.

Methodists came to the Columbia River Indians in 1834, followed by Presbyterians with whom they had worked in Texas, and in 1838 the Catholics. *Pére* de Smet, a Belgian and (real) 'Jesuit of the West', travelled the Oregon Trail in 1841 with a Methodist preacher and they parted friends. In May 1842, *The Tablet* (which Macnamara would have seen) attacked Methodist 'wolves in sheep's clothing' for poaching Catholic mission subjects in Oregon. A Methodist Oregon Emigration Society founded in England in 1838 collapsed in 1840. When its leader offered to set up an 'independent nation' in Oregon, the Foreign Office refused him. Bishop Clancy, deep in schism, urged the last of his followers to 'frequent the Methodist chapels', although in his time Clancy too had called them 'wolves, ravening in sheep's clothing'.

Governor Light held Methodists in high regard for their work with freed slaves and for which they had suffered in Britain. The attempted Second Reformation of the rural Irish in the 1820–50s, 'a civil war of the soul', involved 'methody preachers' whom O'Connell accused of bigotry at home while freeing slaves abroad. The Philadelphia riots in 1844 were reported worldwide as anti-Irish, then indistinguishable from anti-Catholic. Behind the rioters, Samuel Morse reinterpreted the US Declaration of Independence as a Protestant charter against Catholic kings and their missioners seeking to convert the USA; the Irish immigrant 'priest police', to Morse, were 'Jesuits from the Pope's bodyguard'.

Macnamara's tone was harsh, but the churches were at war and language, thankfully, was their weapon of choice; he was accused falsely of being a 'wolf in sheep's clothing' among the Georgetown nuns. Even Pope Pius IX lamented to Bishop Hynes how Catholic missioners were being sent to the West Indies as 'wolves on *exeats* to get rid of them'.[30]

MEXICAN COLONISTS[31]

Before Europeans showed interest, Mexico had tried to colonise Alta California, initially using it as a penal colony. In 1834, a non-criminal colony sailed for California, after Mexico City dissolved, or 'secularised' the missions. *Mexicano* colonist administrators, not *californios*, would administer mission assets and award the land to Indian tenants. The remaining Franciscan missioners would be parish priests, the Spanish-born replaced by Mexicans. Alta California's social and religious profile changed: colonists financed by the former mission Fund, mission property taken and sold for state revenue, and parishes replacing missions. Mexicans, however, were as reluctant to volunteer to settle California as they had been to colonise Texas. Isolation meant that by 1834 both *californios* and *tejanos* saw *mexicanos* as foreigners and by 1836, let alone 1846, as enemies.

Juan Bandini, Alta California congressman in 1834, supported the colony so enthusiastically it became 'Bandini's Colony'. Acting-President Gómez Farías, a liberal 'devout anticlerical', wanted the clergy out of politics and education, and the church's real estate put to use. The Spanish missioners had not supported Mexican independence and mexicanisation would now remove them. Bandini and financier, José Maria Híjar, were friends of Colonel José Maria Padrés, former military *comandante* of The Californias, and Bandini's fellow-congressman (for Baja California). Híjar, Padrés and Bandini had shares in Bandini's new 'Cosmopolitan Company of California'.

In 1833 Governor Figueroa of Alta Calfornia fell ill. Gómez-Farías appointed Padrés as military *comandante*, and Híjar to replace Figueroa as civil governor [*jefe politico*]. Híjar was already colony director [*intendente*] and Padrés his deputy. Colonists were recruited, utopia beckoned, and funding was provided for travel, land, livestock, tools and rations. A send-off ball was held in Mexico City for 300 settlers, appropriately in a derelict convent. Bandini's company donated a ship and issued a prospectus to scotch the image of Alta California as a desert run by wild Indians and shipwreck castaways.

The wagon column stopped at Tepic above San Blas. Bandini remained there, while Padrés and Híjar negotiated transport down at the port. Alexander Forbes hosted the waiting group, which inspired his later plan for European colonists. He saw the threat to company monopolies from traders like Bandini, yet dismissed Bandini's *pobladores* as 'ill considered and foolish, not a farmer among them, just artesans and idlers'. The candy maker, goldsmith and teachers were easy targets, but the idea had been to bring artisans and educators to complement farming. Obviously, a projected new town, an admiralty and a shipyard on San Francisco Bay needed builders. Two more colonies of Germans and Swiss and a reorganisation of the missions were to follow.

Two ships brought them from Mazatlán, a Mexican frigate and Bandini's vessel, which was so decimated by sickness it had to dock at San Diego, while the frigate continued to Monterey with 120 settlers under Colonel Padrés. The sick recovered and continued slowly, ex-mission by ex-mission, along the *Camino Real* [Royal Trail] to catch up.

That summer Santa Anna came out of hibernation, 'El Salvador' to conservatives and clerics, to replace 'Judas' Gómez Farías. In Alta California, Governor Figueroa, healthy again, was ordered by courier to concede nothing to Híjar or Padrés when they arrived. Santa Anna feared California might lean to independence, which Texas already threatened, and he was determined to centralise Mexico's federated States. The courier reached Figueroa in September 1834, as he staked out a site in Santa Rosa Valley for 'Santa Anna y Farías', a mission-sounding, but secular *pueblo* north of Sonoma, the last ex-mission.

Padrés landed at Monterey, two weeks after Figueroa received the order. He asked to remain deputy *intendente*, which Figueroa allowed; Híjar arrived by road three weeks later, and asked to remain *intendente* which would have allowed him and twenty-one *mexicano* administrators to allocate mission revenues to the colony, and to redistribute the lands. Hurriedly, the Alta California Assembly excluded the missions from the colonists' authority, 'lest the Indians suffer'. Reportedly the Indians had welcomed the colonists as liberators. What Wyllie and Forbes later condemned as 'the ancient drones of the hive', the resident *californios* took much mission property for themselves.

Winter found colonists sheltering around San Francisco de Solano mission, Sonoma. In March 1835 Híjar asked for help with the new *pueblo*, but Figueroa lacked money and the colonists lacked brawn. Abruptly the Governor ordered weapons surrendered and expelled Híjar, Padrés and their families back to Mexico on charges of conspiracy. It left the colonists leaderless. Híjar had also been ordered to survey and map California, but nothing happened. The remaining colonists dispersed into the *californio* community, ironically affording the missions some respite.

A decade later, Híjar returned to Alta California as Special Commissioner in Mexico's last attempt to save it. The unfinished business of 1835 prompted rumour that he planned another colony. On 29 June 1845 the London *Times* Mexico correspondent informed his editor of Macnamara's petition to Herrera, but despatches took five weeks to reach the British reader. Nothing appeared in the Mexican press. Foreign Minister Cuevas wrote on 30 July to Mexican ambassador Tomás Murphy in London, ordering him to tell Lord Aberdeen that 'Mexico will receive HM Government's cooperation to prevent the loss of [California] as a proof of the good relations between the two countries.' However, the 'amity' agreed by treaty in 1826 was not an 'alliance'. In Mexico City, two weeks later, on his last day as Foreign Minister and weary after his negotiation with Texas, Cuevas gave Macnamara an introduction to Commissioner Híjar at Monterey. In fact, Híjar was sick and still at Reina de Los Angeles.

11 August, 1845

The Irish priest, Macnamara, goes to that department with the expedition under Colonel Don Ignacio Iniestra, and takes a project for colonisation with Irish families. Among the honourable persons who have recommended this ecclesiastic to me, the most illustrious Archbishop has done so very earnestly. Desiring to gratify them in an affair which may be of advantage to the Republic, I commend him to you, charging you to examine well his project and inform the Government of what he may offer, to follow it to determine what is suitable, and that you facilitate him … and make his residence in the department agreeable. You will speak on the subject with his Excellency the Governor [Pío Pico], so that, on his advice and opinion, the Government may decide the more intelligently.

To Don José Maria Híjar, Monterey.[32]

Five days later, William Parrott, President Polk's confidential agent in Mexico City, wrote to the US State Department of 'McNamarrah', about his colony and his leaving for California. Cuevas' letter and Macnamara's posting to Col. Iniestra's command were signs of Herrera's good faith; in mid-September, immediately after Herrera's election, the Council approved Macnamara's petition. Híjar's death in California in December 1845 cost Macnamara a wise counsellor, but Juan Bandini took his place. In fact, half the departmental assemblymen who agreed to Macnamara's petition on 7 July 1846 had been Híjar-Padrés *colonos*.

US newspaper reports in the British press told of Californian independence already achieved, once Pico, Castro and ex-Governor Alvarado had expelled Micheltorena. Irish newspapers carried the London *Times* report of 6 August on Macnamara's colony; *Freemen's Journal* added, 20 August, 'California has declared itself a Republic like Texas.' Seven million Mexicans could not colonise vast territory without European help, yet Mexican politicians could lose credibility by admitting foreigners. It had cost them Texas. Even when Herrera confirmed Macnamara's concession, he demanded that *latinos*, Mexican or Spanish, settle alongside the Irish. *Mexicanos* and *californios* then wrangled among themselves.

Chapter 5

President Polk Reacts: 1845

President Herrera, scapegoated for losing Texas, sent commissioners to listen to the *californios* and a battalion to defend them. He hoped to avert a second Texas. Eugene Macnamara was attached to the battalion for passage to California to negotiate his land. Pico and Castro's *californios*, meanwhile, had thrown out Governor Micheltorena and his soldiers in March, and were in no mood to welcome replacements (see Plate 7).

INIESTRA'S CALIFORNIA BATTALION

In April 1845 President Herrera planned for three divisions to man the Rio Bravo (US Rio Grande) 'frontier' claimed by the US as the original Texas border, south and west of the Rio Nueces, the former State boundary recognised by Mexico. Herrera also ordered Colonel Ignacio Iniestra to raise an expeditionary *batallón* for Alta California. Two commissioners went ahead to hear *californio* grievances. José Maria Híjar, the ex-colony leader of 1834, would accept complaints about military and financial neglect, about US settlers and the Indian problem. Some 800 *anglo* (mainly US) settlers lived in Alta California with about 7000 *californios*, but Mexican and US newspapers warned in spring 1846 of hundreds more heading from the US to swamp the department. When in 1845 the department Assembly installed Pío Pico and José Castro after their bloodless *coup*, Mexico City delayed confirming them. Híjar achieved little, and he died at Reina de Los Angeles in December.

The second commissioner, Andrés Castillero, mineralogist and congressman, had prospected in Alta California. His brief was to buy Johann Sutter's fort on Rio Sacramento for Mexican soldiers to guard the Sierra Nevada passes. The Rio de Los Americanos was already named for the settlers' ease of access. Sutter, who had been on Micheltorena's retinue, refused to sell, and later threatened to raise the French flag. Castillero then chanced upon diggings near San José from which paint was extracted. He identified the 'ochre' as cinnabar (mercuric sulphide), the quicksilver or mercury ore, and lodged an informal claim with the local mayor. Returning immediately to Mexico City, he secured working rights, reward money and two square leagues (13.5 square miles) of land for colonising, since he had 'improved' California. Neither mine nor land were referred to Governor Pico, nor did Castillero return until 1848 when California was US territory.

Pico and Castro had asked Britain secretly in August 1844 to protect California 'under direct government of one of its [*californio*] natives', on the model of the British Ionian islands. Vice-consul James Forbes transmitted the request to Lord Aberdeen and Prime Minister Peel, who rejected it that December as 'contrary to Britain's good faith' towards Mexico; they warned that Alta California should not place itself under any other power either. 'Direct native government' came in spring 1845: Pico and Castro were both *californio*-born, but Mexico City still ruled overall. It was said that the Hudson's Bay Company helped arm the rebels against Micheltorena, when vice-consul Forbes was company closure agent in California. His enthusiasm and *californio* high expectations, perhaps one the result of the other, encouraged them to approach Britain again. London did not dare leave it to its bailiffs and agents on the ground to respond, given their radical ideas of what British policy towards California should be.[1] Governor Pico mistrusted US intent, and feared 20,000 restive coastal Indians, robbed of their living when the missions ended. Five times that number in the eastern hinterland, affronted by grants, fences and invaders, retaliated with robberies and raids.

Iniestra's force mobilised in May, 1845. 'Two thousand men for California, a splendid division of elite troops! Pay guaranteed for a year' sang *La Voz del Pueblo*. The British ambassador reported it to Aberdeen in July, adding his routine nudge: 'the sale of these provinces to England is talked of, if she would purchase them'. Politicians had denied from the floor of the House of Commons in March, the French and British press reports that Britain had negotiated with Santa Anna in 1844 to buy Alta California. When the California Battalion faltered in the summer, unpaid, unequipped and without ships, *Amigo del Pueblo* attacked Iniestra for corruption and inefficiency; in October, *El Siglo IX* demanded, 'When will he *stop* leaving?' accusing him of bombarding California with trumpets and bands, like Joshua before Jericho.

Ambassador Bankhead had told Aberdeen of Iniestra's expedition 'to aid the present feeble [militia] in California … 12–1500 men, to embark from Acapulco to Monterey'. He warned, 'it has been prevented from going by want of funds,' and added his prompt: 'I should be glad if Mr Macnamara would accompany this expedition with authority from the [Mexican] government, as he could then personally examine the facilities and prospects of a future colony of his countrymen.' Macnamara would be the first coloniser sent to Alta California from the capital since Híjar-Padrés in 1834, but he was foreign.[2]

As Iniestra moved towards Acapulco port in staggered company order, William Parrott, President Polk's confidential agent in Mexico City, informed Washington in July and August that Iniestra lacked money and ships. '[His] military education was finished in France … his command and political influence in California will be turned to French account [by] the French Legation here. He certainly takes with him a large number of Frenchmen.'[3] On 11 August, Macnamara received his introductory letter from Foreign Minister Cuevas to Commissioner Híjar. Five days later, Parrott reported on 'McNamarrah' to Washington as he reported the *Batallón*. Bankhead and the Archbishop, by attaching Macnamara to Iniestra's command, drew him to Washington's attention.

After struggling 150 miles south to Acapulco, the expedition stalled. By November, Iniestra had resigned, the ships discharged themselves and the force was stranded. The London *Times* correspondent felt Mexico had 'tantamount to abandoned Upper California, [already] in quasi-allegiance'. Washington ordered a close monitoring of Mexico's Pacific coast, short of blockade, to deter Mexican troops from reaching California. Shortly afterwards, under a new commander, the *Batallón* remnant set out on a brave, impossible march from Acapulco to California. Commissariat and pay were chronic problems for the Mexican army, but consul Larkin reported from Monterey in July that Barron and Forbes financed Iniestra.

Macnamara had withdrawn from the force, reaching California under his own steam in June 1846, but too late to meet Híjar. 'Híjar did not interfere' remembered Governor Pico. According to Abel Stearns, Larkin's own confidential agent for southern Alta California, Híjar's brief had been 'to [investigate] the reorganising of government, customs and courts'.[4] The old coloniser knew how colonies failed. He might have advised Macnamara to enlist *californio* support, to recruit artisans, and possibly that it was all too late.

Paralysis afflicted Herrera, events overtook his policies, cabinets were reshuffled and popular anti-US sentiment was vented. *Mañana* helped delay consideration of Macnamara's request, but that was Mexico, as Macnamara's *bhlárna* was Ireland. The election to formalise the interim presidency delayed it further, into September. Archbishop Posada y Garduno wrote for Macnamara an introduction to Bishop García Diego y Moreno at Santa Bárbara. The California bishop had put to Híjar in 1845 that the moribund California church should look to Europe for 'zealous and well-educated missioners', which some remaining friars manifestly were not. At the end of September, Commissioner Híjar had appealed to Herrera for 'twenty, thirty or more missioners from France, Italy or some other place in Europe, to extend whatever number of missions the Government think best among the pagan tribes'.[5] When, nine months later, *misionero Apostólico* Macnamara arrived in Alta California with colony proposals which included priests, the *californios* promptly relocated him from the coast to the Indian hinterland where missions had always been meant to go.

MEXICO APPROVES[6]

Herrera's Council of Government, including the archbishop, looked at Project Macnamara on 18 September, two days after the duly elected President was sworn in. They welcomed it. Colonies of 1,000 families (5,000 persons) behind three ports, Yerba Buena on San Francisco Bay, Monterey and Santa Bárbara, were approved. Conscious of the 'foreign' element, councillors pressed, yet did not demand that colonists be mainly Mexican and Spanish. Macnamara's Irish came near to being sidelined. By colonising law, already, foreign settlers had to live at least twenty-six miles (ten leagues) from the coast, for security reasons.

The Council accepted his motives 'to prevent the usurpations [of] the American Confederation, and to procure for [his Irish] families ... a more comfortable life, obedient to our laws and authority.' They allowed a square league [4,428 acres] to each of his 3,000 families, and half that again for marriage dowries, but said nothing of an entrepreneur's land bonus. His colonists:

> in the exuberant fertility of our mountains and valleys [would] build roads and canals by which exports can be made. Our wildest lands occupied by a large population would strengthen our country ... California's massive elements attract ... daring adventurers ... to the borders of the USA and Canada by the Pacific Sea, a position of power ... They have wished for many years to occupy even a single point, like San Francisco port, seen as an article to be bought by bargaining with our Government. The impulse to increase the US population there, an enormous American wave, is irresistible. ... colonisers would make good military auxiliaries, having their own property to defend. Colonising would promote justice and enlightenment, as with the missions and *presidios* [garrisons] in 1823. Since then it has all collapsed. Barbarian Indians wander everywhere and this state of wilderness encourages them to invade our Department, bringing death and destruction with them. The Council has no hesitation in approving the request of Priest Macnamara [for] the usefulness and urgency of colonising California ... and for the Republic's continuing to hold this Department.

Indisputably, the Irish were:

> loyal, Catholic, moral, hard working, sober and brave [and he knowing] the traits and qualities of different European colonists most appropriate to our circumstances, has no doubt that the Irish are the best endowed with these, [but] the Council, while intending that the colonisation should be as full and free as possible, advise unalterable restrictions [...] slavery banned and the public profession of a uniform

religion ... It would be no trouble for the Irish who integrate both sentiments into their very education as most profound convictions.

To admit foreigners indiscriminately, as had happened in Texas, was political suicide.

> The Council approves ... without taking away our declared preference for Mexicans, whatever is agreed in this instance, but feel that some of these families should be Spanish from provinces ... in similar circumstances to the Irish and offered advantageous terms. An invitation should be sent out through our Legation in Madrid [as] proof of strengthening bonds between our nations.

Councillors ignored his facile solution that Irish farmers raise £100 passage money by selling up, and they refused him California's customs revenue. Macnamara said nothing of British government or private funding, but did claim it later in California. The Council offered more direct help:

> for bringing in these families, bearing in mind their poverty as labourers and small-holders of scant means, and that they will [save our maintaining] troops in California. We propose that 50 men from our army be despatched, more than enough to conduct the first 300 families [1,500 persons] from Europe and if possible that one of our Steamers should carry these passengers, ensure their peaceful disembarkation and impose respect for them in those remote and unprotected places.

With this vision of Mexican troops on shore leave at Limerick or Cork from one of Mexico's three (British-built) steam warships, the Council signified its approval to the Foreign Minister, and Supreme Congress. An alert congressman might have spotted that 1,550 passengers and soldiers, with crew, would not all fit on a naval or any other steamer of the day, let alone cross the Atlantic or even do the Monterey run from Mazatlán packed on deck. Brunel's *Great Western*, on the Atlantic mail run since

1843, carried 150 passengers and servants, with sixty crewmen. Gesture mattered, however, as with the token corvette which took Híjar-Padrés colonists to Alta California in 1834.

The Council recommended that 'the Project of the Irish priest Don Eugenio Macnamara be acceded to on the terms laid down,' and that Congress give it 'the most immediate attention and decision'. That was September 1845. Congress did not discuss *Proyecto Macnamara* in recorded open session before Herrera's government fell in December, although Manuel Castañares, deputy for Alta California 1844–5, claimed wildly in 1857 to have thwarted 'Jesuit Macnamara' at closed ('secret') meetings in December 1845.

WASHINGTON AND 'MCNAMARRAH'

In April the new US President, James Polk, appointed William Parrott his confidential agent in Mexico after Mexico severed diplomatic ties over the US invitation to Texas to join the Union. Parrott was 'to reach the Mexican President and high government officers' in absolute secrecy, and report their mood to The Mansion. His private claim for nearly $1 million damages from Mexico was questionable and doubted by US diplomats who examined its detail. *Mosquito Mexicano* blew his cover instantly, calling his arrival 'an insult to Mexico' after his 'shamefully fleeing' creditors there in 1840. Parrott had been a consul, briefly, and his brother John was still consul at Mazatlán, both inclined to exaggerate. His priority despatches, written to impress, went direct to Secretary of State Buchanan and the President, who later regretted appointing him.[7]

Parrott warned in May that the British Pacific fleet was reinforcing to take California, but the Mexican press had merely reported fleet 'collecting' by Admiral Seymour, after arriving on Station. Parrott claimed that Mexico was ready for diplomatic relations, that Herrera's government was stable, and that anger over Texas had abated. 'An envoy from the US might with comparative ease settle over a breakfast' the main points of dispute. He dismissed the war party as a minority which would change tune once a USN squadron appeared at Vera Cruz or a US general on the Rio Bravo. Mexico, he said, was 'embarrassed' at *californio* hostility to Iniestra, and its force on the Rio Bravo was there merely to 'annoy'.

On 16 September Parrott's five August despatches were read to the President and full Cabinet; on 16 August he had recorded tersely (for Parrott):

> The expedition destined to Upper California has not yet left, for want of means, and a young Irish priest, by the name of McNamarrah [sic], is preparing to leave for the same place, ostensibly for the purpose of introducing Irish emigrants.[8]

The next day, Polk reconvened Cabinet in 'special session' to reconsider Parrott's information, reliability and the next move. US and Mexican press reports suggested discrepancies and cabinet agreed that a letter be sent to consul John Black, Mexico City, for confirmation of Parrott's views. Black's last despatch had been on 24 July. At Polk's prompting, another letter was sent to John Slidell, nominating him Envoy Extraordinary to Mexico. Such was the urgency, Polk and Buchanan wrote both letters that evening. The next ten weeks were spent countering the threat of 'foreign colonising' in the shape of 'McNamarrah's emigrants'.

Polk, an unexpected Democrat candidate for the Presidency, had campaigned on securing Texas and Oregon, but not California. After Inauguration, however, he confided in George Bancroft, Navy Secretary, that the acquiring of California would be a mark of his success in office.[9] His Inaugural Address skirted it, mentioning only that 'our people now bring the blessings of self-government in valleys of which the rivers flow to the Pacific [Rio Sacramento; Willamette-Columbia rivers] ... our duty [is] to protect our emigrants wherever they may be on our soil'. From September, he played the California game more intently, but always close to his chest and tight-lipped, even when confiding in his diary.

El Siglo IX had reported in May a British bondholder plan to form a company with 'sovereignty over California, similar to the East India Company's authority in India'. The US Consul in Liverpool wrote to Polk about a bondholders 'mortgage on California'. In July consul Larkin reported that British merchants were paying for Iniestra's battalion; he had already reported French and British consuls appearing in Alta California. The London *Times'* report of Macnamara's colony reached Washington at the end of August. Polk, set on acquiring California, knew that if Mexico could not hold it without Britain, and if Britain was about to colonise it, the self-evident US *right* to it demanded that he act. Texas was virtually secured, Oregon a matter of face-saving, even if by protracted haggling. Nowhere in North America, save in Alta California, was Britain or any other European country threatening to colonise.

Throughout 1845, petitioners wrote to Polk offering to raise regiments to take California: one offered to slake the thirst of the log cabin poor for tea, by seizing California as the direct route to buy it from China. 'The Star of Empire points Westward' rhapsodised another, '[and] before four presidential terms ... California will be populated by American enterprise'. England was conspiring to 'crop a wing of this [US] Young Eagle to keep her out of Texas, California and Mexico ... [She] seeks the footing she has [had] in Portugal and in Spain since [the Peninsular War 1808–14]'.

As citizens reminded Polk of US 'title and right' to everything West, a journalist created the banner-phrase 'manifest destiny' (with no capital initials). John O'Sullivan summarised the medley of romantic, religious and racial assumptions which was US expansionism. With unconscious irony, destinarians saw British imperial expansion as their main enemy, themselves in a mirror: 'the little island 3000 miles away' intruding to 'stop our manifest destiny to overspread the continent allotted by Providence for the free development of our yearly multiplying millions'. Both governments were extreme nationalist: both saw their authority embodied in their nationals, wherever they settled, uninhibited by frontiers, however old – a people, not a nation. O'Sullivan regretted the 'diplomatic blundering' which distanced the US and Mexico, but the fact remained: 'California will next fall away from the loose adhesion [of] equivocal dependence ... the anglo-saxon foot is already on its borders [and the settlers] will necessarily become independent.'[10]

Meeting twice weekly, sometimes more, President and Cabinet sifted California options that autumn: buy it, settle it, foment revolt, take it by force. It was decided to authorise Envoy Slidell to spend $40 million, the most ever tabled by the US for territory. 'Money would be no object', Secretary Buchanan advised him, and San Francisco Bay was the crucial minimum purchase, but at most Slidell was to try for all the land west of the Rio Grande del Norte. Congress should not be informed, lest Britain, France or US Whigs hear of it and intervene under arms, or on the floor of Congress, where Polk's majority was slim. British merchants financing

Iniestra, the bondholder 'mortgage' on California, and the Royal Navy were threat enough, but Macnamara's personal staking out of land for Queen Victoria's subjects was the last straw. On 2 October, George Bancroft, ordered Commodore Sloat at Honolulu to occupy or blockade California if he ascertained a formal war, no local provocation required. US Naval communications sometimes strayed, but Sloat positioned himself at Mazatlán from November 1845 to May 1846, to 'deter' ships from transporting soldiers north. It took private intelligence from a US naval surgeon crossing Mexico, not orders from Washington or a threat from Mexican troops, to make Sloat head for Monterey in May 1846 for the final act.

The tempo of Polk's response quickened as he spoke repeatedly of 'colonisation'. On 17 October he began 'the rough draft of parts of my message to Congress in December', warning against European colonisers. Buchanan wrote that day to consul Larkin at Monterey, 'the President could not view with indifference the transfer of California to Britain'. He also wrote to Sloat, but kept both letters until 30 October when a confidential courier was appointed to take them. Polk told Cabinet on 21 October he would 'reaffirm Monroe's ground against any European power to plant or establish any new colony on the North American continent', emphasising he had Mexican territory in mind. That day, he appointed consul Larkin his confidential agent in Alta California , to watch for 'colonisation by foreign monarchies' and to persuade *californios* that their interests lay with the US, even if only as a 'sister republic'.

At noon on 24 October, the President summoned Senator Thomas Benton to The Mansion. Secretary Buchanan had given Benton an open invitation in September to discuss Oregon with the President. It was their opening topic, before they 'conversed on foreign colonisation'. Polk was wary of Benton at this, their first meeting since Benton backed another Democrat for the presidency. 'Great Britain has her eye on [California]' Polk told Benton, virtually rehearsing his December Message to Congress, 'but the US could not willingly permit California to pass into the possession of any new colony planted by Great Britain ... I [have] California and the fine bay of San Francisco as much in view as Oregon ... If a foreign power were about to possess Cuba we would not permit it. We would place California on the same footing.' Benton cited Frémont's third and current topographical expedition in the West, which he oversaw as chairman of the Military Affairs Committee. Frémont had told him that US settlers moving into the Rio Sacramento valley would 'ultimately hold [California]'. The proposal seems to have come from Benton at this meeting that a presidential courier might pursue Frémont with secret instructions on California. Macnamara and his perceived British role had become a major threat.

Years later, Benton cited *passive* Manifest Destiny: Alta California 'had its destiny to fulfil, to be handed over to the United States'. Frémont invoked Creation: 'the California coast is the boundary fixed by Nature to round off our national domain. From Mexico it was separated by Nature.'[11] Frémont had left Washington in May 1845 for his third and crucial survey expedition to the Arkansas River and Colorado, but in winter 1845 he and part of his company crossed the Sierra Nevada into Mexican California. There he tried to allay *Comandante* Castro's suspicions about his cannon, numbers, wild personnel and reluctance to move on, pleading that they were civilian surveyors bound for Oregon, caught out by the winter. Even Frémont's commanding officer in Washington was uncertain about the purpose and range of his subordinate's activities, but knew they were somehow pre-decided.

Frémont's wife, Jessie, was Senator Benton's daughter. In 1845 the Benton home hosted Cabinet preparations, allegedly to be out of earshot of a suspected Irish spy in Buchanan's State Department. Despatches to Buchanan, including those from Parrott, passed informally through the Benton family. Neighbour Senator John Dix, who spoke Spanish, visited to help. Frémont's wife, her sister and their father, also Spanish-speaking, translated enclosures for Buchanan in attendance. They warned off any official who queried Frémont's activities. 'I had full knowledge of the scope and national importance of these journeys,' Jessie claimed later. 'Strictly confined to the few … Even [the Secretary for War and Frémont's colonel thought] they were only geographical surveys.' Frémont, of course, understood the ultimate purpose of his expeditions, but in 1845 had left Washington before Parrott's 'McNamarrah' alert reached the Benton home and Polk's Cabinet. At the end of his life Frémont described how 'frequent discussions in our home among the men who controlled Government gave me the advantage of knowing [its] wishes and intentions'. He stated explicitly that Macnamara had triggered Polk's ultimatum, citing Buchanan's biographer:

In 1845 ... there was reason to believe that England [*sic*] was aiming to obtain a footing in [Mexican] California by an extensive system of colonisation. Under Mr Buchanan's advice, President Polk ... distinctly declared [against any] European colony [in] North America to make it emphatically applicable to California.[12]

On the evening of 30 October, Polk welcomed Lt Archibald Gillespie for 'confidential conversation' at The Mansion. The young Marine, on sick-leave after suffering tropical heat, was detailed by Benton and Bancroft for a 'secret mission to California'. He was to contact consul Larkin in Monterey and Frémont in the wilds. In his career *resumé* for the Navy Department in 1848 Gillespie called it 'Special Service ... which frustrated British intrigue in California'. Polk noted Gillespie's 'secret instructions', mainly Buchanan's letter for Larkin of 17 October warning of new colonies, foreign designs, and the danger if Britain, 'our principal commercial rival' took San Francisco Bay. Frémont would later hear a memorised version of the letter which Gillespie destroyed at sea before landing at Vera Cruz. He and Gillespie were mandated 'to find out, with a view to counteracting, the designs of the British government in California'. Gillespie's mission was even more dramatic than British consul Admiral Elliot's visit to Mexico in disguise to persuade Herrera to recognise Texas: Gillespie assumed at least two disguises in crossing Mexico, and sailed to Honolulu to simulate a voyage to China.

On 10 November, Polk summoned Parrott for 'full conversation', before sending him back to Mexico, ambition thwarted, as mere secretary to Slidell, who was confirmed that evening as Envoy Extraordinary. Parrott was not even Slidell's preferred nominee. Slidell's second accorded title, 'Minister Plenipotentiary' (ambassador), was Polk's misjudgement, based on Parrott's exaggerated optimism about receptive Mexico. To Mexico, Slidell was re-imposing diplomatic relations unilaterally. He docked at Vera Cruz on 30 November, but was never accredited, nor was Parrott allowed a visa. Gillespie arrived, 12 December, *incognito*, and stayed in Mexico City for some weeks as Herrera's government collapsed around him.

The press stoked the fire. Many US and British newspapers assumed that California had declared itself independent after expelling Governor Micheltorena. On 9 September and again on 1 and 17 October, the London *Times*, optimistic that settlers in Oregon (Willamette River) and California (Rio Sacramento) would 'muster and form an independent country', insisted 'England must interfere [in California] … the lands of California were mortgaged to English bondholders, but so were those of Texas and if the US be suffered to eat Texas, can they not [eat] California with impunity?' *The New York Herald* retorted 'English journalists may talk till they are hoarse, of robbery and plunder, but independent people in California and Texas have an inalienable right to annexe themselves to the US.' Angry California emigrants would give the US 'a 2nd, 3rd and 4th edition of Texas all over again'. *Courrier Francais*, 27 September, in Mexico City, cited a *Union* report that 'important orders' had gone to the US Pacific Squadron to occupy and annexe California which 'England intended to take [as its] *pied á terre* in the Pacific.'

On 2 December 1845, with Slidell and Parrott in Mexico, President Polk sent his Annual Message, the president's most solemn communication, to Congress. He repeated President Monroe's warning of 1823 which Britain had applauded at the time, sealing Spain's withdrawal from any role in the Americas: 'The American continents are henceforth not to be considered as subjects for *future colonisation* by any European powers.' He refashioned it for 1846, with unmistakeable emphasis:

> This principle will apply with greatly increased force should any European power attempt to establish any new colony in North America … It is our settled policy that no future European colony or dominion shall with our consent be planted or established in any part of the North American continent.

He saluted Texas, invited into the Union by his predecessor, President Tyler. It had drawn up a Constitution, 'two peoples acknowledging common values', without coercion, despite 'British and French interference'. Oregon, 'several months away by sea' from Washington, remained a major 'difference', but his real ultimatum was about California and Macnamara's Trojan horse. It could not have been more solemn. Admiral

Seymour read the text at Lima in February and told Captain Blake RN how 'that vagabond president Polk had delivered the most insolent message imaginable ... war is inevitable'.[13] The London *Morning Chronicle*, 27 December, complained that 'Polk threatens us with war and bribes us with peace.'

Neither Congress nor the public, knew of Parrott and Larkin's confidential agencies, of Slidell's mission, of confidential courier Gillespie and his 'secret instructions' to Frémont, or of Frémont's covert role. An unhappy vice-President George Dallas compared Polk to the devious King Charles I of seventeenth century England and in 1847 young congressman Lincoln called Polk's Mexican War 'the sheerest deception', a 'half insane mumbling' and 'a provocation of both countries into war'.

When a *New York Herald* correspondent came to The Mansion on 19 December to 'fish', asking the President to approve his forthcoming articles about California, Polk was laconic: 'I am certain his object was to ascertain the view of the US government in reference to the acquisition of California. This I did not choose to communicate to him. My answers were general and indefinite.' John Slidell's first despatch from Mexico City, 17 December, passed everyone by. 'I cannot learn anything that would authorise the belief that attempts are in the making by any European Power to obtain a cession of any territory on the Pacific coast.' That did not exclude settlements, and Macnamara was personally known to US consul Black in Mexico City. Slidell, in touch with Black, evidently did not link Macnamara with the British government. Royal Navy Lt Peel's arrival in Mexico City on his way home from Oregon Country, sparked some 'curiosity and comment', but Slidell kept it in perspective, 'an agreeable trip for the Premier's son'.

Polk and his envoy Slidell were humiliated, but on 20 January he ordered Slidell to act, were his mission to fail, that 'it would appear that the cup of forbearance would be exhausted'. In May 1846, Polk himself acted, when US soldiers died in a skirmish on the disputed frontier: 'A state of war exists on American soil through the action of Mexico.' He convinced his diary he was 'not going to war for conquest', but 'in making peace we would of principle obtain California and other [territory] ... to indemnify our claimants [and] defray the expenses of the war [Mexico] forced us to wage'. He would fight off 'England or France or all the powers of Christendom' to pursue Mexico. Seven weeks later, the US took Alta

California as its first prize of war. Oddly, neither Polk nor US diplomats seem ever to have challenged Britain across the table about its intentions towards California. Oregon overshadowed everything.

LORD ABERDEEN'S DILEMMA

Mexican diplomacy was more open. Ambassador Tomás Murphy tried throughout 1845 to move Lord Aberdeen to an alliance, beyond the 'amity' of 1826. Alta California would be Britain's prize, whether purchased, protected or colonised, as he begged Aberdeen, 'prevent its loss' to the US. Aberdeen saw only liabilities. War over Oregon, Texas or California and a wider-flung US tariff wall around newly taken territories, could cost Britain much North American business. In a war fought at such a distance, defeat was a real risk, and perhaps for the US too. Worse, it would cost the hard-won friendship of old enemies, the US and France, while the only tangible fruit of a victory would be Alta California: even there, US settlers could not be prevented from trespassing across the Sierra Nevada. Aberdeen was a principled peacemaker who had coined the term *entente cordiale*. He already assured US ambassador McLane in 1845 that Britain had no objection to a US purchase of San Francisco Bay. McLane and Aberdeen were friends, with an understanding about Oregon which, when communicated discreetly to Polk, allowed Polk to focus on California with an easier mind: it had to be taken, if not bought, but Oregon was never going to be worth a war.

Tomás Murphy pressed Aberdeen until December, when the British cabinet adopted a non-intervention policy towards California to save the Oregon talks. Aberdeen listened and generally disagreed. The Foreign Secretary spoke war-like language well, but believed few ambitions were worth a war. Strategically the US was in best position to annexe California. Any protection which Murphy sought would breach Britain's neutrality, in the absence of an alliance with Mexico. Requests for help could only be entertained from an Alta California independent of Mexico.

Aberdeen hesitated just once and Murphy reported the insight to Mexico.[14] Aberdeen and Peel had refused flatly the *californio* request for Greek island-style protection in 1844. On 23 September 1845, ambassador Murphy presented a request from Foreign Minister Cuevas for help with California, written 30 July, a month after Macnamara presented his plan to Herrera. Two weeks after writing to Aberdeen, Cuevas had written to commend Macnamara to Commissioner Híjar in California. On 6 August, *The Times*, seen by Murphy, Aberdeen, US ambassador McLane, the Texas ambassador and other interested parties in London, broadcast Macnamara's scheme: 'A strong body of Irish peasantry on a large grant of productive land ... will be no inefficient aid in helping out British policy in that quarter.' Aberdeen ruled out naval intervention in California, to which Murphy replied that a British colony there would have a *right* to British naval protection against the US. Aberdeen showed or read to him Bankhead's July despatch, just arrived, with consul MacKintosh's colony scheme enclosed and with more news of Macnamara's initiative, first reported in the May despatch. On 9 September and 6 October, the *Times* Mexico correspondent pressed again: 'England must interfere ... [California's] ports of expedition to the Chinese market [are] vital to British interests ... The opinion of all the British community here is that California is mortgaged to the English bondholder.'

Aberdeen pointed out that founding a new colony during the Oregon talks would be an act of aggression, and 'even if we allow an English interest to be constructed in California, this could not be done without exciting the jealousy of other Powers ... I wish it might be possible to act in concert with France'. He shared confidences with the Mexican diplomat which he rarely did with Bankhead. As he showed Murphy out, he warned, 'My good friend, this whole conversation must remain religiously between you and me.' In the evening he informed Peel of the conversation, adding 'we might have established our Protectorate long ago if we had thought proper', referring to the bondholders' land option of 1837 and, perhaps the *californio* Ionian Isles plea of 1844. Peel agreed, but 'the offer comes, I fear, too late ... the hasty establishment of [a colony] would have a suspicious appearance and give a selfish character to our interference'. Aberdeen concluded, 'we have no alternative but to leave the field open to the US'. This was communicated so ambiguously to the Pacific coast – 'no interference *while* California remains part of Mexico, but *see that* they do not seek any other country's protection' – that it was indecipherable to Britain's agents on the ground as a policy.

At sea, Britain's bailiff and enforcement officer, Admiral Seymour, saw an embassy copy of Aberdeen's directive. After reading Polk's ultimatum at Lima in February 1846 and having had no directive from Admiralty or Government for over a year, he fully expected 'John Bull to warm up in consequence [and] that I might find orders to take offensive measures.' In fact, lacking the capital ships as well as orders, he sent only a light frigate, HMS *Juno*, to Monterey with instructions almost as loose as Aberdeen's: 'to counteract any inclinations, in the event of California declaring independence, to place themselves under the exclusive control or protection of any foreign power without the participation of Great Britain'.[15]

A month after Murphy and Aberdeen talked, Murphy told Mexico City that bondholder leaders had approached Aberdeen in October. Vice-chairman John Diston Powles of the Spanish American Bondholders, umbrella for the Mexican Bondholders, showed Aberdeen sample land warrants, valid until 1847. Powles, a partner in Manning and MacKintosh, was accompanied by John Schneider, Mexico's financial agent in England, Powles' in-law and MacKintosh's company agent. Consul MacKintosh in Mexico City had been bondholder agent since April 1845, Schneider acting for him in London. The deputation outlined for Aberdeen a joint proposal by Powles and MacKintosh to raise a company to colonise 50 million acres of Alta California for £6.25 million, at a preferential tariff of $0.5 *pesos* per acre, half again of the former discounted bondholder tariff of $1 *pesos*. MacKintosh must have known of, even lobbied for this further reduction, which became Mexican law in December 1846. Four-fifths of the purchase capital (£5 million, $20 million *pesos*), the deputation proposed, would be met by the bondholders' discount purchase, and the balance (£1.25 million, $5 million *pesos*) would be raised by the new company: the British government would underwrite all. Aberdeen saw the snag: if the US took California and *respected* British settlers, Britain would have no pretext to 'protect'. California was inopportune enough, but unknown to any party 50 million acres of arable public land on the coast was simply not available: in 1850, the proposed new California State's *entire* arable *at most* was put at 63 million acres in the *Memorial* to the US Senate from its shadow-Senators and Representatives.

Autumn 1845 was the last time London listened to Mexican or bondholder offers of California, or proposals of an alliance to defend it, although the offers continued. Aberdeen warned that 'playing Don Quixote' could have incalculable consequences. In December, Peel's cabinet ruled out further discussion, as brinkmanship over California would jeopardise the resolution of Oregon. Personally, Peel was 'not undazzled by the prospect' of having California, but ambassador Bankhead was ordered to prevent a US–Mexican war at all costs. The ambiguities left British representatives in and off Mexico without compass. Had Seymour read Aberdeen's September evening note to Peel, 'California must necessarily fall before the first naval force which appears against there', he might have claimed it as his first clear order.

Seymour was half a world away, oblivious of the 'vacilaciones y dificultades que a tormentar el animo de Aberdeen' described by Murphy, or of the cabinet decision to close ears. His 1844 orders were drawn up before Polk and the US expansionists came to office. Mexico, with a navy of sixty-three guns, was desperate for Britain's warships to defend the California 'flanco débil', but Aberdeen told Murphy consistently that a defence treaty would be a hostile act against America. Admiral Seymour's flagship, HMS *Collingwood*, had left Portsmouth in September 1844 to police the Pacific and secondarily to be a presence off Oregon. The admiral spent 1845 in quarterdeck diplomacy backed by cannon, supporting the independence of the Society Islands, limiting French activity by his presence, and curbing the enthusiasm of his own crew for helping rebels to rebel against anything French. He lacked the ships to visit California until summer 1846, after island tensions eased and after Lt Peel had reported to London on Oregon. Seymour's was not 'the first naval force to appear against there', but he ran close second.

Inexplicably, the merchant colonisers pressing Aberdeen to take California failed to initiate a 'California Colonising Company' which they remained free to do. Powles lamented for the rest of his life having lost out on the 1848–49 Gold Rush. Macnamara and MacKintosh must have mulled over the land option together at some point, given their apparent closeness, synchronised debut and overlap of schemes. In the end, Macnamara secured his contract, but the bondholder hypothecated acres remained just that.

Mañana is a survival strategy for the tropics and life, but temperate zone inhabitants mock it; British politicians even called it 'Spanish Diplomacy'. Aberdeen was close enough to Murphy for humour. In the summer of 1845, he warned the ambassador that Mexico was *rushing* to war by not recognising Texas. 'As you always go slow out of habit, you might do so now as policy [*cálculo*]!' Eugene Macnamara also endured six months of *mañana* after his petition, as Herrera's administration slowly collapsed around him.

DICTATOR PAREDES

Herrera was too liberal, said conservatives, too tolerant of Yankee dollars and of squatters in Texas and California; he could not even get the Iniestra *Batallón* to its ships. In reality, his determination was impressive, sending troops to Texas, breaking off relations with the US, rejecting Slidell's dollars, and committing troops, commissioners and a serious European coloniser to California. The London *Times* thought Herrera 'the only person who kept his temper', knowing how unfit Mexico was for war. US dollars had been on the table for California since 1835, consistently offered by five US presidents, and consistently refused through ten Mexican presidential terms. Diplomatic relations were not resumed until 1848, after the US–Mexican war.

In the Oregon dispute, President Polk insisted publicly on US rights to all Oregon Country up to 54 degrees. California trailed on the Oregon coat tail and Polk risked war with Britain, France and Mexico over Texas, with Britain over Oregon, and with his Whig opponents at home over everything. Britain and France had long pressed Mexico to recognise the loss of Texas, and they hosted its embassies in their capitals. Mexican delegates under Luis Cuevas agreed to recognise the Texas Republic during negotiations in May 1845, but agreed too late to keep it from joining the US. The Texas Republic's transition to US State prompted Waddy Thompson, ex-US ambassador in Mexico, to forecast that California would 're-enact' Texas, and journalist O'Sullivan to warn it would 'fall away next'. Misguidedly, ambassador Bankhead believed that New Mexico and Coahuila (in Mexican Federation days, part of Texas) would be the 'second Texas'. The London *Times* Mexico correspondent in August saw losing Texas as the 'signal for the dissolution of the Mexican republic' with US policy increasingly resembling Russian encroachment on Turkey.

Settlers were squatting in California (not in the volume rumoured and press described or forecast) and Frémont's topographers were mapping it. Britain and the US disputed where and whether to divide the Oregon Country, posturing with warship and threat, real, implied and imagined. *Californio* loyalty was under more strain than ever after four uprisings against central government in twelve years. In March 1845, US ambassador Shannon in Mexico told Washington, 'the natives hold the reins of government [and] they ask for Federation, but Congress will not admit even discussion'. Alta California was closer than ever to breaking away.

In mid-December 1845, General Mariano Paredes y Arrillaga, kingmaker in previous *coups*, declared a *coup* for himself. Supported by fellow generals he marched his Home Army on Mexico City 'to preserve the nation's honour', defying orders to go to the disputed Rio Bravo border, where national honour was actually threatened. As 27th president since 1821, Paredes wanted rule by the elite, the rich, the church and the military, from the centre, whereas Herrera had proposed reviving the pre-1836 Federal States. Mrs Bankhead shrugged, 'Herrera is ill and Secretary of State Cuevas an old woman, something of the Jesuit. You cannot imagine a beautiful country more doomed and hopeless.'[16]

Paredes seized the capital on 2 January 1846. Lt Peel lodged at the embassy during the coup, en route to London to report on the Oregon. Lord Aberdeen's brother, Captain Gordon of HMS *America*, had brought him to Mazatlán after stopping at Monterey. There, consul Larkin duly milked the drama for the *New York Sun*: 'A brother of Aberdeen and a son of Peel in company. We can but wonder at it. Peel and Aberdeen hold more power over the whole world than three or four Kings or Empires.'[17] Lt Gillespie kept himself to himself in the capital, unrecognised in his role as a Cuban merchant, even by US consul Black. Macnamara, young Peel, and Theodor Hartweg, a German botanist from the London [later Royal] Horticultural Society sat out the crisis in the diplomatic enclave on Calle de Capuchinas where the party-loving Bankheads feared the coup might disrupt the Twelfth Night Ball.[18] Macnamara heard little about Alta California save its imminent demise.

Most expatriates, Macnamara included, found a welcome at the Legation and the Consulate. Ambassador Charles Bankhead was assisted by Peregrine (Percy) Doyle, the impetuous Irish *chargé d'affaires*. Highly principled, he walked out on Santa Anna, after a British flag trophy from Texas was displayed at a reception. He refused consul MacKintosh's blandishments to buy dubious new bonds issued in 1846, and had him dismissed from office in 1853. He spoke fluent Spanish and went native, down to 'a suit fastened up the side with silver coins'. His Irish horsemanship matched his Mexican dress sense and won him admirers in a land of horse riders. When he took long overdue leave in April 1846 (US consul Black dramatised it into a dash to London for British help), Bankhead thought the Legation 'quiet as an old convent'. The fastidious Dr Wyllie thought Doyle 'rough'.

Christmas 1845, Doyle wrote to his brother John, at Wroughton Castle near Oxford, of the threat to Eden:

> Notwithstanding the good advice the Mexicans have received for years to recognise Texas independence, they consented too late [June 1845], and unless some other power makes their own arrangement for California, that beautiful country will became US territory. Almost all the Yankee squatters in Oregon have gone lately into [California] and the accounts we receive of the fertility of the soil and the beauty of the climate are really marvellous. This country is going headlong to the Devil. Mexican patriotism simply means 'look after yourself'.[19]

US Marine Lt Gillespie continued to Mazatlán and on to Honolulu by USS *Cyane*, to play the wealthy, disabled tourist before returning to Monterey. He had memorised Secretary Buchanan's instructions to Larkin, not to foment the *californios*, but to offer 'a sincere reception as brethren', just as Washington had welcomed Texas. Gillespie also carried personal family mail for Frémont, including a letter or letters from Senator Benton.[20] Washington seemed shaken by reports that Britain would hold all of Oregon to the point of war, and take California in the process. President Polk, after his December ultimatum to European colonisers, fired a live warning round to underline it when he admitted Texas to the US at the end of the month.

PAREDES' MANDATE

'At 4.00 this morning Paredes' troops occupied our city,' wrote Mrs Bankhead on 29 December. In fact, they surrounded it. Herrera resigned on 31 December and Paredes' men entered the capital early on 2 January 1846. Macnamara's annual visa expired that day and failure to renew within the month incurred a fine, but the New Year *fiesta* and the almost equally customary annual coup halted everything. Next day he read of Paredes' dictatorial powers in the *Diario del Gobierno*.

'The *coup* seems to please the English,' reported US consul Black. Envoy-unrecognised Slidell filled out the wider canvas on 14 January: 'Yucatán virtually independent, Tabasco will be soon, the allegiance of California is nominal, while New Mexico, Chihauha and Durango, without protection [from Indians], will free themselves.' Macnamara's ally, the Archbishop, chaired a Council of Congress to ratify Paredes' dictatorship, and on 19 January Macnamara had a note from Castillo y Lanzas, new Foreign Minister:

> Having heard the opinion of Council [September 1845] the Government in accordance has determined that in view of the necessity for effective measures on that and other concessions proper for the legislature, the matter will be referred to [Congress] together with your memorial ... I state this for your information. [It] will be attended to at a convenient time.[21]

It angered him. In September the Council had requested 'immediate action', when Macnamara was already attached to Iniestra's command. He tackled Castillo y Lanzas' 'convenient time'.

> I deeply regret that the President should so determine, as the case requires in my opinion prompt, strong and *immediate* measures ... the plan which I [submitted] should be considered at once. A statesman should have no other object in view than its benefits to his country. Secondly he should reflect whether these benefits are obtained by immediate action or procrastination: it requires little wisdom to see which course should be pursued in the present instance.
>
> The combined attention of the Americans is now directed to possessing the Californias. Squatters and colonists are passing in thousands over the Rocky Mountains to Oregon which they find barren and unproductive, and they naturally descend into the rich and fertile plains of California. Believe me, no force [of yours] will be capable of checking them.

'Ere long, the Oregon will be the scene of war between the British and Americans. You cannot for a moment suppose that the victors will respect your territorial rights … they will not. Both parties look with wistful eyes at the beautiful bay of San Francisco knowing that the axiom 'might is right' universally prevails. I am aware of the value of your time. I wish to be as brief as possible, yet let me give a candid and free opinion, that before two years The Californias will cease to be an integral part of this Republic, if the plan I propose be not speedily adopted.

Again he forecast accurately: two years later, less a week, Mexico lost Alta California in the draft peace treaty. Macnamara also warned against both hostile parties, the US and Britain. When he did claim British government support later, it was in Alta California, where he could not easily be challenged.

Scold morphed into diplomat, promising a new California, and to double its settlers by 10,000 'Irishmen', even if not to treble, with the 3,000 families (15,000 persons) originally requested:

If the President exercises that privilege which he undoubtably possesses and which I find in *Diario del Gobierno*, 3 January 1846 … exceptional dictatorial powers for the defence of national territory … he has the power of assigning to me the grant of land which I solicit. It will certainly prepare for the defence of the country and, let me add, when hereafter he will review the principal actions of his life, none will bring greater consolation to his bosom than this.

I can bring to California ten thousand Irishmen, a race brave and hardy, loyal and devoted, who never yet proved ungrateful to their benefactors, in confirmation of which I refer you to the historical records of Spain, France and Austria. If my suggestions be carried out, I will render The Californias before five years, the most flourishing portion of this Republic.

With regard to the Council's mind to send the question to Congress, I respectfully suggest that that passage of their judgement be referred back to them by the President for reconsideration. As this is an highly national and patriotic question, I sincerely trust that the present energetic Government will despatch it speedily and promptly.[22]

'Eugene Macnamara, Missionary Apostolic' signed himself 'your very obedient servant', but chafed at the bit.

On 29 January, Castillo y Lanzas referred the case back to Congressional Council which re-endorsed it on 3 February but remitted it direct to Paredes for decree. The purged Supreme Congress did not meet until late May 1846, and left no minute of the Irish colony: a dictator's order did not need its approval. California was on the brink, its expeditionary force aborted, its commissioners dead or absent, and Macnamara the only strand intact from an irreparably damaged rescue rope. The archbishop's lobby and British merchant finance for Iniestra probably softened Paredes' attitude to English-speaking settlers: Texas and his own days in New York explained his mistrust, but unknown to him and to the US Congress, President Polk had proposed payrolling him (to pay his troops) $2 million to buy negotiating space for the purchase of California.

When Macnamara landed in Alta California in June 1846, he explained his delay to a *californio,* possibly Suárez de Real, priest at Santa Clara, who informed Larkin, Polk's agent, who embroidered it to Abel Stearns, Larkin's own agent. 'When Mr Macnamara called on President Paredes to converse on the subject, the latter objected at once, saying the Irish would join the Americans immediately and that he wanted no immigrants whose national language was English.' Larkin reported it to Washington in August, but by then Macnamara's 'call on Paredes' was 'several conferences with Herrera and Paredes'.[23]

ALTA CALIFORNIA

The Iniestra expedition came to nothing, but it took a year. In May 1846, Governor Pico questioned 'the non-arrival of the expedition announced last year. [We] would be most happy to hear of its entry into California, but [not] if sent without sufficient funds for its maintenance.' A sufficiently funded force would ride roughshod over the inhabitants; an insufficiently funded force would fail against the US and still ride roughshod.[24]

Alta California was distant, 'the world's end' of hispanic North

America. It took weeks, even months for letters and travellers from Mexico City to reach Monterey overland. Indians blocked the trails, paper was in chronic shortage, and Mexican newspaper tax meant that 'In all California there is not a subscriber of a Mexican newspaper. The Supreme Government sends the *Diario* and a few Mexicans receive papers from friends in Mexico City. No books for sale here.'[25] Honolulu traders brought the *Polynesian* after 1844, but California's first regional newspaper came only with US occupation. Rumour posed as information, shaped policy and fuelled suspicion in a tiny population thinly spread and isolated. New consuls reporting back to Washington, London, Paris and Madrid had to sieve through much chaff from the rumour mill.

Some 800 *anglo* settlers, mostly American, but including fewer than 100 British, braced themselves for the Mexican military to arrive. Dr John Marsh, one of the few settled in the San Joaquin valley, alerted Larkin at Monterey: 'Mr Híjar of colonial memory has arrived, but with what object? One, two or three thousand soldiers are to follow, but for what purpose? Let them be stationed on the eastern frontier where they can protect us from [Indian] horse thieves.' Marsh had already called on settlers to arm and proclaim independence from Mexican rule. Abel Stearns told Larkin that Iniestra had 'some 15 or 18 *thousand* troops', financed by British merchants. Larkin told Captain Montgomery of USS *Portsmouth* that Barron and Forbes of Tepic financed it, acting for other 'capitalists'. John Jones of Santa Bárbara judged Commissioner Híjar 'a spy who 'governed Pico entirely ... keeping himself quiet, visiting no one'.[26] In fact, Híjar was dying.

In January 1846 word came from Reina de Los Angeles: 'the vessels are all ready at Acapulco to take the troops on board'. John Jones told Larkin, 'General Paredes with 12,000 troops has deposed [Herrera] and declared for a dictator[ship].' In Mexico City, Theodor Hartweg, German collector of seeds and plants for the London (Royal) Horticultural Society, started for the Pacific coast and met Iniestra's remnant heading north. 'They will never reach California, but [are being] kept out of mischief during the [Paredes] revolution.' Hartweg was afraid: no-one in convulsed Mexico would believe 'that a person would come all the way from London just to look for weeds'.[27]

In the first few months of 1846, when not covering Ireland's famine, *La Reforma*, staunchly republican and anti-monarchist, pleaded the case for

Alta California. The editor warned of centralist Mexico's 'selfish torpor and cruel indifference' towards California, 'a year and it will be abandoned'. The Bishop of The Californias, García Diego, requested priests, but *La Reforma* wanted Mexican, not European priests. Harking back to Híjar-Padrés days, it conceded 'colonisation is vital and [a department's] people would be its defenders', but insisted a Mexican military colony was the only solution. As the editor set his type, troops were stood to and stood down, until the final order was given to proceed to Alta California on foot.

RUMOUR AND DISTORTION[28]

Macnamara had more leverage on the new dictator than had Envoy Slidell, lying low since December 1845. Ostracised, he and secretary Parrott took refuge at Jalapa, near Vera Cruz port and the USN Eastern Squadron. Mexican honour was at stake, despite Slidell's $5 million on the table to compensate US settlers in Texas, $20 million for Alta California with San Francisco Bay, $5 million for Monterey and a haggle-ceiling of $40 million to include everything imaginable inland. Polk believed that bankrupt Mexico would be tempted, yet neither Herrera nor Paredes acknowledged Slidell, Parrott or their dollars. When the snubbed and smarting envoys returned to the US in May 1846, Slidell, who had advocated 'chastisement' in December, demanded 'redress'.

Slidell's brief had been to negotiate the new Texas frontier advanced to the Rio Grande to settle US citizens' legal claims – Parrott's included – and to buy Alta California. The US would not buy Texas, instructing confidential agent there, Charles Wyckliffe, to 'counteract British and French attempts to defeat the reunion [*sic*] of the Texas Republic with the US'. Herrera feared appearing to concede to or conspire with the US, yet the alternative was a hopeless war against a powerful enemy in a lost cause.

Consul John Black was the only US listening post left in Mexico City, never part of the diplomatic breakdown. He told Slidell on 19 February that the British ambassador:

> has today passed a note to this Government asking [permission] to land and send through Mexican territory *twenty thousand* [Black's emphasis] English troops on the pretext of passing them to Oregon territory. The English have some fixed and determined project in relation to

Mexico, and Mexico's non-consent will not prevent their landing their troops, which will be done at all hazard. [The US] will be unprepared and find the Oregon dispute tied up with Mexican affairs. People here say they would a thousand times prefer annexation by the US than submit to a foreign prince imposed on them by a foreign power.

The British, to US minds, were capable of anything, but a week later, Black ate his words. 'The number of English troops to pass through this territory has risen from twenty to forty thousand. Many think that no such application has been made.' Paredes was overheard at a British Legation banquet, whispering to ambassador Bankhead, 'I hope your government does not mean to let us be eaten up.'[29]

Bankhead had Paredes' ear. Ever ready to prod Whitehall, Bankhead sent a secret letter to Lord Aberdeen on 10 March 1846 (received 6 May) reporting that 'President Paredes intends to commission a person visiting England to communicate with Lord Aberdeen [about] the monarchy proposal and to put Mexico into the arms of England.' In the end, Paredes did not trust anyone to take the message, although in June, about to be deposed, he begged Great Britain to accept California, in hypothecation or as collateral on a loan, as long as she would protect it. For once, Bankhead did not report to London immediately.

On 19 and 24 February, consul Black reported to Envoy Slidell that 'Paredes made no less than five distinct visits to Mr Bankhead's house in one day, an affair so extraordinary … neighbours concluded that some very important business was about to be transacted.' Calle de Capuchinas was confined and nothing was missed. Slidell already blamed Bankhead's 'interfering in no friendly spirit' for his own snub by Mexico, and notified Washington of 'these repeated unceremonious visits'. Even 'a single visit deviates from established etiquette', making Bankhead 'confidential adviser' to Mexico. Bankhead's embassy was known for intrigue as well as parties, and conspiracy was assumed. 'Everything coming from California excites great interest here in English circles. The British Legation is all alive on such occasions.' Polk's cabinet assumed that Mexico was confident of its British alliance, which helped explain its consistently confident rejection of US money. Macnamara was incriminated by association with the diplomatic ant-heap, while Bankhead was reprimanded by London for ignoring government policy. Despite this atmosphere of suspicion and conspiracy, Black wrote an introduction for Macnamara to consul Larkin at Monterey, once Macnamara took out a visa for California on 12 March.

On the Pacific coast, Larkin wrote to Jacob Leese, 17 April and 21 May 1846, 'England is all powerful, almost able to fight the world. Jonathan [Hickory] will, in a war with John Bull, receive some hard and ugly knocks. He may take them patiently knowing John is growing old, while he is just coming up to manhood.' Rumour stalked the Oregon Trail in May that disguised British soldiers were stirring up Indians against US migrants. Two serving British officers travelled the Trail in plain clothes to test the feasibility of sending troops from Canada and found it impracticable.[30] More prosaically, in 1845, a retired British officer with a London lawyer, William Romaine, were on a trail sabbatical to see the west; Romaine was remembered as 'an imperious fool' and the captain as 'an old woman'. In 1845, Lt Peel reconnoitred several hundred miles into the Oregon by horse, sledge and Hudson's Bay trading posts, which his father duly reported to Wellington with pride.

The French ambassador to Mexico reported to Paris in April on the end of the Iniestra expedition. 'Colonel Iniestra has died. [His successor] has rebelled, taking all the funds.' In May, the French consul at Mazatlán reported 'the Mexican government despatched to Mazatlán part of the proposed expedition. A review was held the other day of little more than 700 men. *Comandante* Gutierrez [of Mazatlán] flattered himself that the English Admiral would lend him ships to transport this force … quite illusory. As for going overland … before 100 leagues, desertions would have decimated the force. The officers and men … have revolted and given Gutierrez 24 hours to leave.'[31]

MACNAMARA TO THE PACIFIC

Macnamara took out *Visa 455, Eugine* [sic] *Macnamara, Religioso, Irlanda, resid. Mexico,* on 12 March. Black gave him the note for Larkin, and Bankhead handed him letters for acting-consul Alexander Forbes. A letter from Bankhead lay at Tepic for Admiral Seymour whenever his flagship should appear at San Blas from Peru; a month later, at Mazatlán, its enclosed estimate of Macnamara, 'so good a testimonial and so strong a recommendation' impressed Seymour.[32]

It was a short walk north from Calle de Capuchinas to the president's and archbishop's adjacent palaces. Manuel de Posada y Garduno was Mexico's first native archbishop, successor in 1840 to a Spanish prelate who died after a fifteen-year absence from his diocese. The Archbishop hoped for a Mexican monarchy with a Spanish bloodline to revive Mexico and the *ancien régime*. Macnamara took the mail for Bishop García Diego and a letter of introduction, confirming church support for the Irish *Proyecto* which might revive the California church and bolster security. Macnamara had a *Facultas* to preach and hear confessions in French and English across Mexico. He added to his pouch copies of his petition, Cuevas' introduction to the late Comissioner Híjar and possibly another from Castillo y Lanzas (see Plates 6 and 8).

Flag Lt Frederick Beauchamp Seymour, nephew and ADC to the Admiral, accompanied Macnamara. Tall and dandy, known in the service as 'The Ocean Swell', young Seymour was his uncle's *confidante* and 'mainstay' on Station. The Admiral heard that the Irish Parisian and the Old Etonian had become good friends on the ten-day ride. Alexander Forbes put them up at Tepic from where San Blas lay a day away, no place to wait and not even a deepwater port, but 'a vast swamp overflowing in the rainy season' as one Royal Navy officer grumbled. Its ruined fort and dockyard hinted of a heyday.[33]

After Macnamara left Mexico City, consul Black told Washington of 'a visit some time since by an Irish priest, a particular friend of the archbishop and with whom I am on best of terms'. The priest 'who had just visited that dignitary', asked Black to look into a delayed consignment of books for the archbishop from New York, but 'turned the conversation to … what course would the US take if a monarchy were established in Mexico?'

Black replied that the US would have 'nothing to say' if that were the Mexican people's will. The Irishman pressed: suppose Mexico were to 'call in foreign aid and intervention to support [a monarchy] and that the federalists [liberals] opposed to monarchy should in like manner call in the US for protection, would the US assist against the established government?' Black referred the priest to Polk's December ultimatum to Europe. 'I have since understood,' Black continued, 'that the archbishop was much disappointed that England had not [supported] a monarchy, and in revenge has threatened "one grand federation, from Canada to Panama inclusive". He is heart and hand in favour of monarchy, panting for the splendour of a [Spanish Catholic] court, as others would be tinctured with heresy.'[34] Macnamara was Black's visitor, the archbishop's protégé and the sole Irish priest in the capital. Clergy from as far as Demerara purchased books from Murphy's of New York, but Black knew the visit was not about books.

A month later, Black reported 'Paredes has a good working relation with the English. England has three objects, territory, exclusive [commercial] privilege, and guaranteed interest on money bonds after deducting the value of territory to be ceded [under bondholder land warrants]. England will hem in the US [from south and west].' Consul Larkin reported in like vein from Monterey.

Macnamara and the politically aware Flag Lieutenant spent some days with Alexander Forbes, probably gratified to see his published advice finally being implemented. Forbes asked the priest to take a letter to his vice-consul, James Forbes (unrelated), in Alta California, requesting 'correct information' about the mercury find on the San José river, south of Santa Clara. Unpaid consuls combined commerce and diplomacy legitimately under Foreign Office rules, and enjoyed the proceeds. Without such concessions, consulates could not be staffed, but Forbes wanted more than intelligence. He asked Macnamara to secure him a business *entrée* to the mine, offering company expertise, 'British Crown protection', and money to buy out its shareholders. Two years later, vice-consul James reminded acting-consul Alexander that 'Mr Macnamara, on his arrival in California, commenced his negotiations to obtain an interest in this mine, as your agent.'[35]

THE SANTA CLARA MINE

Alexander Forbes, Robert Wyllie and consul MacKintosh had all argued that mineral exploitation should finance the colonising of Alta California. Macnamara, a prospective large-scale coloniser from Great Britain, defying Polk's ultimatum, had done enough already to provoke war. Now he was helping British merchants maintain their monopoly on a Mexican resource which might fund his colony in the process. It added to US suspicion of him and of Britain.

The mercury deposits near the San José river were identified and claimed late in 1845 by Commissioner Castillero as the Santa Clara Mine. It threatened the Barron and Forbes monopoly of mercury imports on the

Pacific. Mercury (quicksilver) was the essential amalgam for extracting silver from ore, and for extracting gold from river sand and crushed quartz. Mexico, a prime source of world silver, relied on the Rothschilds in Europe for mercury, particularly from the Almaden mine in Spain. It also imported from China, even when Rothschild imports stood at 600 flasks a month in 1845. The Santa Clara cinnabar was remarkably high yielding, US and British governments knew of it, and consuls and visiting naval personnel paid close attention.[36]

Commissioner Castillero left California for Mexico in March 1846 and his claim was conveyed in May. Crucially it was not put to Governor Pico and was mis-registered as 'at Santa Clara mission', although nearer *pueblo* San José. As principal claimant, Castillero held 12 of 24 shares, while a syndicate held the balance: Padre Suarez de Real, priest of Santa Clara and mine manager, held four; José Castro, military *Comandante* and senior-ranking mine partner, owned four; two brothers Robles, *californios*, who had dug the cinnabar for years as 'ochre', also had four. Alexander Forbes had the money and expertise to buy them out. Consul Larkin in Monterey was also interested, ordering 200 mercury flasks from Mott and Talbot at Mazatlán. On a convenient beach, he showed officers from USS *Cyane* how to 'bake' mercury from cinnabar, after they returned from viewing the mine. Vice-consul James Forbes monitored, but kept his own counsel at home nearby. Paredes ratified Castillero's $5000 and land reward, yet Governor Pico was still not consulted.

Macnamara and young Seymour left Forbes' mansion, 22 April, and boarded *Alexander Grant* at San Blas, for Mazatlán. The 700-ton Liverpool trader took them towards the Gulf of California and through the Marias islands, named for the three Marys of Calvary. Friar Junípero Serra, Alta California's first *Misionero Apostólico,* had travelled this route in 1768–9, co-founding San Blas, re-opening missions in Baja from which the Jesuits were being expelled, and founding Franciscan missions in Alta California. After staying briefly in Baja, Serra dedicated the first Alta California mission to San Diego, a sainted Spanish friar. From there, over half a century, a line of twenty more coastal missions sprouted north towards Sonoma, beyond San Francisco Bay. A thousand Spanish settlers trailed Serra overland from New Spain (later Mexico) to forestall British and Russian invasion threats to the empty coast. Around 300,000 California Indians also had to be 'civilised'. Missions and garrisons (*presidios*), with *pueblos* to sustain them, were the religious and secular arms of conquest, conversion and cultural consolidation. By 1846, Mexican California was barely populated, the friars all but eliminated, their impact on the Indians and the landscape cut short, and *presidios* and *castillos* crumbling around them. Eugene Macnamara entered California as its last 'Apostolic Missioner' and coloniser from old Europe, too late and dated.

Chapter 6

Ration Strength, Royal Navy: 1846

Macnamara had crossed the Atlantic three times, but this was his first voyage on the Pacific. *Alexander Grant*'s British captain would have afforded the aristocrat officer and Irish *padre* the courtesy of the wheel house and the chart table. To starboard, jungle coastline bared to sheer bluffs as the Sierra Madre slid into the Gulf of California. They made Mazatlán in four days.

BISHOP CLANCY'S LAST VOYAGE

William Clancy was also at sea, bound for Ireland, prematurely old at 44. The last parishioners left when Pope Gregory excommunicated him. Of the dozen or more priests he had recruited to Guiana, almost all had fled or died. John McDonnell of Kerry, Macnamara's travelling companion to Rome, was among the last to leave in 1845. He fought a drink demon, joined the Jesuits and worked with coffin ships carrying the first Famine Irish into quarantine at Quebec. He died in New York, 1852.[1]

As Clancy's house congregation dwindled, and Hynes' parishioners held the church next door, Hynes recorded Clancy's movements, the Postmaster checked Clancy's mail and the press recounted Clancy anecdotes. He fired off letters to clergy, laity, London MPs and to Hynes, 'with the most hellish intent. I [Hynes] am not safe near this skulking assassin'. *The Tablet* refused to publish his letter to the Irish bishops claiming the Pope's support.

In the humidity, men drank to blot out boredom, insomnia and life. Clancy drained his finances and lost more in court, including two cases against Macnamara *in absentia* for libel and refund of passage money; he held a yard sale, but few attended; he advertised for lodgers, but Hynes warned publicly the house was not to let. Privately Hynes called Clancy's congregation 'dupes', his services 'musters and demonstrations', and the remaining nuns 'Clancy's women'. The longer the ex-Apostolic Vicar hung on, the more vituperative the Apostolic Administrator's language became.

The 'dupes' dispersed, the singing stopped and Clancy's money ran out. In desperation he sold the roof shingles from the presbytery (March was still dry), the window glass, a water butt and 'two cartloads of trumpery'. A doctor examined him, as parishioners deserted to kneel before Hynes. Clancy advised the rest to become Methodists.

At dawn on 16 April, 'in a hired covered gig, [he paid] his farewell visits. He looked terribly pulled down.' Five days later (as Macnamara left San Blas for Mazatlán) Clancy boarded the steamship *Parker*. 'Not a single white, black or coloured person wished him goodbye. His ruffians possess the house and it is laughable, if melancholy, to see the houseboy wearing Clancy's cap.' Hynes and others forced the gate to reoccupy the house, while Clancy's lawyers ranted in the yard. Police dispersed small demonstrations outside and the sheriff returned the registers to Hynes.

Clancy was easy prey. The captain made him haggle for a ticket on an unseaworthy vessel, and boasted about it. 'In a long voyage, if water were scarce, I could not have had a better passenger … for he never washed.' *The Tablet* was kinder, reporting discreetly in August, 'Dr Clancy has arrived safely at Cork from the tropics.' Clancy died in June 1847 and was buried in the grounds of Cork cathedral, leaving £1,500 to two of his Georgetown nuns 'for their mutual support and the education of poor children'. They were back in Ireland, recovering in sympathetic convents.[2]

At Santa Bárbara, Alta California, Francisco García Diego y Moreno, first and last bishop of the Two Californias, to whom Macnamara had an introduction, took to his bed 'gravely ill and no longer able to attend to this diocese'. On 20 April he assigned his authority to his Franciscan aides, Narciso Durán and José Maria de Jesús Gonzáles Rubio. Ten days later he died 'of tuberculosis aggravated by acute depression'.[3] From Santa Bárbara he had overseen a '700 league [1,820 miles] long' bankrupt diocese, ruined churches and fewer than two dozen priests. A gun salute and genuine outpouring of grief greeted his coffin. Archbishop Manuel de Posada y Garduno died in Mexico the same day.

One month later, Narciso Durán, practical joker and musician, died at Santa Bárbara, leaving Gonzáles Rubio alone as 'governor of the mitre', the last Mexican to oversee the California church. On 1 June, Rome lost its bishop, Pope Gregory XVI, remembered by critics for his misgivings about railways, gaslight and liberals, but by admirers for his missionary enthusiasm, condemning of slavery and restoring of Papal authority after its humbling by Napoleon.

ADMIRAL SEYMOUR AT MAZATLÁN

On Sunday 26 April, *Alexander Grant* sighted Mazatlán, where HMS *Collingwood* had ridden anchors for ten days. The deepwater port was 'full of busy merchants and traders', British and American.[4] HMS *Spy* reported the frigate HMS *Juno*, 26 guns, from Peru, but the Admiral missed nothing: '26 April. Fine weather. Church service. Huge ship off, apparently that mistaken by *Spy* for *Juno*, the *Alexander Grant* of London. Dined in the Ward Room. The Rev. Mr Macnamara dined aboard.'[5]

Rear Admiral Sir George Francis Seymour had started service aged 10 on a fighting deck under the then Captain Nelson, and at 16 on HMS *Donegal* helped mop up after Trafalgar. *Collingwood*, his giant flagship on its first deployment, was a fitting memorial to Nelson's late second-in-command whom Seymour knew well. At 28, he took a disability pension for face wounds (his sideburns were partly cosmetic), which led to a shore posting as ADC to King William IV, and a seat on the Admiralty Board. USN Captain Du Pont, who developed a rapport with Seymour, reported 'a fine old gentleman, one side of his face handsome, the other gashed by a battle scar'.[6] (See Plate 10.)

He was hand-picked for the Pacific Station, primarily to monitor the French, with Oregon as a secondary brief and to watch Alta California in passing. He and the senior US naval officers were veterans of the 1812–15 Anglo-American War. Commodore Sloat, to Seymour 'a steady old officer', was 67 and sick, while Commodore Biddle, 63, had been

Seymour's personal friend for years, the two on trans-Atlantic visiting terms. At 59, Seymour observed, read and enquired, which helped distract him from wounds and gout. His Flag Lieutenant nephew called him 'a *preux chevalier* of the old school'.[7] In 1845, he walked forty miles to inspect a Hawaiian volcano; in 1846, he swam ashore to trek seventy miles to see a silver mine. His royal line boasted Queen Jane Seymour, favourite wife of King Henry VIII, and mother of King Edward VI.

The British Pacific Station totalled 17 vessels, including frigates, sloops and a steamer, but effectively only 'half a dozen ships when I need five times that number'. *Collingwood*, 80 guns, left Spithead in September 1844 to a formal send-off by Prince Albert, the Queen's Consort, and rounded Cape Horn to relieve flagship HMS *Dublin* at Valparaiso in November. HMS *America*, Seymour's other capital ship, an old 72-gun converted to a 50-gun heavy frigate, was commanded by Captain The Honourable John Gordon, brother to Foreign Secretary, Lord Aberdeen. He conveyed Lt William Peel, the Prime Minister's son, to an inland reconnaissance of Oregon Country, while *America* patrolled offshore, its draft too large for the Columbia river. From Peru in March 1845, Seymour requested reinforcements for a 'probable war' with 'offensive and grasping' Americans over Oregon. 'At least two additional line-of-battle ships should be sent to this sea to oppose, hold or check the … US Navy.' He lamented wryly that his two major warships, *Collingwood* and *America*, were 6,000 miles apart on a station stretching from the Falklands to Alaska: 'I get orders by the same ship to go to the Oregon and Tahiti and to put Peru to rights while half a dozen customary revolutions are going on in the American continent.'[8]

To worsen matters, Mexico and Chile currently refused Britain warehousing at Mazatlán or Valparaiso. Alternative facilities were being prepared at Honolulu and the Admiralty requisitioned *Palinurus*, an unseaworthy Liverpool barque, to fill the gap as a victualling transport based on Valparaiso. In January 1846 Lord Aberdeen rattled a sabre he would never draw, warning US ambassador McLane that he would send thirty major warships to the Pacific to meet US bluster over Oregon. The ambassador, whose son was with the USN Pacific Squadron, thought the threat 'menacing'; Britain's ambassador to Washington thought it 'dignified and imposing'. Nine months previously, Aberdeen had judged Seymour's force 'ample' for a war. Seymour's seventeen scattered ships faced ten American vessels concentrated on the Mexican coast and fifteen French vessels far-flung among the islands.[9]

Months later, in June 1846, Aberdeen conceded minor reinforcement, warning Seymour (too late) that 'the acquisition of territory and of ports is for Government consideration [alone]'. The California game required poker faces, but Aberdeen's expression over two years made even the game hard to name.[10] In Washington, slavery darkened every debate about expanding national territory. In December 1845, the new State of Texas became the latest slave state in the Union and abolitionists feared more new territories would swell slaver ranks. In Alta California, cheap Indian labour bordered on slavery, now that Indian rights to Spanish law and mission protection had evaporated.

Seymour's eyes suffered from constant reading, reporting and corresponding, often by candlelight; his face wound brought on toothache and insomnia in 'head-aching weather'. After dining with Macnamara on 26 April and seeing him onto *Collingwood*'s cutter, Seymour worked into the small hours, writing to Forbes at Tepic and to Bankhead in Mexico City, acknowledging letters brought by Macnamara and nephew Frederick.

> Mr Macnamara arrived here today in the English merchant ship *Alexander Grant* from San Blas and I had much pleasure in making his acquaintance. I wish he had taken up the matter of filling California with Emeralders some years earlier, as present prospects hold out greater chance of its being inhabited by people [Americans] whose objects and moral qualities are not of so meritorious a nature ... Mr Macnamara brought me your interesting letter of 11 March on Mexico and US politics which was mislaid at Tepic and not forwarded to me while I was at San Blas. Thank you also for the New York newspapers.[11]

The papers carried US news of 'Polk and his friends in the Backwoods and the West', and some Irish news. Seymour had an Irish estate and a soft spot for 'Emeralders', gentler language than the 'Patlander', 'Mick', 'Potato Head' and Irish-ape cartoons then appearing in London's *Punch* magazine. His Protestant naval *padre*, Nathaniel Proctor from Tipperary, had graduated from Trinity, Dublin. Admiralty instructions to chaplains

1. Mid-morning, 7 July 1846, (L-R) USS *Cyane*, flagship *Savannah* and *Levant* salute US flag raised at Monterey. In Los Angeles, Macnamara was being awarded his land; at sea Admiral Seymour was becalmed, heading for Monterey. *W.A Coulter, 1902. Monterey Public Library, California History Room Archives.*

2. £600,000 in Californian gold and Mexican *pesos* entering the Bank of England, 1849, 'securely transported' by HMS Calypso for British merchants to avoid Mexican dues. Official smuggling damaged Royal Navy discipline and Mexico's ability to repay debt. *Illustrated London News, 20 September 1849, Oxford City Public Library.*

3. Eighteenth century Royal Arms of Ireland over the door of the Irish College, with the tricolour of the modern Irish Republic. The former college is now the Irish Cultural Centre, Paris. *Author.*

4. Bishop John Hynes O.P., Apostolic Administrator, British Guiana, 1843-6, Apostolic Vicar, 1846–56. *M. Gardignani, Rome, 1860. Melbourne Diocese Historical Commission.*

5. Fort Ross[iya], California. A colony around Bodega Bay claimed the area as Tsarist Russian territory in 1812. President Monroe worried about a Russian base in North America. Russia abandoned it in 1842. *Author.*

6. Plaza Mayor, Mexico City. The Archbishop's former palace lies near the top of the side street behind the parked bus between his Cathedral (L) and Presidential Palace (R). *Dan Fox.*

7. Texas Legation, London, 1842-5, down 'No 3' passage, entrance in side of wine shop. The outstanding wine account was settled with the shop by Texas patriots in 1995. Ashbel Smith, ambassador, and Luis Cuevas, former Mexican ambassador, failed to reconcile Texas and Mexico. An independent California would have had a London embassy too. *Author.*

8. Posada y Garduno, Archbishop of Mexico, 1840–46, licensed Macnamara to preach in English and French in Mexico and Alta California. He supported his Project. *Cardinal Rivera Cerrera, Archbishop of Mexico, and Visual Library, E.U.I., Mexico History.*

9. HMS *Collingwood,* 80 guns, flagship RN Pacific Station under Admiral Seymour, 1844-48. *Illustrated London News, 22 March 1845, Oxford City Public Library.*

10. Admiral Sir George Francis Seymour, RN, Pacific Station 1844–48, with HMS *Collingwood* in background. *F. Lucas, 1852. Marquess of Hertford, Ragley Hall.*

11. Wardroom table, HMS *Collingwood* used by Macnamara, Frémont, Somerville, Walpole, Kit Carson, Hertweg, Seymour, consuls and merchants. Sidestays held it in floor hooks in heavy weather. *Marquess of Hertford, Ragley Hall.*

12. Figurehead of former HMT *Palinurus*, wrecked off Scilly Isles while making for London from British Guiana, 1848. Under Navy requisition, it conveyed Macnamara from Honolulu to Mexico in 1846. *Scilly and Tresco Museum: Amanda Martin, Curator Isles of Scilly Museum.*

13. Tullig, an 'unhoused' (evicted) village, near Macnamara's first parish of Kilkee-Killard. Landlords demolished 20% of Clare peninsula inhabitants' homes. *Illustrated London News, 15 December, 1849, Courtesy Oxford City Public Library.*

14. Chilean government agreement to Macnamara's Osorno colony, registered [no date] October 1848. *Archivo Nacional de Chile.*

15. Sluicing for gold on Gold Mines River, Co. Wicklow. Over 800 lbs of gold was found 1796-1802. *Aquatint, J. Bluck after T.S. Roberts 1804. Reproduced by Permission of The Geological Society of London.*

16. Nineteenth century Irish settler graveyard, Great Central Valley, California, *Mike Hornick, Salinas.*

17. John Charles Frémont, c. 1857, *Brooklyn Museum.*

banned sectarianism, summarised as 'preaching church instead of Christ'. On 5 May, after *Juno* arrived, Seymour hosted Lt Smith, a neighbour of his estate at Lisburn, County Antrim.

Four times in two weeks at Mazatlán Macnamara dined with Seymour. The 'intelligent young Irishman educated as a priest' impressed the ship's officers. With Irish gentry and protestant clergy he was at ease, 'a clever and pleasant companion, even our clergyman [Proctor] admits this truth', noted Collingwood's Senior Lieutenant and Acting Commander, Philip Somerville of West Cork. Many of *Collingwood*'s officers and men were Irish, and celebrated their land legs with the Irish on USS *Savannah* by racing hired horses at full gallop through Mazatlán streets. Macnamara's colony scheme drew Seymour's interest. 'I wish Mr Macnamara had better prospects in that direction,' he told Bankhead, 'for it is impossible not to be pleased with his apparent straightforwardness and intelligence. If I can help on his task I shall do so, as he is still here.'[12]

Macnamara was trapped at Mazatlán with other travellers. Commodore Sloat's command frigate, *Savannah*, 54 guns with two escort corvettes, deterred ships from transporting Mexican troops to Alta California, but Seymour warned Sloat that a formal blockade would be an act of war. Sloat blew hot and cold, promising Seymour he would not act without new orders, yet Seymour felt it imperative to curb the Americans. The local population were 'frightened out of their wits', and while Sloat 'says his hostile intentions are greatly exaggerated, I do not know [any] more about his peaceful intentions'. Theodor Hartweg, botanist, had drummed his heels at Mazatlán for a month. 'There is not the slightest chance of ships sailing for northern California. Commodore Sloat told me sharply he could not let his movements be known [despite] their being well known weeks before he sailed!' The LHS rebuked Hartweg for inertia, unaware he had to wait three winter months at Tepic for his scientific baggage to arrive by mule. Now he prepared to return to San Blas on rumour of a schooner for California. Macnamara knew him from Mexico City and possibly they shared a roof in Mazatlán.[13]

On 7 May 1846, the remnants of Iniestra's *Batallón* halted at Mazatlán, declared for Santa Anna against Paredes and invited US warships into harbour. Seymour offered Macnamara 'passage on board *Juno* as soon as she has completed her water', and invited him to what was effectively a working dinner aboard *Collingwood*. William Talbot, of Mott and

Talbot importing mercury from China, was consular agent in Mazatlán, and Robert Walkinshaw was mining engineer and agent for Barron and Forbes, importing mercury from Europe as well as from China. Both companies had handled San Feliciano gold after 1842, and were anxious to cut a deal in the new Santa Clara mercury mine. Forbes had already asked Macnamara to negotiate for him with the mine shareholders at Monterey; Seymour had trekked with Talbot to see Walkinshaw at work at a silver mine, had talked mining with Forbes, and had handled cinnabar brought to Mazatlán from Santa Clara by Captain Mervine of USS *Cyane*. 'Mercury', he warned. 'will increase the US appetite to acquire that country.'

Next morning, 10 May, Hartweg approached Seymour with his introduction from Aberdeen, issued to a foreigner in lieu of a passport. 'More successful was my application,' Hartweg recorded, 'to Rear Admiral Sir George Seymour, who kindly allowed me a passage to Monterey in HMS *Juno*. Towards evening on 11 May I went aboard *Juno* and arrived at quiet little Monterey after 26 days.'

After Seymour had inspected *Juno*, he hosted the two passengers with Patrick Blake, *Juno's* captain, on the flagship. They talked of the flares and bonfires in port the previous night to celebrate the mutiny against Paredes and local *Comandante* Gutierrez. 'They risked a fine if they did *not* illuminate!' Seymour quipped. Gutierrez had boarded *Collingwood* to ask Seymour to transport the late Iniestra's men to California. 'He was seasick and he has not the manners of a gentleman' noted Seymour after refusing. After the celebrations, Gutierrez was taken under close arrest to San Blas.

Seymour did not hide Blake's mission: 'As it was known that Mr Macnamara and Mr Hartweg were to be embarked, I advised Commodore Sloat that *Juno* was going to California to see what is going on ... I have had no ships at California this year.' He did, however, omit details of his order to Blake, 'to examine the landing places on the coast near San Francisco and positions on commanding ground [for] operations which may hereafter become necessary, and to obtain the number of British subjects settled in California and the extent and situation of a quicksilver mine reported in California'. Sloat knew Macnamara was going north and presumably he knew why.[14]

Two weeks later Seymour wrote to his senior captain, Gordon of HMS *America*: 'I sent *Juno* to see whether the *californios* had had the good sense to declare themselves clear of Mexico before it got them into a scrap! But I doubt they have good sense about anything.'[15] He wanted to send HMS *America* as 'a vessel of more respectable size' than *Juno*, but *America*, after dropping Lt Peel at Mazatlán for Mexico City and home in November 1845, took on $2 million of British merchants' silver to deliver to the Bank of England. Consul Barron refused to use HMS *Daphne*, 18 guns, as too lightly armed, although Seymour had detailed it for use. The admiral would receive flag officer's commission for the cargo, but Gordon ignored Seymour's order of 27 April, 'I cannot spare the *America*', and sailed from Valparaiso for England. He was court-martialled later for dereliction of duty. Seymour advised the Foreign Office in June that when acting-consul, 68-year-old Alexander Forbes, retired, consuls should 'be obliged to keep out of trade'. He also asked for Forbes' silence about his going to California, 'so as not to create a supposition that I was authorised to offer that province protection, which is not the case'.

Sloat and Seymour dined together at Mazatlán and played whist. Their respect was mutual. At Honolulu, the previous October, the two had talked Pacific politics into the early hours. At Mazatlán Sloat accepted coal from HMS *America* and loaned *Juno* a chart of the Gulf of California to copy before it left for Monterey. Both flag officers were in the dark about their respective governments' intentions towards California, and Sloat, a sick man, was ready to retire. 'If we are at peace with Mexico, we have no right to take California,' he told Seymour, 'and if we are at war, I do not see what right you have to prevent us.' His orders of October 1845 read 'If you ascertain actual hostilities, take San Francisco port and blockade or occupy Monterey': it lacked the precision of 'if you ascertain war'. Only in mid-May 1846 did Navy Secretary Bancroft order Sloat to take the ports outright, but the order reached the Commodore – courtesy the Royal Navy – only after he had left the Pacific for retirement late in July. No navy could 'take ports' without troops. Seymour had 'scarcely received a word for more than 12 months' from Admiralty or Foreign Office since he arrived on Station. 'It does not lay fair for us.' he told Alexander Forbes, 'until our government takes a decided line on California.' 'If HM Government sends us the orders,' he told James Forbes, 'I shall lose no time in managing them into effect'. The ageing sea-dog straining at the leash was totally and correctly dependent on the politician's word of command.[16]

'Old Ironsides', USS *Constitution*, 44 guns, rode for three months before Mazatlán, retained by Sloat on its way home from the East Indies Station. The 50-year-old frigate, launched by Washington himself, was the talk of British decks: 'in the last war [1812] *Constitution* took three British frigates', marvelled Midshipman Markham, in awe at being so near a legend. Seymour believed the dominating presence of *Collingwood* had sobered US officers, reassuring Mexicans 'that there are larger ships afloat than the Commodore's'. He even took credit for *Constitution*'s eventual departure, supposedly daunted by *Collingwood*'s size.

Alexander Forbes wrote yet again to James Forbes at Monterey for information on the mercury mine. 'I wrote to you, 15 April, by Mr Macnamara, but he ... will go by the next vessel which takes this. Procure information on the quicksilver mine or mines ... of immense interest to Mexico as without it the precious silver mines cannot be worked.'[17] Seymour wrote to the First Lord of the Admiralty about Macnamara:

> Nothing but a large influx of British subjects into California could have had any lasting influence – Mr Bankhead sent me with strong recommendation an active and intelligent gentleman, Mr Macnamara, educated as a priest, who had a scheme of taking 5000 Irish to the country and has gained some influence in Mexico. I ordered him a passage in *Juno* to California, arriving with so good a testimonial from Mr Bankhead and having travelled with my nephew [Flag Lt Frederick Seymour] from Mexico [City] who thought well of him, but I am afraid he is two years too late to be of any use in California. Its situation is irremediable.'[18]

After flagging *Juno* out of Mazatlán on 12 May, Seymour resigned himself and 800 crew to weeks of stand-by: expeditions, shell collecting, alligator hunting, beach cricket, letter writing, hull painting and ruminating. On 24 May, *Collingwood* saluted Queen Victoria's birthday with cannon and flag, and *Savannah* reciprocated. Seymour hoped fresh orders might arrive at Tepic by courier from Vera Cruz. American officers had no such facility, for instance at Panama, to link with Washington, only the use of scheduled civilian vessels. Sloat and the *californios* heard of Polk's war proclamation on 13 May, only at the end of July. If news to departments was slow, it reached ships even more slowly. London knew of the US–Mexican War early in June, but *Illustrated London News*, 6 June, still played it down: history would see 'stranger events than future Polks and Jacksons on the throne of the Montezumas'. Midshipman Markham assumed it had started already: 'The Mexicans are, I believe, at war with the Yankees', but he was always distracted by something, this time by Mazatlán sharks thrashing below the deck rail.

Patrick Blake ran a screw-tight, demoralised ship. He had little time for 'uneducated lower orders' and flogged them. *Juno*'s 250 crew, after forty days at sea from Peru, had six day's rest at Mazatlán, including replenishment work, before another month at sea to Alta California. Two days out, rounding Baja California, they were mustered to witness a marine lashed for insolence. On the first Sunday morning, after muster call, Blake led from the *Common Prayer* book, Macnamara attending, but with no other role in an Anglican service. At 5.00 p.m. they buried Lt Smith overboard, the Lisburn man who had dined with Macnamara and Seymour the previous week.

When coastal fog permitted, they watched desolate Baja California to starboard, 'sterile, but when the shades of evening close around, or before daylight, nothing can exceed the magnificence of the barren peaks and cactus-covered rocks. Feudal castles come to mind.'[19] Home was never far from sailors' minds. Lts Walpole and Peel later saw 'English parkland' between Monterey and San Francisco Bay; Lt Somerville glimpsed 'the hills of Glengariff' above San Blas, and heard 'the bell of Rosscarbery' sound over the Catholic mission at Honolulu. Back home, Commander Eden, briefly *Collingwood*'s second-in-command, had daydreamed of being stranded on The Marias with one dusky Inés and her Cuban bloodhound, Zambro. He exorcised the fantasy with a vividly illustrated novel.[20]

Wine, beer and grog (diluted rum and lime) compensated for barrelled water, and a Friar Mathew medallist could choose tea, cocoa or boiled vinegar water. Three more Sunday services later, they rounded Point Lobos into Monterey Bay. The crew mustered for another flogging: 36 lashes for 'continued dirtiness and stealing clothes'. They dropped anchor on 7 June; 'Mr Hartweg, naturalist, was discharged' into a new habitat of 'verdant fields and pine-covered mountains', apparently oblivious to the street stench and litter of cattle limbs.

Macnamara landed too, but *Juno* remained at his billet. Blake's priority was to meet vice-Consul James Forbes whose home was at San José, but Forbes had gone south to Santa Bárbara for a crucial Convention (*Consejo General*) summoned by the Governor. Blake needed to follow, which limited Macnamara's time for business in Monterey.

THE MINE DEAL

Macnamara took consul Black's letter to consul Larkin's house, but Larkin was away with *Comandante* Castro confronting rebellious US settlers further north. Padre Suárez de Real, whose unrealistic parish stretched from ex-mission Santa Clara to ex-mission San Carlos at Monterey, evidently expected Macnamara. He managed the mercury mine for Castillero, its owner, and *Comandante* Castro, senior shareholder.

The 'Cave' on the Rio San José was known for its vermilion pigment used to paint faces and the walls of Santa Clara church. The Robles family had dug it for decades, but Castillero analysed a mercury yield at 26–35 per cent, making the Rothschilds' Spanish ore from Almaden 'poor' at 16 per cent. In 1847, James Forbes renamed it 'New Almaden'. Mexico produced some mercury, but from uneconomic ore and it depended on imports. A rich find on Mexican territory would unlock the nation's silver, but threaten the Barron and Forbes monopoly.

Word of the find spread quickly. Lt Peel RN visited, November 1845; Captain Frémont spent two days there, January 1846; officers from USS *Portsmouth* and *Cyane* saw it in April, and US consul Larkin sent quills of mercury to Secretary Buchanan and Senator Benton in Washington, just as he and Abel Stearns of Reina de Los Angeles had sent California gold samples in 1842. In April 1846, Alexander Forbes commissioned Macnamara as he passed through with Flag Lt Seymour, to secure him a lease on the mine.

The owners believed Britain would protect the mine against the US if Barron and Forbes co-owned it. Santa Anna in exile in 1845 had placed property and money with consul MacKintosh's wife for 'British protection'. Macnamara, acting temporarily for Alexander Forbes, was carried by a British frigate, and armed with a British colony scheme recommended by Mexico City. Admiral Seymour also told the captain of HMS *Frolic* about 'British merchants whose interests [at Monterey] may want looking after': it must have been the mine, as California hosted no other British commercial interests. In a US judicial appeal in 1859, ex-*Comandante* Castro declared 'Suárez de Real and I considered Macnamara an influential person.'[21]

José Maria Suárez de Real was an energetic 40-year old Mexican friar, sent to California in 1833, just as the missions were ordered dissolved. In 1846, his huge parish was bankrupt. He was isolated and had several uncanonical relationships, what USN officers called 'left-handed wives'. He took responsibility for them as well as the widow and children of his problem predecessor, Padre Mercado. To help feed his dependents, the priest expanded the mine with the help of two *californios* and three Indians. In 1846 he informed Bishop García Diego that he was waiting for a boat from Monterey to Mexico.[22]

The priest could support no-one on the 'ecclesiastical beggary' of offerings and stole fees – even the Bishop loathed them – but it was all the clergy had when their diocese could not pay them. Were he to be disciplined in Mexico, he would lose his families and they his support. *Comandante* Castro, before going to Santa Clara in pursuit of the settlers, had left Suárez de Real three sheets of scarce franked paper. One was a pre-signed lease of the mine to Barron and Forbes; with the second, Suárez de Real bought an orchard; he used the third to convey a mine share in 'voluntary perpetual cession' to Macnamara. A consideration or 'bite' may have been passed on to him from Alexander Forbes.[23]

Macnamara's power-of-attorney of 12 June was pre-signed by Castro and Antonio Osio witnessing each other, and by others when available. Power-of-attorney, like staggered witnessed signing, was frontier practice where communications were poor and distances great. 'Good faith governed contracts in those days', Castro pointed out in court years later.

> I give special, ample and sufficient power to Presbyter Don Eugene Macnamara that representing me and my associates, he may contract with an English company to the exclusion of every other nation [to] work three properties [*pertenencias*] of the mine for nine years, with an extension option of seven years more, the products being one half for their owners [but] free of charges and one half for the English company [or] two thirds to the English company, and one third to the

owners [but] free of charges … or other stipulations will be made. Witnessed by Jose Malarin [*rancher*], David Spence [*JP, Scots settler*], Manuel Diaz [*mayor of Monterey*], Antonio Osio [*JP and rancher*] [*over the signature of*] Jose Castro.[24]

A British warship in Monterey Bay was news, and Larkin returned with Castro in time to catch the visitors before *Juno* sailed. Larkin was disappointed that Blake had no news of hostilities. Macnamara gave him consul Black's letter of introduction and greeted Castro. On 14 June, Larkin, as President Polk's confidential agent, confided in his own agent, Abel Stearns at Reina de Los Angeles. Either Macnamara had played down his approval from Paredes, or Larkin misunderstood:

We have in Monterey the Rev Mr Macnamara who arrived here from Mazatlán in HBM Ship *Juno*. The officers of the ship were prohibited by the captain from bringing letters. Mr Macnamara is a Catholic priest, Irish, and has been in the City of Mexico all 1844 [*sic*] with Herrera; almost concluded a negotiation for the London Emigration Society to land ten thousand Irish in California. Paredes refused to allow any English-speaking emigrant, as the Irish in California would join the Yankees at once.

Mr Macnamara dresses in Citizen clothes, has in my opinion as full government and political information as theological. He and the captain of *Juno* appear satisfied that no British government course can prevent the destiny of California as it now appears to be going.

Mr Macnamara has correspondence for the Bishop; now goes south [to Bandini], will call on the Governor [Pico], I suppose. He brought to me letters of recommendation from our consul [Black] in Mexico City. He has a very good appearance; his actual business I presume to be of a private nature as Agent for his company to find available lands for the Irish. I should think his Government had cognisance of the business; perhaps affords assistance. Will you inform me of his motives and movements.[25]

'LONDON EMIGRATION SOCIETY'?

'The London Emigration Society' left no record, Larkin was partially deaf and Macnamara had a western Irish accent tamed by education and travel.[26] A Clare man's '*Land and* Emigration Society' might be heard by a Massachusetts ear losing its edge as '*London* Emigration Society'.

Britain's '*Colonial* Land and Emigration Commission' was commonly known as 'The Land and Emigration Commission' (or 'Committee', 'Office' or 'Board'). It was a weak government standards office for emigrants to 'healthy' British territory, advising on finance, recruitment, and overseeing health and safety in ports and on ships. In 1841 it refused to help emigrants to Australia delayed at Rio, who asked to stay: 'Protection or redress', it judged, would be impossible in Brazil. It gave futile help in bringing workers to Guiana from Sierra Leone in Macnamara's time; it persuaded the Army Board to send pensioners to farm the Falkland Islands, and in 1847, it opened an office in New York to advise Irish emigrants fleeing the Famine.

Only rarely did it subsidise, for example, emigrants to Guiana after 1840, to New South Wales in 1848, and the Irish Famine Orphans Project to Australia in 1850. Were California to become a British protectorate, the Commission might give moral support, but no finance. Macnamara may have bragged to impress, confident that California would be British territory that year, once he, Seymour and the newly independent *californios* had pulled together. Personal support from Bankhead, Seymour, MacKintosh, Alexander Forbes and London bondholder leaders, may have turned his head. A month later, at Monterey, he told Lt Somerville clearly, 'the Government will bear the expense'.[27]

When Macnamara met Seymour at Mazatlán, the Admiral expected 'probable' war over Oregon and certainly over California. The Irish priest did not tell him of 'London' support, as the admiral would know better, but he had mentioned the 'Emigration Committee' to Bankhead in 1845, which the ambassador duly reported to Aberdeen: 'Macnamara can entertain no hope of money from Mexico, but he seems to think that if an additional grant of land was given in lieu thereof, he could raise money upon that with some aid from the Emigration Committee, to bring over his colonists to California.'[28] Finance was always the *Proyecto's* weakness.

The CLEC dealt routinely with Irish cries for help, but recorded no contact with Eugene Macnamara. 'Large spontaneous emigration from

Ireland means that HM Government will not sanction any aid from public funds.' A pencilled endorsement noted 'Irish families are unacceptable on account of numbers of children.' Sometimes the CLEC haggled fares and kept families together, although few colonisers were willing to set up Wakefield-style 'villages': the CLEC 'will only support emigration of tenants if a bond is put down by the landowners. Villages risk unemployment for sixty families [concentrated] in one spot.' In February 1847 the CLEC rejected a plan for convicts to build log huts in Canada for Scots emigrants. A British consul in Texas warned it about false claims for Texas agriculture by a 'British Mutual Emigration Association', its directors 'without character or influence'.

Overall it was 'no provision to throw great numbers of poor on large tracts of vacant lands', or beyond the empire. The CLEC warned one enquirer not to hope for 'emigration agents to China', another against 'enlistment as soldiers for Ecuador', and in September 1846, it warned a County Monaghan man, 'the Government has not adopted any measure to promote emigration to the Oregon Territory and there are no opportunities for emigrants to engage passage direct to that part of America'.

Larkin reported Macnamara's claim to Secretary Buchanan. 'Mr Macnamara informed me that he was commissioned by a private company in London', but the CLEC was not private, and if Macnamara was referring to bondholder land warrants, he was parroting what he had heard from MacKintosh.[29] Two weeks later at Santa Bárbara, Macnamara expanded to Governor Pico and Spain's consul, Cesareo Lataillade, on his claim to government support, which he then repeated to Lt Somerville.

Robert Crichton Wyllie, of the 1843 *Bondholders Report*, had written from Honolulu to cousin Hartnell at Monterey in March 1844, 'The answer from the London [Mexican Bondholders] sub-Committee to my *Report* may lead me to visit California [from Hawaii] to determine how English settlers there would enjoy greater advantages than in [Mexico's Atlantic departments].'[30] Bondholder committees, however, were investor mouthpieces, not colonising companies. The only decision they could make was whether to form such a company, or to continue sitting on their hands hoping for cash.

John Diston Powles wrote to Lord Aberdeen in May 1846 as Macnamara was sailing to Monterey. He begged that Government intervene in any

US–Mexican war 'to protect bondholders' commercial interests'.[31] Two days later the bondholders endorsed his plea, but too late to save land option *and* cash repayments from events in the Pacific. Powles rued it for the rest of his life. Macnamara had namedropped, banking on a sea change in bondholder attitudes to acquiring land and in what remained of Government thinking on acquiring California. When neither happened, he railed in frustration later, from Honolulu, at 'asinine, stupid old Aberdeen'.

SANTA BÁRBARA: THE ABORTED CONSEJO GENERAL

Captain Blake watered, provisioned and led service on Sunday 14 June, Macnamara his sole passenger. Five days later, *Juno* put in before Santa Bárbara, Macnamara was discharged, but only after ten more men were flogged for insolence. Macnamara was probably glad to exchange his navy cot for a mission palliasse.

He and Blake believed that James Forbes was attending the *Consejo* at Santa Bárbara, but Governor Pico cancelled it even before *Juno* left Monterey. Vice-consul Forbes, under Aberdeen's orders in 1845 to play down *californio* expectations of Britain, had ridden on to the capital, Reina de Los Angeles, to discuss a personal land grant with Governor Pico, also expected there soon. Leading *anglos* and *californios* saw the writing on the wall and queued for grants which Pico distributed legally and dutifully in bulk, through May and June, to reduce unoccupied land and perhaps to build up a meagre defence fund. Defence was the governor's prime, stipulated duty and Pico declared shame at having so little revenue for it. He took nothing from Macnamara and Mexico City sent him no salary.

Ex-mission Santa Bárbara, the late bishop's *cathedra*, was intact, thanks to an Irish settler, Dr Nicholas Den of Kilkenny, mayor of *pueblo* Santa Bárbara, who leased it and its 35,000 acre ranch for an annual $100 rent in gold. It saved the mission from asset-strippers and gave the diocese revenue. Bishop García Diego y Moreno had elected to live there in 1840, instead of at San Diego, the seat Rome designated for the Two Californias diocese. His dreams of monastery, cathedral, girls academy and primary schools, were still piled stones when he died on 30 April 1846.

Padre Gonzáles Rubio, interim head of diocese, welcomed Macnamara and told him of the death on 1 June of Padre Narciso Durán, mission Prefect and champion of the Indians. A proud Spaniard, Durán had refused the oath to Mexico. The Irish traveller and Rubio would have prayed by the two new graves in the altar sanctuary out of respect. Rubio read the Archbishop's letter, and accorded a 'Permit to hear confession and preach in English and French, to the priest Eugene Macnamara, native of Ireland and passing through this diocese, under the same terms as granted by the Archbishop of Mexico.'[32]

Patrick Short, ex-Irish College Paris and Picpus missioner expelled from Hawaii to California in 1831, was now in Valparaiso, the Picpus mission headquarters. In 1837 Durán had asked him to take charge of ex-Mission Purísima Concepción, north of Santa Bárbara. Short declined, left for Hawaii, from where he was again expelled and went to Valparaiso. La Purísima closed permanently.[33] Hartnell and Larkin were still corresponding with Short in 1846.

The *Consejo General* of the seven *pueblos*, summoned by Pico and his Assembly on 13 May, was to have convened 15 June at Santa Bárbara, two delegates per *pueblo*, seven Assemblymen, five soldiers and five clergy. The *Consejo* was poised, it was believed, to debate independence from Mexico; Juan Bandini, Assemblyman for security, would chair. Pico knew that northern members would not attend over *Comandante* Castro's objection, as the north objected less to US protection. Castro was not consulted, but vice-consul Forbes received Pico's confidences with his usual sympathetic ear. *El Expectador* in Mexico heard about it only after the US occupation of Monterey, but on 5 August dismissed it all as 'Quixotic'.

Stearns alerted Larkin from Reina de Los Angeles, 14 May.

> [At the *Consejo*] California will look for friends in another quarter. Overtures have been made by British agents [James Forbes denied it, Macnamara had not yet arrived] to Governor [Pico] of California to declare independence, at the same time requesting to declare itself under the protection of [the British] government with guarantees. This I am certain of.

Stearns also noted that Castro wanted to meet Pico at San Luis Obispo for talks. Larkin suggested Stearns have himself elected to the *Consejo* where they might explain to Bandini that US protection and support for a 'sister republic' was on offer, which was not a threat of occupation. It was Secretary Buchanan's line, dictated to Larkin and conveyed by Lt Gillespie. Vice-consul James Forbes dismissed the gossip as 'entirely false respecting any offer made by British agents. The Governor should give up any idea of looking to England'. Larkin enjoyed a drama. Forbes warned him and French consul Gasquet that London would 'view with much dissatisfaction any other nation that interferes with Californian affairs'. Larkin retorted with small-town bravado, 'Britain is welcome to *view*, but events must have their natural way.'

Admiral Seymour was aware of the *Consejo* when he sailed from Mazatlán to Monterey in June. It was 'to canvas under what power [the *californios*] were to place themselves, [one] eager to get them at any price [the other] not having shown any disposition to do so ... I go to see if *Juno* has taken any part and if the inhabitants seek independence or merely independence of Mexico.'

Comandante Castro was a Paredes man, grudgingly accepting Pío Pico as governor in 1845, when an earlier mood for secession had obtained. Faced with a settler revolt (Bear Flaggers), the US Navy offshore, Frémont's trespassing topographers and the rumours of US settlers heading overland, Castro judged the *Consejo* the final 'treason'. From Santa Clara on 8 June, he mixed metaphors with brandy: 'the insane Hydra of discord aborted ... this most abominable scrawl ... assassinating the bosom of the mother country ... a dangerous club ... this volcano whose lava consumed ... our rights [and] converted liberty into an abyss of evils ... illegal, subversive, anti-constitutional, illiberal.' Martial law was the only 'legal resort' left. Consul Larkin acknowledged Castro's spirit: 'if strong is well, it is well written.' Four days later, Castro himself committed 'treason', transferring his mine holding, through Macnamara, to 'British protection'.

Larkin informed Washington on 1 June, that James Forbes would 'not advise Governor Pico to look to England and would advise [privately] to look to the United States'. Larkin suggested that instead, the *Consejo* request President Paredes to sell California to the highest bidder, since millions of US dollars lay unspent on the table, but by then Envoy Slidell had long left Mexico, Paredes had weeks left, and Polk had already declared 'a state of war exists' due to Mexico. On 13 June the departmental Assembly met at Santa Bárbara to defer the *Consejo* indefinitely, a full week before Macnamara arrived. [34]

THE GOVERNOR'S CONCESSION

Blake sent a courier from Santa Bárbara to James Forbes in Reina de Los Angeles. Once Forbes responded, 23 June, Blake sailed there with a letter from Seymour. He found the vice-consul sick, anxious to return home to San José, and took him aboard. Headwinds slowed their return, but gave them time to talk: 'I have availed myself much of his information.' Forbes insisted on disembarking at Santa Bárbara 'on learning that Eugene Macnamara had arrived there'. The two met 'at the start of July'.[35] They may have talked protectorates, but Forbes' overriding interest was the mine.

Given London and James Forbes' disclaimer of British interest, Pico's continuing confidence in British protection must have been encouraged by Macnamara when they first met at Santa Bárbara. *Californios* always overstated Britain's interest and intent and Macnamara was not subject to Aberdeen's 'hands off' policy. James Forbes was also widely believed to have influenced Pico. After *Juno* sailed south to find Forbes, Pico heard from Castro of the Bear Flag revolt. With that in mind, on 24 June he and Macnamara examined the *Proyecto* documents together, since Foreign Minister Cuevas' letter to Commissioner Híjar had required Pico's close involvement. At Monterey, Macnamara had brokered British protection for Castro's mine; a week after meeting Macnamara at Santa Bárbara, Pico petitioned British protection for California through Blake from Admiral Seymour.

From meeting Macnamara on 24 June, Pico took the colony petition to Reina de Los Angeles for the next Assembly to deliberate. He and Macnamara had agreed to relocate the colony from the coast to a 52-mile deep belt along the entire eastern bank of the Rio San Joaquin, beginning on Rio Cosumnes in the north, running south-east beyond the San Joaquin source, through the Tulares wetlands to Tejon Pass, then southeast into the San Gabriel mountains, San Bernardino and Cajon Pass. The exact area which 'floated' within this 300-mile long frame could only be finalised by survey. In mid-July, once the Assembly supported the concession, Pico increased the area and numbers by 50 per cent. For the first time '*internal peace*', along with 'enemies who might invade', 'the faith', and relief of Irish, Mexican and Spanish poor, was cited as rationale for the colony.

Pico expected to meet Forbes at Reina de Los Angeles, missed him, and doubled back to catch him and Blake on *Juno* at Santa Bárbara.

Securing British protection was his urgent priority. Approaching Santa Bárbara on 1 July, he met Macnamara riding south for the Assembly who needed Pico's approval of outline landmarks obtained after they met on 24 June. The Assembly would need such detail for their deliberation. 'I don't even remember to have conversed with him more than half an hour,' the Governor testified ten years later, 'and my only recollection is that it related exclusively to the land he sought. It was on that occasion I made the grant to him and it is so dated.' Vehemently, he denied discussing British protection.[36] They arranged to meet again in mid-July at Santa Margarita de Cortona, near San Luis Obispo, between Santa Bárbara and Monterey, where Pico and Castro had arranged to meet in twelve days' time. Macnamara would pass by it on his return journey to Monterey, where he and Blake were to rendezvous.

Before he left Reina de Los Angeles, Pico wrote ahead to Forbes. He had seen the Bear Flag proclamation of 14 June:

> a multitude of invaders from the USA have entered [northern California], taking possession of Sonoma and tearing the Mexican flag to pieces. I have not had confirmed news of an open declaration of war with that power. [The American settlers] are trying to have this part of the Republic of Mexico present as sad a picture as the Department of Texas, practically consummating another great theft.

He alleged that the sloop, USS *Portsmouth*, in San Francisco Bay, was supporting Frémont and the Bear Flaggers,

> the shores are unprotected and exposed to American warships. Great Britain will doubtless give her protection. I solicit help for the Mexican Departmental government as a British war corvette [*Juno*] is on the coast, hoping this will be enough to stop the Americans.'[37]

Pico was a patriot and ready to fight. His *californios* resisted the US until January 1847. His optimism about Britain was partly due to the Trafalgar effect, a worldwide, if naive view of British power. Had Pico omitted '*Mexican Departmental* government' and replaced it with 'Californian

Government', then Seymour and Blake would have been permitted, even by their dated London instructions, to protect and defend *independent* California, a damsel in distress, as part of the Royal Navy's world 'policing'. The fruit on the branch would become the windfall for which Aberdeen had once vaguely hoped. Pico believed in some formal Mexican alliance with Britain, so closely tied were the two countries, yet the 1826 treaty was of goodwill and amity, not defence, and the bondholders' land agreement, although a 'treaty' in common parlance, was no such thing. In Pico's mind, California independence was not a necessary pre-condition for British intervention.

On 2 July 'the Governor of All The Californias came on board *Juno* at 12.30. [After talks] the Governor left at 4.30. Saluted him with 15 guns.' The four-hour conference between Pico, Blake and Forbes was not minuted, but Blake told Seymour that Pico, well meaning, honest and generally popular, was governor 'in little more than name'. Naval officers knew salvage law, by which a stricken ship, once abandoned, can be claimed. Formal war between the US and Mexico, however, rendered *Mexican* California a legitimate US prize, but it neutralised Britain. The fifteen-gun salute accorded Pico as he disembarked was the only British powder fired on California's behalf. Forbes handed Pico's letter to Blake for Seymour's considered response.

Cesareo Lataillade, Spain's new young vice-consul at Monterey, was Macnamara's mentor at Santa Bárbara. He spoke of 'robbery by the Indians' a week before Pico spoke to Macnamara of resisting 'invasion of the savages'. *Californio* and *anglo* settlers endured regular Indian hit-and-run attacks from on and below the Rio San Joaquin. In August 1846, US chaplain Walter Colton recorded Indian bands, 60- to 100-strong, horse-stealing and looting near Monterey. At around 100,000, the *Tulareno* Indians outnumbered hugely the 8,000 settlers nearer the coast. 20,000 coastal Indians, ousted from mission lands to be low-paid ranch workers, if lucky, were also restive. California was Indian before Spain came: European-style fenced estates shredded a hunter's space and mindset. Indians managed land their way, not the lost Eden or wasteland construct of European minds. Across Mexico, in Sonora, New Mexico and on the Yucatán peninsula, Indian unrest was a growing concern.

Los Tulares, (The Rush Marshes, or Wetlands) was the 1847 Mexican title for Macnamara's concession, from the seasonal *Laguna* south of Rio

San Joaquin. The *Porziuncula* (now Kerns) and *Tres Reyes* (Kings) rivers pooled their *nevada* snowmelt to create hundreds of square miles of sloughs and rush marshes. The Valley was attractive, as long as ranches could be defended, irrigation engineered, and its shelterless heat endured. Missions had long used the technology of pipes, flumes, canals, dams and aqueducts, but *Tulares* settlements could not be developed while the Indians were in ferment. Of thirty San Joaquin tracts granted 1836–46, some were abandoned quickly and solely on account of Indians. John Frémont's *Las Mariposas* title on the Rio Merced, which he bought from a *californio* in 1847, was still threatened in 1852 by Indians and squatting miners. Black Widow and mosquito, reinforced by cholera and malaria, also defended their territory.

Lieutenant Watson, USN, visited the Santa Clara mine a month before Macnamara arrived. A *californio* rancher showed him the 'vast plain of the Tulare Valley' from the top of the Monte Diablo range. Watson thought it 'the most beautiful view ever beheld by man ... the silvery surface of the San Joaquin just perceivable, the snow-covered Sierra Nevada mountains [beyond] rising thousands of feet reflected in the receding rays of the western sun like a vast inland ocean, and the curling smoke of Indian fires'.[38] The early summer snow-melt seemed tranquil from a distance, yet Hudson's Bay officials had dismissed the Valley and its swamps as fit for trappers and hunters, but not for farmers. USN Lt McLane remembered 'thousands of elks and mustangs'.

Macnamara shrugged off consul Lataillade's warning about the Indians, accepting Pico's assurance, which he related to Somerville at Monterey on 19 July: 'The Indians are harmless, a few tribes only remained uncivilised and fierce. There are not above 25,000 [*sic*] castilians [*californios*] in California which is not so thickly populated as Mexico. The Indians go in tribes from 150 to 300 and use large bows and arrows.'[39]

His roadside petition to Governor Pico on 1 July was for a grant of Texan proportions:

> I contract to introduce in the shortest time possible 2,000 Catholic Irish families, industrious and sober, 10,000 souls [in all], subject to [Mexican] laws, to serve in defence of California against all enemy invaders, to maintain internal peace and dedicate themselves to this country. I solicit the

land selected between the Rio San Joaquin, from source to mouth and the Sierra Nevada. The limits are the Rio Cosumnes on the north, and on the south the extremity of The Tulares in the neighbourhood of San Gabriel [Mission]. I beg your Excellency to look favourably on my proposition, to the happiness of California, to propagate the holy religion we [Irish and Mexicans] profess, and to be helpful to my countrymen.[40]

Macnamara had no sketch map, yet in this ramshackle tradition where even the statutory franked legal stationery was unobtainable, his bid was sound. His new-found confidence caused him to boast to Somerville of '6000 volunteers from Cork, Clare and Tipperary ready to travel'.

In a letter which he carried south for consul Lataillade to Bandini, recommending that the Assembly sub-committee take the project seriously, Lataillade supported Pico's plan to relocate to the east:

a cordon of lands between latitude 38N and 31S (San Joaquin estuary to the Rio Colorado estuary), a secure barrier of holdings in the interior to resist the robbery of the Indians and prevent the secret and scandalous entry of the Americans of which Sonoma [Bear Flag capture, 14/15 June] was a recent example. The land would be the colonists' property, although they would not inhabit for two or three years [five, laid down by Mexico, May 1847] and Great Britain would make sure that no one from anywhere else would squat on their possessions. It would be politic to respect titles already conceded in the Los Tulares area.

He *emphasised* Macnamara's claim to London support.

Macnamara had his difficulties in Mexico because it appeared the costs of the voyage would be incurred by the [Mexican] Government, but in the end the colony will be subsidised by Her Britannic Majesty as regards the expenses, with huge resources placed at the disposition of this colony whenever it shall be agreed by this Departmental Government.[41]

The Irish *empresario* was shooting a line, strengthening his petition, boosting his profile and feeding grist to the California rumour-mill. He had convinced himself, with the help of three British merchant consuls, that London – political Westminster and Stock Exchange bondholders – would annexe California, use their 'mortgage' discount warrants and finance his settlement in the process. Talk of gold, silver, copper, and now mercury, further excited him. Macnamara continued south to Reina de Los Angeles with Pico's approval of his outline landmarks in hand, surely aware that his house of cards could so easily come tumbling down.

Chapter 7

Contract: 1846

After meeting Pico on the road, Macnamara continued to Reina de Los Angeles, eighty miles and three mission stages south. He and Blake were to rendezvous at Monterey on 20 July; en route there from the capital, he would deliver to Pico at Santa Margarita de Cortona the Assembly's approval which Pico would endorse to recommend to Supreme Congress. Far out at sea, trade winds forced Seymour to detour 3,600 miles from the 1,200 charted for San Blas to Monterey. He sorted papers, read Henry Dana on California and marked time on 'a circular journey of learned leisure, as contrary winds took us halfway across the Pacific'.[1]

SEYMOUR TO CALIFORNIA: 'A LOTTERY OF BLANKS'

HMS *Collingwood* had left San Blas on 13 June, immediately the express courier from vice-consul James Forbes at Monterey told of the *Consejo General* due at Santa Bárbara, 'to get a [British] Protectorate'. The majority southern delegation, Forbes reported, wanted British protection and the *Consejo* might vote independence. It was Seymour's green light, 'in the absence of instruction [and] in the open exercise of the duty of looking after British interests and to see if the arrival of *Juno* has inspired the people to seek independence instead of foreign subjection. I have called the greater part of my squadron northward, including [HMS] *America*, which I wanted to detain there until the Oregon was settled. I

150

shall visit that province in no sanguine temper, but to judge if its situation is irremediable.'[2]

Sloat's *Savannah* had left Mazatlán for California a week before Seymour left merely for San Blas: they did not race. Sloat sent *Cyane* to Monterey on 18 May in *Juno*'s wake, after Surgeon Wood's express courier from Guadalajara told him of the hostilities on the Rio Grande.[3] He had already posted USS *Portsmouth* to Monterey with copies of the new Texas constitution to inform any independence negotiation. News of General Taylor's capture of Matamoros across the Nueces strip finally impelled Sloat to sail north, but only on 8 June. Seymour lingered a further week at San Blas hoping for something from London. 'I go with the full expectation of seeing a Yankee ensign flying there,' he told Bankhead on 14 June. 'I have as little authority as I need for making the bite I wished, so it will be of little use that I should open my mouth.' He did not rule out intervening were the US flag *not* visible or were Alta California to declare independence as in 1836, when Governor Alvarado proclaimed it 'free and sovereign' under a Lone Star flag. *Californios* had talked of doing so again, ever since.

In June 1846, a small band of American settlers protested against *Comandante* Castro's 'despotism', demanding principled republican rule. A Star-and-Bear flag with slogan *California Republic* was hoist in Sonoma, but was dismissed later as insignificant by Bear Flaggers themselves. Twenty days later, Captain Frémont put aside his specialist survey role to take charge of the insurgents as a US officer. Its original leader, William B. Ide, was dismayed. Frémont formalised US protection, but US–Mexican politics were not the insurgents' cause and neither they nor Frémont, nor US or British naval commanders knew that formal war had already been declared in mid-May. *Anglos* and *californios* had been developing their own rough-hewn identity in Alta California, neither US nor Mexican, as the California Convention showed clearly in 1849.[4] From San Francisco Bay, the captain of USS *Portsmouth* insisted he was a 'passive spectator'.

Two days out from San Blas, Seymour wrote to a friend in Parliament: 'As our government have not made a footstep, I shall not do so for them, *without a fair chance of doing so finely* [author's emphasis]. I am left to guess my way through the difficulties.' He told Lord Ellenborough, First Lord of the Admiralty: 'I am drawing in a lottery in which nothing remains but blanks, but I take the only chance of retarding the unfavourable result

[US occupation]. If I find at Monterey no good is to be done, I shall not stay longer than necessary for the safety of British subjects.' Ellenborough believed San Francisco Bay 'had facilities of defence hardly to be found anywhere unless at Corfu [Ionian Islands] or Malta'. He had urged Lord Aberdeen to 'obtain possession, while we are about it and while we can, of the key to the northwest coast of America'.[5]

Seymour had shown steel enough since 1844. *Collingwood*'s open gun ports had forced an apology from the Prefect of Callao to the British consul. Patrolling the Sandwich (Hawaiian), Friendly (Tongan) and Society (Tahitian) Islands, he was mindful of Captain Lord Paulet's *gaffe* in 1843, imposing British rule on Hawaii without mandate. Seymour's role was to deter France from extending unwanted 'protection' to reluctant, independent islands, and to curb his men from siding with Tahitian rebels against France. London refused Tahitian requests for British rule and France took charge. At Bora-Bora island, Seymour entered port in defiance of French blockaders, but charged *Collingwood*'s band with keeping the peace. 'If I ever wanted to take a Polynesian island I should certainly put the Clarinets or Trumpets in front, as music has an extraordinary effect on these people.' He understood Pacific lotteries well.[6]

American mess-decks caricatured him, but respect bonded British and US captains in 1846. Seymour was a living (and courteous) link with Nelson, Trafalgar and royalty; Sloat and Biddle had impressive 1812–14 war records. The navies shared charts, supplies and mail deliveries; their wardrooms exchanged visits and shore picnics at Mazatlán, Monterey and Honolulu. Seymour promised that if war broke out, he would offer British subjects in the US Navy passage home, 'to prevent their fighting against their country': Lt Rowan of USS *Cyane* was from Dublin. Seymour would also discharge any Americans aboard his own ship: he had at least one. On 2 July, when Sloat reached Monterey and Macnamara was approaching Reina de Los Angeles, Seymour was becalmed, 'out of the world for many weeks'. Scurvy affected his crew, chair baths were rigged, but mercifully it remained cool and awnings were not needed.[7]

They spotted (and shot) huge brown albatrosses. A rank-conscious crew 'skylarked after Quarters [sunset], the men divided from the petty officers on opposite sides of the becalmed ship'. Skylarking was horseplay, 'sky high' on the rigging or the tops, a safety valve at the end of the day. Midshipman Markham thought *Collingwood* 'a very happy ship', and

Lt Somerville called it the 'last and happiest' of his ten postings. He and Seymour played chess most evenings, but on Sunday mornings Seymour tensed: Chaplain Proctor's preaching was a variant on tedium, 'not plain, and too declamatory'. Somerville, a devout Anglican, refused to attend quarterdeck services, considering them a mockery, and noted without comment the Irish Catholic midshipman punished for mimicking cockcrow to enliven devotions.

The US myth of a 'naval chess game' persisted. Midshipman Wilson on *Savannah* insisted that 'Admiral Seymour had followed us for several months.' Thomas Lancey, on *Dale*, heard that *Savannah* had staged mock hangings at sea off Mazatlán to feign a routine of leaving harbour. Mushrooms in the dark, the crews below American decks recreated the world above. A landsman told of how Sloat had kept news of the Rio Grande hostilities to himself, then sailed *south* from Mazatlán before heading north under cover of darkness: in fact southwest was the only way to round Cape San Lucas from Mazatlán. The gullible Seymour, legend added, pursued Sloat across open sea towards Hawaii and went 'entirely there' before realising he had been tricked.[8]

PROJECT MACNAMARA CONVEYED

On Monday, 6 July, the departmental Assembly convened at Reina de Los Angeles under Francisco Figueroa, either at Pico's headquarter off the Plaza, or at Abel Stearns' and Arcadia Bandini's adobe almost next door. To boost civic pride in 1845, Pico had the town centre buildings limewashed. Assembly accepted his apology for absence, then tabled Macnamara's petition of 24 June and Pico's roadside concession of 1 July. Pico, meanwhile, was heading north from Santa Bárbara to reconcile with Castro after Captain Blake refused him British protection on 2 July.

Of the six Assembly deputies present, Antonio Coronel and Agustin Olvera, cousins, had been Híjar-Padrés colonists, and Juan Bandini their promoter.[9] They heard Macnamara's petition, referred it to committee, then tackled the day's agenda. The committee of two, Bandini and brother-in-law Santiago Arguello (Olvera's father-in-law), both from San Diego, met later with Macnamara, probably at *el Palacio* Stearns, where all would have lodged. An open house allowed Stearns to monitor intelligence on consul Larkin's and President Polk's behalf (see Map E).

On the morning of 7 July, in Extraordinary Session, the committee recommended *el Proyecto Macnamara* as 'essential to the Department'. One square league of land (4,428 acres) was confirmed to each of 2,000 families (10,000 persons), with public plots to be left vacant between grants,

> without prejudice to any [existing] third party, on [*sobre*] the Rio San Joaquin in the direction of The Tulares, beyond the southern extremity of the Laguna Tulares, then up to the Sierra Nevadas, and then [in extension south east] on [*sobre*] the Rio de Las Animas [Mojave] to the [southern] mouth of the Cajon de Muscupiabe [Cajon Canon] on the north, to near San Bernardino. [*see Map D.*]

US lawyers complained later that 'Over There' was precise by comparison with customary landmarks, yet without survey, landmarks were everything. Macnamara's 13,500 square miles, increased by Pico to 20,280 a week later, 'floated' in a 30,000 square mile frame from the Rio Cosumnes to the Rio Mojave. Bandini acknowledged existing grants in the frame, such as Alvarado's *Las Mariposas*, later bought by Frémont; Laguna Tulares in full snowmelt also took hundreds of square miles out of use. In the north, Rio Cosumnes neighboured the ominously nicknamed Rio de Los Americanos, the southern boundary of Johann Sutter's New Helvetia colony and a major access for US settlers. In the south, San Bernardino neighboured Bandini's San Salvador colony of New Mexicans guarding his cattle against Indian raiders.[10]

In 1847 a Mexican Congress committee described Macnamara's *Los Tulares* concession as a *firme antemural* (strong bastion) against US squatters and Mojave raiders. Its southern part included former lands of ex-Mission San Gabriel, near Reina de Los Angeles, as far inland as San Bernardino, its ex-*asistencia* or sub-mission, sixty miles east.

Bandini stipulated that Macnamara's land was not to go to other foreigners without approval, and was to be allocated only as colonists appeared. Supreme Congress should be asked for customs exemption at Yerba Buena (renamed San Francisco in 1847) and San Pedro (Reina de Los Angeles), the access ports for the San Joaquin valley and San Bernardino, but given Alta California's meagre revenue, it was tokenism. The Assembly notified its agreement in letters to Pico and secretary

Moreno from Figueroa and senior assemblyman Narciso Botello, letters which Macnamara took north: 'This body agrees with the sentiments expressed by your Excellency in your official [note] of 24 June [from Santa Bárbara], expressing your opinion and great desire that the said enterprise be carried into effect.'

The *diputados* convened that morning under Mexican rule and rose under US rule. A USN parley team had landed at Monterey, 340 miles north at 7.30am. They went to the home of Captain Mariano Silva to invite surrender, but he disclaimed any authority to do so; 225 sailors and marines landed from USS *Cyane* at 10.20am. After a bilingual proclamation by Captain Mervine, the US flag was raised on the Custom House flagpole.[11] Only later did Sloat, Pico, Macnamara, Bandini and Seymour learn of a state of war since May, which Sloat had simply assumed.

The end-date for *californio* authority in Alta California remained moot. 13 May 1846 (US declaration of a state of war) was deleted from the Peace Treaty of 1848 by the US; 7 July 1846 (capture of Monterey) was tacitly accepted by the California Land Commission and appeal courts in the 1850s. The day itself, however, began as just another warm morning in Reina de Los Angeles, with apprehension, but not war in the air. The Assembly continued to legislate until 10 August, and resistance continued until Pico's brother signed the surrender before Frémont in January 1847, at Cahuenga (Hollywood). *Californios* inflicted bloody noses on US forces, most notably at San Pascual in December, but even before 7 July they had lost control of Alta California north of Santa Bárbara, due to the Castro–Pico feud.

A sketch map was required of a private grant, but this contract was unprecedented, and no colonising authority existed to advise. Bandini advised:

> Firstly, whether of the land requested from the Rio San Joaquin inclusive up to the extremity of The Tulares on the south, you hold a plan or outline sketch [*diseño*]. Please consider sending copies. Secondly, how many square leagues do you consider it indispensably necessary to have, to fulfil the colonising contract ? If initially you do not have such a document, there should be at least a manifest of some sort, indicating which are summer grazing lands, the extent of

colony lands in square leagues, the rainfall, watering places, irrigated land, rivers, streams, wells.[12]

He also drafted a proclamation (*bando*) or circular. Alta California had no newspapers or printers, but a surviving draft document proclaims Macnamara's conveyance and California's minerals. Bandini was a prospector and the world first heard of serious California gold in 1842 through Bandini and Stearns. Delegates due to have attended the *Consejo General* at Santa Bárbara needed an update. The flyer must have been composed shortly after the Assembly as it says nothing of a US–Mexican War, of the capture of Monterey or of Pico's 50 per cent enhancement of the conveyance a week later.[13]

> I hasten to inform you of an event of real importance to take place … A colony of 10,000 Irish people has requested the Mexican government to be allowed to come to this country to cultivate vacant land under Mexican law.
>
> The contractor, Macnamara, an Irish priest, has appeared before the Departmental *Diputación* with special recommendations from the Supreme Mexican authorities to find out the extent of wasteland available for colonising. This Assembly recommends favourably to the Mexican Government so that the Padre *empresario* can return to Mexico to agree with Congress the concessions allowed this type of colony. Note the general advantages to California, to all the social classes, given how vast and fertile it is, as well as a terrain for industries, its minerals already discovered such as silver, gold, copper and mercury. All these raw materials are hidden in the entrails of this virgin earth which will produce whatever man wants to cultivate [and] will not require laborious industry, but will disgorge from its depths with little labour.
>
> The Mexican government, to contain the greed and ambition of the US *del Norte*, needs to promote colonisation and, I believe, as the first step is made for the arrival of an Irish contingent, the government will continue to protect

every claim proposed, by justified and fair concession. I pass you this important advance notice so as to be prepared in case someone decides to take and profit from the wealth and abundance of this country.

Juan Bandini retired on 8 July. He wrote to consul Lataillade in Santa Bárbara and vice-consul Forbes in Monterey, both courtesy Macnamara riding north. 'I have done what I believe necessary,' Bandini told Lataillade, 'to the good despatch of priest Eugene Macnamara'. He handed Macnamara a memorandum of California's 'immense quantity of minerals. Besides gold, silver, copper and iron, semi-metal [mercury], or in Indian tradition "white water" which you could not keep in your hand, was found between 30-34 [degrees] latitude, not far from the coast.' Macnamara shared it with Seymour, who noted, 'Bandini is at work in a copper mine which promises much with indications of gold and silver, but scientific miners are not available and he experiments.'[14]

El Palacio Stearns was the most notable house in town (see Map E). In 1842 its dance floor hosted the diplomatic ball for USN Commodore Jones after he apologised to the governor for annexing California. Stearns was close to Bandini, as son-in-law and business partner. On 8 July he informed Larkin in Monterey, 'Mr Macnamara is here and leaves for Monterey. He has presented to the government for 2000 leagues [13,520 sq miles] in the interior and on the Rio San Joaquin, commencing North at *arroyo* Cosumnes and South or Southeast as far as the interior of San Gabriel. The Assembly has recommended his plan of colonisation. The Governor will probably decree in his favour. He obligates himself to bring in 2000 families [totalling] 10,000 souls, which will be quite an addition to our population.'[15] Unknown to Stearns, Sloat held Monterey and Larkin was now an ex-consul.

It remained to convey the land to Macnamara for presentation to Supreme Congress. Pico had ridden north from Santa Bárbara with secretary Moreno and soldiers to parley with *Comandante* Castro, marching south, at Santa Margarita de Cortona. This former property of mission San Luis Obispo belonged to Pico's cousin who was also Castro's uncle. Its 4,500-square foot store-chapel could billet Pico's and Castro's combined 400 militiamen. The two reconciled on 13 July and discussed Sloat's letter of 9 July to Castro requiring him to surrender at Monterey, before they headed south together for Reina de Los Angeles.

Macnamara met them at Santa Margarita on or around that day, five days and six ex-mission stages from Reina de Los Angeles, from where he brought the Assembly's formal agreement. By 17 July he was at Monterey on Seymour's flagship with Pico's conveyance in hand, 'on plain paper for lack of official such', pre-addressed as from Santa Bárbara, 4 July. Pico's secretary Moreno had prepared and packed his secretariat chest before leaving Santa Bárbara for the three-stage ride north on or around 4 July. It was also the feast of Our Lady of Refuge, patroness of The Californias diocese, which coincided with US Independence Day.[16]

At Santa Margarita, the Governor increased the number of settlers to match Macnamara's original request. *Three* thousand families, totalling *fifteen thousand* persons, were to have a square league each, totalling 13.3 million acres, or 20,280 square miles. Macnamara told *Collingwood*'s officers on 19 July of his '12 million acres'. Like Bandini's customs fling, it was Pico's handout,

> considering the advantage to [Mexico] from settlement in those regions, hitherto deserts, in agriculture, commerce, arts and industry, and in the propagation of the faith. It would also secure the Department from the frequent incursions of the savages … and that the increased number of settlements would preserve national integrity … Having made diligent examination and using the powers conferred on me in the name of the nation, and with the advice of the Departmental Assembly, I hereby concede for the colonisation of Irish families the land solicited by the said Padre Macnamara, *reserving it for the approval of the Supreme National Government* … in the interior beyond the twenty boundary leagues on the Rio San Joaquin, from its source to its mouth, and the Sierra Nevada, the boundaries being the Rio Cosumne on the north, and on the south, the extremity of The *[Laguna] Tulares*, in the vicinity of San Gabriel, without prejudice to paths, roads and public use.

If the Irish had too much land, others would join them; if too little, 'they are limited to what is found. Should fewer than 3000 [Irish] families arrive, excess land may be allotted to Mexican families.' Pico's decree was recorded in 'the proper book and delivered to the interested party for his security and use'. José Moreno countersigned, copied it to Macnamara and entered it in his Land Register.[17]

Pending formalities in Supreme Congress, the Irish missioner had secured 13 per cent of the later US State of California, or one third of the land estimated as arable by California shadow-representatives in their Memorial to Congress for Statehood, March 1850. The then Alta California Department stretched hundreds of square miles east of today's California–Nevada boundary. In County Clare a farmer was rated 'strong' with thirty acres or more, 'middle' with 10–30, and 'small' with fewer than ten. The average at Kilkee-Killard was six limestone acres, while the cottier and labourer had a potato patch. The San Joaquin concession, by Irish standards, was beyond imagining, and by California and Texas standards still extraordinary in its extent, and for its encouragement by a Mexican government.[18]

When asked in court in 1859 why Central Government 'referred Macnamara to you and left you to make him the grant of land for the colony?' Pico shrugged. 'They did. I do not know what its motives were.' The court pressed. 'How many grants of land in California do you know of made by Mexico City?' He answered plainly, 'I don't remember any, other than the one I have mentioned [Castillero's thirteen square miles at New Almaden], except the one to Castillero and Carillo of [Santa Cruz] island.' In 1859 the US government contested an appeal over ownership of the New Almaden mine, claiming Pico had acted *ultra vires* [in conveying] on another occasion, in conveying, backdating and 'falsely addressing' the Macnamara contract to defraud. The notorious Limantour title claim, thrown out on appeal in 1857, was fresh in mind, concocted in Mexico by *californios* including an ex-governor, in 1852. The Pico dossier, taken by Frémont to Washington, disappeared after publication in 1848, and secretary Moreno's working register with it. Bewildered, sick, but essentially honest, Pío de Jesús Pico spoke truthfully in 1859: *Proyecto Macnamara* really was unprecedented, and virtually Mexico's last hope of keeping California out of US hands.[19]

HMS COLLINGWOOD ENTERS HARBOUR

Commodore Sloat expected *Juno* and *Collingwood*, but *Juno* had passed northwards on 10 July to drop Forbes at Yerba Buena. Blake anchored for a week in San Francisco Bay, discourteously aloof from the US captains there. Larkin warned that *Collingwood*, with three times *Juno*'s firepower, would 'look down on *Savannah*, 54 guns, unless *Columbus*, 74 guns, is here as a shew off'.[20] USS *Columbus*, under Commodore Biddle, was far away, visiting Japan. Seymour, however, was frustrated that Captain Gordon had not appeared with HMS *America*, depriving him of his only other capital warship. He did not know, yet, that Gordon had departed the Station altogether (see Plate 9).

Collingwood came in from the northwest on 15 July, to anchor off Santa Cruz, out of view from Monterey. Lt Somerville was woken early on 16 July by Midshipman Markham, 'to attend Quarters, when the guns were shotted, and again secured'. *Collingwood*'s hull was scrubbed and sails repaired, to impress. Late that afternoon, Walter Colton watched Britain's largest warship 'enter harbour under a cloud of canvas, majestic on the wave', furl sails and drop anchors alongside *Congress* (newly arrived) in line with the other US vessels there, *Savannah*, *Cyane* and *Levant*. Despite their 'warlike appearance controlling the anchorage', *Collingwood*'s 200-foot deck and 2,600 tons dwarfed them. 'She came up beautifully,' thought USN Captain Du Pont of *Congress*; 'she handles like a yacht,' Seymour explained modestly. Commodore Sloat went aboard, anthems were played and salutes fired, for which cannon, powder and wadding were run out.

Midshipman Wilson watched from *Savannah*: 'Admiral Seymour who had followed us for several months [*sic*], arrived the 16th. Commodore Sloat sent orders, as I understand, to be in readiness in case the Admiral be entering with hostile intentions, leaving the impression that the Admiral intended to prevent our squadron from taking possession of California.' (Lt Walpole and other British officers were 'astonished' that the US had done so.) Captain Du Pont commanding Commodore Stockton's *Congress*, summoned all hands from shore to quarters: 'foreign interference was still anticipated ... and as if in confirmation [Seymour] arrived. Whatever the original intention, the game was blocked'. British officers would see immediately that the US ships were cleared for action, save for muzzles forward of open ports; it was harder for US officers to see the state of *Collingwood*'s high decks. USN Lt Beale later told a Senate

Committee, 'we felt insecure, sent our men to quarters and prepared for action'. Joseph Revere of USS *Portsmouth* in San Francisco Bay, spoke of 'Seymour's conditional orders to take the country as security for British holders of Mexican bonds.' As late as September, Captain Kellett RN reported that *Portsmouth* treated HMS *Herald* as a hostile vessel, with calls to arms and drumming to quarters.[21]

Midshipman Toler, Sloat's ADC who had twice raised the flag over Monterey, accompanied Sloat onto *Collingwood*, though evidently was not present when the commanders met. British lieutenants told him that Seymour had stamped his foot and thrown down his hat on seeing the US flag onshore, and had greeted Sloat with, 'You have played on me a Yankee trick', a British proverb for a double-cross. In fact, headache, insomnia, London's silence and Gordon's behaviour upset Seymour more than any American. Mischievous young British officers sending up a cocky US midshipman whom they knew already may have been behind the legend. (Officers of both flagships had mixed socially for weeks at Mazatlán.) Seymour had no illusions and showed stoic courtesy. Even had he fought, he was outgunned on the water and faced an elevated shore battery, built after the Jones incident and hastily refurbished by Sloat. Du Pont heard a markedly different greeting: 'I am sorry for it, but it is no business of mine.' Sloat found Seymour 'amiable and polite', his visit 'very serviceable to our cause in California, as the inhabitants [had] fully believed he would take their part'. Commodore Stockton had brought news from Honolulu of hostilities on the Rio Grande, but nothing of formal war, although his crewmen were learning Spanish in anticipation. His chaplain, Walter Colton, found Seymour 'a boon companion, of great amenity of deportment'.

Seymour's flag received every courtesy: 'Our band greeted her with *God Save the Queen* which she returned with *Hail Columbia*.' British line (capital) ships outgunned US line ships, which in turn could outrun them – battle lines were avoided. Similarly, British frigates, outgunned by US frigates, could nevertheless outrun them. The British had the advantage (and experience) in full-facing battle lines; the Americans looked to avoid set-piece fighting. Seymour complimented Sloat on *Savannah*'s being the best-armed frigate he had seen, but warned him that his annexation of California was against the US Constitution and the Law of Nations: it could be no more than a 'provisional occupation'. Commodore Stockton, Sloat's successor, took careful note. Upon taking over the US Squadron on 23 July, he declared a temporary occupation, 'not a moment longer than is necessary'. Honour satisfied, Seymour noted the now 'modified pretentious proclamation'.

Macnamara boarded *Collingwood* on 17 July, with Forbes' whereabouts. Seymour summoned the vice-consul to Monterey 'in the interests of HM subjects resident in California ... my stay will be very short ... Mr Macnamara informs me [*Juno*] will be here 20 July. Captain Blake will convey you from San Francisco Bay if you prefer.' Blake had discharged Forbes at Yerba Buena on 11 July, and moored *Juno* in the lee of USS *Portsmouth*, but he was no Seymour. He despised Americans, Mexicans and uneducated Bear Flaggers. 'Aggressors step forward as the aggrieved. A proclamation was published at Sonoma by an uneducated person called Hyde [Ide], part of a lawless gang of invaders and adventurers. There are few British subjects, but many British-born individuals, most from the lower walks of life.' Seymour's courier failed to contact him, and after four days, without returning a courtesy visit from USS *Portsmouth* which he saw was 'prepared for engagement', Blake left for San Blas, bypassing Monterey altogether. Macnamara was stranded outside the US blockade of Mexico, unable to keep appointments with Alexander Forbes, Commissioner Castillero or Supreme Congress.

Vice-consul James Forbes despatched from San Francisco Bay to acting-consul Alexander Forbes on 14 July, angry at the US invasion, 'by base intrigue, subterfuge and open violation of the law of nations, of a country whose native inhabitants sought in vain the protection of Great Britain and who still flatter themselves that England will rescue them'. Alexander Forbes forwarded it to Bankhead who sent it to Aberdeen on 14 August by the despatch sloop from Vera Cruz, adding his own last prompt, that Britain had lost 'one of the most valuable possessions in the habitable globe whose resources are yet imperfectly known'. By the time it reached London in early October, Aberdeen had gone, Palmerston was Foreign Secretary, and Alta California instant history.

Seymour placed visitors before pain. 'Mr Macnamara, David Spence and Hartweg aboard. Visited by Commodore Stockton and [Commander] Du Pont. The latter gave me the Honolulu newspapers.' Spence, a Scots beef rancher who supplied *Collingwood*'s 'blood boat' at dawn, brought a copy of Sloat's proclamation and welcomed the new law and order. Macnamara told of Pico's conveyance and of returning to Mexico. Hartweg (Seymour and Somerville still called him 'Hardwick') had been stranded in Monterey without completing any research. 'The fields and woods which were covered in flowers [in June] are now drying up from total absence of rain.' Lt Somerville found the place revolting, 'roads and streets strewn with bullocks' heads and legs, the smell not pleasing'. Seymour returned respects to Sloat on *Savannah* at the end of a full first day.

He conferred again with Sloat, Du Pont and Stockton (of a new generation, 'eager for notoriety') on 18 July, while *Collingwood*'s crew scrubbed hammocks on deck and cut spars ashore. Seymour landed as Britain's first official visitor to US California, to see Spence's *vacqueros* at work and to visit Friar Junípero Serra's grave at ex-mission San Carlos. *Collingwood*'s officers were also the first British to hear of Macnamara's success. 'He has got a grant of 12 million acres, but this the Yankees will dispute' noted Somerville after Macnamara boasted '6000 [*sic*] Irishmen from Cork, Clare and Tipperary would readily volunteer'; Westminster would pay and the Indians were harmless. Du Pont wrote that day 'the Californians are with us, but cannot declare until they ascertain our government is determined to hold on this time, and not give up as did Commodore Jones'.

As the evening heat (and the stench) grew bearable, US and British sailors crowded to watch Frémont's soldiers and Bear Flaggers canter through Monterey. Lt Walpole saw 'the wildest wild party in file, two and two, riding out of a cloud of dust', led by Frémont and Kit Carson, scout and deputy, 'as well known in the prairies as is the Duke [of Wellington] in Europe'. Du Pont counted '131 American Arabs of the West', Frémont claimed '162', including six Delaware Indians. Walter Colton thought 'the ground trembled' as the files paraded through town two abreast, two horses apiece, to the tempo of *Savannah*'s band. Du Pont compared 'the thrilling sight' of Frémont's arrival to that of Captain Cook on Hawaii, 'as a sort of demigod', with an escort column larger than life against a backdrop of sunset behind the warships.

The company bivouacked above Monterey among the pines, 'the sea breeze and shade welcome', while crewmen of both nations crowded around. 'Sir George Seymour made the first call' on 19 July, remembered

Gillespie, 'yet the feeling on the part of Commodore Sloat was not [that] we had a right to respect ... had he waited a few short weeks, the whole country would have been under a well-organised government.' Sloat had ordered them into town ostensibly to defend Monterey against Indian marauders, but really to bring them under Navy control. Frémont, Carson and Gillespie had blood on their hands, after murdering *californios* and Indians who hindered their already questionable covert operation. US naval officers expressed concern: Lt McLane, the London ambassador's son, seconded to Frémont as second-in-command, thought him 'an ambitious Ass, persevering and cunning'. Dubliner Stephen Rowan on USS *Cyane* dismissed his battalion as 'a gang of filibustering outlaws'. Commodore Sloat began to interrogate him on board *Savannah*, but stormed out of the cabin in anger. Even Frémont admitted Sloat was 'greatly disturbed' that he, (Frémont) had acted 'without any authority from government'.

'Many of my men', wrote Frémont forty years later, 'had never seen the ocean or the English flag. They looked on HMS *Collingwood* with the feeling of the racer who has just passed the winning post. Seymour recorded 'Visits from Messrs Frémont and Gillespie. The trappers were ready to show their skills as marksmen on shore.' Towards the end of Seymour's week there, with Macnamara safe aboard *Collingwood* on Admiral's Retinue rations, Frémont and Gillespie climbed on deck, 'in blouse, leggings and felt tights'. Frémont denied later that they ever wore such costume, save in paintings, but at court martial in Washington, he did remember, 'Macnamara was on board *Collingwood* when I arrived at Monterey'. Lt Somerville recorded, 'Frémont came on board and a rascal named "Ide" who hoisted a Bear Flag near San Francisco.'

The brief encounter with Seymour and the Irish *empresario* could have been awkward, the champions of Manifest Destiny confronting the British threats to it in person. Navy beer and even a cigar (frowned upon by Seymour) might have helped. Frémont did not mention the Irish colony project in his letter of 25 July to father-in-law Benton, although eighteen months later, in a Senate hearing, he invoked it as the prime reason for 'his' Bear Flag rising (see Plate 11).

Seymour needed distracting from pain. The sharpshooting 'delighted the officers of *Collingwood* while reducing their store of silver dollars'; trappers fascinated them. Walpole saw 'the class that produced the heroes of Fenimore Cooper's best works'. Somerville cited Cooper's 'Bee [wild honey] Hunters', thinking them 'depraved, desperate and restless, needing to be humoured'. Commander Eden, late of *Collingwood* and a Pacific veteran, but left behind in Portsmouth, knew them as 'mounted herdsmen, or *vacqueros*, [cowboys], but believed "trapper" more clearly conveyed their style and manner'. For the rest of his life Frémont carried the Cooper accolade, 'Pathfinder'.

To Seymour, trappers were like brown albatrosses and Governor Gutiérrez of Mazatlán, curiosities meriting courteous interest. Chaplain Colton met Seymour 'several times on board *Congress*. He and most of his officers are of the English nobility, but assume no airs. He had no instructions from the British monarchy to raise the English flag in California, a mere assumption warranted by not a solitary fact. When we had harpooned the whale, they left us to make the most of the blubber and the bones.'

In the early hours, as the trappers bivouacked noisily on Monterey heights, Seymour wrote to his soldier son, Francis, just back in London from several weeks leave on *Collingwood* and with mother and sisters at Valparaiso:

> The presence of *Collingwood* and *Juno* here has been unnecessary, but that would not have been the case had the people the good sense to declare independence in time. I feel I was entitled to instructions on a subject which I called to [London's] attention at various points beginning in March 1845 when I predicted what has since happened. I have not had a single syllable in answer. I am writing as you will see in bad spirits. Things have gone wrong in both the quarters which have principally occupied me. I do not want to stay in these seas a day longer than the usual period. 'Jonathan' [US] has improved his position, but I hear of 23,000 Mormons coming to California disenchanted with the state.

James Forbes joined *Collingwood* after dark on Monday 20 July. Next morning, he and Seymour discussed 'California affairs', before the cutter took them to Sloat on *Savannah* about to relinquish flag command to Stockton on *Congress*. Ex-consul Larkin dined on *Collingwood*, where

Macnamara sought his legal opinion, now California was under new authority. Larkin knew nothing of Mexican colonising law, only of the ceiling to a governor's grant of land to individuals. Twice he reported their conversation to President Polk:

> Mr Macnamara informed me that the Governor and Legislature gave him a deed for 3000 square leagues of land dated 4 July, 1846. This approval was in Mexico to be confirmed and made into a grant and title. He engaged to place there within a specific time 10 thousand [Pico raised it to 15,000] Irishmen. He applied to me for my opinion of his rights now our flag was [wove] over California. I replied that a Governor of California had no power to grant over eleven [sq] leagues in a single deed. This act shows a new feature in British policy to obtain a title to California [and is but a change of other plans], although Mr Macnamara informed me that he was commissioned by a private company in London. Consul Black in Mexico City was well-informed about these emigration plans and I presume has informed the State Department.

That evening James Forbes joined Macnamara, Spence and Hartweg at the Admiral's table. Forbes had his eye on the mine; Spence had formally witnessed the share transfer to Macnamara; Macnamara hoped for mine revenue for his Project; poor Hartweg, after outlining the hazards of wartime botany, had little to add.

The US blockade meant Macnamara could only return to Mexico on a British naval vessel. Seymour was keen to see his wife and daughters at Valparaiso, and offered to take Macnamara to Honolulu, his next port of call, and there find him a Navy passage for Mexico. Macnamara accepted, assuring James Forbes by letter that he would keep him posted of the Project and the mine deal. Forbes had evidently played close to his chest at Santa Bárbara and at Monterey, letting Macnamara do the talking. In August, for a fee to Padre Suárez de Real, he took over the managing of the mine.

In 1887, Frémont remembered sitting on the beach one evening in July 1846,

Looking out over the bay, the dark hulls of the war vessels and the slumbering cannon still looked ominous and threatening. But the Cross of St George hung idly down from the peak of the great [*Collingwood*], the breeze occasionally spreading out against the sky the small red patch which represented centuries of glory. There lay the pieces on the great chessboard before me with which the game for an empire had been played. At its close we had four pieces [ships in Monterey Bay] to one, but that one was a Queen [Victoria]. I was but a pawn and like a pawn I had been pushed forward to the front at the opening of the game...

His letters at the time said nothing of this cosmic gaming board, but forty years on he remembered the ensign. Seymour, however, sailed under The Blue Ensign on the Pacific, until his promotion to Admiral of The Red at Rio de Janeiro, on route home in 1847. Frémont also recalled writing to father-in-law Benton that '[*Collingwood*'s sailing] ended my mission as well as that of Macnamara', yet the letter made no mention of Macnamara [whom Frémont had just met]. Eighteen months later, he swore before the Senate Committee that he knew of Macnamara in June.

On *Collingwood*'s final day in harbour, 22 July, as British-born trappers, including one Royal Navy deserter, bantered with British matelots onshore, Seymour finished off correspondence, advising James Forbes of 'a provisional occupation only, pending future decisions on the outcome of the contest. I recommend to you the strictest neutrality, prudence and circumspection.' A copy was sent to Sloat to show the correctness of British behaviour. Sloat provided *Collingwood* with mast spares and provisions; American officers passed on books and US newspapers reporting the 'great distress in Ireland'; mail was also exchanged for delivery on word of honour that it contained nothing 'prejudicial'. The Royal Navy even conveyed Washington's sensitive state correspondence to its own Squadron. Seymour summarised the atmosphere at Monterey to Bankhead: 'Animosity here, but no conflict.'

On the morning of departure, 23 July, Seymour replied to Governor Pico, courtesy James Forbes, after seeing Pico's letter of 29 June. They never met. 'I regret deeply [the US attack on Monterey] but as the

Province remained under the authority of Mexico at the time of the attack, and as the officer of a nation which is in amity with Mexico and the US, I could not be justified in interfering in the hostilities.' Pico acknowledged from Reina de Los Angeles on 29 July, when hope of British help had faded. As late as 9 August, *Comandante* Castro informed James Forbes of his correspondence with Commodore Stockton, Sloat's successor, 'as proof of my behaviour, and to inform [your] nation': Castro refused to surrender or even parley. Seymour had deserved better than the 'lottery of blanks' and London's silence, just as Sloat in June had protested against Washington's 'humiliating and mortifying want of communication'. Sloat and Seymour, left to their own devices, acted as statesmen; Pico and the *californios* were more used to being hung out to dry by their government.

Diplomacy, repairs and casking completed, Seymour paid respects to Stockton. To chaplain Colton's amusement, 'many British officers had clothing onshore in the hands of washerwomen, which they hurried off, some half ironed, some half dry and some in suds'. *Collingwood* weighed anchors after noon, setting course for Honolulu, some 1,900 miles away. USS *Congress*'s band saluted its wake. Two hours later it was becalmed in fog, crewmen crowding the rails to watch 'mountainous black fin whales sporting around the ship', and another legend was born. US Surgeon Duvall was adamant that Seymour hovered below the horizon, beyond the fog, to attack US ships at anchor. He was right about Seymour's taking twenty-four hours to clear the Bay, but not why. Seymour's Signal Log recorded meticulously that he was becalmed from 'sunset 23 July' until 1 pm 24 July, and only at 6.00 pm did he lose sight of the US ships. Du Pont observed that *Collingwood* remained 'two days in sight of harbour'. A weary Seymour watched the whales and retired to his cabin with Dana's *Two Years Before the Mast*, and Frémont's 1842 expedition report, loaned by Du Pont. Somerville found the Admiral an irritable chessmate.

'Air comparatively warm at night. Mr Macnamara gave me the verses in the [New] Testament, I Corinthians 3, 13-15; Matthew 5, 26, on which Catholics found their doctrine of Purgatory.' Whenever Macnamara, Proctor or the devout Somerville touched on religion in Seymour's hearing, it would have to be good-humoured, as Naval Regulations (and Seymour) forbade sectarianism. Midshipman Markham thought Proctor 'a very good old fellow, very low church and anti-Tractarian', but Somerville disapproved of 'Proctio's' contempt for O'Connell and

Friar Mathew, central figures in Macnamara's life. Purgatory, the purging of guilt after life, a metaphor for divine mercy, was neither top rung nor literal on the Catholic ladder of belief, but it had surfaced with the 'Romanisers' in Great Britain's established Protestant churches. Devout Irishmen, thrown together, might have touched on many such topics, but the Famine was their most shared concern. *Collingwood* even held a relief collection. Village life on board the giant flagship, with its gentry, crew, goats, clergy, hens, geese, the Admiral's cow and evening fiddle music, a cross between Noah's Ark and Windsor Castle, afforded the two clerics and Somerville promenade space and escape from the wardroom.

At the end of July, Seymour withdrew altogether. 'The sudden change in weather has weakened me', he told his diary between reports. Pilot, his dog, and Somerville at chess were his company. His report for The Admiralty on California did not name Macnamara, but was consistent. 'In addition to a considerable force, a large body of emigrants on whom reliance could be placed would be necessary to establish any British ascendancy, *but without these* I think it preferable that no attempt should have been made to connect the honour or the interests of Great Britain with the possession of California.' Seymour was low: the fruit he had been expected neither to shake, nor pluck, but to pick up only if and when the wind felled it, had been picked up first by a less scrupulous rival.

A final witness testified in *Collingwood*'s sternwake. Louis Gasquet, French acting-consul, spent fifty-one days under house arrest in Monterey, a 'troublesome functionary', for refusing to recognise US authority and for inciting French citizens against the US. Evidently he met Macnamara. To Europeans, a priest acting politically was a 'Jesuit', but a 'Jesuit agent' acting for Protestant Britain was gothic nonsense. Facts, however, never shook Gasquet. Duflot de Mofras, French explorer, had reported in 1840 that California, with 4000 [*sic*] inhabitants, could be taken by a man-o-war and 200 men. Gasquet believed it, and fifteen French naval vessels were at hand on the Pacific.

> *Juno* had brought an Irish priest, M. Eugene Macnamara, a Jesuit whose worldly manners, spirit of intrigue and dexterity in affairs show him to be of the same family with other members of the celebrated order. He had come to ask of the Governor and [obtained] an immense tract of land,

nearly eighty [*sic*] square leagues for an Irish colony. This gentleman said quite loudly that his action was uninfluenced by the English Cabinet, although all his steps had been well planned in advance, and I believe that he undertook nothing of his own motivation. England and her agents have not lost the hope of establishing themselves in California. They regard the American occupation as precarious and they are putting themselves in a position to replace them. M. Macnamara has laid a stepping stone; the others will soon follow. This must be well understood in France if it is to be opposed and if advantage is to be taken of the good will that [the Californian] chiefs and population manifest for us.

BONDHOLDERS AWAKE[22]

For months, the London Stock Market feared a US–Mexican war and British involvement. Sixteen Mexican finance ministers came and went in 1846 and bondholders raised no colonising company. Their land option would expire on 1 October 1847. The gambler's hopeless dream of cash persisted, but briefly the pro-colonising minority had their moment: Wyllie the theorist, MacKintosh the agent, Powles the spokesman.

The latest re-scheduling of the debt proposed in 1845, did not extend the land offer, but consul MacKintosh agreed the new bond issue with Mexico's Finance Minister in March 1846. £4.5 million worth of bonds reduced to 60 per cent of face value, would be exchanged for new stock carrying 5 per cent interest. At a stormy meeting on 18 May in *The City of London Tavern*, bondholders objected to the bias in Mexico's favour. Two weeks later, when news of the war focussed minds, bondholders considered a revised offer brokered by John Schneider, Mexico's financial agent in London – and agent for Manning and MacKintosh – ambassador Tomás Murphy, and Guillermo O'Brien, Mexican consul in Paris. George Robinson and John Diston Powles presented the revised offer to the meeting: the *entire* debt was now offered in new stock, still devalued to 60 per cent, but all with 5 per cent interest. It reduced Mexico's liability by £1 million, to £10.2 million, but it was sweetened for investors. However, Consul Francisco de Lizardi and son Manuel, Schneider's predecessors as agents, had so oversold the 1837 stock, it could not be exchanged one for one for the new.

The agreement reached Mexico in August 1846, as war intensified. Vice-President Gómez Farías rejected it, perhaps bribed by de Lizardi junior. He dismissed Schneider in favour of de Lizardi; he dismissed Murphy and O'Brien from negotiating altogether and Murphy from the ambassadorship, but the new issue bonds had already gone on sale. MacKintosh had bought heavily and after Mexico cancelled, was unable to sell them on. In October, Mexico suspended all talk of re-schedule, which earned a scathing *Illustrated London News* editorial, 17 October: 'To refuse to owe is a great improvement on to refuse to pay … let us hope Santa Anna returns with more wisdom.' He did return, and reversed the annulment in 1847 at Britain's (effectively MacKintosh's) request.

The bondholders asked Aberdeen to intervene lest the war be 'protracted and sanguinary' and that British mail ships be allowed through the blockade. The US considered them such a vital link they were admitted into Vera Cruz. The bondholders overbanked on British mediation: they had gambled on the latest *refacción*, 'on the express ground that British interference on behalf of Mexico might be relied upon'. The last four decades had seen many precedents for such intervention on behalf of traders, creditors and settlers overseas, through direct warnings, diplomatic pressure and as last resort, the show of force, but crucially, it did not happen for the Mexican bondholders in 1846.

Charles Graham, business partner to Powles, asked Aberdeen late in April 1846, to buy California for its harbours and its gold. America had made several offers and if she seized California, Graham argued, 'she would [have enough mineral wealth to] repudiate the whole of the debt of Mexico'. He put his experience at Aberdeen's disposal. The prospect of the US waging war on prostrate Mexico was as unpopular in England as among US opposition congressmen and critical US officers. In June 1846 the umbrella Spanish American Bondholder Committee begged Aberdeen to consider the losses to Britain from such a War, and 'to protect their communal interests', but Aberdeen only announced his agreement on Oregon to Parliament on 29 June. Over the following year, the US rejected British mediation in Mexico, although consul MacKintosh and *chargé d'affaires* Percy Doyle, secured cease-fires in the summer of 1847, by presence and pragmatism.

After the War, when Doyle and MacKintosh secured for bondholders nearly a sixth of the $16.8 million US 'consideration' (including interest) paid to Mexico for California, MacKintosh pocketed $600,000 in fees, recouping his 1846 loss on the cancelled bonds. Meanwhile his company obtained textile import licences, exempting them from the very customs earmarked to repay bondholders. Private smuggling by public servants in government ships, rife to the point of being tradition, deprived bondholders and Mexican citizens of revenue, and compromised Britain's integrity. The alarming case of HMS *America* deserting Station with two million *pesos* for the Bank of England, ended in a court martial conviction for insubordination. USN Surgeon Wood had watched Captain Gordon haggle at Mazatlán, 'chaffering for percentages ... dishonest and degrading', which he justified by blaming 'the wretched laws of the country'. *El Libertador de Vera Cruz*, 29 November 1846, reported cargoes even larger than *America's* $2 million. HMS *Talbot* off Mazatlán in May, 'fished' for silver smuggled from night-time beaches. Lt Somerville judged it 'most dishonourable, trafficking treasure to serve private individual ends, so derogatory to the British nation'.

Henry Parish, bondholder and old Spanish America hand, wrote from Caerphilly Castle in July to Lord Aberdeen, to protest at losing 'New Albion, San Francisco, which belongs to Great Britain in virtue of its having been discovered by Sir Francis Drake and formally conceded by the native chiefs to Queen Elizabeth.' It was a *cri de bourse*. For months Mexican bonds stagnated on the Exchange, reported in *The Times* as 'flat ... heavy ... depressed'. When London finally learned of the US taking of California, *The Times* protested, 1 October, that 'the rights of mortgagees ... our lien on a mortgaged territory ... should not be demolished by unscrupulous ... piratical invaders [seeking] to square off territory ... by coolly seizing it.'

HAWAIIAN INTERLUDE

Fourteen days out of Monterey, *Collingwood* anchored at dawn in Honolulu Outer Roads. As the only capital ship standing off, it was immediately surrounded by 'two or three hundred wooden canoes full of noisy natives with fresh eatables. Our old tortoise on board awoke and wantoned on the fresh food.'[23] Somerville and Macnamara ended five months companionship with 'a long chat' and the earnest Somerville's gift of 'a pair of Repeal Buttons which Macnamara has promised to keep for my sake'. The repeal of direct Westminster rule and a restored Irish

Parliament was O'Connell's cause, Michael Comyn would have approved, and even Chaplain Proctor, with reservations.

Consul Sir William Miller greeted and briefed Seymour. Macnamara took the cutter into Honolulu where he may have lodged with Picpus *Père* Louis Maigret at the mission, or at Miller's consulate nearby. Lt Walpole RN, 'deplored much of what missioners have done' to Hawaii, but excepted Maigret, 'of whom, no eulogy would be too high'.[24] USN Lt Watson echoed him, praising the Picpus priests' 'laborious, praiseworthy and philanthropic work'. Lt Somerville, reminded of Rosscarbery and home by Maigret's mission bell, stayed in touch with Macnamara onshore.

Seymour had business with the Sandwich Island King, whose new Foreign Minister was Robert Crichton Wyllie, the bondholders' mentor on colonising California. Wyllie kept in touch with cousin Hartnell in Monterey, and in closer touch with vice-consul James Forbes managing Santa Clara mine. Consul Miller complained to Aberdeen, 'Forbes does not write to me, as I have requested him to do, *and this* [Miller's emphasis] is the more remarkable since he never fails to write to [Wyllie].' Forbes pressed Wyllie for mine labourers, after the unemployed miners he brought from Sonora were turned back by the US blockade. Seymour, like Miller, found Wyllie pretentious and long-winded, but the King amused him by describing the Admiral's deep voice as 'speaking from his bottom'. To son Francis, Seymour confided about the 'gang of scoundrels who have installed themselves as [the King's] ministers. Wyllie is the most out and out specimen [...] The Sandwich Islands are a hornets' nest, but will be a fine Yankee colony one day.'[25] On 11 August the Admiral learned that HMS *America* had left the Station for England, 'without orders, with money'.

Macnamara dined on *Collingwood* on 16 August, and Somerville visited him ashore several times. On 6 September they held a farewell dinner on the flagship prior to sailing. 'I gave Macnamara a letter for my sister, a large journal which I scarcely expected to send, but he took charge of it *via* Vera Cruz. We had a large dinner party, Macnamara, [merchant Robert] Janion, [palace surgeon, Dr] Rooke and Lt Walpole: toasts and sentimental speeches washed down with champagne. Under weigh at 6.30 p.m., our guests gave three cheers as they parted.' One toast, presumably, was raised to Project Macnamara. In Mexico, Paredes y Arrillaga was deposed and Santa Anna invited back from exile.

Seymour stood for Valparaiso in early September, after discussion with his old friend Biddle, returning with USS *Columbus* by Honolulu. News had come through of the Oregon settlement and neither commander felt needed in California. Macnamara's expressed loathing for Honolulu on 27 September (below) may be explained by Biddle's crew having shore leave *en masse* to recover from scurvy. In 1847, the American editor of *Polynesian* wrote a feature on the Irish colony project: 'Most readers recollect Eugene Macnamara, a Jesuit, who arrived here last August [1846] in HBMS *Collingwood* on his way to Mexico City to negotiate land in California.' *Polynesian* was a government paper, cold towards Britain after Paulet's brief annexation, towards Washington after Polk included Hawaii in the Monroe Doctrine, and towards Catholics after an Hawaiian bill of rights for Catholic missioners. Macnamara may have been remembered just for being there when California was the talk of Honolulu.[26]

Late in September, Miller forwarded to Lord Aberdeen (now displaced by Lord Palmerston) a letter from the captain of HMS *Modeste* at Vancouver. 'Nothing of importance has occurred in the Oregon Territory … excepting the near approach of about 3000 more immigrants from the US, part of whom vary their route for California, a system of squatting by irresistible numbers.' William Romaine, who brought the letter, was a London lawyer touring the Oregon Trail. Miller duly reported:

> Mr Romaine proposes leaving here with Mr Macnamara, a young Irish priest, for San Blas or Mazatlán. Mr Macnamara came here in *Collingwood* and recently obtained from the Mexican Government the grant of a valuable and extensive tract of land in California which was conveyed to him two or three days only previous to Commodore Sloat's taking possession of that country. Mr Macnamara tells me that it *was* [Miller's emphasis] his intention to have brought out a great number of Irish emigrants to California.[27]

At the same time, Macnamara expressed impatience to James Forbes in a letter sent courtesy of a US merchant vessel to California:

> I send you a few hurried lines [as promised]. Here I am still, very much annoyed at being detained in this half savage

place, having nothing to do and my anxiety to reach Mexico amounting almost to madness. I am daily, nay hourly, expecting the arrival of *Palinurus*, transport ship, which is to carry me to San Blas.

He was bitter about the Oregon treaty, as Seymour had been, 'giving what we were ready to give two years ago, without the bluster':

England gives up all the good harbours of the northwest coast and gets nothing in return. The country has again been sacrificed by the asinine stupidity of old Aberdeen. Every Englishman with whom I have spoken on the subject seems utterly disgusted at the whole proceeding and none more so than the officers of HM's Navy who looked forward with pleasure to a brush with the Yankees, but who now must hide their diminished heads, while 'Jonathan' [US] may well boast, if not of his bravery, at least of his superior sagacity.

Oblivious that James Forbes was already receipting ore production to share proceeds with the diggers at Santa Clara, Macnamara confided in him:

I fully expect to leave before a week, and soon to enjoy a *palaver* with our mutual friend Mr [Alexander] Forbes. I am most anxious to form a company to work the mines of Santa Clara. In the event of my succeeding, of which I have very little doubt, would you consent to take charge of the whole concern ? Pray let me know in your next letter. I am [also] very desirous of doing something about that [colonising] grant of land. I will give the Yankees as much annoyance as I possibly can in the matter. Write to me by the very first opportunity to Mexico [City] under cover directed to Mr Bankhead. I enclose a letter [from Bandini] for you which I got at Los Angeles, but which I forgot to deliver when we last met [at Monterey]. I shall write to you again from Mexico City.

I forgot to mention that by last accounts the Americans were rapidly advancing into the very centre of Mexico, and it was even feared they would overrun the country if England or France did not interpose. The *ilustre sangre Mexicana* seemed to be below par. I remain, my dear Mr Forbes, Your very sincere friend, Eugene Macnamara.[28]

HM Transport 27, *Palinurus*, the requisitioned stores barque, supplied ships between Valparaiso, Mazatlán and Honolulu, until Seymour condemned her unfit for service in February 1847. On 2 October, her seconded officers, Lt Lucas and Lt The Honourable Arthur Cochrane, brought bread into Honolulu, before replenishing for Mazatlán. Romaine and Macnamara spent four weeks on board with the two lieutenants. Arthur Cochrane's father, a retired admiral, had once liberated Chile and in 1846 was corresponding with his son. Young Cochrane may have told Macnamara that Chile, like Mexico, was anxious for colonists, and spoken of the Picpus mission at Valparaiso. Old newspapers helped pass the time on board, and dog-eared copies of *El Mercurio de Valparaiso*, then much preoccupied with colonising, may have been available (see Plate 12).

Summer 1846 had seen Romaine pursuing buffalo 'as if foxes in his native Surrey'. An American traveller thought him 'overboiling with conceit', adding for good measure his 'glaring want of courtesy and good sense'.[29] *Père* de Smet, Jesuit missioner on the Oregon Trail, was kinder, 'fond of travel, already seen four quarters of the globe, estimable in many respects, but with so many prejudices against the Catholic religion. I treasured one of his beautiful reflections: we must travel in the desert to witness the care of Providence over the wants of man.'

Perhaps Romaine, a vicar's son, shared reflections with his second 'Apostolic Missioner' travelling companion, but more likely each wearied of the other's bravado. Romaine had experienced the Oregon Trail, Macnamara the California crisis. Of similar age, both were opinionated and neither short of words. Romaine, later known as 'the eyes of the British Army' in Crimea for his remarkable long-sight, would have spied Mazatlán first. On 9 November Lucas brought *Palinurus* into the bay to provision HMS *Herald* due down from Oregon and California. *Herald*, under Captain Kellett, carried Berthold Seeman, a German botanist:

We sailed on 21 November for San Blas, Mr Romaine and Mr Macnamara passengers. The latter, a Roman Catholic priest, intends founding in California a colony of Irishmen who would swear fealty to Mexico and resist the further encroachment of the Americans. The project nearly forestalled the occupation by the US and would in all probability, either have led to the establishment of an Irish colony or compelled the British government to occupy the country.

The colony was slipping even further into the past tense.[30]

Favourable following winds took them quickly to San Blas. Macnamara carried a letter for Alexander Forbes from Kellett and one from James Forbes sent in September. Kellett warned that after a six-month occupation, 'it would require a fleet to turn [the Americans] out of California'. Mormons, 'all mechanics' were swarming into the new territory, 'well armed and with the intention, it is said, of settling on the San Joaquin River'. Kellett moored briefly at San Blas to water while delivering and collecting mail.

[23 November] Mr Romaine and Mr Macnamara landed immediately and a courier went up with them to Tepic to bring our letters, good news from a far country. Tepic is 22 miles direct from San Blas and 2900 feet above sea level, but by road it is 56, tedious and fatiguing.[31]

Chapter 8

Demon Macnamara: 1846—48

Macnamara spent a week in Tepic under Alexander Forbes' roof. *Comandante* Castro was also resident, having failed to raise funds in Mexico City for the *californio* resistance. His mine shares more than earned him Forbes' welcome.[1] He and Pico had left California together in August to seek outside help, but Pico failed to reach Mexico City and his appeal letters for a counter-invasion achieved nothing. Mexico had its own invaders and Mexican newspapers derided him for seeking help from a government he had once rejected.

On 28 November, before a notary, Macnamara exercised his power of attorney for Castro, Suárez de Real and the Robles brothers, handing to Barron and Forbes a nine-year lease (*habilitación*, entitlement) on the mine with an optional further six years. Proceeds were to be divided between lessees and shareholders. The *californios* were assured, although not in writing, that this newly anglicised business had Queen Victoria's protection. Alexander Forbes' rank and wealth warranted their trust and no doubt word of his brother's role as Queen's Physician helped.

'Old Mr Forbes' shared James Forbes' September letter with Macnamara.[2] The California vice-consul had claimed-jumped them both, managing the mine since August and securing two of the Robles' shares. Macnamara took serious umbrage and later wrote 'bitterly' to Suárez de Real who had sold his role as site manager to James Forbes for a fee which he and his dependents needed.

Alexander Forbes asked Macnamara to deliver his November despatch to Bankhead. Like Miller, he complained of hearing nothing from vice-consul Forbes, but made no mention of his own leasing of the mine. Normally legitimate, it was out of order for a consul in wartime, especially when Seymour and Aberdeen had warned against even *perceived* breaches of neutrality. Barron and Forbes' offer of 'British protection', ruled out by London for anything else Californian, was a commercial confidence trick. The company pursued the lease and shares in a buyer's market created by war panic. After an expectedly brief war, they calculated, their share control, long lease and expertise would make it impossible to dislodge them. All they needed for the present was Macnamara's silence when he returned to the diplomatic enclave in Mexico City.

As Macnamara conveyed the lease and fumed over James Forbes' deceit, Castro sold his shares piecemeal between December and March to Alexander Forbes at between $800 and $1300 *pesos*, 'terms by no means ruinous to Tepic'. A canny prospector, Forbes had already played down the mercury mine to one of silver with a vein of low-grade cinnabar. In January he informed James Forbes about Macnamara's obtaining lease rights for the company, reminding him 'as you have two shares, your help will be to your advantage. You will leave to me the regulation of affairs'. He offered him $600 *pesos* each for the two shares. Far from selling, James Forbes advised that Bankhead be involved, so that 'British protection of the mine' might feature in any peace treaty. It was a veiled threat to reveal all which forced Alexander Forbes to stay his distance. In December 1847 the Robles brothers sold James Forbes their remaining two shares for $3,860 *pesos* in total; within months he sold them on to Robert Walkinshaw, Barron and Forbes new mine manager in his place, for $3,500 *pesos* each.

In January 1848, Padre Suárez de Real sold three of his four shares to A. Forbes for $1500 *pesos* each, but complained of having been short-changed, probably after hearing what the Robles had received. He headed for the Sierra Nevada southern mines with the gold seekers, to continue providing for his dependents. In August 1849, after violence broke out in the mines and as demand for mercury rose in the gold fields and in post-war Mexico, he returned to the coast and sold (or re-sold) his (or Macnamara's) remaining share to Walkinshaw.

THE MIDDLE MAN

No-one ever admitted to buying Macnamara's share, but in spring 1847 he complained that it had been poor remuneration. Walkinshaw's purchase from Suárez de Real in 1849 also conveyed the 'power to reclaim the share from any person living'. No one, however, knew whether Macnamara was dead, alive, or even who might have his share.

He had probably sold it to Alexander Forbes in November 1846. He needed money and his work for the company as well as his forthcoming silence at the embassy warranted generous treatment. Once there, realising he had been short-changed by both Forbeses and that the mine would never subsidise his colony, he wrote to Suárez de Real at Santa Clara. James Forbes saw the letter, which threatened to blow the whistle on him, and accordingly wrote to Alexander Forbes from Santa Clara on 14 July 1847.

> I have seen a letter from Mr Macnamara to Padre Real complaining bitterly that he has not received enough for his services; that he ought to have had one share from each [shareholder]; that I wrote inaccurate statements to you; and a furious tirade telling Padre Real that he has great influence with HM [ambassador], his most intimate friend; that I had better be cautious or I will lose my official situation! ... I have no copy, as Padre Real is absent. The letter was evidently written that I should learn its contents. I am ignorant as to how my letter to you [September 1846] could have given the Reverend gentleman such umbrage and I beg a copy of that letter, and also to inform me whether Mr Macnamara is still in Mexico.[3]

Macnamara was out of his depth and New Almaden, as James Forbes renamed the Santa Clara mine, was mired in dispute for many more years. Barron and Forbes invested in neither machinery nor workforce until well into the Gold Rush, and Alexander Forbes and Walkinshaw first visited it only late in 1847, after Mexico City fell. James Forbes ceded the management to Walkinshaw, but railed against Alexander Forbes for profiteering through Macnamara, on terms least favourable to the [shareholder] owners and most favourable to you. It raises doubts about the validity of the contract and Eugene Macnamara's right to the one share offered him for the due discharge of his agency to obtain for the owners a beneficial contract. [You have not] conciliated the mine owners to this undue proceeding of Mr Macnamara, Rev. Real having appointed me to manage the one share promised to Mr Macnamara on the condition stated. I trust you have not purchased that share from the last named person?[4]

The share 'consigned' to Macnamara in June 1846 was never 'offered', 'promised' or 'conditional'. Retrospectively in 1847, Castillero 'remedied' Macnamara's 'lack of legal formality'. Only when significant gold surfaced in California in 1848 did James Forbes complain that 'the interests of the owners should have come first'. He claimed to have bought out all four Robles shares and claimed power of attorney over Suárez de Real's three. California's gold boom boosted the mercury trade to some degree, but the simultaneous Mexican silver boom returned the real profit: exports. In 1846, however, the owners were desperate in the face of a US invasion and blockade. After 1848, when the mine was up and running, they forgot why they had ever scrambled to make it a 'British protectorate'.

At the end of November 1846, with Pico's conveyance, perhaps money for his share and a consideration (*mordida*, bite) from Alexander Forbes, Macnamara began the two-week journey to Mexico City. Alongside him, pilgrim columns descended on the Virgin of Guadalupe shrine from every wintery direction and he arrived in the capital on 12 December the feast day itself of the 'Empress of America'. Archbishop Posada y Garduno was dead; General Paredes had been deposed; US forces had taken Monterrey, 600 miles to the north, in September; Santa Anna, back from exile, was about to be president again, just as Washington was raising a new army to invade from the Mexican Gulf. *Californio* resistance had stiffened but irregulars could not continue on courage alone, and Britain would not intervene. Mexico City made a futile concession in August: the restoring of the Federalist constitution to win over unhappy California and Yucatán to Santa Anna.

Former commissioner Castillero was ready to sell. On 16 December, he and Macnamara met to confirm Macnamara's 'special but full' power of attorney and 'to effect the contract for which he was empowered'. They signed on the following day before a notary, after Castillero promised to obtain 'explicit consent' from all shareholders. He conveyed five of his dozen shares to Alexander Forbes for $5000 *pesos*, along with his two leagues of settlement land, and conveyed gratitude that 'my island of Santa Cruz [off Santa Bárbara] as well as the quicksilver mine may also appear as an English possession under the protection of HBM Government'.[5] By mid-1847, Alexander Forbes had Castillero's five shares, Castro's four, perhaps Macnamara's one and was pressing James Forbes for his secured Robles' two to complete the twelve-share holding required for ownership. Far from selling, James Forbes took power of attorney (he claimed) over the remaining two Robles shares as well.

New 'Almaden produced mercury for decades, outstripping other sources in Europe, China and the Americas, but it brought little joy. James, branded as a liar in court, shuffled shares like a cardsharp, selling each for as much as $35,000 in 1855. Alexander retired to England, before his understating of the ore-yield came out in court. Castillero's title, submitted to the Land Commissioners in 1852, was invalidated in 1855: he had rights to the mercury, but the mine was not on public land, nor at Santa Clara as registered, nor was it or its land-for-colonising agreed by Governor Pico. Murder, perjury and the withholding of evidence dogged appeals right up to the Supreme Court in what the *New York Times* called 'one of the most remarkable civil actions in this or in any century'. When, in 1863, the final appeal faltered, President Lincoln nationalised the mine for the Civil War effort. Alexander Forbes was dead, but his company received $1.7 million compensation. New Almaden closed in 1912 and is now a County Park.

Macnamara was well-rid of a distraction, and his need for project funding was increasingly academic. California surrendered to the US occupation in January 1847, after six-months' resistance; Mexico was invaded by sea in spring 1847; Gómez Farías became provisional President, freeing the brave, proud, vain and romantic President Santa Anna to become *generalissimo* to 18,000 troops facing the invader. Macnamara was sidelined in Mexico City, where he lived under a diplomatic roof on Calle de Capuchinas, either at MacKintosh's consulate or at the Legation.

He may have been there all along from 1844. Charles Bankhead was invalided home through US lines in October 1847. Dr John Baldwin, who helped General Scott negotiate, once US troops had secured the capital in September, told the Senate Military Committee, six months later,

> I made the acquaintance of priest Macnamara and I was credibly informed that, under the auspices of the British Legation, he had projected a plan to colonise California with Irish emigrants. It was asserted that his ulterior views were to promote British, not Mexican interests. His project approved by the Mexican government, he went to California. A fierce opposition was contemplated by the republican [centralist] members of Supreme Congress on his return with his matured plans from California. This resistance became unnecessary with the conquest of California by US arms. Macnamara lived in the family of either the British consul or *chargé d'affaires* in Mexico.[6]

Irish *chargé* Percy Doyle worked with MacKintosh to broker local ceasefires, although the US rejected Britain's formal offer to mediate. Macnamara may have been warned by his hosts not to compromise their neutrality. The Mexican government confirmed his colony formally in May 1847, but events reduced him to just another stranded expatriate in need of help. In Britain, too, Mexican debt and California were eclipsed by another crisis.

THE IRISH FAMINE

George Bancroft, Polk's Navy Secretary, succeeded ambassador McLane in London:

> The British government will not attempt to direct Mexican affairs, although on the ceding of The Californias to the US, some consideration may be asked for such rights as British subjects pretend to have acquired there. This Government has preserved in the whole matter the most profound silence. Another cause exists for the great disinclination of England to interfere with foreign nations, a disinclination

which in comparison with her past history can only be called extraordinary. That cause is Ireland.[7]

The only 'rights' British subjects might 'pretend' in California were Macnamara's land and Alexander Forbes' mine. British investment there was non-existent and bondholder warrants would expire in October 1847, unused and with few mourners.

By 'Ireland' Bancroft meant the Famine. The Church of Ireland invoked the collect-prayer *In Time of Famine* in the winter of 1845 and newspapers took it up. Admiral Seymour read of it with disbelief in June 1846, in old US papers: 'US newspapers always contrive.' A collection was held on *Collingwood*, although one Irish senior rating openly refused to contribute. Under a stark 'FAMINE IN IRELAND' front-page headline, *The Tablet* told of 'the most entire famine known for hundreds of years in any considerable quarter of Europe'. Famine dominated the London *Times* in the autumn and winter of 1846 and the sympathetic *Illustrated London News* reported direct from Skibbereen and Clonakilty in west Cork; in 1849 it reported from Macnamara's old parish of Kilkee-Killard in Kilrush Union, 'another Skibbereen'. On 1 January 1847, Bishop Hynes asked the Demerara clergy 'to arrange a subscription for relief of the distress in Ireland'. Lt Somerville's sister wrote from Cloyne of 'Famine staring in the face the poor who are already crying out for food', and of Catholic and Protestant clergy working together.[8]

'Famine' described the first two years of airborne spores which blighted the Irish potato crop for yet another three and more. Potatoes blackened in the ground and in store: the smell was rank. A greatly increased population had come to depend on an efficient nourishing tuber which could be grown on a patch of poor soil. When it failed, life failed. Twice during Macnamara's youth, the Clare crop had failed, but from rain and rot; the consecutive failures (1845–9 and beyond) were from blight, and were nationwide. Doonbeg village was so bad in 1847, 'a wretched nest of filth, famine and disease', that Michael Comyn gave up Baltard House in protest. He had already given up alcohol until the Union should be repealed.

Peel's public workfare and imported 'brimstone' maize gave way to Lord Russell's 'self-help' and free market forces. Hungry, sick people could not build roads, some of which actually led nowhere. Westminster, paralysed by the scale of famine, appeared pitiless. In contrast, the public were moved. Despite her aloof government, Queen Victoria donated a personal £2,000 ($8,000) to relief. The Turkish Sultan offered £10,000 ($40,000) and a food convoy, but Westminster advised that £1,000 might be more appropriate, lest Victoria's donation be outshone. British residents of Mexico, Macnamara among them, collected in their war winter of 1846: Palmerston thanked them for '£523 [$2092] relief of their fellow subjects at home, the distressed Irish'.[9]

US President Polk sent his 'personal mite' of $50, but vetoed a $500,000 Ireland relief bill in Congress. Two US Navy vessels, less their cannon, were spared for civilian hire to transport private relief supplies to Cork. One, the rebuilt prize, USS (ex-HMS) *Macedonian*, was delayed while ruffled British political feathers were smoothed. The Pope donated through dioceses and missions, appealing by encyclical to Catholic bishops worldwide for prayer and for 'liberal Alms'. Choctaw Indians, Protestant SPG missioners, Scots Presbyterians, Methodist ministers, Jews and memorably the Quakers contributed, as did French slaves in the Carribbean. Arawak Indians at John Cullen's river mission in Guiana sent $44.88. Some donors stipulated that their money go to 'all religions'. The Famine wasted a million Irish lives through starvation, cholera and typhus; poor records hide tens of thousands more. It accelerated the flight, mainly to the US, of another million by 1850. The rest of the century saw four million leave for the US, Canada, Australia and Britain.[10]

Some claimed to know God's mind. The anti-Irish saw famine and flight as Nature's sifting of the fit from the flawed. Some clergy and bishops spoke of 'judgement' on lax religious observance, or of God's plan to evangelise the world through an Irish diaspora. US Chaplain Colton reported oddly in his Monterey newspaper in September 1847, 'the Irish have kindly consented to starve'. British Secretary of State Trevelyan decided that God's visitation should not be impeded. Daniel O'Connell, in his last days, attacked Irish landlords for not paying the rates to help the poor and for being neglectfully absent; he savaged London financiers and middlemen for diverting Irish estate revenues from tenants' needs. *Punch* mocked, saying O'Connell was Ireland's blight, and it cartooned the Irish as ape-figures. Only late in the 1840s did *The Times* accept that the Irish peasantry needed exceptional help and law reform, not benevolence. As late as 9 July 1849, it sniped at the refugee-emigrant: 'Since so many of our fellow British subjects must join a foreign alliance ... the Celt will probably pass from being a bad subject to a good ally.' The landed class suffered, losing revenue (and in a few decades, their lands) as tenants fled, were evicted or died. Emigrants saw their flight as forced exile – Famine made such distinctions academic anyway. An 'American Wake' for the virtual dead was held well into the twentieth century, and the mythical 'West' had always been where souls headed after death. In turn, the 'departing dead' felt guilt at deserting their own, as did their own for needing them to leave to take pressure off the land.

Impossible to exaggerate, the Famine was often oversimplified.[11] Like religion or England, it was the alibi for too much. All emigrants, even before the blight, were famine victims. All landowners were pitiless, rich Protestants starving the Catholic poor. The truth behind the halving of the population was more complex. The emigration syphon had been flowing long before 1845, with over a million gone since 1820, and those by no means all Catholic. In the worst of the Famine, Protestant clergy ministered among starving Catholic peasants and several dozen ministers died of Famine-related typhus and cholera. 'Souperism' abuse by extremists was largely confined to the west and condemned by many Protestants. A Clare parish priest wrote to Canterbury of his 'gratitude and love for my Protestant brethren' after the Archbishop's relief collection in England. Michael Comyn ran a soup kitchen with his Church of Ireland counterpart at Kilkee (see Plate 13).

Catholic middlemen and landlords rack-rented and evicted tenants as cruelly as any proverbial Protestant, while some Protestant gentry and aristocrats bankrupted themselves in giving relief. No religion or class monopolised humanity. The harsh public workhouse system, built for poor relief pre-Famine and against Poor Law Commissioners' advice, could not cope with a disaster it was not designed to face, but it became 'proof' of conspired underplanning. When workhouses overflowed, the lucky ones received the boat fare to England; the unlucky were sent home. Emigrants re-invented themselves like holiday romancers, playing victims of famine or of politics, safe in faraway lands where stories could not be checked.

Eugene Macnamara's California scheme was conceived early in 1845, before any famine, in response to the general European (and Irish) land shortage and growing population. Nothing was heard about him in Europe after he left Guiana in 1844, save the London *Times* report of 'an Irish priest's' California project in August 1845, copied to some Irish newspapers. Throughout winter 1845, the famine reports reaching Mexico added powder to his charge. *La Reforma*, 15 February 1846, staunchly republican, identified famine as a hazard of living under a monarch. That the British could import indigestible maize into Irish ports while allowing wheat and barley to leave the same ports astounded all Mexican editors, whatever their politics. It happened at Limerick and Kilrush on the Shannon, east of Kilkee-Killard. Others in Mexico, besides Macnamara, began to talk of bringing the Irish to California.

THE ENTICING OF US IRISH DESERTERS

In August 1846, José Salas, interim President after Dictator Paredes, promised an Office (*Dirección*) and a Congressional Committee (*Comisión*) in charge of colonising. Meanwhile, an interim *Junta* would 'promote foreign immigration for the security of the republic'. The *Dirección* and *Comisión* were established in November, but like Iniestra and Macnamara, came too late to save California. Two Britons of Irish background approached the *Junta* in September. Nicholas Synnott, founder of the *Academia Inglés* on Santa Isabel, teamed up with Isaac Murray, an Irish blanket manufacturer from Puebla retailing in Mexico City. They presented 'humble services to the Government in this honourable war' and named their price.[12]

One third of the US Army, they claimed, was Irish. (It was a quarter.) They insisted that religious bigotry led the US Irish to desert. (Brutality, arbitrary and indisciplined junior officers and low pay were cited far more.) All of General Taylor's deserters, they vouched, since he crossed into Mexico, were Irish. (This was also untrue.) Desertion, however, was real enough. USM Lt Gillespie saw US deserters in Mexico City as early as January 1846, when Taylor was still only at Corpus Christi. In front of Monterrey, in September 1846, Taylor faced a Mexican artillery company of US Irish deserters, the first *Batallón de San Patricio* in action. In the summer of 1847, *Batallón* veterans, re-badged in a larger infantry 'Foreign Legion' composed of several nationalities, defended Mexico City.

The two entrepreneurs asked that Synnott be commissioned as interpreter to the Army Command, where his gifted English would help entice Irish deserters. After the war, they proposed that veterans be given their horses, arms, six-months' pay and land in California. Transformed from combat unit to colony militia, they would be committed to defending their territory, as deserters could expect no quarter from the US, whose future role in California, however, was not explained.

They also proposed that families and single young women be brought from Ireland: family responsibility would turn footloose ex-soldiers into providers. The law would allow Synnott and Murray twenty square leagues bonus land. Murray's commercial links meant that he could source provisions, tools and certainly blankets. He offered to inject his own capital and, while Synnott lured the deserters, Murray would stake out plots in California and organise supply channels. '*Un precio modesto*' would ensure his cashflow and he would be governor (*jefe*) and military *comandante* combined, Pico and Castro in one. Land would be awarded by rank and length of service. Interpreter-captain Synnott might receive 2,000 acres for a year's service, 1,000 more for a second year, plus bonus land and pay as colony supervisor (*intendente*).

Both men knew that Mexico could not afford subsidies and that Alta California was virtually lost, but they also seemed unaware of their own lack of credibility commanding war veterans. At least they considered the worst:

> If through one of war's fatal mischances, the Government were forced to cede California to another power, the colonists would be entitled to make their home in another frontier department, on the same conditions, giving them and the undersigned a similar amount of land.[13]

A sceptical *Junta* advised Supreme Congress not to allow Murray his monopoly; greed stifled colonies just as British manufacturers like him had stifled domestic production in Puebla with smuggled or exempted imports. On 2 October, Synnott informed them that Murray was withdrawing from the scheme and the blanket maker headed for Cuba. Synnott secured a role at Mexican Army HQ and in November US desertions seemed to be more systematically encouraged and with more sophisticated language. Broadsheets were distributed to encourage 'co-religionists and lovers of freedom' to desert, even citing O'Connell. However, Santa Anna suddenly dismissed Synnott: 'he would not work unpaid [and] we have enough interpreters'. Early in 1847, Congress abandoned the deserter project, but those already in uniform fought on.[14]

BATALLÓN DE SAN PATRICIO TO LEGIÓN ESTRANJERA

Galway-born John Riley, (spelled Reilly on the *San Patricios* monument in Mexico City), deserted from the British Army in Canada and from the US Army in Texas. He was allowed to form a Mexican Army company of about fifty Irish-Americans who had deserted. They defended Monterrey as *Batallón de San Patricio* gunners, probably named after the first Irish settlement in Texas. Irish brigades and legions of 'wild geese' mercenaries were a tradition in the Spanish empire and in the wars of independence fought by emerging Latin American states. An Ultonea (Ulster) Regiment helped garrison New Spain (later Mexico) in the 1770s; O'Connell's son fought with Bolivar's Irish Legion. By mid-1847, Riley's *Batallón* had grown to two companies, redesignated *Legión Estranjera de San Patricio*, 200 strong and about half Irish, but still only a fraction of over 9,000 US deserters. President Polk worried about a conflict of loyalties for Catholic US soldiers fighting in Catholic Mexico. He was concerned enough to consult the Bishop of Baltimore, who chose two Spanish-speaking US Jesuits to advise the US Command. They were not chaplains.

US generals in Mexico tried to prevent troops despoiling the vividly Catholic culture around them, promising Mexicans that Catholicism would be as respected as it was in the US. The Philadelphia 'Bible' riots of 1844 were fresh cautionary memories, yet a Protestant pastor there had offered shelter to the Catholic bishop, and in October 1846, Polk himself gave the Presbyterian minister of Philadelphia, short shrift at The Mansion, as 'a knave, fanatic and deranged' when he visited to protest against 'Jesuit chaplains' and to demand his own appointment. Some US soldiers found Mexico sinister, but the abhorrence was mutual. *El Trueno* spoke of 'the Protestant prejudice which animates our northern neighbours', a Mexican assumption on which Macnamara had once played. The Army Jesuits' warning that Mexican Catholicism was a 'pagan distortion', was echoed in *The Tablet*: 'Reformation is needed among the Catholics and the clergy there.'[15]

Relatively few Irish soldiers pleaded that religious prejudice caused them to desert. Promotion, pay and land tempted, but Mexico had no religious toleration to offer. The prejudice behind Manifest Destiny took many forms – careful Calvinist versus feckless Catholic, virtuous republican against corrupt monarchist (and Pope), Latino and Irish against Anglo-Saxon. With its backdrop of Spanish mission churches, wayside shrines and place names redolent of pre- and counter-Reformation piety, the stage on which the Mexican war was played, was haunted by Spain. The Pilgrim Fathers, radical English Protestants who colonised America, had also brought folk memories of the 1588 Armada crusade against England and bequeathed hispanophobia.

In November 1846, Mexican priests attending the wounded under truce at Monterrey tried to entice US soldiers. At Puebla and Jalapa in spring 1847, as a US army marched on the capital, priests were accused of leading peasant guerrilla units. Cenobio Jarauta's name became a by-word in the autumn, 'styling himself a priest, the coldest, bloodiest Guerrilla chief in Mexico'. He fought on after the draft peace of February 1848. The Americans captured and executed him, but buried him with military honours. A priest was arrested in Guadalupe for enticing deserters, but overall, few priests were implicated, despite the indignation in US ranks. General Scott ordered his men to salute all Mexican officials, including priests in cassocks.[16]

US envoys and correspondents vented prejudice freely. Nicholas Trist, Washington's Envoy after Slidell withdrew, reported to Secretary Buchanan on 'lazy, ignorant and stupid monks [in a] round of animal enjoyments, [greedy] for money and property, idol worshippers, fanatics and candle burners'.[17] In 1848, the same Trist joined young congressman Lincoln, Lt Ulysses Grant and USN Captain Du Pont to express shame at the entire war, 'an abuse of power on our part'.

In the spring of 1847, Lt Robert Anderson wrote home of new 'addresses in bad English calling on fellow Volunteers to desert, promising them rich lands'. By then, Synnott and Murray were long gone. Ralph Kirkham, with Scott at Puebla in the early summer, described 'rascally priests living off the fat of the land'. It was campfire stereotype. 'If a Mexican buys a[n] American horse, he pays the priest to bless it,' Kirkham also reported, but the ritual antedated the US itself, whatever nationality the horse. Hearsay quickly became fact. 'The Mexican government's most promising plan was to buy up Scott's Irish soldiers through the priest Macnamara, recently conspiring in California, and facilitate their desertion, by having Santa Anna attack Puebla.'[18]

Inevitably Macnamara's name was linked with any talk of settling Irishmen in California. American soldiers demonised him, yet priests-at-war, like priest politicians were a Mexican tradition: Aztec priests fought Cortés, Miguel Hidalgo and José Morelos led the fight for independence from Spain. Ireland too had seen fighting priests in the 1798 uprising, just before Macnamara was born. In April 1847, José Ramírez, Durango congressman and late Foreign Secretary, told the governor of Durango that Secretary of State Baranda was 'getting secret aid from the English residents of the city, particularly from an Irish priest who for some time has been planning a colonisation project in California, in my opinion as a secret agent of England'.[19]

After General Scott took Mexico City in September 1847, Anderson reported Scott's *Order of The Day* which appeared in the Army newspaper *American Star*, 'informing us of a company headed by some cowardly officers and false priests to assassinate our brave little army. The principal conspirator is said to be an Irish priest called Macnamara who had been tampering with our soldiers, offering them lands in California if they desert. I hope, if the evidence is conclusive against him, he will be hung [*sic*].' Macnamara provided a name for an otherwise anonymous threat, but his guilt was produced by camp gossip. As an Irish British subject, Catholic and Mexicophile, he fitted the rogue part well. Scott, however, did not mention him, only 'conspiracy by several false priests who dishonour the holy religion they profess, to entice our gallant Irish Catholic soldiers to desert under a promise of lands in California … already conquered and for ever a part of the US'.

Anderson was a fair man who respected Mexican religious practice, despite stereotype Macnamara. Captain Kenly, another fair-minded US officer who would 'make no reflection on the Church and its clergy – they have done wonders in reclaiming an idolatrous people', acted as defence lawyer for the curate of Naolinco, charged with 'helping corrupt the rank and file of the US Army by money and promises'.[20]

As Anderson inveighed, Scott's negotiator, John Baldwin, met Macnamara in the surrendered capital. British diplomats mediated between Scott in the capital and the Mexican provisional government at Querétaro, 150 miles away. It is unlikely the diplomats would have tolerated a subversive guest when neutrality was British policy and peace their commercial priority, yet the the provincial occupation newspaper,

American Flag, on 5 April 1848, still accused them all of rigging or 'fathering' the final peace treaty:

> It has many fathers. It was manifest that Mr MacKintosh, with Mr Thornton, *chargé d'affaires*, Mr Eugene Macnamara, the ecclesiastic, and others, exercised considerable influence in imposing guarantees for their alleged rights and for the interests of those whom they represented.

José Maria Mora, liberal reformer and priest, was called out of exile in Paris late in 1847 to be Mexican Envoy Extraordinary in London. During preparatory talks in November, Mora invited Britain to combine buying California with brokering peace terms for Mexico. In a 'nota confidencial' he reminded Lord Palmerston of Paredes' deal with Macnamara, when 'the alienation of a part of the territory of California in the name of England was agreed in your favour. Previously, less explicitly, you made the same or similar insinuations to General Santa Anna'.

US peace negotiators, out to secure California 'respectably' before a critical world, disclaimed US right to it, save by purchase. In the end, the $15 million with interest paid in 1848 to cover minor debts and private US claims, was not a purchase, but a sweetener 'in consideration of having California': it just seemed like purchase. Mora argued that the US disclaimer of all but purchaser's right, meant that Mexico had a corresponding vendor's right to a preferred customer, '*en favor de la Inglaterra*'. Britain's commercial interest in Mexico would justify her seat at peace talks without her breaching neutrality. Her California purchase money could pay '*par parte considerable*' Mexico's debt to the bondholders. It was not easy for proud Mexicans to plead: Mora called it *triste, tristisima, pero inevitable*, but Palmerston remained silent, as he did when Mora also requested that consul MacKintosh be dismissed for profiteering from so-called British interests.[21]

The *San Patricios* were on the losing side and no mercy was shown them on surrender. Congressman Ramírez thought them 'generous but luckless'. Fifty of the hundred taken prisoner were executed when Mexico City fell, the rest lashed, face-branded, yoked and dismissed the Army they had deserted. The survivors were demobilised by a Mexican government too poor to pension them and powerless to reward them with

California land. It had already paid out $1700 *pesos* to 17 ex-*San Patricios* in 1847 and in 1848 borrowed from consul MacKintosh to help more. His consulate distributed $50 *pesos* each, in lieu of land, to thirty-four veterans of the 'Foreign Legion of St Patrick' and John Riley was allowed a Mexican army pension in 1850. A bankrupt government acted honourably and the *pesos* were more than any other Irish would-be colonist for California would see.[22]

PROJECT MACNAMARA ENDORSED[23]

In mid-1847, as Scott's army moved west, inland from Vera Cruz, Mexico's new congressional *Comisión* for colonising scrutinised Governor Pico's conveyance to Macnamara. US newspapers mocked them for fiddling while Mexico burned. The conceding of territory to foreign colonists when all Mexico had been seized by foreign force was now even more humiliating and politically charged. The *Comisión* confirmed that Dictator Paredes had acted within his emergency powers by approving the project without Congress, in sending Macnamara to California, and in ordering Pico's cooperation. It only needed President Santa Anna's signature.

Macnamara had said little about paying for the land, but the *Comisión* acknowledged his good faith, upholding his right to settle 'the location known as *Los Tulares*, as a firm bastion against barbarous Indians and north American adventurers'. It was the eastern bank of the Rio San Joaquin, from Rio Cosumnes south east across nine major tributary river valleys, two of them with upper forks, to beyond Laguna Tulares, through Tejon Pass, across Rio Las Animas (Mojave) to the mouth of Cajon Pass and down to San Bernardino. Only Mexicans and Spanish would be allowed to settle alongside the Irish.

The 'disastrous circumstances of the Republic and the sad state of The Californias' were no time to talk money and a tariff would be decided later. Land prices were inconsistent: the bondholder option of April 1837 discounted an acre from the then $2 *pesos* to $1 *peso*; a law of desperation in December 1846 reduced the acre to $0.5 *peso* and in California to $0.25 *peso* considering its isolation. In April 1847, a more businesslike $1.25 *peso* tariff was introduced. The *Comisión* was the first official body to mention Macnamara's and the bondholders' land in the same breath, although he had openly boasted of private as well as governmental support. Consul MacKintosh had also proposed a $0.5 *peso* tariff to Aberdeen in September

1845 through John Schneider, and characteristically may have worked behind the scenes on Mexican politicians to achieve it in law. Macnamara lived on Calle de Capuchinas at consulate or embassy. If a bondholder overlap or link with Macnamara existed, the bondholders could have had a flying start, their hypothetical 250,000 acres in California, riding on the back of Macnamara's 13,284,000 firmly secured acres.

The *Comisión* costed his acres across the tariff range, rejecting the lowest ($0.25 *peso*), yet aware that the '*muy miserable*' condition of Irish settlers had to be a consideration: poor colonists buying cheaply were preferable to an enemy confiscating.

At one point the Committee toyed with increasing each of the 3,000 family concessions from one to eleven square leagues each, the maximum allowed in a personal land grant by the governor. It turned Macnamara's 20,000 square mile concession into 231,000 square miles, 25 per cent more than the land mass of later US California State, but possibly feasible in the much wider area of Alta California. Hostile US news editors mocked 'a calculation more curious than constructive', but it was a measure of Mexico's desperation about its frontier.

Macnamara admitted that Pico's legal untidiness made his conveyance 'lack due force'. The scheme, conceived, hatched and bred under three governments, was without precedent. Pico's records were in enemy hands in Washington and the sole evidence before the *Comisión* was Macnamara's conveyance copy, yet Pico had clearly made a colonising conveyance, not a personal grant, which made fraud almost impossible. Crucially Pico had left the final word to Central Government, which healed everything. As Dictator Paredes had acted constitutionally without Congress – it convened under his rule only on 29 May 1846, when Macnamara was long gone and at sea for Monterey – the conveyance needed only Santa Anna's signature, not a congressional debate or vote.

Comisión registered its coded decision: '*Permita al Eugenio Macnamara, naturel de Irlanda y súbdito de S.M. Británica, el establecimiento de una colonia ... denominado Tulares.*' Santa Anna appended his signature shortly afterwards. Macnamara's land had to be occupied within five years, but summer 1852 was far away and California's future uncertain.[24] Significantly, no doubt because MacKintosh was close to him, Santa Anna agreed in May to reinstate the new bond issue agreed in London 1845/6, which had been cancelled when war broke out.

FRÉMONT'S 'BRITISH AGENT'

John Frémont's youthful independent command was privileged. From humble origins, he served at the Coastal Survey Office below Capitol Hill, mixed in Washington society and married the daughter of Senator Thomas Benton, chairman of the Senate Military Committee. Benton oversaw Frémont's topographical surveys of the West and Frémont understood well the destinarian nature of the expeditions. Benton was a leading expansionist. The soldier-surveyor 'Topogs' explored The Rockies, the Columbia, Nevada Territory and eastern California. Their third expedition, 1845–6, was the most charged, both in the surrounding volatile political atmosphere, and in the numbers and nature of the team, complete with cannon.

Frémont took a team section across the Sierra Nevada to Fort Sutter and on to Monterey, via the Santa Clara mine. President Polk's Cabinet, alerted to Macnamara's and Admiral Seymour's activities, was determined to have California by any means, including insurrection or war, should offers of money fail.

Comandante Castro grudgingly allowed Frémont to winter inland, after being assured that the surveyors were civilians not US soldiers. Frémont then went on to goad Castro, at one point hoisting the US flag on a defensive height. The bait was not taken and Frémont turned north for Oregon Country, accused by William Ide, who was soon to lead the Bear Flag revolt, of 'leaving us [settlers] to the wrath of the authorities'.

At Klamath Lake, in Oregon Country, Lt Gillespie, Polk's confidential courier, who had crossed Mexico in disguise and detoured via Honolulu to hide his tracks, caught up with Frémont to instruct, 'Watch US interests in California'. 'Watch' in a Washington order was as wide a remit as 'See that' in a London directive. Gillespie had memorised a letter from Secretary Buchanan to consul Larkin before destroying it at sea outside Vera Cruz in December 1845. He also brought Frémont family correspondence. His journey had started after 'confidential conversation' with the President. Buchanan had urged tact and persuasion with the *californios*, had warned of active British interest and a threat of colonising. He advised that a contented protectorate was preferable to a mutinous possession. Frémont later claimed the family letters were crucial, notably the one (or more) from Benton, apparently one of friendship and family details, [but] a trumpet giving no uncertain note [which] in the light of many conversations with him in Washington, clearly made me know I was required to find out and counteract any foreign schemes in relation to California ... at last the time had come when England must not get a foothold, that we must be the first. I was to act, discretely, but positively. His letters made me know distinctly that.[25]

Frémont and Gillespie turned south, where a handful of *anglo* settlers had already risen against Castro, taken hostages and his militia's pool of horses, then raised a Lone Star flag at Sonoma in June. Three weeks after it started, Frémont commandeered the uprising as a US officer, virtually ignoring Buchanan's more pacific instructions. Ide's proclamation demanded 'republican government' (constitutional rights, even independence, but not necessarily US rule), an end to Castro's 'military despotism' and to the corrupt selling of mission land. Ide also addressed 'all good citizens of California', by definition *californios* as well as *anglos*, and his principal hostage, General Vallejo, supported him. Independence was the rebels' threat, but not their objective. Whether through ambition or being dazzled by his high contacts and sense of importance, Frémont reinvented their aims and Ide resented it. The Lone-Star-with-Bear flag was recognised by no-one and disappeared immediately US forces occupied Alta California. It was passing theatre.

Frémont's company became the small mixed battalion of 'Topogs', trappers and Bear Flaggers which Seymour and Macnamara watched parade through Monterey. Sloat ordered it designated a Navy Mounted Battalion, which soon became 'California Battalion'. Frémont and Gillespie took it to Reina de Los Angeles, where Gillespie provoked a *californio* backlash. Major Frémont had to take reinforcements south again, where he styled himself local 'Governor', convoluting an already complex chain of naval command. General Kearny brought a column of US volunteers overland into southern California to secure the trail from Mexico. Frémont defied an order from Kearny to disband his force and to stop, as Lt McLane, his second-in-command, put it, 'playing Governor'. His 'governorship' lasted forty days. Remanded to Washington for court-martial, Frémont was convicted of mutiny and insubordination in January

1848. President Polk approved the verdict, but overruled the mutiny conviction. Frémont was allowed to remain in the Army. In protest, he resigned his commission, while father-in-law Benton blamed Polk and jealous West Pointers. Samuel Du Pont, already cynical about Polk's War, disagreed: 'Frémont's astuteness and Benton's influence have not been able to put down honesty and truth.'[26]

The brittle friendship between Benton and Polk snapped. The President had attended Benton's younger daughter's marriage to William Carey Jones in March 1847, but rejected both Benton and Jones's petitions for the bridegroom's diplomatic preferment. In June, Jessie Frémont and Kit Carson visited The Mansion to show Frémont's letter to Benton, written after the insubordination incident. They hoped Polk would veto the inevitable court martial, but carefully he 'evaded approbation of her husband's conduct'. Benton snubbed Polk routinely at church and in December 1848, Polk noted, Benton 'has not called on me or spoken the last twelve months'.

A redeemed, if civilian Frémont bounced back to claim $700,000 reimbursement for expenses incurred and pay due to his 'Topogs', credit suppliers, Bear Flaggers and trapper irregulars. Before the Senate Miltary Affairs Committee, chaired by Benton with his allied senators Dix and Rusk by his side, Frémont stated on oath in February that 'his' Bear Flag revolt achieved California's independence from Mexico, thereby saving it from Britain, and before he learned of the Mexican War. He claimed that on 7 July 1846, he had handed to the US the fruits of 'the revolutionary movement. The peaceful possession of California checked *californio* designs to put California under British protection and prevented the great grant to Macnamara, the original papers of which I have here.'[27]

He remained evasive about June–July 1846 for the rest of his life, although he tried frequently to explain it, as did his wife. He had obeyed Buchanan's directive 'Watch', but was also instructed directly by Gillespie from the President himself and obliquely by Benton, virtually in code. The covert mission, whatever its make-up, remained classified for his lifetime and the rushtide of events which followed nearly overwhelmed him, as Benton family secrets overlapped and muddied those of the President.

For reimbursement of his considerable expense, Frémont had to prove that he had defended US interests against a grave foreign [British] threat, when the reality was that a junior officer and his company had abused their welcome on Mexican territory and involved themselves without official US mandate. Benton's 'trumpet note' and the President's secret dealing remained classified as they too lacked authority. It was all a *gaffe* more serious than Ap Catesby Jones' attack on Monterey in 1842, more conspiratorial yet distinctly more to Washington's (and the expansionist party's) advantage. It could also be traced back to Washington. Project Macnamara, coincidence or not, offered the President every reason to believe in, or at very least to proclaim a British threat to the US. He welcomed it at a time when mistrust of Great Britain was in the very air Americans breathed.

Witnesses lined up to speak for Frémont. 'The *californios* designed to create a large British interest … to convert public or Mexican property in California into British property' was true of the Santa Clara mine, Santa Cruz island and Macnamara's 20,000 square miles, but that the grant to Macnamara 'was appreciated by the Bear Flag [revolution]' was suspiciously vague. The courtroom chorus sounded other flat notes. Gillespie generalised: 'the transfer to England, and Mr Forbes' and Macnamara's influence in it, was common conversation throughout the country after the rising of the settlers in the north'; the aborted *Consejo General*, 'arranged by James Forbes and Macnamara, had been prevented [by] the rising of the settlers. All this intrigue of British agents was broken up by settlers under Captain Frémont'.

Witnesses confirmed hearsay. All mentioned the British settlers, Workman and Reid, receiving grants in the last weeks of Alta California: the more British interests, the more likely British conspiracy. Sam Hensley, four years in California, knew of 'general report that the authorities were about to grant land for a British colony to an Irish priest who came in a British warship. My impression was that the timely movement of the settlers, Frémont and others, prevented the transfer'. Macnamara's close involvement with the Royal Navy (on four naval vessels) justified Hensley's impression. Seven 'Topogs' insisted that 'the Bear Flag revolution put a stop to such grants' and USN Lt Loker remembered 'a good deal of talk of England taking possession of the country. England had a mortgage on it. A British man-o-war on the Oregon coast would be down in the summer to take possession of California'.

HMS *Collingwood, America, Juno* and *Herald* might be conflated into one warship, but a ship could not harness a territory. Seymour knew better than US Navy Secretary Bancroft and Commodore Stockton that to hold land required troops. Pressed on Macnamara, Midshipman Wilson of USS *Savannah* remembered seeing him 'at Monterey engaged it was said in negotiations with Admiral Seymour over a grant of land made to him by the Mexican government'. Lt Minor of *Savannah* knew 'from sources entitled to confidence' that most *californios* expected British protection once 'the British frigate *Juno* landed an English subject named Macnamara, who had obtained as I believe one third of California'. Minor was on shore patrol at Monterey when Frémont's column arrived: 'they made a strong impression on the British admiral and a happier one on the American officers.' USN Lt Rowan, however, wrote from USS *Cyane* of 'filibustering outlaws, insurgents, not a man in California over twelve months', while Lts Walpole and Somerville RN reported from shore to Seymour that they were 'loafers and a lawless gang'.

The Military Committee asked each witness, 'what effect did the Bear Flag revolution have in stopping the sales and grants [by Pico, to keep] missions and public lands out of American hands?' All testified to hasty grants at nominal prices and to Macnamara's being 'conversation in all the intelligent circles of California'. Colonel Russell conjectured, 'I fear Seymour intended to prevent our taking California and, but for Frémont, such would have been the result.'

Frémont was awarded his expenses, but one debt came back to imprison him in London (of all places) in 1852.[28] William B. Ide, Bear Flag leader, did not testify, but accused Frémont of distorting the Flaggers' vision of freedom. Frémont's influence and pen can be seen in the *Memorial* for Statehood presented by Californian representatives, including Frémont in 1850. Its explanation of events in 1846 was evasive to the point of incoherence:

> Settlers in 1845 constituted the basis from which sprang the train of causes which led to the ultimate subjugation of the country [when] a united force of emigrant settlers under Colonel Frémont and naval force under Commodore Sloat raised the US standard.[29]

His father-in-law Benton was more economical: 'California became independent by the revolt [1845] of the Pico [brothers against Micheltorena] and independent of them [the Picos] by the revolt of the American Settlers.'[30] Frémont's activities spurred Sloat on to take California in the absence of instructions, but on 19 July the Commodore was angered to hear Frémont admit he had acted on Washington 'expectations', not orders. Successor to Commodore Jones, Sloat understood political sensitivity. To Captain Du Pont on 6 July 1846 he had acknowledged the huge gamble in taking Monterey without knowing of a state of war, yet 'I prefer being sacrificed for doing too much than too little.' Frémont, however, produced and portrayed Macnamara and Seymour as Goliaths to his David. For 'proof', he cherry-picked the *Proyecto Macnamara* dossier from Pico's captured archive in Los Angeles which the Military Committee appended to its *Report* without comment.

Eight years later, the 'Pathfinder's' biographer declared, 'Macnamara would have put the whole country under British protection. The American flag floated over California in consequence of Frémont's achievements. The whole Macnamara scheme, Irish colony and British protectorate, was scattered to the winds. Frémont secured California and prevented a disastrous collision [with] Great Britain.'[31]

Senator Benton gilded the lily: 'Frémont put himself at the head of the people to save the country from the British. For 200 years [*sic*] British eyes have been on California [and Frémont prevented] transfer of the public domain to British subjects, via consul Forbes and emissary priest Macnamara ruling and conducting everything, their plans so far advanced.'[32] Forty years later, Frémont saluted Macnamara, but when the priest was long dead and the demon had served its purpose.

DEMON MACNAMARA

Eugene Macnamara was reported by John Baldwin to be in Mexico City in Sepember 1847. Rumour had his travelling to Europe 1847–8 and his dying somewhere east of Cape Horn. William Rudall, British consular agent in Guaymas, wrote to José Velasco, the chronicler of Sonora, late in October 1849. He knew one 'Dr Delis, a practical miner', of Mr Whiting's miner group in California, which in July 1849 'was ruined by the strong opposition of Americans to Mexicans, Chileans etc,' in the southern mines. Ithamar Whiting was Barron and Forbes' cotton mill manager at Jauja near Tepic, who had gone or was sent to the goldfields. He and many key workers at the mill were US citizens, as Delis may have been. Delis had written to Rudall from San Francisco where he and others retreated in August from the violence between *latino* and *anglo* miners in the mountains.

Safe back in Guaymas, Delis talked to Rudall in October. He forecast California's population would double by 1850 and gold found would total 'larger than the income of Great Britain'. He had seen the Forbes mercury mine at work, realising a daily profit of $1000 even without mechanisation. His assumption was that heavily dependent California would import food and manufactures from Britain. Rudall reminded Velasco,

> that a tract 70 leagues long [182 miles, 50 per cent understated], was granted by Pío Pico to Fr Macnamara to establish a foreign colony. It runs north to south between the latitudes of Monterey and San Diego, and it will probably lead to litigation, as Dr Delis, a friend of Macnamara, told me. It was granted by Pico before the Americans entered in 1846 and confirmed in Mexico City by President Santa Anna before last year's April [*sic*] armistice [1848]. According to what I have learned, Macnamara is currently in Europe pursuing his claim.[33]

In the first New Almaden appeal hearing, in 1858, James Forbes stated,

> Macnamara is dead, as I have been informed. He died, as I have been told, in 1847, but it must have been later, because in 1847 he left the [west] coast of Mexico and went around Cape Horn. I had intelligence, 1848 or 1849, that he was dead.[34]

Nothing more was heard from Macnamara, for all his threats to 'make mischief', 'pursue his claim' and 'litigate'. Once Mexico lost Alta California, Project Macnamara was irretrievable, a utopian memory, 'no such place'. A Clare priest in the US, Macnamara's contemporary, denied in 1878 that the Macnamara saga had ever happened, and a Franciscan mission chronicler in 1896 accused the dead Frémont of having invented it.

Another Washington appellant invoked Macnamara in 1848. The

rebel Mexican department of Yucatán had declared independence several times since 1821 and the kindred Texas Republic supported it in 1841. It revolted yet again in 1846. As draft peace terms were negotiated between the US and Mexico, Justo Sierra O'Reilly, Yucatán Commissioner to the US, pleaded repeatedly that independent Yucatán was free of Mexico and that the US should be defending it against both Mexico and Britain. The Royal Navy had attacked and blockaded Yucatán, protected the nearby Meskito Kingdom (Belize and Honduras), and armed the native Maya of Yucatán for a race war against the authorities. O'Reilly asked Washington to follow through Polk's 1845 ultimatum against Britain, 'which employs its strength according to any rules other than those of morality', seizing Yucatán ships and threatening to bombard on behalf of the Meskito King. In an attractively wild sketch, he warned that

> The Two Californias and the State of Yucatán were hypothecated for the payment of the English [bondholder] debt [in a] secret treaty in 1836 [*sic*], England to take possession of those countries after a certain lapse of time, since corroborated by certain incidents, not least the authorisation granted by the Mexican government to a certain Irishman, individually, to colonise an immense quantity of square miles in The Californias, the extent of which embraced nearly the whole [*sic*] of those provinces.[35]

O'Reilly's interests chimed with those of the expansionists on the Senate Military Committee, Benton of Missouri, Rusk of Texas, a former independence fighter, and Dix of New York. As Frémont's expense claims were being heard, and with them the revelation of recent British threats and attempts on California, Rusk warned against Britain during a debate over just how much of Mexico the US should retain. Britain, he warned,

> never fails to redress the grievances of the lowliest as well as the proudest of her subjects: British agents are always at work ... for the last 10 or 12 years Mexico has been practically under the control, directly or indirectly, of the British government ... A threefold operation [since 1846] by official or unofficial British agents [has included]

transfers of land from individuals and from churches, a *Junta* summoned by the Governor [to vote] the inhabitants independent of Mexico and on seeking the protection of the British government, a stupendous scheme and been devised by an RC priest named Macnamara ... to secure a grant of 3000 square leagues. He was transported to Monterey by a British national ship. Had it not been for Frémont, California would have belonged at this moment to subjects of Great Britain and the British flag would have been flying on all her forts.[36]

Senator Dix, helpful neighbour and *confidant* of the Bentons, was more judicious. Frémont had kept California 'out of the hands of British subjects and perhaps out of the hands of the British Government'. Dix had conferred with O'Reilly, citing the British on the Meskito Coast where the Isthmus offered suitable levels for a canal. Congress (and Polk) had restricted Monroe to north America, but O'Reillys'concern was central America. Macnamara's scheme, Dix claimed, was typical British expansion, from house, through ditch, fort and colony, to perpetual occupation, of which India and Canada were the results.

Dix criticised the Irishman's 'stigmas cast upon us and on one of our most respectable religious sects'. 'Methodist wolves' had just been published by the Committee in the Macnamara documents appended to the Frémont Claims *Report*. Dix, however, thought it was calculated rhetoric, not Macnamara's belief. He described Macnamara's rapport with the Royal Navy and Pico's hasty grants of May and June 1846 'to British subjects' with legal delicacy. Macnamara was 'so connected with the movement of public vessels and public agents of Great Britain as to raise a strong presumption that he was secretly countenanced by the British government. We are constrained to believe that the British commander was fully appraised of Macnamara's objects and that he was there co-operating.'

He then dropped his guard to tell of the wider conspiracy, what President Jackson had called the 'iron band of British influence around the USA':

The Oregon crisis, the [Meskito] Kingdom and the Macnamara scheme were a deliberate design to surround us with British colonies and to shut us out of the Pacific and its commerce. [In California] the drama of the Meskito Coast would have been re-enacted. A California Governor, above the grade of King of the Meskitos in respectability, but on the same level of subservience, would have been put in the forefront, while British subjects would have occupied the country. Thus shut out from the Pacific, our own people would have been met at the Sierra Madre or further east, and the tide of emigration and settlement been turned back on the Atlantic coast.[7]

GOLD

In January 1848, days before the draft peace treaty conceded Alta California to the US 'in perpetuity', one of Johann Sutter's men found 'goald' in a sawmill race at Coloma on the Rio de Los Americanos. The next river south was Rio Cosumnes, Macnamara's northern boundary. The other gold site, announced in 1842 in San Feliciano canyon, south of Tejon Pass, was on Macnamara's southern boundary. Gold drew immigrants in numbers of which Mexico had only dreamed: the world rushed into empty California in 1848 and stampeded there in 1849.

Word of gold reached the eastern US seaboard in April 1848. The exodus from San Francisco port to the mountain mines began in May, leaving a harbour choked with abandoned ships. Their canvas sails became the raw material for Levi Strauss's working denims. President Polk informed Congress in December of an 'abundance of gold as would scarcely command belief'. The first few thousand miners came from the USA, Hawaii, Mexico, Panama, Peru and notably Chile. Fortune hunters came by sea, overland and across the unhealthy Panama Isthmus. The influx made a transcontinental railway and a canal to the Pacific absolute priorities. The flow of goldseekers swelled to an estimated 90,000 in 1849 and from further afield, China, Australia and Europe. The tidal wave subsided only in the mid-1850s. California's chronic lack of people was resolved and the resulting immigrant mix was likened to flakes and nuggets melting in the heat of a miner's iron smelting pot.

Gold offered only fragile security. The strongest, hardest and luckiest survived, minorities and the weak went under. *Anglo* prejudice against *latinos*, particularly Mexicans and Chileans, showed in San Francisco ghettoes and in the southern mines. Macnamara's and Rudall's friend, Dr Delis, who withdrew from the mountains to San Francisco, did so because of 'strong opposition' and violence, particularly from gangs of discharged American veterans. His mining company leader, Ithamar Whiting, Barron and Forbes' mill manager, died in a San Francisco hospital on 31 August 1849, possibly of injuries.[38] *Chilenos*, the largest ethnic goldseeker minority, also began to return home to Valparaiso. Behind its 3,500 mile long coastline, Chile was barely inhabited and largely unproductive. It had few attractions like gold or mercury to commend it over any other Latin American wasteland, and like Mexican Sonorans, the hopefuls who had left Chile in their thousands for California, late in 1848, were unwittingly depleting their own small population.

After the peace treaty was ratified in May 1848, bankrupt Mexico borrowed honourably from consul MacKintosh to help discharged foreign veterans, but was manoeuvred into paying millions of dollars through him to the British bondholders, which Mexico could ill-afford. California was now out of Macnamara's reach and Mexico had nothing left to offer. Spurred by continuous, relentless famine reports from Ireland, he sailed south to Chile.

Chapter 9

'New Irelands': 1848–52

On 2 February 1848 draft peace terms were signed at Hidalgo in the shadow of the Virgin of Guadalupe Basilica, northern Mexico City. The treaty ceded directly over half a million square miles of Mexico to the US, which already had Texas since 1845, a third of a million square miles more. Alta California was obtained 'in consideration' of $15 million in instalments, with interest, to settle private claims and nearly $3 million of debt. $2.5 million was immediately earmarked for the London Bondholders through deft dealing by consul MacKintosh for a fee of $600,000. Mexican politicians, news editors and British diplomats bayed for his removal. Washington agreed the treaty of Guadalupe-Hidalgo in March, with adjustments; Mexico City agreed in May, and ratifications were exchanged immediately. The Mexican Concession brought to the US more Catholics, *latinos*, abolitionists and resentful Indians; the spread or prevention of slavery in the new territories became a long-burning political issue. Congress was divided over whether to accept California and New Mexico at all, while President-elect Taylor wanted California and Oregon to be independent nations instead, outside the US.

EL PROYECTO MACNAMARA II, CHILE

Macnamara lodged a colony petition in Santiago de Chile, summer 1848. He would have left Mexico *via* Tepic, San Blas or Mazatlán, landing at Valparaiso for Santiago, before perhaps rounding Cape Horn for Europe.

James Forbes testified in 1858 that he heard Macnamara had gone that way in 1847 or 1848. Robert Walkinshaw, who took over managing the New Almaden mine from Forbes, may have told him. William Rudall noted in October 1849 that Dr Delis thought the priest was '*currently* in Europe pursuing his claim', but which claim, and how pursued, was unclear.

Macnamara knew something of Chile. The Picpus Fathers were based on Valparaiso from where Patrick Short, ex-Irish College and Rue Picpus, corresponded with consul Larkin and the Santa Bárbara clergy through the 1840s. Lady Seymour and daughters stayed there during the admiral's tour and navy personnel socialised ashore. On HMT *Palinurus*, Macnamara messed for a month with Lt Cochrane, son of Admiral Thomas Cochrane, British commander of the Chilean Navy during the Independence war. In 1818 as Cochrane sailed to serve under Irish-Chilean *supremo* Bernardo O'Higgins, he considered freeing Napoleon from St Helena to be President of a new South America Federation, based on Valparaiso. A liaison officer found the ex-emperor too ill to consider it.

General William Miller, consul in Honolulu when Macnamara passed through, had been the military commander in Cochrane's seaborne force when they took Valdivia, the last and crucial fortified Spanish port in south America. Seventeen forts commanded the Pacific approach from Cape Horn and hostile Indians inland. Seymour had supported Cochrane when he was wrongfully cashiered and jailed. Lt Somerville had heard Lt Cochrane talk openly about his father, long reinstated and incidentally a Mexican bondholder. Hardly an issue of *El Monitor de Valparaiso* appeared without some article about colonising. Lt Walpole of *Collingwood* who, with Lt Somerville, befriended Macnamara, was nephew to Colonel John Walpole, British consul in Santiago. The British and Irish connection with Chile was historic and pervasive, from Queen Mary Tudor's title 'Queen of Chile' on her marriage to Philip of Spain, to Chile's eighteenth-century Irish leaders and Charles Darwin's Chilean narrative of 1840 which made science a best-seller.[1] (See Map F.)

Chile's coast stretched 3,500 miles to Cape Horn, its hinterland no more than 150 miles deep and its hispanic population largely located between Coquimbo and Concepción. After independence, a civil war and a campaign to drive the Mapuche (Araucanian) Indians to the edge of their homeland, the new republic enjoyed a peace which Mexico did not. Frontiers remained fluid, the far south consolidated in 1843, the north only decades later after a war with Peru; the eastern mountain belt bordering Bolivia and La Plata (Argentine Federation) took longer to stabilise. Chile had empty wastelands, but its borrowing through London bondholders of £1 million had been a far cry from Mexico's £6.5 million.

In July 1837, as Mexico offered to sell land to its Bondholders, the US *chargé d'affaires* in Santiago, warned that Britain 'in all likelihood' would purchase the Chilean bondholder claims in London of about £4 million ($10 million *pesos*) 'and get the cession of Chiloé Island in payment' of the claims.[2] He warned 'It would give England great advantages over us in our intercourse with the Pacific and power in this sea which, in case of war between us, might be seriously felt by us.' In the background lurked John Diston Powles, leading Mexican and Spanish American bondholder. Chile's mining of silver, copper and nitrate had suffered, like Mexico's mining, in the London financial slump of the 1820s, but after that, Chile looked to industrialise and colonise. President Manuel Bulnés turned to Europe in the 1840s for Spanish recognition, for academics to found a university, and for colonisers. He regretted that 20,000 Catholics left Europe each year from Germany, Britain and Ireland, but none came to Chile.

In 1845, Congress allocated him an 8000-square mile colonising zone in Western Patagonia. It was largely temperate rainforest, yet advertised as deforested lakeland. The access ports, Valdivia and Ancud (on Chiloé), had never served the hinterland as trails were few and navigable rivers even fewer. The Valdivia–Osorno *camino real* had not been maintained for forty years, since the last Irish settler left Osorno or died. Each year on 1 June, Bulnés promised Congress an infrastructure, roads, canals, ports and a steamship line (one vessel appeared in 1851) to link Concepción, Valdivia and Chiloé with Valparaiso, but it was grand vision in slow motion. Osorno would be the supply depot and urban focus for Irish and German communities, with river gold and cheap Indian labour as added attractions. In July, 1848, outline approval was given for a German settlement, and instructions followed in August. Its recruiting *empresario*, Bernardo Philippi, Berlin-born, a naturalist and a Protestant, left for Germany in December and his first recruits arrived in 1849.

In October, just before Chilean newspapers broke the California gold news, Manuel Vial, Foreign and Interior minister, issued detailed instructions to 'Don Eujenio [*sic*] Macnamara' previously 'comisionado' to settle 3,500 Irish families east and south of Osorno.[3] This decayed city was known to the Irish whose folk memory was partly shaped by Spanish exile. In the eighteenth century, many Irish 'wild geese' settled in Spain and its empire. Ambrosio O'Higgins from Sligo, after working with John Garland, Irish-born Governor of Valdivia, became the last Captain-General of Chile, and was created Marquis of Osorno for rebuilding the derelict city in 1792. He appointed Juan Maqena [MacKenna] of Drogheda its governor in 1796, and in 1798 two dozen Irish artisans trickled into New Osorno with skills to offer, but their contribution died with them. Ambrosio's son, Bernardo, ordered Cochrane to dislodge the Spanish from Valdivia's forts in 1820, and created him Marquis of Valdivia in thanks. Bernardo became Supreme Director of a virtually independent Chile in 1817, but five years later was overthrown by *ranchero* landowners, while still urging both Chile and Mexico to take Irish colonists. In March 1848, while en route home, Admiral Seymour took HMS *Spy* inshore to inspect Valdivia, Corral ('one of the best anchorages on the coast … unsilted since Fitzroy surveyed'), and to probe Osorno department, a 'most fertile' hinterland of 'fine woods, but scant population'. Darwin had described the landscape scientifically and dispassionately, but it was no more attractive for that: high forest, hard cane stem undergrowth, tree-trunk trackways, lake shores of black volcanic sand, and pervasive damp from heavy rainfall which hindered clearing by fire.

Manuel Vial's instructions to Macnamara were brisk. 500 Irish families (2,500 persons), would embark in Scotland.[4] Farmers and rural artisans would colonise the 'lake district' near New Osorno, twenty-five acres for each father, for each son over 10 years of age, and for a daughter as a dowry, but 100–150 acres per family was a far cry from the 4,428 acre lots of *Los Tulares*. Phillippi's Germans would have slightly larger plots than the Irish, direct entry through Ancud, provisions, a priest guide to Reloncavi Bay, a road to Lake Llaniquhue, and a ferry to bring livestock from Osorno. That was the brochure. The lake road, promised annually to Congress, was still unlaid in 1858, by which time 800 Germans had settled (see Plate 14).

As in Mexico, the Irish settlers had to take *chileno* citizenship. Chile would salary two priests ($329 *pesos* each p.a.), two teachers versed in Spanish ($200 *pesos* each p.a.), and a doctor ($500 *pesos*, p.a.), all with 42-acre bonuses. Each colonist would pay $15 *pesos* per five acres towards travel, initial subsistence and seed, stock and tools purchased in Ireland. The fund would be administered by a committee chaired by the priests, and accounts would be audited. It was nearer Wakefield's vision of community than Pico's 'bastion', but it was never El Dorado or Val de Paraiso.

As Macnamara considered his instructions, a serious criminal conspiracy was uncovered. 3,000 Chileans already held *ranchos* in the colonising zone on land seized from the Mapuche Indians. Colluding with speculators from Valparaiso and Osorno they forged claims to land adjoining their holdings, to sell to settlers at inflated prices. They lorded over what Guillermo Frick called [their] 'unsurveyed islands in a fiscal lake' and beyond them. Policing and settling Osorno department with its resentful Indians, overgrown landmarks and absence of roads, was impossible enough, without this new discouragement.[5]

An announcement that independent colonists would be allowed to settle alongside contract colonists inflated prices further. 'Not a single inch of land [existed] without some imaginary owner,' complained *Intendente* Vicente Rosales in 1849. Word of the fraud spread to Europe, making it harder to recruit Germans to what Rosales had already disparaged as the 'vast fog-shrouded region of Valdivia [with its] primaeval forests and hamlets: forgotten Valdivia, La Union, a half executed sketch of a town, and Osorno, heaped rows of overgrown dirt'. The US was always attractive and California gold made it more so to the Chileans who settled the 'southern mines' in and around Frémont's Las Mariposas grant. In 1850 the Chilean press indicted the toothless colonising programme for its empty boasts. Local people feared cheap labour and Protestants; German settlers faced opposition at home to emigration on principle: Catholic bishops opposed a Protestant *empresario*, Protestant politicians feared a Catholic destination; both warned of Osorno's *mato grosso* isolation. Nevertheless settlers continued to arrive from Germany, cleared the forest and left their mark long-term, but no Irish had appeared by 1850, let alone by October 1852. After years of famine and with little capital, Irish settlers might have baulked, even had they wanted to volunteer.[6]

Nothing is known of Macnamara's movements between Chile 1848 and his arrival in France in December 1851–January 1852. President Bulnés' address to Congress, 1 June 1849, trumpeted 'favourable accounts from commissioners sent to Europe to promote immigration of colonists to Valdivia [and] missions of Valdivia entrusted to newly arrived missioners from Europe' which may have included *misionero Apostólico* Macnamara and his two contracted priests, as well as Protestant missioners leading other groups. Bulnés, however, was known for trumpeting. Macnamara may have gone to Ireland in 1849 to recruit, as Philippi went to Germany six months after his instructions. Inflation, cholera and revolution convulsed Chile, 1849–51 and California gold drew Chileans to emigrate; Macnamara may also have begun to sicken after years of stress. Suddenly, in March 1851, Washington offered a new and unexpected deadline, which may have raised his hopes or added to his stress.

CALIFORNIA TITLES: FLAWED OR FRAUD?

The gold seekers swamped California, 'as if the world rushed in'. The Mexican-bequeathed civil administration under a US military governor was overwhelmed. Wrangling in Washington log-jammed all decisions about the status of California and other ex-Mexican departments. Congress never accepted California unanimously, but after the gold rush California law and order became a pressing political priority. Hundreds of thousands of new arrivals (100,000 by 1850, 300,000 by 1852) clashed with each other, and with 8,000 pre-war, pre-gold settlers, over land and gold claims on unsurveyed territory.

In theory, Mexican property titles were safe under US rule. The Treaty promised 'Property shall be inviolably respected' (*Article 8*). However, 'all grants of land made by the Mexican government shall be respected as valid' (*Article 10*), was deleted in the US ratification as too sweeping and lax. In its place the US negotiated a Protocol: 'Grants ... which were legitimate titles under Mexican law in California ... up to 13 May 1846 ... preserve the legal value which they may possess' (*Protocol of Queretaro, 2*), which paved the way for re-scrutiny in the future.

Mexican frontier administration had to be pragmatic given poor communications, few lawyers, no surveyors and lack of franked paper. To depart from the letter of Mexican law was not necessarily to reject its spirit or to act in bad faith, but it did leave *californios* open to criticism by outsiders. Conquerors read 'customary' as 'fraudulent', and preferred their own 'tidier' Anglo-Saxon tradition.

Between 1833 and 1843 an average of fifty-three land grants a year were made in Alta California by Governors with the Assembly. In 1844 it leapt to 122. Pío Pico, the first *californio* and last Mexican Governor, conveyed a *finale* of 146 grants (2.5 million acres), some even after US occupation. In 1847 John Frémont acquired from ex-Governor Alvarado the Las Mariposas grant, between the Rios San Joaquin and Merced, rising to Yosemite. It 'floated' inside Macnamara's concession frame. Title to Las Mariposas land and minerals was challenged by goldseekers working in the new 'Southern Mines'. Frémont persuaded the US Senate Military Committee in his California Claims hearing that Pío Pico had disposed of land, hurriedly and corruptly in the last months of Alta California, yet Pico had a governor's duty to populate and defend California, but lacked the people and money to carry it out. The money from grants was virtually his only administrative revenue and he expressed shame that often he did not even receive that, nor had he even been paid as Governor. He certainly had nothing from Macnamara.[7]

Frémont's testimony to the Senate Committee coincided with the draft peace treaty and the seismic California gold find. The draft treaty's respect for all pre-War Mexican grants was reduced, perhaps understandably, to pitting the spirit of Mexican frontier legal practice against the spirit and letter of Mexican legislation, but at least not against alien US law. Two years later, as land disputes intensified, it was argued that the new California State's authority might be strengthened by a judicial review of all land held under Mexican titles. Land also entitled owners to vote.

California was a constitutional no-man's land, 1848–50, a military governor and staff overseeing a kaleidoscope of law administered through local mayors. It would have worked, had California remained the empty outpost of 1846, or under full US military occupation, but that stopped with the treaty and the instant population drawn in by gold. Abolitionist and slavery lobbies made it impossible for Congress to agree even Territory status for California, let alone Statehood. Battle was joined over how far the whole Mexican Concession would line up over slavery. Texas had led the way, freed from Mexico's ban. Ironically, President Polk, driven to acquire California and desperate for it to be secured by Statehood, was helpless before a tied Congress rejecting all compromise.

To add to his troubles, on 30 September 1848 *The New York Herald* reproduced a letter written in August by Senator Benton 'to the people of California' through the press. It prompted five hours of Cabinet discussion. Benton exhorted Californians to call a convention and form an independent government with Frémont as governor, until a decision from Congress. Creaking laws, expired military edicts from the likes of Kearny (Benton's *bête noir*) and others, were not helping and their current status was a constitutional fiction. Polk thought the letter 'Arrogant, offensive and calculated to do much mischief', suspecting yet another Benton family conspiracy. Cabinet called it 'a revolutionary movement' and Polk feared another 'California republic' (*sic*) which he amended immediately to 'Pacific republic'. Two envoys reached California with the President's counterblast in February 1849, but too late. The new *Alta California* published Benton's rallying call in January.

In March 1849, Henry Halleck, California Secretary and uniformed ADC to Governor Mason, reported on increasingly chaotic and fraudulent land claims.[8] Mason's successor, Governor Riley, cut through the Washington *impasse* by calling a Constitutional Convention on his own authority to 'organise civil government and establish social institutions'. Elected in August, forty-eight delegates convened at Monterey. Frémont's brother-in-law and court martial defence lawyer, William Carey Jones, in California to make a report for the US Land Office on title chaos, joined father-in-law Benton, Secretary Halleck and a wide spectrum of the great, the good, former enemies, and the ambitious. The optimism was tangible. Frémont observed, but took no part, devoting time to a sick wife. Polk's fears of a Benton family *coup d'etat* in the west were not realised. The world moved on from the Benton era, and ex-*Comandante* Castro was spotted in Monterey, keeping a low profile but looking miserable. Baia California compensated with openings for him, Pico and Bandini, who had all invested there when Mexico sold off the missions and opened it to colonisers.

Thirty-six delegates made for a quorum at Colton Hall. Six *californios* attended, including General Vallejo, the Bear Flaggers' hostage, Captain Carillo, whose lancers savaged US forces at San Pascual (he co-owned Santa Cruz island under spurious 'British protection'), and his brother-in-law José Covarrubias, a Híjar-Padrés colonist. *Anglos* included ex-consul and Presidential agent, Thomas Larkin, merchant Abel Stearns, Hugo Reid the Scottish rancher at San Gabriel cited by Frémont as a British conspirator, and Johann Sutter, Swiss coloniser. Robert Semple presided, a giant ex-Bear Flagger complete with coonskin hat. No Indians were represented, save one mixed race (*mestizo*) delegate who later lost his citizen status. *Latino* and *anglo* delegates alike warned against excluding Indians from their homeland yet again, already displaced once by colonial invasion and more recently expelled by Mexico from their mission tenancies. Thirty six delegates, however, came from the eastern US states and the Convention was a child of its time: Indians, along with Africans and women were ruled out from franchise or citizenship, which was exclusive to white US males, although a last-minute possibility was agreed that individual Indians might be considered. From the outset, slavery was firmly excluded.

Delegates were generally united by possibilities and few topics were barred. Prayer was led on alternate days by the *padre* from Carmel (Friar Serra's burial place) and a US Congregationalist minister. Halleck produced a *Digest of Laws* to explain discrepancies between US, Mexican and frontier legal cultures. The assembly looked beyond topical concerns about population and land, to taxation, to sharing territory with New Mexico, and at census-taking and education. Gold, a population dream come true, and a beef trade (not just hides) fuelled the general optimism. Semple boasted during the education debate that gold allowed California to buy the 'President [*sic*] of Oxford University'. A poll in November chose William Gwin, veteran of the Texas Republic congress, and John Frémont, as Senators-elect, the slaver and the abolitionist respectively. Gwin's rise to influence was meteoric, a devout Methodist of Welsh descent, who spotted and grasped a career opening in the new California. He voted against slavery, although against his grain, and delegates made the point that California's extended dry heat would make plantations economically and practically impossible.

Statehood came in September 1850 when Congress adopted and President Taylor supported a compromise initiated by Senator Clay and taken to conclusion by Senator Douglas. It postponed the slavery decision piecemeal throughout the Mexican Concession. California would become an abolitionist State immediately. Nevada, Oregon, Arizona, Utah and New Mexico (then including Arizona) would become Territories, with self-determination about slavery guaranteed when eventually they became States. Texas remained a slaver, its debts assumed by Washington, and the Fugitive Slave law was strengthened, (prohibiting sanctuary for slaves on the run throughout the US). Britain was accused of offering slaves asylum in British North America (Canada) and long-distance exhortation to slaves to rise against their owners.

IF MACNAMARA HAD PRESENTED…?

Slavery was Washington's issue, California's was land rights. William Carey Jones reported to Washington and once seated at their Senate desks, Frémont and Gwin competed to devise a new law. Jones' report on Mexican law in Alta California argued that procedures which seemed irregular to outsiders were customary here, dictated by frontier circumstances. Technically 'defective' grants were incomplete, not illegal; back-dating, relay-witnessing, unfranked paper, and lack of sketch maps were acceptable in such extreme circumstances. Senators Benton and Frémont supported Jones and his light touch. Frémont proposed that if any land commission ruled against a Mexican title, only the claimant, not the new settler, should have the right to appeal, but his Bill failed and with it his Senate career. Senator Gwin took a strict line and his California Land Act was adopted in March 1851.[9] July 7 1846, when Sloat took Monterey, was recognised as the terminal date for Pico's authority to make grants to townships and from that, it was tacitly assumed to apply to all grants. The date 13 May 1846, when war became formal, which was laid down in the Querétaro Protocol, was quietly shelved. The communications lapse was bridged.

Jones' report had clarified the role of a Mexican governor, authorised since 1833 to use 'all measures to assure colonisation and the secularising [dissolving] of the missions [properties]'.[10] A governor could grant eleven square leagues to an individual, but could also contract and convey larger tracts to colonisers, with Assembly agreement, on condition that he submitted them to Supreme Congress for confirmation, as Pico did for Macnamara. In May 1847, the Congressional *Comisión* for Colonising found Pico's conveyance defective, but remedied it because defence was his priority and he had sought ultimate confirmation from Mexico City. It worked both ways. Commissioner Castillero had not submitted the Santa Clara mine claim to Governor Pico, yet Supreme Congress confirmed the colonising land and bonus which came with it. The unremedied irregularity came back to haunt the mine owners after Gwin's Bill put a limit on how much 'frontier untidiness' was acceptable. The New Almaden title was eventually declared void.

A US California Land Commission was formed to judge land titles up to 7 July 1846 against Mexican law. Defects and untidy procedure characterised many grants, but did not make them fraudulent. Concepts introduced by Jones and others of 'inchoate ownership', 'incipient rights' and 'rudimentary entitlements', were accepted by the Land Commission. Jones insisted 'the great Macnamara grant *or contract* of which the principal papers are on file in the State Department', was a conveyance, not a grant. It was so vast it could not be measured with a yard (*vara*) chain and unmeasured land could not be mapped, save by a list of visual landmarks. Unprecedented in California, its 15,000 Irish settlers would have trebled the settler population of 1846.

While Jones' report tempered the harshest judgements, Senator Gwin's Bill still required all pre-1846 landowners to prove title, or forfeit, leaving a cloud of suspicion over all Mexican titles. The Bill came into force on 1 March 1851, after which claims were due before a three-man panel in San Francisco or at San José between 2 January 1852 and 1 March 1856. New Almaden, the only mine claim, was presented in September, but dragged on until declared void in 1863. Three quarters (604) of the 813 titles presented, were validated, 190 rejected, and 19 withdrawn. Validation, usually after appeal, took on average seventeen years and many petitioners gave up, bankrupted by legal fees, interest on loans and land lost to mortgage or sale to meet mounting debt. Blatantly forged titles were declared forfeit, like the Limantour ranch claim in Central Valley, drawn up in Mexico City in 1852 by *californio* conspirators and supported by the perjury of ex-Congressman Castañares. Fraud reinforced anti-hispanic prejudice; failure to locate a paper trail from times when paper was simply not available undermined many claims. Destiny was never far away: Senator Benton described Gwin's Land Commission as 'redemption' for those whom Manifest Destiny had decreed conquered.

Had Macnamara presented to the Land Commission, *Los Tulares* would have been closely scrutinised and courtroom drama guaranteed. His paper trails led straight to Mexican Presidents, Supreme Congress and the US Senate. Lawyers could have demonstrated that Pico's apparent backdating, '4 July' for '7 July', confirmed 12/13 July, was no subterfuge, but down to secretarial procedure. News of war or even of occupation had not reached Reina de Los Angeles on 7 July 1846; the Assembly was unhurried and its procedures minuted, dated and lawful.

Pico had given careful consideration to his final conveyance. The Land Commission and later appeal courts validated grants lacking the required sketch maps, but the size of Macnamara's conveyance was unique, and by 1852 positively quaint given the flow of immigrants into California.

Unique or outdated was still not illegal or fraudulent. New Almaden was unique, but not rejected for that reason. The Mexican time limit placed on Macnamara in 1847, to produce colonists by the summer of 1852, was automatically annulled by the conquest of California, but unexpectedly revived by the creating of the new Land Commission and its deadline. It allowed Macnamara the possibility of realising his *Proyecto*, even if in reduced form. 'They are limited to what land is found', was as binding in any review of Macnamara's contract title as when Pico stipulated it in his conveyance.

IRELAND'S EXODUS

In 1850, the new California State had a population of at least 100,000, ever-rising and already thirteen times the settler population of 1846. It dwarfed the confirmed colonies of Híjar-Padrés, Sutter and Macnamara. Boundaries were drawn by teams of US and Mexican surveyors turning the customary landmarks of Mexican departments into a US State and several US Territories.

Settlers, including British and Irish, rushed in before Macnamara would or could ever have recruited his '6000 ready volunteers from Cork, Clare, Limerick and Tipperary', let alone taken them to the Pacific. The Irish who came for California's gold had usually acclimatised back east or in Canada. Few refugees landing in the eastern USA direct from Ireland could have faced the trek west, the breaking of soil, fighting Indian raiders, and restarting life in such remoteness and extremes of climate.

In 1842, *The Emigration and Colonial Gazette* (published by the CLEC) castigated America as 'a charnel house of humanity'. It advertised alternative settlements at San Patricio and on the Red River in the Texas Republic. In 1849, *The Emigrant* acknowledged California with a crude map and an uncanny forecast. 'A new nation is suddenly planted where we thought solitude would reign. [Before gold] California's attractions went unheeded. Now all the products of the USA, apples, oranges, potatoes and sugarcane may soon be produced in the valleys of the San Joaquin and the Sacramento.' The frame in which Macnamara's concession floated later came to include the Southern Mines, Yosemite, 'Laguna Tulares', the Central Valley fruit and vegetable ranches, and even Hollywood.[11]

The Irish Famine was entering its third year when Santa Anna endorsed Project Macnamara in 1847. Irish and Scots emigrants often followed a priest or minister and passages were advertised through parishes and newspapers. Emigrants crowded the roads to the ports. In Clare, evicted tenants crowded the Limerick road to embark:

> Women and children sat on beds and boxes with swollen eyes and wet cheeks, while with downcast looks old and young men marched slowly by their sides. On the morning of the sailing of the emigrant ships, along the roads as far as the eye could see, came trains of carts after travelling all night, often in rain.

Policemen were devastated by what they saw, but constables did not always have the Gaelic. Macnamara's brother John served with the Irish Constabulary in western Ireland throughout the Famine. Evidently they corresponded. On Fridays, hungry Catholic peasants on the move were ashamed to take meat offered by well-meaning Protestants on the roadside. Provocatively, Scottish troops were quartered on Ennis, where there was literally no stomach for revolt. The vessels which took the refugees to the US and Canada were called 'coffin ships'.[12]

Travel agents in market towns asked the clergy to explain sailing timetables to parishioners, but the clergy were divided over emigration. Michael Comyn begged the Famine Relief Commission to develop Doonbeg, Killard, whose people would be 'better on the unprofitable wastes of their own native land than compelled to emigrate to some hostile distant country to swell the ranks of Britain's enemies'.[13] Comyn could not win. The London *Times*, no friend of the Famine Irish, accused clergy like him of protecting their populist power base. Friar Mathew feared emigrants would be 'lost in large cities'; some clergy discerned a plot to decimate and disperse the Irish, others, particularly in Limerick, urged emigrants on to a new life.

At the receiving end, in the colonies and the US, Irish immigration was seen as a Papal plot or as Britain's dumping of its unwanted. In 1850 Bishop Goold of Melbourne thanked the Queen publicly for overriding local opposition and re-settling 4,000 Famine orphans, mainly girls. Some churchmen strained credulity to make sense of losing the young and their energy, 'a scattering of the blessings of Catholicism over distant lands'. In desolate Butte, Montana they were reminded by their priest that exile was their 'via dolorosa'; in California, another pastor called it their 'terrestrial Paradise'. A Kenmare priest, begged by parishioners to take them to America, could not face it. The abbot of Mount Melleray considered moving the abbey to Iowa and an advance party of monks embarked. A Wexford priest organised his parish in groups of 300 to lead them to Arkansas, but lost control of the first group at Liverpool. A Carlow priest founded the Leinster Emigration Society, advertising for colonists to found 'New Carlow on the Mississippi': they did not even reach Liverpool. By the 1850s, these priests, occasionally eccentric, sometimes unworldly-wise, generally honourable and desperate for their people, were a dated species, helpless on a tide. A colony went to Andalucia, a group headed for Lima, the Argentine colony of La Plata was generally welcoming, but nomadic rural colonies were in decline. The exodus of individuals and families, largely rural, to urban industrial destinations and not wide vastnesses, was a growing reality. Priests could neither explain it away, nor prevent it, only share it.[14]

MACNAMARA'S LAND

Mark Twain's early newspaper career took him to the most inhospitable parts of California and Nevada. He forecast that the inhabitants of Central Valley, on reaching Hell, would beg the Devil for blankets. Today agribusiness has earned it the sobriquets 'Factories in The Fields' and 'Garden of the Sun'. In 1846, hostile Indians, mosquitoes, elk and mustang were almost its only inhabitants, and a handful of settlers. Some thirty land grants on either side of the San Joaquin and to its south, mixed speculation with defence.

When the California Land Commission asked former Governor Alvarado in 1852 if he had thought it 'safe or expedient' before July 1846 to occupy 'Las Mariposas on the San Joaquin, because of Indian depredations' he was unequivocal. 'It was not safe or possible.' He had not even been able to select, survey and stake out his floating entitlement. Lt Walpole RN saw Indian attacks near Monterey: 'Mexican rule could not protect against increasingly bold Indian aggression.' Frémont bought Las Mariposas from Alvarado in 1847, but told the Land Commission in 1853 that it was still 'too dangerous for occupation until nearly the present day, in constant danger of destruction'. By then the US had held California for seven years.

As late as 1830, most of San Joaquin Valley was thought to be wetland, hence the name *Los Tulares*, 'Tule Marshes', for Macnamara's concession.[15] Early Spanish scouts named the two Central Valley rivers after the Sacrament and St Francis, but folklore conflated them into one fictional 'Rio Buenaventura' (a thirteenth-century friar Cardinal) emptying from the Sierras into the Pacific through San Francisco Bay. Place names came from the feast day on or near which an explorer made a sighting, or from *sierra* and *pampa* landscapes reminiscent of Spain.

The Franciscan missioners came from San Blas along with Alta California's first, belated colonisers in 1769, but their first task was literally to ship out the Jesuits from the twenty missions which they had run in Baia since 1697. In 1767 the King of Spain expelled Jesuits from all his territory (Portugal had already done so), and the Pope dissolved the whole Society soon afterwards. Junípero Serra's friars founded one new mission in Baia, then headed north while Dominican friars occupied the Jesuit missions and added nine of their own. In Alta California, the Franciscans founded twenty-one missions over the next half century, from San Diego to Sonoma. The British invasion which Spain feared and which brought the missioners and soldiers there in the first place, did not materialise.

Mission strategy was to establish a base, win over and civilise the Indians, then move on, allowing each mission to grow into a European-style parish ministered by secular priests. A whole countryside of matured missions would become a European-style diocese, the one model European missioners knew. Alta California extended far to the east, which the Baia peninsula patently did not, but the coast-bound missions in Alta never left the coastal strip to expand east. All missions had unmanned *asistencias* or sub-missions with chapels and storehouses, like European chapels-of-ease. San Gabriel's *asistencias* lay the furthest east of all, but a proposed mission at Castaic *asistencia* near Tejon Pass, was abandoned, and the specific 1834 plan to make San Bernardino, the easternmost *asistencia* by the Mojave Trail, a mission, came too late.

'If the Mexican republic had been bred in peace, California might have had a new chain of missions in the very heart of paganism' wrote Padre Duran, mission president, to Mexico City in 1837.[16] An outreach was planned at San Juan Bautista, but Indian hostilities stayed it at the point of piled bricks. Several missions interacted with and baptised Valley Indians; San José, Santa Clara and Solano missions called themselves 'the

Gentile frontier'. Finally, Rome elevated The Californias into a bishopric in 1840 and freed it from the Mexican Sonora diocese. Macnamara had the support of the primate of Mexico, but it was Pío Pico, born and bred at San Gabriel Mission, who remoulded Macnamara's land to meet defence needs, colonisers' dreams while retaining a whisper of the former church aspiration to go east.

Governor Alvarado had owned Las Mariposas east of the Rio San Joaquin. Frémont had reconnoitred from Sutter's Fort south to *La Porziuncula* and *Tres Reyes*, (half Macnamara's concession frame) and wintered near Laguna Tulares. Macnamara's contract was for ill-defined, undeveloped land, which his colonists would have to break and defend. William Kelly from Sligo did not think much of it, despite Frémont's 'timbered mild and genial', and settler John Marsh's 'very inviting field for emigration'. Kelly thought Lansford Hastings' description of 'a great extent of fine country' was hype. It had 'only a few highly favoured localities where wheat might be raised if peopled with enterprising settlers from the old country, but I saw no grain and heard only vague missionary traditions of its having once been grown there'. Los Tulares, he concluded, was fit only for rice, wild horses and a little vine culture. Frémont, however, spoke from experience as did Dr Coulter who in 1835 judged San Bernardino *rancho* 'the only point south of San Francisco [Bay] capable of sustaining a large population'.

Had all Macnamara's 3,000 families gone to Central Valley and the San Gabriel extension, they would have run out of land. The 3,000 unsurveyed square leagues (13,284,000 acres, 20,280 square miles) were allocated at one square league (4,428 acres, 6.8 square miles) per family. The floating concession frame, extending fifty-two miles east of the San Joaquin and north-west to south-east from Rio Cosumnes to Tejon Pass, and on to San Bernardino amounted at most to about 75 per cent of Pico's final 'gesture' award. Wetlands at their wettest took away hundreds of square miles as did ranches granted before Macnamara's time, vacant Mexican plots between Irish plots, not to mention the twenty-six-mile coastal belt closed to foreign colonies. There was not enough land in the entire frame to meet Macnamara's conveyance and Pico knew it would fall short. Accordingly, he declared, settlers 'must be content'.

Shadow-Senators Frémont and Gwin reported to Congress in March 1850 that California had at most 62,820 square miles of arable and pasture land, mainly in 'the two great [central] valleys and the small lateral valleys that pierce their rugged sides', the Sacramento and the San Joaquin valleys. Lt Minor of USS *Savannah* described the 20,280 square mile Irish grant to the Senate Military Committee in 1848 with curiously coincidental accuracy as '*one third* of the richest portion of California'.

PLOUGHSHARE AND SWORD

Macnamara's Irish were to defend the unpopulated belt between Sutter's 'New Helvetia' and Bandini's 'San Salvador', but they were not Wellington's or Bolivar's veterans. No Mexican regulars garrisoned California. William Hartnell's *Compania Estranjera* at Monterey in 1832 was a scratch militia; Castro's standby militia was threadbare and Iniestra's relief column never arrived. The danger from the Indians was real and Macnamara deluded himself that they were divided and 'harmless'. At the Weber (Stockton) ranch in 1847 settlers built houses in a brick and timber fort formation. Others built blockhouse homes, with rifle ports, and fortified bunkhouses. One ranch fired a cannon at night like a crowscarer. Corrals for cattle and fences for crops were a priority as the Indians rustled both. Bandini's San Salvador was founded to help protect stock. The US later concentrated the Indians into a Central Valley reservation and, after a serious revolt in 1853, transferred them to another near New Tejon Pass.

Arable, watered valleys were an Irish smallholder's dream. Vicente Rosales, Chilean *Intendente* for the 'two closed valleys' of Osorno, rated them 'comparable with the valleys of California, in a permanent springtime'. Valleys, however, had to be cleared and defended against the Indians from whom they were taken. Supreme Director of Chile, Bernardo O'Higgins, agreed to settle Irish colonists on his property south of Rio Biobio (Concepción) in 1825, but nothing happened and the Indians retained it. 'The poor Irishman will not find the climate superior to his own and will soon find that he must hold the ploughshare in one hand and his sword in the other' warned a British Consul.[17] From exile, O'Higgins sounded President Vitoria of Mexico to take Irish settlers, 'beginning with California, then continuing with Texas: the first colony should be established in San Francisco Bay, California'. Mexico had already put out feelers. Vitoria's silence spurred O'Higgins: 'I still believe the leaders of Mexico will approve as they understand the importance of colonisation by such industrious and brave people, who will [defend] that nation against Russians and North Americans.' (See Plate 16.)

John Diston Powles with Robert Crichton Wyllie pressed London bondholders until 1846 to take up the California land offer. Powles' greatest failure, the Topo river settlement in Venezuela, Gran Colombia, in 1826, had been well-organised, but ill-briefed, despite its ventilated ships, games for children and Spanish lessons for the adults. A Scots pastor and doctor led thirty families, shepherds, shopkeepers, weavers, a blacksmith, joiner and gardener; 140 lodged in a company long house, two rooms and separate entrances per family, a transit hostel for future arrivals, but 300 Irish settlers simply failed to appear on a second site. The British consul monitored from Caracas and crop talk was of indigo, cotton and coffee, but a year later, goats ruled. The pastor-*Intendente* burned himself out; they cleared and cultivated 120 acres, but the soil was toxic and clean water five miles distant. Powles' Columbia Agricultural Company, which had formed the Colombia Immigration Society to bring 300,000 immigrants, disowned its settlers and left Topo to the weeds. In 1843 Macnamara had seen Powles' second failure under the Tropical Emigration Company in Guiana.[18]

Powles, Wyllie and Macnamara lacked investment and publicity, their timing was bad and they were identified with the British government. The US taking of 55 per cent of Mexican territory in 1848 ended bondholder dreams of colonising. William Robertson, fact-finding in Mexico for the bondholders that year, was advised by George Robinson, chairman of Spanish American bondholders, and Powles his deputy: 'There is no objection [here in London] to making new deferred bonds recoverable in payment for land, should any bondholders be inclined to buy land in Mexico. The provinces should be specified on the bond.' Robertson, on the spot, was more upbeat: 'Mexico should be to England a place of planting colonies without the expense of keeping them. There is room for ten times its population,' but Mexico never repeated its offer.

In 1863, chairing the South American Bondholders committee, and advocating a similar land option in New Granada, Powles regretted publicly the bondholders' loss:

California was one of the places specified in part satisfaction of Bondholders claims [in 1837] and warrants were issued.

The Bondholders failed to organise to take up those lands. They trusted to a chapter of accidents to give – one day a [cash] value to their bonds. California subsequently fell into the hands of the United States, and the British Bondholders lost out by not having taken possession when they might have done without hindrance. They would by this time [1863] have had ample indemnity [gold 1848–55] for all the debt arrears they would have given up to the Mexican government. Let not that lesson be lost.[9]

Like Mexico and Chile, New Granada, (Colombia), had assigned 4.3 million acres of unpopulated land to offset its bond debt. In 1850, Dr Edward Cullen, of mirage survey fame, recommended it to Irish newspaper readers.[20] He advised sawmills to clear forests, and the growing of cotton, coffee and cocoa in a climate 'corresponding to Demerara', where his priest brother John served in Macnamara's time. He assured recruits of military protection, and proximity to a river or town. An Irish priest had assured him, 'all that is needed is gentlemen officers, a mason, carpenter and blacksmith. The rest would be native labour'. In 1863, through John Diston Powles, New Granada invited its bondholders to choose 1.5 million acres below the Colombian Sierra Nevada, from which snowmelt watered rich soil. Fifty British families would occupy temporary housing in the foothills in the sowing season. Claims would be confirmed after five years, once everyone arrived. The colony would then clear the plain for tobacco, cocoa, coffee, sugar and cotton, in a location uncannily like the San Joaquin Valley and foothills, but more evenly watered and in a temperate climate. Bondholders would profit within ten years.

In 1851, as Macnamara weighed his options and perhaps his health, Bishop James Goold sailed from Australia to Ireland by way of South America. He was curious about the ex-colonial Spanish church adrift among the new republics of Latin America. At Callao, he noted:

Emigration from Ireland to Peru had long occupied attentions and is now on the eve of being tried. As to its success, I am not sanguine. The Irish labourer has little sympathy to expect from a Government unsettled and jealous of strangers, a serious disadvantage; a strong settled government [is] necessary to the welfare of the poor and struggling colonist, on whom the unprincipled ... are disposed to [prey]. Again, the climate is very trying on constitutions accustomed to the moderate summers of Europe.[21]

The *Los Tulares* Irish were to be in place by June 1852, the Osorno Irish by October 1852. Mexican US California titles had to be submitted for judgement from January 1852. It was a year of deadlines, but by then, more Irishmen than Macnamara could have imagined, including gold and silver miners from Wicklow and Tipperary, had made California their home. Discrete rural national colonies gave way to the melting pot, strangers from different countries levelled by the fresh starts and new horizons of California, the Irish among them in strength, certainly, but no longer in agricultural colonies.

Chapter 10
Death and Requiem: 1852

At the turn of the year 1851–52, Eugene Macnamara landed at a French port, possibly Le Havre, 'on his way home, when he took ill'.[1] A new railway joined Le Havre to Paris, a hundred miles away.

DEATH

He died in Paris on 19 January 1852, days after the US Land Commission convened in California. A greengrocer neighbour and a local coal merchant (it was winter) reported the death at Rue Duphot 19, to the Mayor of the 1st (now 8th) Arrondissement that afternoon: 'Eugene Macnamara, bachelor, Irishman, of independent means, aged 38'. No cause of death was required or given. The body was apparently buried shortly afterwards, as next of kin were sought in Ireland only in late March.[2]

Rue Duphot is a street of First Empire apartment buildings five and six storeys high. Balzac used it as the setting for Mme Rabourdin's apartment in *Les Employés* (1841), describing large salons, marble fireplaces and private courtyards. A lawyer, an academic musician and a regional tax inspector, as well as the greengrocer, had apartments at Number 19. Macnamara's arrival in Paris was unscheduled, and he may have been sickening for some time. A doctor would sanction burial; a *juge de la paix* would seal personal effects, pending claims; a foreign will would be translated by a notary under oath.

At the end of March, Dr Thomas Kane, Lord Mayor of Limerick, 'received a communication from Paris stating that a Roman Catholic clergyman named Eugene Macnamara, a native of Bawnkile near Corofin where his mother is living, died and left a sum of 1.2 million francs'. Kane located John Macnamara of the Irish Constabulary, Limerick, the priest's 'only surviving brother, to whom the immense wealth which the reverend gentleman amassed by working the silver mines in Mexico, now reverts'.[3] John Frémont arrived in London that week to begin a social round of receptions at Buckingham Palace, Downing Street, The Mansion House and tea with the Duke of Wellington, but was arrested and imprisoned on 7 April for a bad debt incurred in California, 1846. He was bailed the following day.

Macnamara, 'through his connection with some close relatives engaged in mining speculation in Mexico and elsewhere, became possessed of property to a very considerable amount in lands and money in a foreign country and was on his way home when he took ill and died intestate, in Paris'.[4] There, 'some good friend … supposing him from papers in his possession to be from Limerick', contacted Lord Mayor Kane. 'The fortunate John Macnamara, a fine young man of interesting personal appearance, has reason to bless his stars and thank the Mayor.' £48,000 (1.2 million francs) was immediately available. In May 1853, Bishop Hynes of Guiana wrote 'to Mrs Mary Macnamara, mother of Rev'd Eugene, in answer to her queries about the property left by her son'.[5]

Macnamara's 'papers' would include two colonising dossiers. He must have considered raising a colonising company for Chile and had an unexpected new opportunity to validate his California title. In Mexico City, consul MacKintosh was liquidating his assets, including his palatial Consulate and furniture, to ward off insolvency. He was dismissed from office in 1853, but his portfolio of mine investments was worth tapping during a boom in Mexican silver mining: even his failures were attractive, the annulled rail and canal rights over Tehauantec, the cancelled 1845–6 bond issue, and the five million acres for colonising in Tamaulipas which he could not sell. MacKintosh probably dispersed his assets in what some suspected was a dubious insolvency. Macnamara may have been about to redistribute his own funds in Co Clare, directly where needed. He had seen enough hats passed round in Mexico, California and on HMS *Collingwood* for the Famine poor. His 'good friend' in Paris, probably a lawyer or justice, looked to Limerick because of letters from policeman brother John found among Eugene's papers.

The British and Irish press found that 'Wealthy Priest' made a good headline; the *Belfast News Letter* barbed it into 'Poor Priesthood?'; the 'Fortunate Constable' was a journalist's bonus. Editors watched the *Limerick Examiner* for more. In early October, solicitor Joseph Murphy of George St, Limerick, spent a fortnight in Paris 'on behalf of the deceased's surviving relatives, one of whom, a brother, is very well educated, well conducted and meritorious member of the Irish Constabulary'. A will was found, despite first reports of intestacy. 'The seal of the will was broken with great formality. The will is written in the Spanish language.'[6] *The Tablet* and Battersby's *Directory* (1853) missed Macnamara's death, despite the reports in provincial newspapers, but they had lost him already in 1845, even as the London *Times* reported and other newspapers syndicated his project.

THE GOLD RUSH IRISH[7]

No part of nineteenth-century California was ever named 'New Ireland'. The 'countess', 'poet', 'gentleman' and 'virtuous woman' recorded on State census sheets, were trying to forget Ireland and sometimes mocked their roots. Macnamara's colonists arriving in 1852 would have faced anti-Irish 'lynch' and 'shillelagh' law in San Francisco. 'British subject' was an Irishman's nationality, not his race, and a Mexican *Comisión* called Macnamara, '*natural de Irlanda y súbdito de S.M. Británica*'. President Polk's 'English subjects in Ireland', 1848, nearly caught it. When the gold rush Irish took US citizenship, they abjured Queen Victoria, but remained ethnic Irish. In tense moments in the mines an Irish name or accent could pass as Scots, Welsh, Cornish or Manx; a strong accent against the roar and rock tumble of a mountain snowmelt also affected the enumerator's hearing. Miners would refuse to give personal details, censuses were state interference and UK miners remembered the intrusive first census of Great Britain and Ireland in 1841. A prudent California enumerator would guess and ride on, pencilling 'Fitzpatrick' as 'Fritz Patrick' and 'Eamonn' as 'Almond'.

In 1870, 54,000 Irish-born, consistently 10 per cent of California's total population since 1850, formed 29 per cent of California State's foreign-born. In 1850, they had complained of the California mosquitoes, but welcomed crows as if from home. They hesitated to farm, as land had once cost them their confidence. Their descendants waxed about an Ireland they never saw, vicarious nostalgia caught from the pioneers when old age made them talk. A Dublin, a Limerick, a score of Irish Hills, Cemeteries and Creeks and even a Shandon dot the California map. One historian has spoken of 'the Uncounted Irish', but they had been as well-counted in Ireland as they were California. Many censuses, church registers and wills were destroyed in Dublin during The Troubles (1916–23). Had they survived, the story of Irish migration would have been told in detail long ago. Colonist 'families' of five persons could include a bachelor band of brothers, a network of cousins or a lone mother with a brood of daughters. Eventually, the feet of *Los Tulares* Irish settlers would have itched, distant growing *pueblos* would have beckoned, mineral *bonanzas* tempted and coastal breeze enticed. They could not have been detained in Central Valley forever by an *Intendente*, or even an Apostolic Vicar.

Once settlers had the means to survive, they needed respect, from themselves and others. 'To be decently buried without undue ostentation' one dying Irish miner requested in Sutter County in 1878, 'but with proper regard to my station in life'. Long biographical inscriptions on wood or stone markers cost money, even when a fellow Irishman cut them. Thomas Kerr, out from Londonderry to California in winter 1849–50, wept into his diary: 'I regret coming here. I have shed floods of tears. I have earned nothing to what my expenses were.' Miners died young, went back east or turned to other livings. Gold was a delusion, and relatively few made fortunes from it. In 1852, William Kelly ended *Stroll Through the Diggins* [*sic*] with a virtual epitaph: 'some crawled away from the [gold mining] experience marred and shaken to the inmost'. Most turned from mining gold to 'mining the miners'.

Those with means published short autobiographies in leatherette-bound 'County Histories', obituaries sanitised in their own lifetime. Some recreated themselves, and not every 'victim' of famine and oppression had experienced either. Respectability cost $50 an article and no one cross-checked. Copies were freighted to Europe to impress. In one classic case, when nothing more could be wrung out of his life story, an émigré boasted that his parents back in Ireland 'would also have been industrious and patriotic Americans, if they had come here'. There was no charge for being listed in a census, which allowed those without means also to proclaim or to puff their pedigree, from a 'Blennerhassett-Chute of Chute Hall, Co Kerry' to 'a landowning Smyth of Co Cavan'.

Some Irishmen brought skills and experience, from the Goldmines River in Wicklow, where a second 'rush' occurred in 1841, and from Silvermines mountain in Tipperary, also active that year when Macnamara was curate nearby at Borrisokane (see Plate 15).

> Gold is obtained by continual washings, but a spot on which to labour is a matter of chance. The clay is conveyed to a wooden trough, through which runs water, and the clay is raked. Any gold will sink and the result after half an hour is scarce enough to fill an iron bowl which is continually shaken, examined and the gold detected by its colour.[8]

Smallholding and mine might cross-subsidise on a single California claim, but 'farmer' rang better than 'miner' on the *Great Voting Register*. The speech of the Irish was a figure of fun: direct Gaelic thought patterns cut across 'roundabout' courtly English when expressed in that language, while paired languages breed the 'pun'. When miners wrote home to Gaelic-speaking parents, they sprinkled the earlier letters with Gaelic phrases heard in childhood.

The 'California Letter' became proverbial for the emigrant letter, not necessarily from California. It brought good news, often unfounded optimism, and sometimes a remittance. Of hundreds and thousands of such letters, at least five substantial correspondences with the UK survive from California itself.[9] Letters from the Sierra Nevada sometimes enclosed gold dust, but more commonly bankers orders and news of relatives and former neighbours. Remittances from the US to Ireland totalled $6.8 million in 1854 alone, a record figure largely attributed to California gold. Emigrants also begged money from home to invest in a rumoured *bonanza*, a new railway, or to tide over a difficult patch.

They spoke of returning home, as if from seasonal work. They knew (and felt) the pain their departure had caused, and the finality of severing with home was often too much. They had after all, attended their own 'American wake'. They grasped straws, as real life around them took over. The single temporary emigrant became a married (if occasionally homesick) settler; a promise to visit home replaced talk of return, and visits were postponed until they turned into a wishful sigh to retire there. Finally they wished merely to see home, just once, before dying. Men died in their eighties with White Star brochures beside them.

William Clarke of Colusa County, a God-fearing Donegal Presbyterian and teetotaller, left a fulsome diary, found in a barn decades later. He chased wolves rather than waste bullets on them, 'although they would like to have tasted good Irish blood'. Perhaps he was a poor shot who told a good story. He treated people as wolves, with fists and sometimes (prodigally) with a bullet, even in the courthouse. In 1873 he killed himself.[10] Suicide often resulted from memories looming large in later, leaner years. When a tiny minority chose the razor, bullet or poison, the coroner recorded their last words from witnesses or a note, often their only known words. Thanksgiving, 4 July and St Patrick's Day were days of serious, lonely, and sometimes alcohol-fuelled nostalgia.

In the economic depression of the 1850s, a Hibernian Benevolent Society was founded in Tuolomne and Calaveras counties, inside the Macnamara concession frame. The HBS allowed the 25 per cent Irish-born of both counties to *feel* in touch with home, without being so, and provided social support. After the US Civil War, a Fenian or Irish Republican Brotherhood formed in the same communities. It raised money, words and bands, but not one volunteer for rebellion in Ireland or the Fenian attack on Canada. Macnamara's colonists would have been no different and just as remote.[11]

IN FADING MEMORIAM

Isaac Hartmann, a San Francisco attorney, unleashed venom on ex-Governor Pico, as corrupt, non-English speaking, negroid, dwarfist and *latino*.[12] Loathing of *latino* and Irish was endemic in City Hall, and sometimes victims suffered what they had once meted out. Irish gravestones at Mission Dolores pray 'May God Forgive our Persecutors' and 'Remember Not Our Offences'. The Mexican War bred a prejudice still audible in Land Commission transcripts. Territorialism donned religious garb and in 1849 Mexicans, Chileans and Irish became the perceived intruders into former New Spain, *latino*, catholic and both. Hartmann went for Macnamara:

more bitterly hostile to the American people than any other foreigner who ever visited California. [He and James Forbes] undertook the pleasant task of serving themselves. The pen of history has not yet written any account of the subsequent Apostolic Missionary labours of Fr Macnamara and here we lose sight of him.

Others wrote of him in passing or in a Land Commission hearing, but knew nothing of his death or his life before Mexico. Castillero was Mexican consul briefly in San Francisco, 1848; James Forbes resigned office, 1850 and Ewen Mackintosh was dismissed, 1853. Alexander Forbes died in England, 1863; Juan Bandini died in 1854; Manuel Castañares, ex-congressman, described to the *San Francisco Bulletin* in September 1857 how he had 'opposed the grant of 300 leagues [*sic*, 2000 square miles] to the Society of Jesus which had asked for that amount through one of its priests, Padre Macnamara'. Ex-Governor Pico 'barely remembered' Macnamara, objected to being questioned about him, and said nothing of him in his memoir.

In 1878 Pico's son-in-law, John Forster of San Diego, remembered that Seymour had 'raced' to Monterey to raise the British flag, 'as arranged beforehand between the California and British governments, through an Irish catholic priest named Macnamara'. It was the received version. Forster had attempted a colony of his own on Pico's old home ranch, but 'Forster City', near San Onofre, grew to three buildings and a field of footings before it was abandoned.[13]

Comandante Castro, senior syndicate shareholder, whose mine Macnamara put under 'British protection', remembered that he once thought Macnamara 'influential'. Barron and Forbes left no archive, nor did the London Mexican Bondholders, and Macnamara is not mentioned in the Manning and MacKintosh archive at U.T. Austin. James Forbes referred to him in several court appearances during the New Almaden appeals. In 1877, Eusebio Galindo, Forbes' father-in-law and Santa Clara magistrate, remembered Macnamara's 'concession on the Sacramento [*sic*] to counteract the Protestant Americans. It is believed by some that Macnamara was an agent in this country of the English who have been accused of having ideas for taking possession of it.'[14] Witnesses to Macnamara's power of attorney in June 1846 did not mention him again:

David Spence, beef dealer who also met him on *Collingwood*, and Antonio Osio who chronicled the end of Mexican California. Admiral Seymour did not refer to him again in writing after 1846, even when annotating his 1846 *Diary* in 1851, but then he had met many such colourful characters.

Those who did mention him later spiced their memories with hearsay. Thomas Lancey, formerly of USS *Dale* off California in December 1846, wrote about Macnamara third-hand, thirty years later. His Macnamara, fresh from London, had met Pico in 1844 [*sic*], bypassing Mexico altogether. Lancey tried exorcism by doggerel:

> The English transport *Palinurus*, instead of taking the good Father to Van Diemen's Land [Tasmania, British convict settlement], left him at Mazatlán about December 1846, and in 1847 he went round [Cape] Horn in a ship and soon afterwards died. *Go tell your Queen and Parliament, to Aberdeen make known, That Macnamara's little scheme, by Frémont is o'erthrown.*[15]

John Ross Browne, from Dublin, reported the California Constitutional Convention, 1849, for Congress. Macnamara and the old 'foreign threat' were not mentioned in the discussions about California's future, or by Frémont in 1850 when he and fellow interim Senator Gwin penned their *Memorial on California* for Congress. Belatedly and feebly in 1869, Browne made a passing spat at Macnamara's coming to Mexico on HMS *Herald* from London, for 'making such a noise about founding his giant colony of Irish refugees in the Tulares Valley of the present State'.[16]

Narciso Botello, senior deputy in the former Assembly, had listened to Macnamara on 6/7 July 1846 in Reina de Los Angeles and penned a recommendation for him to take to Pico. In 1875 he remembered him, but meanwhile had turned against Pico and Bandini for lining their pockets:

> [Macnamara] came to Los Angeles recommended by Central Government and brought a project to establish a colony of Irish Catholics, asking for that purpose a land concession. This business went through the procedure of the Assembly and there was conceded to him a land title in

northern California near Cape Mendocino [*sic*]. This was in
June and July 1846.[17]

Botello's mistaken location was understandable. Mendocino and its
hinterland was still charted in Seymour's day as New Albion, to mark
Drake's claim for his Queen in 1579. Antonio Coronel of the Assembly
had formally recommended Macnamara's plan to Pico. Thirty years later
he remembered that Macnamara came to put a British colony of Irishmen
in the way of the Americans, 'to enable England to protect her subjects'.[18]

When these memories faded, California was settled and tranquil.
The Irish could distance themselves there from the Boycotts and Bence-
Joneses of the Land War at home. Distance and US constitutional
neutrality towards religion helped fade, if not erase Old World grievances,
but some needed time to lay aside their crowns and boasts of being
doubly persecuted for race and religion. Hugh Quigley was a Clare priest
from Tulla, fifteen miles east of Ennis and Corofin; he was ordained for
Killaloe diocese seven years after Macnamara. Quigley, who arrived
in New York in 1848, criss-crossed California to record the 'Milesian
nobility of soul' behind every 'fine Irish face' in that 'terrestrial Paradise'.
Erratic, pompous, sentimental and gullible, he published *The Irish Race in
California* in 1878, between green, gold-tooled covers, to boost immigrant
self-respect, an Irish version of the California *County Histories*.

Quigley dismissed the Macnamara story as 'apocryphal, only true
in part', exhumed from 'dusty old books'. As a new American, he was
embarrassed by Macnamara's 'Methodist wolves' which, he argued,
would not have been representative of opinion in 'liberal Mexico'. He
knew nothing of Mexican law forbidding Protestant worship in public.
Mexican liberal reformers in the *Dirección* for Colonising had pressed for
civil over religious registration from the mid-1840s, to make Mexico more
attractive to settlers. They cited US success in drawing immigrants, as due
in part to religious neutrality, but Mexico agreed tolerance only in 1862.
Quigley defended an imaginary golden-age Mexico, and knew nothing of
the longstanding tension between liberals and the church there. It was, he
claimed

> unlikely that Mexico which had granted lands so freely to
> non-Catholics would concern itself about the religion of

immigrants, Protestant, Catholic or atheist. The Mexicans wanted settlers, not enquiries about their religion. More land went to Protestants than to Catholics. Protestant and atheist receive the same liberal treatment [in Latin America] as if they were the most orthodox Catholics, but if a colony of Catholics applied to any liberal Protestant government, would they be as successful? The Macnamara story needs confirmation. It has no proof beyond rumour. England was, however, negotiating to possess California and an English fleet was on its way to take it. England could not have held the country for a month. Kearny and Stevenson's Irish New York Volunteers would have made short work of the 'redcoats' had they landed in California.[19]

Quigley's 'redcoats' were not just the Royal Marine detachment on each of Seymour's warships. Tactlessly, even bravely, Quigley had once preached in a garrison church in Glasgow on Repeal of the (Irish) Union with Britain and had to be moved back to Ireland for his safety. As a curate in County Clare, he reported on the worst of the Famine for *The Tablet* in 1847.

Hubert Howe Bancroft, the father of California history, dealt in detail with the Macnamara story during Frémont's last years, but attacked Quigley for 'painting [Irish] wealth and influence in glowing colours', although his own palette could be equally lurid when he described the Irish. He agreed with Quigley that the Macnamara story was suspect, but on different grounds. Reasoning from the disturbed and defiant Ireland of the 1880s, not from the prostrate Ireland of the 1840s, he was certain that no *Irish* colony in California 'would have commended itself to the favour of Her Britannic Majesty'. Without access to British archives, he was cautious about the Macnamara project. Pico's 'granting' of the land in 1846 he dismissed as beyond a governor's authority, therefore fraudulent, but Frémont's claim of a serious British threat from agent Macnamara he also dismissed as a 'bugaboo', invented to scare, distract and provide an alibi for covert expansionist activity.[20]

Friar Zephyrin Engelhardt, fervent, vinegarish chronicler of the missions, had the last word in 1896. He accused Frémont, six years dead, of 'shady transactions in historical affairs' and of 'more to do with the wording of [Macnamara's] petition as it exists [published by the Senate, 1848] than Macnamara'. Engelhardt knew that Frémont had taken Governor Pico's files to Washington in 1847 to support his expense claim, yet Frémont's first volume of *Memoirs* in 1887 applauded Macnamara's 'nobly conceived plan' as 'among the great ideas which affect nations'. Engelhardt ignored or overlooked it; his Mexico of the 1890s was revolutionary and secular, no love lost between church and state, a once devout country destroyed by 'liberal Voltairists'. The Macnamara story, he concluded, was 'a suspicious [later] interpolation by an irreligious and anti-Catholic nation' and Macnamara was 'very ignorant not to know that Catholic institutions in the US went unmolested'.[21]

Bancroft's work on the crucial California years (1846–8), and John Frémont's unfinished *Memoir*, stirred embers. The *Boston Pilot* was Catholic, Irish and alive to British wickedness. It once claimed that John Riley the Galway commander of the *San Patricios* was a 'fiction of anti-Catholics', and in reality had been John Ryder, an Englishman. Its activist Fenian editor, who had suffered for his political principles, judged Macnamara zealous, honest but too naive to see 'behind his well-meant design, a deeper well-laid scheme of English government to seize the country'. Frémont, whatever he felt about Britain in 1848, had accepted by 1887 that Macnamara's was a communitarian and church scheme, not a British conspiracy. The *Pilot*, however, was in permanent polemical mode and conspiracy theory held. A 'slow moving' Admiral Seymour had been ready 'on the slightest pretext to plant his flag ashore'; Project Macnamara would have led to 'incalculable misfortune, had California fallen into the hands of England'. Macnamara was 'too lofty and unselfish to appreciate English cunning … [his project] was no loss to religion or human freedom'.[22]

FRÉMONT'S LAMENT

Forty years after Frémont and a troupe of witnesses swore to a Senate Committee that he had saved California from Britain and Macnamara, he published a retrospect to tie up life's loose ends. His ex-*californio* grant, Las Mariposas on the San Joaquin, which he sold in 1860, had kept him faintly mindful of Macnamara, whom he had met on *Collingwood*. By the time he wrote he had left California, with profits from his mineral rights and sales of land plots, but only after years of contesting Forty-Niner claims. When his *Memoirs* appeared in 1887, agribusiness was beginning to tame his and Macnamara's valley and water was the new gold over which farmers and towns fought. Ecologists and tourists had claimed Yosemite canyon with its '500 psalms of waterfall' on the upper Merced, above Frémont's grant. The Valley Indians had all but vanished and the *Los Tulares* wetlands were evaporating (see Plate 17).

Frémont lamented the lost British *utopia* of Irish farmers as an interrupted vision. He saw it as an attempt to revive the missions, and to serve the Indians better, 'nobly conceived in the interests of Macnamara's Church'. No more was said of British agents, protectorates or of Papal missioners. Frémont was wiser, poorer, chastened and old, no longer the ambitious young officer in the limelight, ducking, weaving and choosing his words before court martial or Senate Committee. In 1887 he no longer needed an alibi, as his and Jessie's fluency still served them well.

Under Macnamara's direction, colonists would have spread over the whole beautiful San Joaquin valley. Farms would have occupied the river lands, and the plains between them would have been cattle ranges. Among the springs and streams of the foothills, up to the snowline, happy and prosperous homesteads would have arisen. Under an intelligent and stable authority the old oak groves and the pine forests would not have been swept away. With its climate, soil and abundant streams, the whole valley would have presented a picture of agricultural beauty unsurpassed on earth. The mountain Indians would have been reclaimed as useful herdsmen and labourers, and the abandoned missions along the coast would have been restored on a higher level, as centres of productive labour. The Indians would have had firm government [and] the advantages of civilisation [not just] its vices … a reality created by the missions when the country was very remote and the resources came from within themselves. In 1846, when the colonisation project failed, I wrote from the quiet of the ruined old Carmel Mission to Senator Benton of the events which had brought me [there]. *Carmel Mission, 24th July 1846* … ended my mission as well as that of Macnamara.

Age and hindsight frayed whatever consistency the old 'Pathfinder' had ever had about California events, but it no longer mattered that his letter from Carmel had been dated 25 July, and had never mentioned Britain, Macnamara or colonising. At the time he had merely logged: 'I found Admiral Seymour in charge of HBMS *Collingwood*.' The rest only mattered in 1848 when he needed them. In 1886 a young man's scheming and posturing gave way to an old man's generous, almost affectionate salute to Macnamara:

> We cannot fail to sympathise with the grief of a mind which had conceived a project so far-reaching and which had experienced the shock of overthrow in the moment of its complete success. The time, the thought, the labour of solicitation, the patient endurance with slower or inferior minds – all had resulted in the blank of absolute failure.[23]

Notes

INTRODUCTION

1. Bill and Penny Anderson own and edit *The California Territorial Quarterly* in Paradise ('Dogtown' in 1849), northern California's sole independent history journal, peer-reviewed and of high scholarship standards. I value their friendship.

2. *The Times*, 6 August 1845, '*The Affairs of Mexico*', Mexico correspondent, 29 June; Bankhead's report on Macnamara: Despatch 52, 30 May 1845, TNA FO, 204/88, 483–4. The British Legation in Mexico City, Calle de Capuchinas 5, later demolished for Avenida Venustiano Carranza, was one block south of Presidential and Archiepiscopal palaces on Plaza Mayor. Charles Bankhead, ambassador 1843–47 and Peregrine (Percy) Doyle, *chargé d'affaires* (1843–50), both Irish, supported Macnamara. *The Times* Mexico correspondent demanded in September 1845 that Britain occupy California.

3. Archivo General de la Nación, Mexico City, *Gobernación, Caia 4, 1845–6, Expediente El Proyecto Macnamara*.

4. Hubert Howe Bancroft, *History of California, 1884–92*, (7 volumes), *Volume 5, 1846–8*, (Works of H.H.Bancroft, Vol.XXII, San Francisco, The History Company, 1886), pp.215–223; J.C. Frémont, *Memoirs of My Life* (NY, Chicago, Belford, Clarke), I, p.560.

5. Mary Karam OP, *Elusive Entrepreneur; Eugene Macnamara's California Land Grant and Colonisation Scheme of 1846*, (Dissertation, University of San Francisco, 1967).

6. Ignatius Murphy, *The Diocese of Killaloe in the Eighteenth Century* (Blackrock, Four Courts,1991); *The Diocese of Killlaloe, 1800–1850* (ibid.,1993); *The Diocese of Killaloe, 1850–1904* (ibid.,1995); *A Starving People:Life and Death in West Clare, 1845–51* (Dublin: Irish Academic Press, 1996), which coincidentally analyses Macnamara's first parish.

7. Admiral Sir George Seymour's Papers, Pacific Station, 1844–48, TNA, FO/5 and 418; Admiralty 53, logbooks of HMS *Collingwood, Juno* and *Herald*; Seymour of Ragley Papers, Warwickshire Record Office, Warwick, UK, CR 114A, 374, 23 and 24; 380; 412–418; 421–422.

8. Michael J. Costeloe, *Bonds and Bondholders:British Investors and Mexico's Foreign Debt, 1824–88*, (Westport, Ct, Praeger, 2003); *Bubbles and Bonanzas:British Investments in Mexico, 1821–60* (Lanham, Md: Lexington Books, 2011). Costeloe also published *To Bowl a Mexican Maiden Over: Cricket in Mexico, 1827–1900, Bulletin of Latin American Research*, 26, 1, January 2007, pp.112–124.

9. D.J. Weber, *The Mexican Frontier* (Albuquerque, New Mexico: U.P., 1982), p.206: 7300 *californios* in 1845, 700 foreigners mainly US, and 500 on the trail, summer 1846; D.J. Weber, *Spanish Frontier in North America*, (Newhaven Conn., Yale U.P., 1992), p.263:

300,000 Indians in 1783, reduced to 200,000 by 1821, with 21,000 mission Indians, and 3200 *californios*. After 1848, California, 'an Hispanic Siberia' became 'an American Mecca' (p.341).

CHAPTER ONE

1. '225' US sailors and marines landed at Monterey: Lt Stephen 'Paddy' Rowan, Executive Officer, USS *Cyane*, was there and recorded the number: C.M. Zemke, *Stephen C. Rowan and The US Navy*, PhD Thesis (Utah State University, 2012), p.35. Midshipman Robert Duvall, USS *Savannah*, logged the same figure, *CHSQ*, Vol.3, 2, July 1924, pp.105–125.

2. Robert Ryall Miller, late Professor of Mexican History, CSU at Hayward, informed author that 'Lone Star' flags originated as Texan militia pennants in 1835. In 1836, rebel *californios* used a red-star-on-white flag for the 'Free State of Alta California', proclaimed by Governor Alvarado, Pío Pico and *Comandante* José Castro, 7 November, 1836: copies of the proclamation in Mexican National Archive, Huntington and Bancroft Libraries. Waddy Thompson, former US ambassador, called the US taking of California 'a re-enactment of Texas', *Recollections of Mexico* (New York: Wiley & Putnam, 1846), p.232. William B. Ide's 'settler revolt' in June 1846 added a grizzly to its Lone Star, and legend *California Republic*. He did not demand a 'Republic', but republican freedom from Castro's despotism. Frémont took command after twenty-five days, which Ide called an 'entering wedge' for US occupation. He disliked Frémont's crediting himself for the uprising, and was not called for evidence of a 'British threat' to support Frémont's expense claim on the Senate. John Bidwell, another Bear Flagger, described British influence as 'not open, but felt, and not a few [hoped] that England or France would one day seize and hold California': *Echoes of The Past about California* (Chicago: Lakeside, 1890), p.100.

3. A commemorative plaque on St James Street, Westminster, marks the Texas Legation to Great Britain, 1842–5; others opened in Paris and Washington, also likely allies. Had California become independent, it would eventually had its ambassador at the Court of St James.

4. M.A. De Wolfe Howe, *Life and Letters of George Bancroft*, Vol. I (New York: Scribner; 1908), pp.279–80, 25 August 1845 to William Sturgis.

5. E. Nelson & A. Probart, *A Man Who Can Speak of Plants, Dr Thomas Coulter* (Dublin: E.C.Nelson, 1994), p.112: Coulter added that the Indian would not survive without the missioners after 'secularisation at the hands of scoundrels'.

6. P. Cushner, *Why Have You Come Here? The Jesuits and the first Evangelisation of Native America* (Oxford: Oxford University Press, 2006), p.62. For new work on the California Indian culture in mission times, see S.W. Hackel, *Alta California: Peoples in Motion, Identities in Formation, 1769-1850* (California UP, 2010). For a general view of the California missions, see Alison Lake, *Colonial Rosary, The Spanish and Indian Missions of California* (Ohio UP, 2006); for the mission viewpoint, see M. Geiger, *Franciscan Missionaries in Hispanic California, 1769-1848, Biographical Dictionary* (Huntington Lib. San Marino, 1969); M. Gonsalez, *Religion and the Impact of Islam on Spanish and Mexican California, 1769-1846*, in *California History: Journal of the California Historical Society*, 90, 1, (2012), pp.18–39.

7. Santa Bárbara Mission Archive, 1034 and 1038, letters Patrick Short to *Padre* Duran, 1836, where Short reports the Pope's planned journey from 'authoritative' sources cited in the US press. For the wider world mission movement, see *The Missionary College of All Hallows, 1842-91*, K. Condon, (All Hallows, Dublin, 1986); Colm Cooke, 'The Modern

Irish Missionary Movement', *Archivium Hibernicum*, 35,(1980), pp.234–246; ibid., p.38, The Archbishop Murray Papers (3), 66, 43–127, 106, (1983); Colin Barr, 'Irish Episcopal Imperialism', *English Historical Review*, CXXII, (2008), pp.502, 611–50; *The Tablet*, 20 March 1852, 'Reviews', p.87.

8. F.B. Olguin, 'Bernardo O'Híggins and Irish Immigrants in Mexico', *Irish Immigration Studies in Latin America*, 5, 1, (2007), pp.59–60; *British Consular Papers from South America*, Peru, Camden 3rd Series, Vol.63, June 1940, p.168 and *n*.3; Catalogue of the *J.E. Hernandez y Davalos Mss* Collection, (University of Texas Library: C. Castanada (ed.), 1954) pp. 325, 394, citing *La Diplomacia Mexicana*, II, (Sec. Relaciones Exteriores; Mexico;1910), pp.276–7, No 2079, 7 March 1824, to Mexican ambassador, London, offering land to Irish paper makers and weavers.

9. Seymour Papers, WRO CR 114A, 374, 17, *Diary*, 17 October 1840. For Irish emigration, see K.A. Miller, *Emigrants and Exiles* (New York, London: OUP, 1985).

10. David Sinclair, *The Land That Never Was: Sir Gregor MacGregor and the Most Audacious Fraud in History* (London: Review, 2003).

11. Pedro Ó Crouley y ÓDonnell, *A Description of the Kingdom of New Spain, 1774*, trans. by J. Howell (Dublin: Allen Figgis, 1972).

12. Michael P. Costeloe, *Bonds and Bondholders:British Investors and Mexico's Foreign Debt, 1824–88* (Westport Ct, & London: Praeger, 2003) is an indispensable study which underpins this author's treatment of the bondholders. For 'Mexicomania', see M.P. Costeloe, *Bubbles and Bonanzas: British Investment in Mexico, 1821–26* (Lanham,Md: Lexington, 2011), pp.11, 53, 142; R.J. Salvucci, *Politics, Markets and Mexico's 'London Debt', 1823–87* (Cambridge UP, 2009) tackles pertinent questions raised by the lack of bondholder archives.

13. G.L. Rives, *The United States and Mexico, 1821–48*, Vol.2 (New York: Scribner, 1913), pp.94–100; L.H. Jenks, *Migration of British Capital to 1875* (New York: Knopf, 1927); E.W. Turlington, *Mexico and her Foreign Creditors* (New York: Columbia UP, 1930); B.A. Tennebaum, 'Merchants, Money and Mischief', *The Americas*, 35, 3, (1978–9), pp.317–329; H.J. Heath de Bohiges, *British Commercial Houses in Mexico*, PhD thesis, (London School of Economics, 1988); H.J. Heath, 'British Merchant Houses in Mexico', *Hispanic American Historical Review*, 73, 2, April 1993, pp.261–290; D.C.M. Platt, 'British Finance in Mexico, 1821–67', *Bulletin of Latin American Research*, 3, 1, January 1984.

14. Patrick Milmo, one of two brothers from County Sligo, was a cousin of William Kelly, also from Sligo, an Irish writer on California in 1849: J. Fox, William Kelly, *California Territorial Quarterly*, Winter 2005, pp.24–36.

15. M.P. Costeloe, *Bonds and Bondholders* (Westport,Ct: Praeger, 2003) p.152.

16. Heath de Bohiges, ibid., pp.160, 269, 275.

17. José Castro, testimony in *US vs Castillero, New Almaden Mine*, Transcript Vol.4., p.2629, November 1859.

18. J.A. Hawgood, 'A Projected Prussian Colonisation of California', *Southern California Quarterly*, 48, 4, December 1966, pp.353–368.

19. Mexican Government response to the Macnamara Project, September 1845: 1845–6 *Gobernación*, Caja 4, 1846, *El Proyecto Macnamara*, ff 3–9 and verso, Archivo General de La Nación, Mexico.

20. Edward Gibbon Wakefield, *England and America: The Art of Colonisation*, II, (London: Bentley, 1833), p.243.

21. Ibid., pp.56–7; Waddy Thomson, *Recollections of Mexico* (New York: Wiley & Putnam, 1846), p.239.

22. H.R. Key, *Topo: Story of a Scottish Colony Near Caracas, 1825–27* (Edinburgh: Scottish Academic Press, 1988).

23. Seymour Papers WRO CR 114A, 374, 23, *Diary*, 1846, back flyleaf.

CHAPTER TWO

1. Ignatius Murphy, *Diocese of Killaloe, 1800–1850* (Blackrock: Four Courts, 1993), pp.95–98; TNA, Foreign Office, 204, 88, ff.483–4, Despatch 52, Charles Bankhead, Mexico City, to Lord Aberdeen.

2. C Chevenix Trench, *Grace's Card: Irish Catholic Landlords, 1690–1800* (Cork: Mercier Press, 1997); J.G. McCarthy, *Henry Grattan* (London, 1886), p.44; D.H. Akenson, *Small Differences: Irish Catholics and Protestants, 1815–1921* (Dublin: Gill & Macmillan, 1991), pp.3, 22, 81–4, 112–126, 218, n107, 225, n13, 226, n18.

3. S.J. Connolly, *Priests and People in Pre-Famine Ireland, 1780–1845* (Dublin: Gill & Macmillan; New York: St Martins Press, 1982), p.11; W. Fitzpatrick, *Life and Times of Dr Doyle, Bishop of Carlow*, Vol.2 (Dublin: Gill, 1880), p.5.

4. John Hynes' *Diary* (B. Condon (ed.), Melbourne Archdiocese, 2002) 20 December 1852, private Papal audience; *ODNB* articles, *John McHale* and *Paul Cullen* (2004) illustrate the Irish bishops' self-assertion and struggles between Ultramontanists and 'Castle bishops'. C. Barr, 'Imperium in Imperio:An Empire Within the Empire, Irish Episcopal Imperialism', *English Historical Review*, Vol.123, 502 (2008), pp.502, 611–650, shows Irish missionaries shaping many communities within the British Empire. In 1864, Pius IX issued a *Syllabus* condemning eighty perceived post-revolutionary human '*Errors*'. 'Bad pear' was gentler than the 'blot' or 'abuse' uttered by some bishops.

5. Akenson, ibid., p.3.

6. Brian Merriman, *The Midnight Court* (1787), trans. by D. Marcus (Dublin: Dolman Press, 1953).

7. E.T. Craig (adaptation), *An Irish Commune, The History of Ralahine* (Dublin, 1919); E.T. Craig, *An Irish Commune: The Experiment at Ralahine 1831–33*, with additional essays (Dublin: Irish Academic Press, 1983); W. Thompson, *The Distribution of Wealth, The New System* (London: Longman, 1824); H.W. Weir, *Houses of Clare, Rathlakeen House* p.224 (Co. Clare: Ballinadesha Press, 1999).

8. Irish College Paris, Archives, Ms A2.d. 1, *Register, Entrée des Eleves,*1832; Ms A2.d.3, *Comptes des Eléves* 1832–40. Six students enrolled in 1828, tripling registrations 1826 and 1827; ten enrolled in 1829 and again in 1830; twenty-two joined in 1831 and again in 1832, Macnamara among them; thirty-three joined in 1833, and twenty-five in 1834. Pre-Revolution students (on two sites) had numbered 200. In Rome accommodation was limited: fewer than twenty enrolled in 1832, more than forty in 1834, and over sixty after 1840: *ODNB* article, *Paul Cullen* (OUP, 2004). For the cholera epidemic, see Commission Nominée, *Rapport sur la Marche et les effets Du Cholera-Morbus dans Paris, 1832* (Imprimerie Royale, 1834); Galignani's *Guide to New Paris*, 1830, 1841 and 1851.

9. L. Swords, *The Irish French Connection, 1578–1978: Irish College Paris* (Paris: Irish College,1978); R. Hayes, *Biographical Dictionary of Irishmen in France*, (Dublin: Gill, 1949); P. Boyle, *The Irish College, Paris*, (Dublin: Gill, 1901); W. Fitzpatrick, *Life of Dr Doyle*, Vol.1 (Dublin: Gill, 1880), p.441; Vol.2, pp.38, 87; Dublin Diocesan Archive, *Archivium Hibernicum*, 45, (Maynooth, 1990), pp.36, 45; Murray Papers, ibid., 37,

(Maynooth, 1982), p.58; Irish College Rome, Archives Online, *Cullen Papers*, CUL/87, A. Quinn to Cullen, 27 May 1833.

10. Pope Gregory XIV, *Mirari Vos*, 15 August 1832, Denzinger Schoenmetzer (Freiburg: Herder, 1965), 2730–32 (abstract).

11. Irish College, Paris, Archives Online, *Register, Sortie des Eléves*. J. Schuster, Picpus Order Archives, Rome, 1-91-2, Hd ff1-2, and typed narrative, 238; S.B. Dakin, *Lives of William Hartnell* (Stanford UP, 1949); H.A. Whelan, *The Picpus Story* (Pomona, CA, 1964); L. Jore, 'Picpus Fathers', *Southern California Quarterly*, 46, 4, December 1964, pp.194–301; The Picpus authorities took pity on Irish 'penniless aspirants', and their college, robbed by revolutionaries of funds and properties'. They fed them in the 1820s, but their own numbers quadrupled. In 1837–8 a new Picpus superior terminated the philanthropy. The College at Rue Picpus 33 was demolished 1905. In *Les Miserables*, Hugo used it as Valjean's and Cosette's refuge when fleeing.

12. Macnamara told fellow Irishman Lt Somerville RN he was 'educated at Trinity College, Dublin': H.A. Kay, *HMS Collingwood, Journal of Lt Somerville* (Edinburgh: Pentland Press,1986), p.184, 28 April 1846. Chaplain Proctor, BA, Trinity, conferred in 1837, might have commented. From 1794 Trinity admitted Catholics, but RC theology was not offered, RC bishops warned increasingly attending against it, and Macnamara is not in *Alumni Dublinenses 1593–1846* (London: Butchel & Sadleir, 1924). Archbishop Slattery of Cashel graduated from Trinity in 1804 before training for the priesthood, and graduated MA in 1832. Three years of Macnamara's training, 1834–37, remain unaccounted.

13. Sources for Macnamara's first posting: Charles Lever, *Jack Hinton* (Dublin: Curry, 1843) and *ODNB* article, *Charles Lever* (OUP, 2004), who cast Comyn as 'Fr Tom Loftus'; W. Battersby, *The Complete (Irish) Catholic Directory, Almanack and Register, 1838* (Dublin: Battersby); S. Lewis, *A Topographical Dictionary of Ireland*, (London: Lewis, 1837), to which Comyn, Birmingham and Bishop Clancy's brother contributed; H.W. Weir, *Houses of Clare* (Clare: Ballinadesha Press,1999): Baltard House has been demolished; I. Murphy, *Before the Famine Struck; 'Life in West Clare, 1834–45* (Dublin: Irish Academic Press, 1996) analyses Comyn's parish; 'H.M. Commissioners for the Poor, Ireland', *First Report, County Clare 1835*; I. Murphy, 'Building a Church in Nineteenth-Century Ireland', in *The Other Clare: Shannon Archeological and Historical Society*, 2, 1978 pp.20–26; *Illustrated London News*, 15 and 22 December 1849, called Comyn's parish, Kilrush Poor Law Union, 'the new Skibbereen'.

14. T.P. O'Neill, 'The Catholic Church and The Relief of the Poor, 1815–45', *Archivium Hibernicum*, 31 (Maynooth, 1973), pp.132–45.

15. J. Birmingham, *Memoir of Very Rev. Theobald Mathew* (Dublin, 1840): the list of clergy involved (London edition, p.76; US edition, p.106), was badly typeset from the manuscript; *ODNB* article, *Theobald Mathew*, (OUP, 2004); 'John F Quinn, Temperance in Tipperary, Archbishop Slattery and Fr Mathew', *Tipperary Historical Journal*, 14 (1995), pp.133–9.

16. B. Macnamee, 'The Second Reformation', *Irish Theological Quarterly*, 33, 1 March 1966, pp.39–64.

17. C.J. Riethmueller, *Frederick Lucas* (London: Bell and Daldy, 1862); E. Lucas, *Life of Frederick Lucas,MP,* (London: Burns & Oates, 1886); *ODNB* article, *Frederick Lucas* (OUP, 2004).

18. For Bishop Clancy, see J. McEvoy, *Carlow College, 1793–1993* (Carlow: St Patrick's College, 1993), entry, *William Clancy*; P. Guilday, *Life and Times of John England*, 2 Vols, (New York: American Press, 1927); Pat Carey, *An Immigrant Bishop* (US Catholic Hist. Soc.,Vol.

36,1982);ODNB article, *John England* (OUP, 2004); 'John Hynes' *Diary* (Melbourne Diocese Hist. Commission; B.Condon (ed.), 2002); *The Tablet*, 15 and 29 May, 1841, '*Catholic Intelligence*'; *Shorrocks Manuscript*, Jesuit Archives, London and Georgetown, Guyana; *The Tablet* Online Archive.

19. Ignatius Murphy, Vicar General and historian of Killaloe diocese, could not find Bishop Kennedy's report of Macnamara's offence in Propaganda Fide archive, Rome. Patrick Connors, SJ, of Georgetown cathedral, Guyana, saw a copy, since mislaid, described to the author as 'vague and bland'. Francis Clancy MD's hostile summary was 'proven seduction'. Bishop Clancy, who had retained the *exeat*, sent a copy to the Colony Secretary in Georgetown in 1844 to undermine the newly promoted Vicar Administrator. Macnamara's mother Mary and brother John were living in 1841, the year John joined the Irish Constabulary.

20. *The Tablet*, 29 May 1841, *Catholic Intelligence* and *Mr Langdale MP's Dinner*.

21. *Annals of North Presentation Convent*, Cork City, 10 and 17 June 1841 (Mss, Presentation Order Archive); John Hynes' *Diary* (Melbourne, 2002), p.37, 17 December 1843, on the 'elopement'.

CHAPTER THREE

1. *The Tablet*, 29 May 1841; *Royal Demerara Gazette*, 3 July 1841; Sol Benjamin, US consul in Guiana, British Library, SPR, Mic. B 22 (144). Selective passenger lists were published in *The Tablet* and *Demerara Gazette*.

2. *The True[sic] Tablet*, 5 and 12 March 1842, under '*Colonial Correspondence*'. William Nightingale, Guiana, to Charles Weld, barrister and *Tablet* trustee, 31 July and 20 October 1841, excerpts published at Weld's request. *The Tablet* retitled itself briefly, *The True Tablet*, February–December 1842.

3. TNA, CO 111, 203, 371, Henry Light, *Report on The State of Religion in British Guiana*, September 1843.

4. Irish College Rome Archive Online, *Cullen Papers, Trinidad & British Guiana Supplement 1837–48* (CUL/TBG), 4.

5. *The Tablet*, 12 March 1842, '*Colonial Correspondence*', Nightingale to Weld. Snuff was believed to fumigate the body.

6. J. Bernau, *Missionary Labours in British Guiana* (London: Shaw, 1847), p.5; A. Trollope, *West Indies and The Spanish Main* (London: Chapman & Hall, 1859), pp.167–8; B. Premium, *Eight Years in British Guiana* (London: Longmans, 1850), p.26.

7. Georgetown RC Cathedral Archive, Macnamara to Clancy, and Clancy to Light, 15 December 1841, abridged.

8. *The True [sic] Tablet*, 5 March 1842, '*Colonial Correspondence*', above Nightingale's first letter.

9. Ibid., 30 April 1842.

10. Ibid., 4 June 1842.

11. TNA, CO 111, 203, 372, Henry Light, *Report on State of Religion in BG*, September 1843. The clergy of the established churches of England (Anglican) and of Scotland (Presbyterian) clergy, were state-subsidised in the colonies, as were Catholic clergy after Emancipation; Methodist and Congregationalist clergy were not.

12. TNA, CO 112, 25 & 26 *passim*, *Correspondence, British Guiana*.

13. TNA, CO 111, 185, 25 May 1842.

14. TNA, CO 111, 189, 24 June 1842; ibid., 191, 22 July 1842.

15. For Guiana immigrant schemes, see W. Ireland, *Demerariana* (Georgetown: Baldwin, 1896), pp.52–3; B. Premium, *Eight Years in BG* (London: Longmans, 1850), pp.38–9; H.G. Dalton, *History of British Guiana* (London: Longmans, 1855), pp.127, 444–6, 452; *Emigrant and Colonial Gazette*, 1, 22 August (CLEC,1848); M.Menenez, *The Portuguese of Guyana* (S.I., 1993); B. Moore, *Guyana after Slavery* (*Caribbean Studies*, Book 4: Routledge, 1987); J. Rodway, *History of BG,1668 To Present*, III, Chap. 29 (Georgetown: Thompson, 1894); *Shorrocks Manuscript*, pp.69–70, Georgetown Cathedral Archive; F. Millroux, *Emigration á la Guyana Anglaise* (1842); TNA, CO 111, 229, September 1845, enclosure from Dr Charles Stilwell of London; W. Dupouy (ed.), *Diary of Sir Robert Ker Porter, Caracas, 1830–41* (Caracas: Archivo de la Nación, 1966); N. Perazzo, *La Immigración en Venezuela, 1830–50* (Congreso de la Republica, 1982); J. Rodway, *The Story of Georgetown*, pp.71, 83–88 (Demerara: Argosy, 1920); Hynes' *Diary*, p.171, 20 September 1848; V.T. Daly, *A Short History of the Guyana People* (London: Macmillan, 1975), p.174; Richard and Robert Schomburgck, *Travels in British Guiana 1840–44* (Weber: Leipzig, 1847; trans. by W. Roth for Georgetown *Daily Chronicle*, 1922), I, pp.182–7, describes the Schomburgcks' Irish-Indian welcome from the Cullen brothers at Santa Rosa. Immigration from Madeira ended in 1842.

16. TNA, CO 111, 208, 500, 29 February 1844, Light to Stanley with enclosed, *Private and Confidential.*

17. All Hallows College, Dublin, Archives, *Hynes Correspondence*, BG 2, 1 September 1842, Hynes to Archbishop Murray; BG 12, 30 November 1843, Hynes to Rev. Hand; BG 14, same to same, 26 February 1845. In BG 18 (1846) and BG 20 (1848) Hynes details a missioner's manner and garb: 'docile, obedient, gentlemanly, respecting the episcopal character', wearing 'white cotton socks and shirt, light frock coat, black trousers, standing collar, half boots, broad hat'.

18. *The Tablet*, 8 July 1843, '*Catholic Intelligence*', letters, Clancy and War Office.

19. Irish College Rome Archive Online, *Cullen Papers*, CUL/TBG, 24.

20. *Royal Demerara Gazette*, 16 May 1843; 3 June 1843.

21. TNA, CO 111, 203, 375-6, Henry Light, *Report on State of Religion in BG*, September 1843. Clancy dismissed the committee overseeing mission finances.

22. Bishop John Hynes, *Diary* (B. Condon (ed.), Melbourne Archdiocesan Historical Commission, 2002), p.182, 23 November 1848; p.223, 23 March 1850. The Pope shows 'more civility than the merest understrapper at Propaganda'.

23. Ibid., pp. 2 & 3, 1, 6 and 11 May 1843.

24. Ibid., p.21, 20 August 1843.

25. *The Tablet*, 26 August 1843, '*Catholic Intelligence*'; TNA, CO 111, 217, 138 enclosure, printed letter Francis Clancy to Lord Stanley, August 1844, copy also sent by Francis Clancy to Hynes, January 1844; *Shorrocks Manuscript*, p.76, Georgetown RC Cathedral Archive; TNA, CO 111, 208, 495, 29 February, 1844.

26. Propaganda Fide Archives, Rome, *SRC Americas*, 1, *Antille* vii, 339–400, in B. Condon, *Letters and Documents of Nineteenth-Century Australian Catholic History* (Melbourne Archdiocese, 2001) 'compiled by Eugene Macnamara and John McDonnell , priests of British Guiana, to the best of our knowledge, June 1843'. They calculated that Bishop Clancy had received $38,786 between his arriving in 1838 and January 1843, of which $23,000 (59 per cent) could not be reconciled. This was 'exclusive of annual grants by the Colonial Office'. The US and Mexican dollar/*peso*, 4 to £1 sterling, were international currencies.

27. Macnamara's week in Rome is reconstructed from Hynes, *Diary*, pp.11, 21, 24–5, 1 July, 20 August, 2–14 September 1843.

28. The missioners' return from Rome is reconstructed from: *Shorrocks Manuscript*, pp.86–7, 145, Georgetown RC Cathedral Archive; *Royal Demerara Gazette*, November 1843–October 1844, notably 14 November, 1843, 20 August 1844, 3 September and 17 October, 1844; *The Tablet*, 18 November 1843, 22 June, 31 August, and 19 October 1844, 'Catholic Intelligence'; *Cullen Papers*, Irish College Rome Archive Online, CUL/TBG, 26–30 (November–December 1843), 32–3 (January 1844), 35, 37 (February 1844), 38–9 (August 1844), 44 (November 1844); Hynes, *Diary*, pp.31–55, 1 November 1843–12 July 1844; Hynes, *Correspondence*, All Hallows Archive, BG 10–23, 1842–48.

29. TNA, CO 111, 208, 495–7, Light to Stanley, 29 February 1844.

30. Propaganda Fide Archives, Rome, SRC *Americas*, 1, *Antille*, vii, 501–2, 14 November 1843, in B. Condon, ibid., above, *n.*26.

31. Stanley's endorsement on Despatch, above, *n.*29.

32. The Colonial Office and Governor of Guiana's role in adjudicating on claims to oversee the Guiana Catholic mission can be followed through TNA CO 111, 208: 493, 495–7; 209: 302, 306–9, 312, 317, 319, 494; 210: 64; 211: 192, & enclosures, 206–8; 211, 326; 212: 167; 215: 524; 217: 130, 138–9, 498–9, 500, 503. *The Tablet*, 19 October 1844, under 'Colonial', documents Hynes' case before Court of Policy, 23 August 1844. James Rodway, colonist and historian of Georgetown, concluded, 'The Roman Catholics, respected by all the churches, have had a brilliant record since Dr Clancy's departure', *Story of Georgetown* (Demerara: Argosy, 1920), p.90.

CHAPTER FOUR

1. M. Orozco y Berra, *Historia de la Ciudad de Mexico Hasta 1854* (Mexico: Sec. de Educación Pública, 1973). Macnamara's date of arrival, M.P.Costeloe, private correspondence.

2. TNA, FO 207, 19, *Consular Miscellany, Mexico City*, 98,1845.

3. The huge convent, largest in Latin America, was half-demolished in 1856. Macnamara preached February 1845 – March 1846, Sundays,11a.m.,in the Servite chapel (now demolished) in the convent church atrium: *El Siglo IX*, 14, 16 and 21 February 1845 (advertisements) ; Hynes, *Diary*, p.53, 8 June, 1844, his meeting with John Urquhart just in from Mexico.

4. Hansard, Series 3, LXXVIII, pp.430–432, 7 March 1845. After Santa Anna was deposed, December 1844, his captured correspondence reputedly revealed talks with the British ambassador. Peel and Palmerston together denied in Parliament that Britain had ever offered $5 million, £5 million or even 25 million piastres for San Francisco Bay. The exiled Santa Anna's property was 'protected' by consul MacKintosh, 1845–46, under his Mexican wife's name.

5. W.J. Fitzpatrick, *Correspondence of Daniel O'Connell* (London: Murray, 1888), II, pp.206–210, to Joseph Sturge, abolitionist, 26 August 1839.

6. TNA, FO 204, 89, 30 May 1845, 588–90, *Despatch 52* (Letterbook), or FO 204, 88, ff.483–4 (received original), 30 May 1845, Bankhead to Aberdeen. Hynes' letter to the Archbishop has not been found.

7. Hansard, Series 3, LXXXVIII, pp.978–95, 24 August 1846.

8. F. Calderon de Barca, *Life in Mexico* (London: Chapman, Hall, 1843), p.13.

9. RGS, *Clements R Markham Papers*, CRM, 12, 55. As cadet and midshipman in training,

Markham copied *Collingwood* charts showing the Cape Mendocino hinterland as *New Albion*. Drake's 1579 claim prompted Spain to begin a short-lived survey.

10. A. Forbes (Sir John Forbes (ed.)), *California: A History of Upper and Lower California* (London: Smith,Elder, 1839), pp.152, 310–11, 314, 321; *El Siglo IX*, 14 April 1844 and 13 May 1845; Short's and Richard Hartnell's reservations about colonies, S.B. Dakin, *The Lives of William Hartnell* (Stanford: Stanford UP, 1949), pp.245, 259. J.A. Hawgood, 'A Proposed Prussian Colonisation of Upper California', in *Southern California Quarterly*, 48, 4, December 1966, pp.353–368. The Prussian ambassador to the US thought California suitable for military training and commerce, but soon realised Prussians 'think in acres', Mexicans 'in degrees of latitude'.

11. R. Thompson, *London Commercial Directory* (1844).

12. H.H. de Bohiges, *British Merchant Houses in Mexico*, PhD Thesis (London School Economics, 1988) pp.42–3; M.P. Costeloe, *Bonds and Bondholders* (Westport, Ct: Praeger, 2003), p.37ff. The US *chargé d'affaires* in Santiago, Chile, warned Washington, 12 July 1837, that Britain would press Chile to repay its bondholders and might take Chiloé island in lieu: W.R. Manning, *Diplomatic Correspondence of The US*, Vol.5, (Washington: Carnegie, 1935), *Chile and Colombia*, Doc. 1669, pp.130–1.

13. This author's treatment of the bondholders owes much to M.P. Costeloe, *Bonds and Bondholders* (ibid.), and his scholarly generosity. Currency exchange rates varied slightly, but generally the US dollar and Mexican *peso* had parity, the pound exchanging for four.

14. On Powles' regret about losing California, especially after the Gold Rush, see Chapter 9, *n*.19. Schneider died 1851, Powles his main beneficiary. On the bondholder loans, see M. P. Costeloe, ibid.; R. Salvucci, *Politics, Markets and Mexico's 'London Debt', 1823–87* (New York: Cambridge UP, 2009); E. Turlington, *Mexico and Its Foreign Creditors* (New York: Colombia UP, 1930); C. Fenn, *Compendium of Foreign Funds* (London, 1837), p.77; earlier treatments of colonising California, are found in: G.L. Rives, *The US and Mexico 1821–48*, II, (New York: Scribner, 1913), pp.85–101; R.G. Cleland, 'Early Sentiment for the Annexation of California', *Southwestern Historical Quarterly*, 18, 1, July 1914, pp.1–40; 18, 2 October 1914, pp.121–161; 18.3, January 1915, pp.231–260; R.G. Cleland, *A History of California* (New York: Macmillan, 1922), Ch 14; E.D. Adams, 'English Interest in California', *American Historical Review*, 14, 4, (1909), pp.744–63; L.G. Engelson, 'Proposals for Colonisation of California by England', *CHSQ*, 18, 2, June 1939, pp.136–148; S.G. Jackson. 'Two pro-British Plots in Alta California', *Southern California Quarterly*, 15, 2, Summer 1973, pp.105-112, describing a *californio* approach to British vice-consul Forbes, 1844; ibid., *The British and The California Dream, Rumours, Myths and Legends*, 57, 3, Fall 1975, pp.251–270.

15. R. Salvucci, ibid., p.67.

16. Sir G. Simpson, *Narrative of a Journey Round the World, 1841–2* (London, 1847); S.R. Bown, *Merchant Kings* (London: Conway, 2010), pp.193–237. James Forbes, British vice-Consul in Alta California, was HBC's last representative there, 1845.

17. R.C.Wyllie, *Mexico:Report on its Finances since Independence* (London: Baily, 1844) pp.70–74; 267. Tasker's annotated copy of Wyllie's *Report* is in the British Library, London. In 1849 the California Constitutional Convention declared the California climate too dry for plantations, and therefore for slaves.

18. Susanna D. Bryant, *The Lives of William Hartnell* (Stanford UP, 1949), pp.259–70; Bancroft Library, California, *Vallejo Papers*, CB 33, 369; CB 34, 2, 10, 13, 14, 16, 17, 26, 28, 72.

19. R.C. Wyllie, *Letter to G.R. Robinson, Chairman of Spanish American Bondholders* (London: Baily, 1840) pp.9–12.

20. C. Sellars, *James K. Polk, Continentalist, 1843–46* (New Jersey: Princeton UP, 1966), p.332.

21. Hansard, Series 3, LXXXVIII, 978–95, 24 Aug 1846. The terse record ends, '*Subject Dropped*'.

22. M. Castañares, *Documentos Relativos al Departamento de California* (Mexico: La Voz, 1845); H.H. Bancroft, *History of California*, Vol.3, 1825–40, (San Francisco: The History Company, 1884), pp.411–17; ibid., Vol.4, 1841–45, (ibid.,1885), pp.27, 77, 191, 518, 524; ibid., Vol.5, 1846–48, (ibid. 1886), pp.191–223; *US vs Limantour*, 1857, N. California District Court, SFo,Transcript, p.429. Castañares' self-inflating interview in *San Francisco Bulletin*, 12 September 1857 with H.D. Barrows: H. Barrows and L. Ingersoll, *Memorial and Biographical History of The Coastal Counties of Central California* (Chicago: Lewis, 1893), pp.42–45.

23. Archivo General de la Nación, Mexico City, Gobernación, S/C Caia 4, *El Proyecto Macnamara*, ff.12–16 and *verso*, 1846, Document A/1, secretarial script, signed by Macnamara, undated, here abridged for rhetoric and repetition. This verifies three of the five papers in Pico's captured archive printed as Appendix to John Frémont's California Claims, 1848, *Senate Committee Report 75*, pp.19–21, 77–79. As the *californios* retreated south in 1846, Governor Pico hid selected archive items, including the Macnamara papers and land registers. When US soldiers found them, Frémont extracted the Macnamara papers to take to Washington as his alibi for supporting the Bear Flag revolt without authority: a serious British threat from Macnamara and Seymour would exonerate him. The Senate printed the dossier with its *Report* on Frémont's Claims, March 1848. The Pico papers then disappeared. Macnamara's own documents were found at his death in 1852, but have also disappeared.

24. *La Voz del Pueblo*, 5 February 1845.

25. Macnamara demanded priority consideration around the end of July. MacKintosh's proposal was sent in full copy by diplomatic bag to London: TNA, FO 204, 88, 30 July 1845, 622–4, Despatch 53, Letterbook Copy, with MacKintosh enclosure, 625–31.

26. Archivo General de la Nación, Mexico City, Gobernación, S/C Caia 4, 1846, *El Proyecto Macnamara*, 10-11 and *verso*, in secretarial script, amended and signed by Macnamara, undated; *The Times* (London) 6 August 1845, '*The Affairs of Mexico*', Mexico 29 June 1845, on the Irish colony scheme, Macnamara not named; G.L. Rives, 'Mexican Diplomacy on The Eve of War with The United States', *American Historical Review*, 18, 2, January 1913, pp.275–294.

27. R.J. Scally, *The End of Hidden Ireland* (New York: Oxford UP, 1995) describes this exceptional assisted emigration from Crown lands in Roscommon; Kerby A. Miller, *Emigrants and Exiles* (New York Oxford OUP, 1985), pp.48–50, 195-197, 237, 295.

28. I. Hartman, *Brief in Mission Cases* (San Francisco: National Print, 1859), pp.63–5; Z. Engelhardt, *Missions and Missionaries of California* (San Francisco: Barry, 1915), Vol.4, Upper California, (Pt. 3), pp.548–9.

29. M.M. Quaife, *Polk, Diary*, 2 November 1845; R. Stark and R. Finke, *The Churching of America* (New Brunswick, NJ: Rutgers UP, 1992) p.275, cited in K. Phillips, *American Theocracy* (New York:Viking, 2006), pp.107–8.

30. W. Shepperson, *British Emigration to North America* (Oxford: Blackwells, 1957), p.135; S. Lewis, *Topographical Dictionary of Ireland* (London: Lewis, 1837); *The Tablet*, 15 May 1841; 21 May 1842; 11 March 1843 and 1 June, 1844; S. Morse, *Imminent Dangers to The*

Free Institutions of the US of Foreign Immigration, (1835; republished New York: Arno, 1959), pp.8–10; C.M. Drury, 'Protestant Beginnings in California', *CHSQ*, 26, 2, June 1947, pp.163–74; C.A. Milner *et al.*, *History of The American West* (New York: Oxford UP, 1994), pp.368–369; I. Whelan, *The Bible War in Ireland* (Dublin: Lilliput & Wisconsin UP, 2005); Hynes, *Diary*, 19 April, 1858, Papal audience.

31. H.H. Bancroft, *History of California*, Vol.3, pp.259–90 (San Francisco:The History Company, 1886); C.A. Hutchinson, *Frontier Settlement in Mexican California: The Híjar-Padrés Colony and its Origins* (New Haven: Yale UP, 1969); A. Osio, *History of Alta California* (1851 Mss, published translation; Madison Wisconsin UP;1996), Chapters 6–7; Agustin Jansens, *Libro de Mia Vita* (1953 ed.), Chapters 2–4; *La Reforma*, 22 January, 10–15 February 1846; D.J. Weber, *The Mexican Frontier, 1821–46* (Albuquerque: New Mexico UP, 1982), pp.180–90, 198–204; S.W. Hackel, *Alta California, People in Motion* (Berkeley: UCP, & Huntington Library, San Marino, 2010), pp.133–48, a view from within the native Indian culture. The missions died before maturing.

32. Cuevas to Híjar, 11 Aug 1845, Document D (Spanish) and E (English), Appendix to Senate Committee *Report* 75, 1848, above, *n*.23. Macnamara presented it to Pico at Santa Bárbara, 24 June 1846, and Frémont took it from Pico's archive to Washington, 1847. The original has disappeared. Híjar died in December 1845 at Reina de Los Angeles. For Cuevas to Murphy, see G. L. Rives, ibid., 93–100.

CHAPTER FIVE

[Note: The Seymour of Ragley Papers, Warwickshire Record Office, UK, include Admiral Seymour's letterbooks, diaries and signal journals 1844–48: WRO CR 114A. British National Archive (TNA) holds naval logbooks and final-version received letters. President Polk's conversations Sept.–Dec. 1845 are recorded in James K. Polk's Diary, 1845–9, 4 Volumes, ed. Milo Milton Quaife, 1910, McClurg, Chicago.]

1. S.G. Jackson, Two pro-British Plots in Alta California, *Southern California Quarterly*, Vol. 15, 2, Summer 1973, pp.107–112. The second 'plot', the General Council at Santa Bárbara in June 1846, was a departmental Assembly initiative: Macnamara and *Juno* arrived well after it was cancelled.

2. H.H. Bancroft, *History of California,1840–45* (SFo: History Company, 1886), Vol. 4, pp.523–33; British Library, Additional Mss 43170, 24, Bankhead to Aberdeen, *Private*, 30 July 1845, Letterbook *précis*; *La Voz del Pueblo*, 4 June 1845; TNA FO 24, 88, 520–1, Despatch 74, Bankhead to Aberdeen, 30 July 1845. Herrera's concern about foreign colonists may be why Macnamara was apparently not reported in the Mexican press.

3. W.R. Manning, *Diplomatic Correspondence of The US, VIII, Mexico 1831–48* (Washington: Carnegie, 1937) Parrott to Secretary Buchanan, 5 August 1845, Doc 3606, p.745.

4. M. Cole (ed.), *Don Pío Pico's Historical Narrative* (Glendale: Clark, 1973), p.122, dictated by Pico, 1878; G.P. Hammond, *The Larkin Papers, III* (Berkeley UCP, 1951), p.244, Stearns to Larkin, 19 June 1845.

5. F.J. Weber, *Writings of Francisco García Diego y Moreno* (Los Angeles: Weber,1976), pp.173, 180, letters to Híjar 18 August, and to Herrera, 27 September 1845. The bishop spoke of 'a new chain of missions in the interior and to the north'. In April 1845, Herrera restored mission funds and property, but his November order halting sales of mission land never reached California.

6. Archivo General de la Nación, Mexico, Gobernación, S/C Caia 4, 1846, *El Proyecto Macnamara*, 3–9 and verso. The Council response was not tabled in Supreme Congress,

September–December 1846: J. Mateos, *Historia Parliamentaria de Los Congressos Mexicanos, 1821–51,* (Mexico, 1877–86).

7. P.M. Jonas, 'William Parrott, American Claims and The Mexican' War, *Journal of The Early Republic,* 12, 2, Summer 1992, pp.212–240; F.A. Knapp Jr, 'Biographical Traces of Consul John Parrott', *California Historical Society Quarterly,* 34, 2, June 1955, pp.111–124.

8. *Diplomatic Instructions of Sec of State to Special Missions, 1801–1906,* Vol.1, US NARA Microcopy 77, Roll 152; *Despatches from US Ministers to Mexico to Secretary of State, 1843–47,* Vol.12, Parrott to Secretary of State, 5, 16, 23, 26, 29 August 1845, Microcopy 97, Roll 13, only three of which (5, 23 and 26) appear at all, and those heavily edited, in W.R. Manning, *Diplomatic Correspondence of the US, VIII, Mexico* 1831–48 (Washington: Carnegie, 1937), Docs 3606–3608, pp,745–747. Diaries and memoirs, but no minutes recorded cabinet deliberations in Washington and London: H.B. Learned, 'Cabinet Meetings under President Polk', *American Historical Association Annual Report,* I (1914), pp.229–242.

9. J.T. White (ed.), *National Cyclopedia of American Biography* (New York: White, 1898), Vol.5, p.55, G. Bancroft, article *Polk, James K.*

10. W. Cutler *et al., Correspondence of James K. Polk,* Vol. IX, 1845, pp.244, 369, 397; Vol. X, 1846, pp.97, 114, 168, 183, 220 (University of Tennessee, 1996, 2004). John O'Sullivan, Annexation, *United States Magazine and Democratic Review,* 17, 1, July/August 1845, pp.5–10.

11. M.M. Quaife, *James K. Polk's Diary, 1845–9* (Chicago: McClurg, 1910), 24 October 1845; T.H. Benton, *Thirty Years View* (New York: Appleton, 1856), 2, p.693; J.C. Frémont, *Memoirs of My Life* (Chicago: Clark, Belford, 1886), I, p.535.

12. Jessie B. Frémont, 'The Conquest of California', *The Century,* 41, 6, April 1891, pp.919–20, edited in John Frémont's name from his manuscript and notes. It cites G.T. Curtis, *Life of James Buchanan,* I, (New York, 1883), pp.579–625. Frémont died in July 1890 leaving this article and Volume II of his *Memoirs* unfinished. Jessie declared that British policy was 'Verified by the great Macnamara grant'. She claimed to know the confidential nature of the expeditions, see Jessie B.Frémont, 'Origins of The Frémont Explorations', *The Century,* 41, 5, March, 1891, pp.766–771. For Buchanan's despatches to Black, Larkin and Frémont, see J.B. Moore, *Works of John Buchanan,* VI, 1844–6 (New York: Antiquarian Press, 1960), pp.260, 275, 294–306.

13. James K. Polk, *State of the Union Address, 2 December 1845,* pp.10–17 (Washington, Senate: Ritchie and Hall, 1st Session 29th Congress); W.R. Manning, *US Diplomatic Correspondence* VIII, Mexico 1831–48, (Washington: Carnegie, 1937), Doc 3636, p.777 (extract) 17 December, Slidell to Buchanan; M.M. Quaife, Polk's *Diary* (1910), 13 May 1845, the day war was declared, and 31 May. The London *Times* called Polk's Message to Congress 'hostile'. WRO CR 114A, 417 (2), Seymour to Blake, 27 Feb 1845; to Bankhead 17 April 1845. D.K. Goodwin, *Team of Rivals* (New York: Schuster, 2006), pp.120–4.

14. Archivo General de La Nación, (1925), Publications 15, *Lord Aberdeen, Texas y California* (1925), 42–54, Murphy to Pena y Pena, 1 Oct. and 1 Nov. 1845; W.D. Jones, *Lord Aberdeen and The Americas* (Athens: University of Georgia Press, 1958), for Murphy's reports in general; G.L. Rives, 'Mexican Diplomacy on The Eve of War with the US', *American Historical Review,* XVIII, 2, January 1913; G.L. Rives, *The US and Mexico, 1821–48,* II, 94–100; British Library, Add. Ms 43064, Aberdeen to Peel, 23 September 1845, written immediately after the conversation with Murphy.

15. J. Ramírez, December 1845, correspondence collection in Mexico During the War with the

US, *University of Missouri Studies*, 23,1, (1950) p.15; *Lord Aberdeen &c*, p.61, Murphy to Foreign Minister, 1 January 1846; Sir Arthur Gordon, *Lord Aberdeen* (London: Dent,1905), pp.182–4; WRO 114A, 417(2), Seymour to Admiralty, 13 June 1846, at sea for Monterey.

16. All Souls College, Oxford, Vaughan Papers, Bankhead Correspondence, C 20/3, Mrs B. to Sir Charles Vaughan, 29 October 1845; Gene M. Black, *Mexico Views Manifest Destiny, 1821–46* (Albuquerque, New Mexico U.P., 1973), p.139; M.P. Costeloe, *Generals Santa Anna and Paredes y Arrillaga in Mexico, 1841–3* (Bristol UP, 1989), pp.2, 9–10; Waddy Thompson, *Recollections of Mexico* (New York: Wiley & Putnam, 1846) p.239, with Santa Anna and Paredes in mind as effective rulers.

17. B.M. Gough, 'Lt Peel, British Naval Intelligence and The Oregon Crisis', *Northern Mariner*, IV, 4, October 1994, 8, 1–14; B.M. Gough, 'The Royal Navy and The Oregon Crisis', *British Columbia Studies*, 9, Spring 1971, 15–37; W.R. Manning, *Diplomatic Correspondence, of the US, VIII, Mexico 1831–48* (Washington: Carnegie,1937), Doc 3612, pp.755–56, Larkin to Buchanan, 29 September 1845, '[Gordon and Peel Jr] were vexed at seeing so many Yankee settlers in California'. Lt Peel reported to the Admiralty that US settlements in the Willamette Valley would join those in the Rio Sacramento Valley, effectively conveying Oregon and California together to the US. Hudson's Bay Company had excluded settlers from Oregon, but its authority weakened in later years. Lt Peel advised Britain's keeping Vancouver Island at all costs.

18. All Souls College, Oxford, ibid., C20/4, 29 December 1845; C/20/1, 29 October 1844.

19. Ibid., Vaughan Papers, Doyle Correspondence, 2, Percy Doyle to brother Sir John, Wroughton Castle, Banbury, UK. November 1845.

20. J. Hussey, 'Origin of the Gillespie Mission', *California Historical Society Quarterly*, 19, 1940, 43-53; G.W. Ames, 'Gillespie and the Conquest of California, Letters to Navy Secretary Bancroft, 11 February 1846 – 8 July 1848', *California Historical Quarterly*, Vol. 17, 2, June 1938, pp.123–140; ibid., Vol.17, 3, pp. 271–284; ibid., Vol.17, 4, pp.325–350; R.R. Stenberg, 'Further Letters of Archibald Gillespie, 20 October 1845–16 January 1846', ibid., Vol.18, 3, June 1939, pp.217–228. Oral instructions from Polk and Buchanan are unknown; Gillespie memorised Buchanan's (known) letter to Larkin; contents of family letters delivered to Frémont are unknown; A. Brooke Caruso, *The Mexican Spy Company, US Covert Operations in Mexico, 1845–6* (Jefferson, NC: McFarland, 1991); John Frémont, 'The Conquest of California', *The Century*, 41, 6, April 1891, claimed the letters from Secretary Buchanan and Senator Benton were 'a trumpet giving no uncertain note [that] I was to act'.

21. Archivo General de la Nación, *El Proyecto Macnamara*, 17, draft letter from Castillo y Lanzas, with amendments not in US Senate version, Document C, English and Spanish versions, Frémont Claim Papers, 30th Congress, 1st Session, Senate Report 75, 1848, 22 and 79. (See Chap. 4, Note 21).

22. Ibid., 18–19 and *verso*, written and signed in English by Macnamara, with Spanish translation.

23. G.P. Hammond, *The Larkin Papers*, Vol.5, pp.53–4, Larkin to Buchanan, 18 June 1846; Larkin to Stearns, 14 June, Stearns Collection, SG Box 40, The Huntington Library; Hammond, ibid., Larkin to Buchanan, 19 August, 1846; M.M. Quaife, *Polk's Diary* (Chicago: McLurg, 1910), 8 May 1846. $40 million would secure everything west of Rio Grande and all Alta California. After the War, the US cancelled Mexico's $3 million debt to private individuals and paid $15 million (with $1.8 million interest). $3.1 million of this went to the bondholders through consul MacKintosh, who took $600,000 commission. By 1850 California had produced gold for the US vastly exceeding the pre-War US bid for California; total gold production in 1858 was estimated at $500 million.

24. G.P. Hammond, ibid., Vol. 4, 13 May 1846, 370–374, in Pío Pico's proclamation of the Santa Bárbara *Consejo General*.

25. Ibid., Vol.3, 31 May 1845, pp.215–220, Larkin to editor, *New York Sun*.

26. Ibid., Vol.3, 7 July 1845, from Marsh, pp.259–260; from Stearns, 19 June 1845, 244–45; from Jones, 10 June 1845, 231–232.

27. Ibid., Vol.3, from Jones, 21 September 1845, pp.358–360; ibid., Vol.4, from McKinley, 23 January 1846, pp.180–1. *Hartweg Correspondence*, Royal Horticultural Society, Linley Library, Hartweg to LHS, 21 December, 1845, Queretaro, as Herrera tried to disperse the army; Hartweg's *Journal*, 2 July 1846, Monterey. Californian sequoia trees still barb the English rural horizon, the literal fruits of Hartweg's and others' travels. Until a twentieth-century reconciliation, the *sequoia gigantica* was known in UK as *wellingtonea* and in US as *washingtonea*; Dr Thomas Coulter brought the sequoia back to Glasnevin, Dublin.

28. W.R. Manning, *Diplomatic Correspondence of the US, VIII, Mexico, 1831–48* (Washington: Carnegie, 1937), 19/24 February 1846, Black to Slidell, annotated to Doc 3651, p.816, Buchanan; J. Smith, *The War with Mexico*, (New York: Macmillan, 1919), pp.102–121; British Library, Add. Mss 43170, 26; TNA FO 204, 91, 453, Bankhead to Aberdeen, May 1846, reminding Aberdeen 'of a colonisation plan to secure that fine country' mentioned in his despatch 30 July 1845; *Diplomatic Correspondence of the US, VIII, Mexico*, Vol. VIII, (Washington: Carnegie, 1937), Docs. 3651 and note, 3650 and note; Parrott to Buchanan, 2 September 1845, and still valid. Bankhead's Legation and MacKintosh's Consulate (*El Palacio*) were at former Calle de Capuchinas, 5 and 10, two blocks south of the Zócalo and Presidential palace.

29. All Souls College, Oxford, Vaughan Correspondence, C20/5, 29 May 1846.

30. M. Wale (ed.), *Journals of Francis Parkman* (London: Eyre and Spottiswoode, 1947), entries for May 1846; W. Jacobs (ed.), *Letters of Francis Parkman* (Oklahoma UP, 1960), I, 38 and note; B.M. Gough, *The Royal Navy and the NW Coast of North America, 1810-1914* (Vancouver: Br Columbia UP;1971), pp.68-71.

31. A. Nasatir, 'French Consulate in California 1843–56', *California Historical Society Quarterley*, March 1933, 12, pp.35–64; Paris Foreign Office, Political Correspondence, Mexico, Chapeau to Guizot, from Mexico City, 29 April, 1846, pp.281–4; Gerault, to Mexico City from Mazatlán, 13 May 1846, pp.323–4.

32. TNA FO 203, 19, Mexican Consular Records; Seymour Papers, 418, 2, 166ff, Seymour to Bankhead, 26 April, 1846; 245, Seymour to Ellenborough, 13 June 1846.

33. F. Walpole, *Four Years in The Pacific* (London: Bentley, 1849), p.181; L.W. Hastings, *The Emigrants Guide to Oregon and California* (1845, Princeton UP facsimile, 1932), pp.138–9. Walpole served on Seymour's flagship, HMS *Collingwood*, 1844-6, before transferring to HMS *Juno* at Honolulu in September.

34. *Diplomatic Correspondence of the US, VIII, Mexico, 1831–48* (Washington: Carnegie, 1837), Black to Secretary of State Buchanan, 21 April 1846, Doc 3666, pp.844–5. In 1821, in the first flush of independence, Mexican leaders envisaged a Greater Mexican Empire, stretching north to Alaska: M. Meyer and W. Beazley, *The Oxford History of Mexico* (Oxford: OUP, 2000), p.316.

35. *US vs Castillero*, Case 420, San Francisco Northern District Court, July 1858, p.88, deposition of James Forbes, Exhibit 181, Letter from J. Forbes to A. Forbes, 28 June 1848.

36. See Chapter 6, sub-section, *The Mercury Speculators*; Rothschild Archive, AR 2008, 27ff. Larkin sent wild turkey or buzzard quills containing mercury to Washington for assay.

CHAPTER SIX

[Note: Warwickshire Record Office, Warwick, UK, holds The Seymour Papers, WRO, CR 114A, 373 23–26, 412–24 containing all the admiral's paperwork from the Pacific Station.]

1. Jesuit Provincial Archive, New York. Cullen went to La Plata colony, Argentina, 1853.

2. *The Tablet*, 22 August 1846. Clancy's grave is marked in Cork cathedral car park. For his bequest, *Annals of Presentation Convent, Midleton*, Cork, 27 January 1848.

3. F.J. Weber, *Writings of Francisco García Diego y Moreno* (Los Angeles: Weber, 1976); Letter to Clergy, Santa Bárbara, 20 April 1846; also Introduction, p.21.

4. B. Seeman, *Voyage of HMS Herald* (London: Reeve, 1853), Vol.1, pp.122–25, November 1846.

5. WRO CR 114A, 374, 23, *Diary*, 26 April 1846.

6. R.S. Du Pont, *Extracts from Private Journal-Letters of Captain S.F. Du Pont* (Wilmington, Del.: Ferris, 1885), p.30, from Monterey, 18 July 1846.

7. A.H. Markham, *Life of Sir Clements Markham* (London: Murray, 1917), p.99, citing Flag Lt Frederick B. Seymour: see *n.*16.

8. WRO CR 114A, 418(2), both citations from letter, 15 January 1846, to Admiral Inglefield at La Plata.

9. '17' from Midshipman Markham, *Clements R. Markham Papers*, Royal Geographical Society, CRM 10, pp.100-101; TNA, FO 5, 461, 56, Seymour to Aberdeen, 6 March 1845, Payeta, Peru; Seymour Papers, WRO CR 114A, 418, 3, Aberdeen to Seymour, 13 June 1846.

10. J. Barnes & P. Barnes, *Private and Confidential: Letters from British Ministers in Washington to Foreign Secretaries in London, 1844–67* (Selinsgrove, Susquehanna UP; London Associated UP, 1973), pp.26, 31.

11. WRO CR 114A, 418, 2, 196, Seymour to Bankhead; ibid., 374, 23, *Diary*, 18 April 1846; TNA ADM 52, 2713, Logbook, HMS *Juno*.

12. For details of *Collingwood*'s crew, RGS, Markham Papers, CRM 9: one officer wore top hat and personal lightning conductor in thundery weather. WRO CR 114A, 418 (2), 166, Seymour to Bankhead, Mazatlán, 26 April 1846; ibid.,374, 23, *Diary*, 2 May 1846; ibid.,418, 186ff, Seymour to Bankhead, Mazatlán, 6 May 1846. H.A. Kay, *HMS Collingwood, Journal of Lt Somerville* (Edinburgh: Pentland, 1986), p.184.

13. Royal Horticultural Society, *Hartweg Correspondence*, Hartweg to LHS, 8 April; *Hartweg Journal*, March and April, 1846. Seymour called the LHS 'Royal' but in 1846 it was still 'London'. H.S. J. Fox, 'Weeds Not Worth Picking Up', Theodor Hartweg, Botanist in California', *CTQ*, 28, Winter 1995, pp.6, 41-45.

14. WRO CR 114A, 374, 23, *Diary*, 11 May 1846; ibid.,418 (2), 207, to Sloat, 11 May 1846; ibid.,412 (2), *Journal*, 12 May 1846.

15. Ibid., 418 (2), 201, letter to A. Forbes, 6 May 1846.

16. RGS, Markham Papers, CRM 50, 205, and 182-257. Markham's *Journal* and nautical *Log* survive for Mazatlán and San Blas, but only his *Log* for *Collingwood*'s time at Monterey and Honolulu, 1846. USS *Constitution*, launched by Washington in 1797, is moored at Boston, the US equivalent of HMS *Victory* at Portsmouth. It took or destroyed five British warships in 1812. In 1886, Admiral Frederick Beauchamp Seymour was contacted by Admiral Clements Markham to answer Josiah Royce, California historian: 'Did Seymour *race* Sloat to Monterey?' F.B. Seymour consulted his journal: 'Sir George treated me with confidence and I was completely *au fait* of all questions with which he had to deal. I know for certain

he never had orders to hoist the flag, neither was there a race between him and Sloat to Monterey.' (*The Century*, 40, 5, September 1890, p.794.) F.B.S.'s *Journal* eludes this writer. Sir George did not have orders *not* to hoist the flag over California, but had discretion to do so, however dated his standing orders. WRO CR114A 418 (2), Seymour, Mazatlán, to A. Forbes at San Blas, 9 April, 8 May 1846; ibid.,to J. Forbes, Monterey, 10 May 1846.

17. Letter exhibited in court, *US vs Castillero, New Almaden Mine*, Land Case 366, Appeal Case 420, Transcript, Vol.1, p.382 (San Francisco: A.Peachy, F.Billings *et al.*, 1859).

18. WRO CR 114A, 418 (2), 245, to Lord Ellenborough, 13 May 1846.

19. B. Seeman, *Voyage of HMS Herald* (London: Reeve, 1853), Vol.2, p.158, March 1849.

20. Charles H. Eden, *Ralph Somerville, A Midshipman's Adventures on the Pacific* (London: Ward, 1876), is Tarzan and Jane, not Selkirk and Crusoe. Eden fell ill and was replaced as Captain in 1844, but knew the Pacific.

21. *US vs Castillero, New Almaden Mine*, Land Case 366, Appeal Case 420, Transcript, Vol.4, p.2629, November 1859; WRO 114A 418 (2), Seymour to Captain Hamilton, HMS *Frolic*, 15 June 1846.

22. F.J. Weber, *Writings of Francisco García Diego* (Los Angeles: Weber, 1976), Letters 190, 191, 192; M.J. Geiger, *Franciscan Missionaries in Hispanic California, 1769-1848* (San Marino: Huntington Library, 1969), pp.164, 249–51, 261–2. Geiger treats scandal and success evenly. The quality of later missioners declined after secularisation and the loss of Spanish-born clergy. Junípero Serra's original vision of 1769 was both narrowed and broadened by successors in the missions' 65 years. W.V.Wells, 'Quicksilver Mines of New Almaden' (visited 1857), *Harper's New Monthly* Magazine, Vol.27, Issue 157, June 1859, pp.25–41; ibid., J.R. Browne, 'Down in the Cinnabar Mines', Vol.31. Issue 185, October 1863, pp.545–561.

23. Exhibit, San Francisco District Court, 1859, *US vs Castillero, New Almaden Mine*, Transcript Vol.1. pp.485–8.

24. Ibid., Vol.4, pp.2637–9, here abridged. The friar's vow of poverty disabled him from owning, but not from holding property; Macnamara, a secular priest, was not under such a vow.

25. Stearns Papers, SG Box 40, Huntington Library, San Marina, California, omitted from Hammond's volumes. Larkin also reported it to Secretary Buchanan, G.P. Hammond, *The Larkin Papers*, Vol.5, p.41, 18 June 1846.

26. H. Hague, D.J. Langum, *Thomas O. Larkin*, (Oklahoma UP, 1995) p.37; F. Hitchins, *The Colonial Land and Emigration Commission* (Philadelphia U.P., 1931). The Commission published *The Colonisation Circular* each spring, 1824–50, and its records are in TNA MH 12, CO 295 and 318. It supported schemes in Guiana during the 1840s depression. See *British Parliamentary Papers, Emigration*, 5, (1847–9); 21 (1842–3); 22 (1843–53).

27. H.A. Kay, *HMS Collingwood, Lt Somerville's Journal* (Edinburgh: Pentland, 1986), p.202.

28. TNA, FO 204, 88, 484, Despatch 52, Bankhead to Aberdeen, 30 May, 1845.

29. G.P. Hammond, ibid., Vol.5, p.218, Larkin to Buchanan from Los Angeles, 23 August, 1846 mentioning again (following letter, 19 August) Macnamara's approach for opinion in July.

30. Vallejo Papers, Bancroft Library, CB 34, 14, 17 March, 1844.

31. TNA, FO 5, 461, 213, Powles to Aberdeen, 2 June 1846.

32. *Facultas* (licence), registered by Gonzales Rubio, Santa Bárbara, 29 June, Libro Primero de Gobierno, Los Angeles Archdiocesan archive. In 1864, Rubio reminisced about plans for *Tulares* missions frustrated by revolution against Spain, poverty and secularisation: 'zealous missioners would have been left among the savage tribes roaming the vast

Territory called *Tulares* by the priests', cited in F.J. Weber, ibid., (Note 22).

33. On Patrick Short, see H. Whelan, *The Picpus Story* (Pomona, Ca., 1964) pp.7, 53, 121; Santa Bárbara Mission Archive, Letters 1034, 1038, Short to Durán, 1836.

34. G.P. Hammond, ibid., Vol.4, p.370, Larkin's copy of Pico's proclamation, 13 May; Vol.5, pp.9–10, Castro's colourful response, 8 June; WRO 114A, 418 (2), Seymour, at sea, to Consul Miller,13 June 1846,

35. TNA, FO 5, 462, 99–115, three letters from Blake to Seymour, July 1846. On *Juno*, Forbes explained to Blake that Lansford Hastings' *Emigrants Guide to California and Oregon* (1845; Princeton U.P. facsimile, 1932), had triggered eastern US interest. Hastings made much of California's mineral wealth and Macnamara probably knew the book. *US vs Castillero, New Almaden Mine*, Transcript, Vol.2, p.841, for Forbes at Santa Bárbara; TNA, ADM 53, 2713, Logbook, HMS *Juno*. The encounters June–July at Santa Bárbara are reconstructed from testimony for Land Commission case, New Almaden Mine, 1852–1863.

36. *US vs Castillero, New Almaden Mine*, Transcript, Vol.4, (1861), Pico's account, pp.2531–42. He was sick when giving evidence in October 1859, evidently with a pituitary tumour: I. and J. Login, Governor Pío Pico, *Pituitary*, 13 (1), March 2010, 80–86. He disliked questions about Macnamara, 'matters not to do with this case', and 1846 had been his *annus horribilis*. He thought they met *before June* in Los Angeles, and on the road near Santa Bárbara 'at the end of June or beginning of July'. He '*probably* became well-acquainted with him'.

37. Letter from Pico to Forbes, see E.A. Wiltsee, 'The British Vice-Consul in California and the Events of 1846', *California Historical Society Quarterly*, 10, 2, June 1931, pp.114–15. Document F, Frémont's printed *Claims Papers*, Senate Committee Report 75, 30th Congress, 1st Session, 1848, refers to a note from Pico about Project Macnamara to his Assembly, 24 June, presented to the Assembly, 6 July, and acknowledged by committee, 7 July: *Legislative Record*, Vol.4, 363, Bancroft Collection, Bancroft Library. The original Assembly records were destroyed in the 1906 San Francisco earthquake. Pico's later dating of the Macnamara conveyance, 4 July 1846, was seen as fraud by nineteenth-century historians, but Project Macnamara was never tested before the US Land Commission. Bancroft accused him of signing and backdating in mid-July at Santa Bárbara, but by then he was at Santa Margarita de Cortona, his stationery dated and addressed from Santa Bárbara before he left. Only in 2010 has he earned a serious biography, but more remains to be uncovered: C.M. Salomon, *Pío Pico, Last Mexican Governor of California* (Oklahoma UP, 2010). Captain Montgomery of USS *Portsmouth* in San Francisco Bay since 3 June, victualled Frémont and his Topographers as US servicemen abroad, but reassured Castro, 18 June, that Frémont had no US authority for supporting the rebels and that he, Montgomery, was not *collaborating*: F.B.Rogers, *Montgomery and The Portsmouth* (San Francisco: Howell, 1958), p.44. Bandini's 7000 acre colony is remembered in 'Spanish Town', Riverside, San Bernardino.

38. C.R. Smith, *Journals of Marine Second Lt Henry Watson* (Washington: Marine Corps, 1990), pp.107–8, 29 April 1846.

39. H.A. Kay, *HMS Collingwood, Journal of Lt Somerville* (Edinburgh: Pentland, 1986), p.202.

40. Printed Document D, Frémont Claims Papers, 1848, Macnamara to Pico, 1 July 1846, on the road, and note from Pico, 1 July, courtesy Macnamara to the Assembly due to meet 6 July. Stearns Collection (see *n.*25) has a 'contemporary copy', dated 2 July, in secretarial script, unsigned, possibly given to Bandini by Macnamara prior to the Assembly meeting.

41. Bandini Mss, Bancroft Library, CB 79, 83, Pico to Bandini, 23 June; 84, Lataillade to Bandini, 2 July.

CHAPTER SEVEN

1. WRO CR 114A 417, 1, 306ff, to J. Forbes Monterey, 17 July, and to son Francis Seymour, Monterey, 19 July; Francis visited *Collingwood*, at Mazatlán, March–April. Henry Dana, *Two Years Before the Mast* (London: Moxon, 1840). USN Lt Stephen 'Paddy' Rowan rode the 650 miles and 13 mission stages from San Diego to Monterey in 7 days, 1847. Ex-mission rancho 'stages' and plentiful horses allowed rapid travel on the coast, C. Zemke, *Stephen C.Rowan and the US Navy*, PhD Thesis (Utah UP, 2012), p.52.

2. WRO 114A 374, 23, *Diary*, 13 June, 1846; ibid., 418 (2), Seymour to Ellenborough, from San Blas, 13 June.

3. W.M. Wood, *Wandering Sketches* (Philadelphia: Carey, Hart, 1849) pp.368–9, sent from Guadalajara, 7 May, to Sloat, delivered, Mazatlán, 17 May.

4. Bear Flag mystique is to California what The Alamo is to Texas. William B. Ide headed the Bear Flag uprising of at most 50 US (*anglo*) settlers and trappers in June after Castro ordered all without Mexican passports to leave on pain of death. Ide complained that settlers had been promised 'republican government' by Mexico, which Castro had debased into 'military despotism'. The rebellion echoed Texan and attempted *californio* secessions, but Ide never *spoke* of a 'California Republic'. John Bidwell, rebel, said the flag was 'not adopted or considered important', but its lone star, pig-like grizzly and 'California Republic' slogan merely brightened an empty Sonoma flagpole. Just as a dozen *tejanos* helped defend The Alamo against Mexico, and a *tejano* vice-President formally agreed the Republic, the Bear Flag rising demanded freedom for all settlers, including *californios*, but not necessarily union with the US. Ide knew it would be an 'entry wedge' and Larkin that 'the ball has been rolled'; General Vallejo, their *californio* hostage, supported US annexation. Ide accused Frémont of opportunism, ambition, and of perversely excluding *californios*. Bidwell called it 'a pretence to justify [Frémont's] premature beginning of the war'. Frémont claimed that after defending them against Indians and Mexicans, '*in effect* in command', he took formal command, 4 July, 'by common consent', when settler irregulars swelled his regular company into a small battalion. Later, Frémont claimed on oath before the Senate a clear British threat from Macnamara and Seymour. Ide died in 1852, without speaking or testifying publicly about Frémont, but he left a manuscript, published by his son, Simeon Ide, *Biographical Sketch of The Life of William B. Ide* (Claremont. Subscribers, 1880). See J. Bidwell, Frémont in 'The Conquest of California', *The Century*, 41, 4, February 1891, pp.519ff and Frémont's posthumous article, ibid., 'The Conquest of California', 41, 6, April 1891, p.924, citing George Bancroft, Polk's former Naval Secretary, in retirement: 'you were absolved as an explorer and became an officer of the US Army, warned by your government of your danger … the great wish of the President as to California was made clear to you [by Benton, via Gillespie, on Buchanan's order].'

5. WRO CR 114A, 418 (2), to Bankhead, 14 June; to Horace Simpson, 15 June; to Ellenborough, 15 June. A. Hamilton-Gordon, *The Earl of Aberdeen* (London: Dent, 1905), pp.4, 183.

6. Midshipman Markham painted Pacific flags in his *Log*, 1845, RGS, CRM 66, Tahiti with French tricolour in the upper hoist quarter, and Hawaii (Sandwich) with British Union Flag in same quarter: it features still on the Hawaii State flag.

7. WRO CR 114A, 374, 23, *Diary*, May–July 1846, *passim*.

8. W.M. Wood, *Wandering Sketches* (Philadelphia: Carey, Hart, 1849), pp.368–9; T.H. Benton, *Thirty Years View* (New York: Appleton, 1856), Vol.2, p.652.

9. Cuevas gave Macnamara the letter to Híjar, 11 August 1845, a day before resigning office; Macnamara presented it to Pico, Sánta Bárbara, 24 June 1846, from whose captured archive it ended up in Washington: *Frémont Claims Papers*, Appendix, Document F, Spanish and English, Washington, 1848. Bandini's committee verdict, approved by the Assembly, 7 July, 1846, *Legislative Record*, Vol.4, 364–68 (original Spanish text 20–24), and Bandini Mss, Bancroft Library, CB 68, 87, with Bandini's comments.

10. W.D. Putney, *et al.*, San Salvador, a New Mexican Settlement in Mexican California, *Southern California Historical Society Quarterly*, 59, 4, Winter 1977, pp.353–364; Bandini also agreed a ranch grant to Scotsman Michael White (*Miguel Blanco*), at the southern mouth of Cajon Pass. He fortified it, but quit after nine months having lost all his cattle to Indian raids.

11. The US landing party figure, '225', is from USN Lt Rowan, C. Zemke, ibid., p.35, who helped lead it under Captain Mervine. Extracts from the Log of Midshipman Robert C Duvall, USS *Savannah*, 1845–6, CHSQ 3, 2, July 1924, pp.105–125; E.A. Sherman, *Life of Rear Admiral John Drake Sloat* (Oakland: Carruth, 1902), see *n*.23. As Spanish-speaking ADC to Commodore Jones, Toler had hoist the US flag, 19 October 1842 and struck it 21 October with apologies. He was then 14. As ADC to Commodore Sloat, he raised the flag again, 7 July 1846. *Californio* Militia Capitán Mariano Silva responded on both occasions, but was dead when Toler hoist it yet again at Monterey, 7 July 1896, aged 70.

12. Bandini Mss, Bancroft Library, CB 69 86, note, 7 July; R.H. Becker, *Designs on The Land: Diseños of California Ranches* (San Francisco: California Book Club, 1964).

13. Stearns Collection, Huntington Library, San Marino, California, SG Box 42, two pages endorsed, unsigned and undated. It may even be a draft of the letter from Bandini to British vice-consul James Forbes, sent on from Honolulu by Macnamara, October 1846 after forgetting to give it to Forbes at Monterey in July.

14. Bandini Mss, Bancroft Library, CB 69, 88 to Cesareo Lataillade; Seymour Papers, WRO CR 114A 374, 23, *Private Diary*, 1846, blank end pages. *Californio* dominance and *anglo* minority was the reverse of settler proportions in Texas.

15. G.P. Hammond, *The Larkin Papers*, Vol.5, p.117, Stearns to Larkin, 8 July, 1846, carried north to Monterey by Macnamara.

16. Frémont Claims Papers, Washington, 1848, printed Document E, Pico Concession; *Pico's Historical Narrative* (Glendale, Ca.: Clark, 1973), pp.130 ff. In US California the diocesan feast of Our Lady of Refuge was changed to 5 July in 1982, to avoid US Independence Day, but in Mexican Baja California diocese it remains 4 July. G. Tays, Governor Pico's Letters, 1846–48, CHSQ 13, 2, June 1934, pp.110–149, Letter V, p.110, 13 July 1846, San Luis Obispo.

17. J. Moreno, *Documentos para la Historia de California*, Bancroft Library, CD 17-18, 38ff. Volume 8, *Toma de Razon* (Land Register) no longer exists. US soldiers captured Pico's archive in Reina de Los Angeles, August 1846. As Moreno's working register from May 1, it recorded Macnamara's title: see J.N. Bowman, *The Lost Toma de Razon*, CHSQ, 21, 4, December 1942, pp.311–20.

18. W. Oberste, *Texas Irish Empresarios and their Colonies* (Austin: von Boeckmann-Jones, 1973); Shadow-Senators Gwin and Frémont, *Petition and Memorial to Congress on California*, March 1850, gave estimates of arable land.

19. *US vs Castillero*, San Francisco Northern District Court, Appeal Case 420 against Land

Board Case 366, New Almaden Mine, Transcript, Vol.4, pp.2538–41, Pico's evidence, 20 October, 1859. José Maria Mora, Special Envoy to London, 1847–8, was the last to ask officially for Britain to protect California.

20. G.P. Hammond, *The Larkin Papers*, Vol.5, Larkin to Stearns, 10 July 1846.

21. *Sources for Monterey, July 1846*, J.D. Sloat, *Report to Congress on California*, Exec. Doc 52, 2nd Session, 30th Congress, 31 July, USS *Levant*; G.F. Seymour, *Report to Admiralty on California*, 28 August, Honolulu, WRO CR 114A 307; ibid., 374, 23, *Diary*, July–August, and end pages. Ibid., 417 (1), to James Forbes, 17 July, to son Francis, 19 July, to Pico 23 July. Walter Colton, *Deck and Port* (New York: Barnes, 1851), pp.298–304; Extracts from The Log of Robert C. Duvall, *CHSQ*, 3, 2, July 1924, pp.105–125. F.B. Rogers (ed.), *Marcus Duvall, Navy Surgeon in California, 1846–7* (San Francisco: Howell, 1957), pp.54–5. E.A. Sherman, *Life of Rear Admiral John D Sloat* (Oakland: Carruth, 1902), with sources for Toler, Du Pont, Sloat and Montgomery. F.B. Rogers (ed.), *Montgomery of The Portsmouth* (San Francisco: Howell, 1958). J.P. Downey, *Cruise of The Portsmouth* (New Haven: Yale UP, 1958). J.W. Revere, *A Tour of Duty* (New Year: Francis, 1849); ibid., *Keel and Saddle* (Boston: Osgood, 1872). Commodore Stockton's Despatches, California, Summer 1846, (Washington Senate: February 1849). C.R. Markham, RGS, CRM 66, *Log*; also observations on *Collingwood* crew, RGS, CRM 10, 24. J.C. Frémont, *Memoirs of My Life* (1887), Vol.1, pp.487–90, 532–563. M.L. Spence and D.Jackson (eds), *Expeditions of John Charles Frémont* (Chicago: Illinois UP, 1973), Vol.2, pp.471–2, 476 *n*. W.D. Phelps, *Fore and Aft* (Boston: Nichols, Hall, 1871), p.295. F. Walpole, *Four Years in The Pacific* (London: Bentley, 1850), pp.204, 251. H.H. Bancroft, *History of California*, Vol.4 (San Francisco: The History Company, 1885), pp.263–73; ibid., Vol.5. (San Francisco: The History Company, 1888), p.214; TNA, ADM 53, 2278, Logbook, HMS *Collingwood*; ADM 52, 2713, Logbook, HMS *Juno*. TNA, FO 5, 462, 99–115, Blake to Seymour, 5, 17 and 30 July. RHS Library, T. Hartweg's *Journal*, 2 July 1846. Captain H. Kellett, *Letterbook*, N.M.M., London, to Seymour, 21 January 1847. G.P. Hammond, *The Larkin Papers* (California: Berkeley, 1951) Vol.5, pp.204, 215, Larkin to Secretary James Buchanan, 19 and 23 August. E.A. Wiltsee, *The British Vice-Consul in California and The Events of 1846*, *CHSQ*, 10, 2, June 1931, pp.99–128. British Library Add. Ms. 48575 and 49968, James Forbes to Aberdeen, 14 July from California, cited in J. Ridley, *Lord Palmerston* (London: Constable, 1970) pp.304–5; G.W. Ames, 'Gillespie and The Conquest of California: Letters to Navy Secretary, George Bancroft', *CHSQ*, 17, 3, September 1938, pp.271, 282; *Illustrated London News*, 8 November 1845, Life aboard HMS *Collingwood*. J. Fenimore Cooper, known in Britain for 'Wild West' novels, was an ex-US Navy officer and naval historian. R.V. Hine and S. Lottinville (eds), *Soldier in the West, Theodore Talbot's Letters, 1845–53* (Norman: Oklahoma UP, 1972). J. Monaghan (ed.), *Private Journal of Lt Louis McLane* (Santa Bárbara Hist. Soc., 1971). Senator Benton's myth was that Sloat was 'watched and pursued by Seymour', and Seymour arrived 'to find Frémont's riflemen encamped over the town', *Thirty Years View*, II (New York: Appleton, 1856, pp.691ff.); C.M. Zemke, *Stephen C. Rowan and The US Navy: Sixty Years Service* (Ph.D. thesis, Utah State UP.;2012). *Stephen Rowan, USS Cyane*, Documents Relating to the US Navy 1775–1920, File 3, Antebellum Navy, 1815-61, Online; ibid., *Extracts from Private Journal-Letters of Captain S.F. Du Pont, 1846–8* (Wilmington, Del.: Ferris, 1885). Journal of Lt S.C.Rowan, *Recollections of the Mexican War*, US Naval Institute Proceedings, Vol. XIV, 46, 1888, pp.539–40. A. Nasatir, 'The French Consulate in California, 1843–56', *CHSQ*, 12, 1, March 1933, pp.35–50, citing Ministry of Foreign Affairs, Paris, Box *Monterey*, Dossier 21. Duflot de Mofras, *Exploration de Territoire del*

Oregon, des Californias, 1840–42 (Paris: Bertrand, 1844). W.R. Manning, *Diplomatic Correspondence of the US*, Vol.6, France (Washington: Carnegie, 1935), Doc 2477, pp.453–4, Buchanan to French ambassador, 16 July 1847, with Sloat's report of 2 June 1847 on consul Gasquet in Monterey in 1846. Seymour called Gasquet 'a Pritchard in Vinculo' after British consul Pritchard was imprisoned by France on Tahiti, and for whom Seymour extracted compensation: WRO, CR114A, 418 (2), Seymour to Bankhead, 3 September 1846.

22. M.P. Costeloe, *Bonds and Bondholders* (Westport Ct.: Prager, 2003), pp.59–62, 177–94, 288, 298, 307, underpins this account; TNA, FO 5, 460, 129-35, 26 April, Graham from London; W.R. Manning, *Diplomatic Correspondence of the US*, 1831–60, Vol.7, Great Britain (Washington: Carnegie, 1937), Doc. 2684, 14 May 1846; TNA, FO 5, 461, 2 June, Powles to Aberdeen, and 14 July, Henry Parish to Aberdeen; Clements Markham, RGS, CRM 50, 181, *Journal*, April 1846, on HMS *America* and others smuggling silver bullion for Barron and Forbes; H. Alison Kay, *HMS Collingwood, Journal of Lt Townsend Somerville* (Edinburgh: Pentland, 1986), p.185, 2 May 1846. USN W.M.Woods, *Wandering Sketches* (Philadelphia: Carey, Hart, 1849) p.336. Silver-running captains received a percentage and the Commander in Chief an honorarium. USN Lt McLane called US naval smugglers a 'disgrace', and Sloat's officers threatened to report them to the Navy Department. France forbade the practice.

23. F. Walpole, *Four Years in The Pacific* (London: Bentley, 1850), Vol.2, p.221. Walpole consciously named few people, Somerville and Markham happily named everyone. H.A. Kay, ibid., 5 August, pp.205–6.

24. Ibid., p.249; C.R. Smith (ed.), *Journal of Marine Second Lieutenant H.B.Watson, 1845–8* (Washington: US Marine Corps, 1990), p.30. Maigret's bullet point journal is in the John Charlot Collection, Manoa Library, pp.35–6.

25. J.D. Raeside, 'The Journals of Dr Wyllie, A Minor Hawaiian Mystery', *Hawaiian Journal of History*, 18, 1984, pp.87–95. The forty-volume memoir was apparently burned in house-clearance. Reputedly Wyllie could split a hair enough times to make a wig: G. Davis, *Shoal of Time, A History of the Hawaiian Islands* (Hawaii UP, 1968) p.110; WRO CR 144A 374, 23, *Diary*, 14 August; ibid., WRO 114A, 694, 4, to Francis, 3 September 1846.

26. *Polynesian*, 14 August 1847. The August–September 1846 editions did not mention Macnamara's arrival. He would have said mass publicly at the mission. *Polynesian*, 23 July, 1846, merely reported 'the corvette Juno off the coast "observing" [*sic*], and the whole English squadron supposedly not far behind it'.

27. TNA FO 331, 11, 246-7, Miller to Aberdeen (Palmerston by then Foreign Secretary), 28 September 1846.

28. San Francisco *Bulletin*, 17 July 1858 for Macnamara's letter, 27 September 1846, produced by James Forbes in *US vs Castillero, New Almaden Mine*, Case 420, Northern District Court, San Francisco, July 1858, Transcript Vol.2, pp.841, 950. Forbes thought it 'came in November 1846, probably by trading vessel'. He denied Macnamara's link with the mine, but witnesses testified to his general dishonesty.

29. M. Wade (ed.), *Journals of Francis Parkman* (London: Eyre and Spottiswoode, 1947), entries, May–June, 1846; W. Jacobs, (ed.), *Letters of Francis Parkman*, (Norman: Oklahoma U.P., 1964), Vol.1, p.38; Vol.2, pp.236–7. *Palinurus* sank off the Scillies, December 1848, all hands lost, with its cargo of Demerara rum and molasses for London; figurehead in the Valhalla collection, Tresco: *Ships, Shipwreck and Scilly* (1999), 71–2; *British Parliamentary Papers*, LXV, 573.

30. TNA, ADM 53, 1919, Logbook, HMS *Herald*; B. Seeman, *Voyage of HMS Herald* (London: Reeve, 1853), Vol.1, pp.122–5.

31. H. Kellett, *Letterbook*, National Maritime Museum, London, Kellett to A. Forbes, 16 November 1846.

CHAPTER EIGHT

1. The saga of the New Almaden mine, the invalidating of its title by the US California Land Commission and subsequent appeals in San Francisco District Court and in the Washington Supreme Court, is found in the four-volume *Transcript, US vs Andrés Castillero, New Almaden Mine* (San Francisco: A.Peachy, F. Billings, P. della Torre *et al*, 1859–61) consisting of over 3,000 pages and available Online, at *archive.org*. The original land title Case 366, is recorded in Volume 1; the appeal Case 420 is found in Volumes 2–4. The transcript also details Macnamara's dealings in California with Pico and Castro as well as in Tepic and Mexico City with the mine owners. No Barron and Forbes company archive survives.

2. *US vs Castillero, Transcript*, Vol. 1, p.540, J. Forbes to A. Forbes, 22 September 1846; TNA, FO, 201, pp.124–9, A.Forbes to Bankhead, November 1846. For Macnamara's lodging in Mexico City, Report of Senate Committee 75, 30th Congress, 1st Session, 1848, Frémont's California Claims, pp.46–9, John Baldwin's testimony echoed in Frémont's posthumous *Conquest of California*, in *The Century*, 41 (6), April 1891, pp.917–28, stating 'Macnamara was a guest of the English consul MacKintosh in Mexico City'.

3. *US vs Castillero*, ibid., pp.540–2, J. Forbes to A. Forbes, 14 July 1847.

4. *US vs Castillero*, Vol.2, pp.957–9, J. Forbes to A. Forbes, 28 June 1848.

5. *US vs Castillero*, Vol.3, pp.2489–90; Vol.4, p.3048.

6. See *n.* 2 above.

7. W.R. Manning, *Diplomatic Correspondence of the US, 1831–60* (Washington: Carnegie, 1936), Vol.7, *Great Britain*, Doc. 2853, pp.289–91, G. Bancroft to Secretary Buchanan, 4 January 1847.

8. *The Tablet*, 9 September 1846, '*Famine in Ireland*'; Clements Markham, *Notes on Officers and Men, HMS Collingwood 1844–48*, RGS, CRM, 9, 7; Philip Somerville, *HMS Collingwood, 1844–48* (Edinburgh: Pentland, 1986), 6 February 1847, letter dated November 1846; J. Hynes, *Diary* (Melbourne, 2002), 1 January 1847; I. Murphy, *Life and Death in West Clare* (Dublin: Irish Academic Press, 1996), p.45; *ILN*, 13 February 1847, '*Sketches in the West of Ireland*'; 15 December 1849, '*The Condition of Ireland*'.

9. TNA, FO 203, 91, Palmerston to Bankhead, 30 June 1847.

10. For the Pope's Encyclical, *The Tablet*, 8 May 1847, '*Foreign and Colonial*'; for the Sultan's donation, *ILN*, 3 January, 1849, '*Address from Ireland to The Sultan*'.

11. Irish Famine literature is extensive but modern: C. Woodham-Smith, *The Great Hunger* (London: Hamish Hamilton, 1962) was a pioneer, while C.Ó Murchadha, *The Great Irish Famine, 1845–52*, (Hambledon; Continuum; 2011) is one of the latest. On Irish emigration and famine, K.A. Miller, *Emigrants and Exiles* (Oxford UP, 1990) pp.280–344; D.H. Akenson, *The Irish Diaspora, A Primer* (Toronto: Meany, 1993); R. Scally, *The End of Hidden Ireland* (Oxford UP, 1995); Murray Papers, 1845–51, Parts 4-6, *Archivium Hibernicum*, Vols 39–41 (Maynooth, 1984–6). William Kelly, London lawyer and textile mill owner in Sligo, discussed the Famine in 1849 with pre-1846 Irish Californians who 'evinced strong sympathy and sorrow on the miseries of their suffering brethren at home, starving and dying on green fields while they in a foreign land had enough and to spare':

W. Kelly, *A Stroll Through the Diggins* [sic] *of California* (London: Simms & M'Intyre, 1852), p.232. See J. Fox, William Kelly, *CTQ*, Vol.64, Winter 2005, pp.36–44.

12. *Diario de Gobierno*, Mexico City, 30 November 1846; *El Siglo IX*, 7 and 16 April 1845, advertising Murray's blanket and textile outlet and Synnott's *Academia*. USM Lt Gillespie wrote on from Mexico City to Navy Secretary Bancroft of having seen US deserters arrive in the capital as early as 16 January 1846: R. Stenberg, 'Further Letters of Archibald H. Gillespie', *CSHQ*, Vol. 18, 3, June 1939, p.255.

13. G. Thompson, *Puebla,* (Oxford University; PhD Thesis; 1977), pp.199 ff; V. Gómez Farías Papers, Benson Collection, University of Texas at Austin, pp.56–62, 18–24 September, 1846.

14. J. Smith, Letters of General Santa Anna (US Hist., Mss Commission 1917; Washington; Government; 1920), p. 392 and *n.* 5, 1 January 1847, from HQ.

15. For Polk's anger with the pastor, M.M. Quaife (ed.), *J.K. Polk's Diaries* (Chicago: McLurg, 1910), Vol.2, pp.187–9, 14 October 1846, and Vol.3, pp.102–3, 29 July 1847. *El Trueno*, 12 February 1847; *The Tablet*, 31 October, 1846.

16. H.Wise, *Los Gringos* (New York: Baker, Scribner, 1849), p.249; W.H. Callcott, *Church and State in Mexico, 1822–57* (Durham: Duke UP, 1926), p.156; J. Smith, *War With Mexico* (New York: Macmillan, 1919), Vol.2, pp. 221, 314.

17. W.R. Manning, *Diplomatic Correspondence of the US*, Vol.8, Mexico 1831–48 (Washington: Carnegie, 1937), Doc. 3733, pp.958–964, Trist to Buchanan, 25 October 1847; J.Z.Vasquez, *La Gran Bretagna, Frente al Mexico Amenezado, 1835–48* (Mexico: Sec. de Relaciones, 2002), p.132. Trist advised that some money for California would soothe 'Mexican vanity'.

18. R.R. Miller (ed.), *The Mexican War Journal and Letters of Ralph Kirkham* (College Station, Texas: A & M UP; 1991), p.21 to his wife from Puebla, 1 June 1847; J. Smith, *War With Mexico* (New York: Macmillan, 1919), Vol.2, p.81; R.Anderson, *An Artillery Officer in The Mexican War* (New York: Putnam's, 1911), pp.80, 314.

19. J.F. Ramírez, *Mexico During The War With The US* (Univ. of Missouri, *Studies*, 23, 1, (Missouri: Columbia, 1950), p.127. He had property in Alta California. Lack of evidence prevents any serious correlating of the attempts to entice deserters.

20. J. Kenly, *Memoirs of a Maryland Volunteer* (Philadelphia: Lipincott, 1873), pp.300, 381.

21. M.L. Solares Robles, L.S. de la Torre, *Entre La Lejanía y La Incertidumbre: Correspondencia de José Maria Luis Mora, 1847-48* (Mexico: Instituto Mora, 2001), pp.21–27, Mora to Palmerston, 15 and 30 November, 1847.

22. The *San Patricios* are well researched in R.R. Miller, *Shamrock and Sword* (Norman: Oklahoma UP, 1989); M. Hogan, *The Irish Soldiers of Mexico* (Guadalajara: Fondo Editorial, 1997); P.F. Stevens, *The Rogues March: John Riley and The St Patrick's Battalion, 1846–8* (Washington: Brassey's, 1999). Professor Miller of CSU Hayward shared his scholarship generously with the author. TNA FO 203, 88, 155, 156 record the sums paid to 51 deserters, 1846 and 1848. On St Patrick's day, 17 March, and 12 September, the anniversary of the executions, Mexico honours publicly the 112 *San Patricio* dead, at their monument in Plaza de San Jacinto, Mexico City, a tradition begun in 1848 when Colonel Riley was still begging in Puebla: TNA, FO 203, 94, 110.

23. *El Monitor,* 21 May 1847, pp.2–3, 'Dictamen' [Verdict]; also Hawaii *Polynesian*, 14 August 1847; San Francisco *Californian*, 29 September 1847; ibid., *California Star*, 2 August 1847. Travellers and newspapers crossed between California and Mexico via Honolulu during US blockade, 1846-7. James J. Jarves, US editor of *Polynesian*, called Macnamara a Jesuit, believed he came directly from Britain, and warned Mexico that Macnamara could only

have his land 'Uncle Sam permitting'. The Mormon editor of *California Star*, Sam Brannan, appended the 1837 bondholder land agreement to 'prove' Macnamara was their agent.

24. Project Macnamara's status as a dictator's *fiat* smoothed its passage. Congress did not meet under Paredes between 1 January–29 May 1846, although it had met daily under Herrera. It met regularly again 30 November 1846–16 January 1847, before finally retreating to Querétaro and more frequent meetings 5 October–24 November 1847. Deputies were cut off from travelling by the war; meetings were often inquorate and cancelled: H. Labestida, *Mexican Congressional meetings: Guia Hermografica de Los Debatos de Senada, 1824–53* (Mexico, 1994). Seven presidents ruled 1846–47, and Santa Anna resigned when the capital fell. The historian Justo Sierra looked back wryly: 'our statesmen should have considered how best to give away, literally, the land we could never occupy, by inviting the whole world to colonise it, Russians, French, English, Spanish, Chinese, erecting a Babel of peoples as a dike to stem the tide of US expansion': *The Political Evolution of the Mexican People*, 1900–02 (trans. by C.Ramsdell; Austin: Texas UP, 1969), p.212.

25. J.C Frémont and J.B.Frémont, 'The Conquest of California', *The Century*, Vol.41 (6), April 1891, pp.917–28, edited by Mrs Jessie Benton Frémont from the manuscript and sources of *John Charles Frémont* [*sic*, as if signed by JCF]. Frémont died in 1890 and 'his' account needs cautious reading. Senator Benton's list of papers carried by Gillespie is unreliable: 'a letter of introduction [from Sec. Buchanan], some letters and clips of newspapers from Senator Benton and family and some verbal communication from Buchanan that Frémont should watch and contest any foreign scheme on California': *Thirty Years View* (New York: Appleton, 1856), Vol.2, p.682. In March 1848, after Frémont's California expense claims were heard by Benton's Committee, opposition senators demanded that Buchanan's correspondence as conveyed by Gillespie in writing to Larkin and memorised for Frémont be made public. They suspected that it 'contained instructions to produce a revolution in California before Mexico commenced war against the US and that Col. Frémont had the authority to make that revolution': J.K. Polk, *Diary*, 21 March 1848.

26. S.M. Du Pont, *Extracts from Private Journal-Letters, 1846–8* (Wilmington: Ferris, 1885), p.377.

27. *California Claims,* 30th Congress, 1st Session, Senate 'Representatives Committee 75, 23 February 1848, Frémont's evidence.

28. A $19,500 draft drawn by Frémont in Los Angeles, 1847, on Secretary Buchanan was not settled, as it had been sold on to a debt collector. On 7 April 1852, during a celebrity visit to London, Frémont was arrested and imprisoned overnight for debt. He also had a London agent selling plots on his Las Mariposas estate to British settlers and gold speculators.

29. *Memorial of the Senators and Representatives Elect from California … Requesting the Admission of California into the Union*, tabled in 31st Congress, 1st Session, 18 March 1850, published as House of Representatives Misc. Document 44 and as Senate Misc. Document 68.

30. T.H. Benton, *Thirty Years View* (New York: Appleton, 1856), p.693, where he noted, 'California had its destiny to fullfil, to be handed over to the US'.

31. C.W. Upham, *Life, Explorations and Public Services of John Charles Frémont* (Boston: Ticknor, Fields, 1856), pp.240–1.

32. T.H. Benton, ibid., p.691.

33. J. Velasco, *Noticias Estadisticas del Estado de Sonora* (Mexico: Cumpido, 1850), 13, 255, 258, 289, 306–310. A 'Dr Daly', known in Mexico City, 1844–52, started mining at

MacKintosh's El Real de El Oro mine in 1845: TNA FO 207, Consular Miscellany, showing several Irish 'doctors' in Mexico. In Sonora Camp, southern mines, a Dr Dealy acted briefly as peace broker. 'Dr Delis' (pronunciation and nationality uncertain) remains unidentified. See Chapter 10 for Macnamara's having 'relatives' in Mexican mining.

34. *US vs Castillero, New Almaden Mine*, Transcript Vol. 2, (San Francisco: A.Peachy, F.Billings *et al.* 1861) pp. 842, 846, testimony of James Forbes, June 1858.

35. W.R. Manning, *Diplomatic Correspondence of the US, Vol.VIII, Mexico, 1831–48* (Washington: Carnegie, 1837), Doc. 3752, pp.1061–8, J.S. O'Reilly to Buchanan, 15 February 1848. The commissioner wrote at least eight times to Buchanan between November 1847 and June 1848, protesting against the exclusion of Yucatán 'a neutral country', from proposed peace terms with Mexico, but his plea was ignored in the final Treaty.

36. *Congressional Globe*, 30th Congress, 1st Session, Appendix 87, pp.362–5, 15 February, 1848.

37. Ibid., pp.558–60, 29 March 1848; pp.561–2, 4 April 1848.

38. *San Francisco Chronicle*, 13 September 1849, '*Obituaries*'.

CHAPTER NINE

1. Admiral Thomas Cochrane, 1775–1860, cashiered and jailed for fraud after exposing corruption in the Royal Navy, took mercenary command of the Chilean Navy in 1817. Britain later exonerated and reinstated him. His former midshipman, Frederick Marryat, pioneered the maritime novel and Cochrane inspired *Hornblower* and *Master and Commander*. For Chile and Britain, W. Edmundson, *A History of the British Presence in Chile*, (London: Palgrave Macmillan, 2011).

2. W.R. Manning, *Diplomatic Correspondence of the US*, Vol.5, Chile and Colombia (Washington: Carnegie, 1935) Doc. 1669, pp.130–1, US Consul Pollard to Secretary Forsyth, 12 July 1837. Chiloé had been offered to Britain in 1826 by the last Spanish enclave entrapped there.

3. Archivo Nacional Historico de Chile, Santiago, *Fondo Ministero del Interno*, Vol.78, 4, ff. 3–5, October (no day) 1848. No further record of the scheme has been found.

4. '*Ecossia*' indicates Glasgow, which received an average 1,000 Irish refugees a week in 1848, rising to 3,000 a week January–April. Scotland also suffered potato blight.

5. The report of land fraud is in *Fondo Ministero del Interno*, Vol. 78, 5 f.5-7. Surveyor Frick advocated Trumeo at the confluence of the Rios Negro and Bueno where the Bueno becomes navigable to the sea, as a deepwater *embarcadero* for colonists; see *Mercurio de Valparaiso*, 17 and 18 December 1849, features by Frick.

6. 'La tenativa de buscarlos en irlanda no dio resultado alguo', I. Domeyko, *Memoria sobre la colonización en Chile* (Santiago: Belin, May 1850), pp.6, 10, well before Macnamara's deadline. Cholera outbreaks in 1849 and 1851 did not help. A revolution and civil war in 1851 blocked the entry ports of Valparaiso and Concepción, while British and French 'neutral' navies blockaded, TNA, FO,16,73,35. For immigration to Chile: V.P. Rosales, *Essai Sur le Chili* (Hamburg: Nestler & Melle, 1857), pp.254–265, 455; *Times Gone By* (New York: OUP, 2003, ed. & tr. J. Polt and B. Loveman), p.303; D. Barros Arana, *Un Decenio de la Historia de Chile, 1841–51*, (Santiago: Imprenta Barcelona, 1906), II, pp.527–8; idem, *Historia General de Chile*, 16 Vols, (Santiago, 1902) XI, pp.257–8, XIII, pp.590–1, XIV, pp.528–30; G.F. Young, 'Bernardo Philippi, Initiator of German Colonisation in Chile', *Hispanic American Historical Review*, 51, 3, August 1971, pp.478–96; G.F. Young,

The Germans in Chile (NY Centre for Migration Studies, 1974), pp.70–77, 90, *notes* 14 & 18; G.H. Bucher, *Emigrantes y Imigrantes en Chile, 1810–1915* (Valparaiso;Univ. de Playa Ancha, 2001); J. Mayo, *British Merchants and Chilean Development, 1851–86* (London: Westview, 1987); M.M. Beos, *Presencia de Chile en la Patagonia Austral, 1843–79* (Santiago: Andrés, 1971); G. Frick, Valdivia Province, *Mercurio de Valparaiso,* 17 and 18 December 1849. Bernardo O'Higgins died in 1842. V.P. Rosales' uncle, Francisco Javier Rosales, Chilean ambassador in Paris, processed European colonists. Macnamara's project did not feature in British consular reports from Chile, 1847–51, TNA FO 16/61-74, 16/165, 158, but 4000 German settlers by 1874 and the clearing of the Lake District into today's major timber and agricultural estates indicates how it could have developed.

7. Pico's reputation was shredded by politicians, lawyers and historians in US California. Former colleagues accused him and Bandini of embezzling land sale revenues. Pico returned from Mexico after the Treaty of 1848 to become a loyal US *californio*; he died much respected in 1894: C.M. Salomon, *Pío Pico* (Norman: Oklahoma UP, 2010) is a welcome biography.

8. H. Halleck, *Report on Land Titles in California,* 1 March 1849, Senate Executive Document 17, 31st Congress, 1st Session. In his subsequent *Digest of Laws,* July 1849, Halleck allowed that the Governor and Assembly of California could convey public land for colonising, subject to Mexican confirmation. The debates in Monterey and Washington which shaped Gwin's eventual Land Act included requests that the ex-missions be treated as fairly as if they were US Protestant churches, and that defenceless *californios* and displaced Indians be protected. The 'British threat' was no longer a concern. John Ross Browne, *Report on The Debates in the Convention of California, Sept–Oct 1849* (Washington, 1850).

9. W.C. Jones, *Report on Land Titles in California,* 9 March 1850, ibid., Document 18, 14; Griswold del Castillo, *Treaty of Guadalupe Hidalgo* (Norman: Oklahoma U.P.,1990), pp.72–7.

10. Jones, ibid., pp.24, 29; Legislative Record, Vol.4, 7 July 1846, Article 2, Bancroft Library, Berkeley; C. Burchfield, 'The Golden State's First Senator', *California Territorial Quarterly,* 85, Spring 2011, pp.22–7; Lately Thomas, *Between Two Empires: California's First Senator* (Boston: Houghton Mifflin, 1969).

11. *Emigration and Colonial Gazette,* 8 January, 21 May, 1842; *The Emigrant,* Vol.25, 1, January 1849. 'My hunch is that if Macnamara had lived 150 years later, he would have felt at home in Tinseltown', M. Day, reviewing J. Fox, *Macnamara's Irish Colony* for *La Prensa San Diego,* 2 June 2000.

12. S.T. Hall, *Life and Death in Ireland, 1849* (Manchester: Parkes, 1850), p.197.

13. I. Murphy, *A Starving People: Life and Death in West Clare, 1845–51* (Dublin: Irish Academic Press, 1996), p.18.

14. O. McDonagh, 'The Irish Catholic Clergy and Emigration during the Great Famine', *Irish Historical Studies,* 5, 20, September 1947, pp.287–303.

15. E.G. Gudde, *California Place Names* (Berkeley: CUP, 1949); John Robinson, adviser *California Territorial Quarterly,* helped with river names – the Mojave or *Las Animas* (All Souls) river. The 'Laguna' once many hundreds of square miles of wetland at its seasonal widest, is now subterranean, small and controlled, near Bakersfield. Water control and distribution has been the great issue in Central Valley. See R.W. de Roos *The Thirsty Land* (Stanford, Ca.: SUP, 1948); W. Smith, *Garden of the Sun* (Linden, 2003); G. Haslam, *The Other California* (Nevada UP, 1994); D. Hornbeck, *California Patterns* (Palo Alto, Ca.: Mayfield, 1983). Rain and snow provides much winter water, offset by long hot dry

summers. The Sacramento half of Great Central Valley has two thirds of the State's rain and snow on one third of its arable; the San Joaquin half has one third the water, on two thirds the arable. Today both waterways are highly engineered for irrigation.

16. G.W. Beattie, 'An Inland Chain of Missions in California', *Southern California Historical Society Quarterly*, 14, 1929; Stephen Hackel, *Alta California: Peoples in Motion* (Berkeley, Ca.: California UP, for Huntington Institute), pp.74–110. F. Weber, *Writings of Francisco García Diego y Moreno, Bishop of The Californias*, (Los Angeles: Weber, 1976), cites González Rubio's reminiscences in 1864. For Kelly's and Hastings' comments, see W. Kelly, *A Stroll through the Diggins* [sic] *of California* (London: Simm, M'Intyre,1852), 2 Volumes. Not all *asistencias* have been identified. The projected Mission Los Tulares would have been some fifty miles east of Fresno /Bakersfield, in the Sierra foothills.

17. Camden 3rd Series, Vol. 63, Royal Historical Society, *British Consular Reports from South America*, Peru, p.168, and *n.* 3; Fabian Bustamente Olguin, Bernardo O'Higgins' Plans: Irish Immigrants in Mexico, *Immigration Studies in Latin America*, 5, March 2007, pp.59–60 (abstract).

18. H.R. Key, *Topo, Story of a Scottish Colony Near Caracas, 1825–7* (Scottish Academic Press, 1988).

19. William Parish Robertson, Correspondence, Appendix, *The Foreign Debt of Mexico* (London: Smith and Elder,1850) II, p.45. Robertson also asked Palmerston for 'a vigorous interference' in Mexico on behalf of bondholders, II, pp.96–7, which did come, but a decade later. On Powles, see J.D. Powles, *New Granada, Its Internal Resources* (London: Baily, 1863), p.31; *ODNB*, M.Deas, *John Diston Powles* (Oxford UP, 2004); C. Richardson, *J. D. Powles* (London, 1854).

20. Bishop John Hynes, *Diary*, 21 June 1850, Goold Archive, Melbourne, B. Condon (ed.).

21. Bishop James Goold, *Diary*, 6 July, 1851, Goold Archive, Melbourne, B. Condon (ed.).

CHAPTER TEN

1. *Limerick Reporter*, 16 April 1852.

2. Ville de Paris, 1st Arrondisement, Register 200, No 155, Deaths 1852, f. 184; TNA, Miscellaneous British Military and Foreign Death Returns, 1846–52, RG 35/11, 184. The five-yearly French census returns, including 1851, were destroyed in the siege of Paris, 1871, with many public records. Absence of clerical title may reflect French secular administration, his 'citizen dress' or relative anonymity. His falling sick at Le Havre, Bordeaux or elsewhere is not recorded in British Legation or Consulate papers, TNA, FO 561, 1851–2 (Thomas Pickford, Consul General in Paris). His body seems to have been buried in France, but evidently not in any of the big four Paris cemeteries.

3. *Limerick Examiner*, 14 April 1852, and *Morning Post*, London, 19 April. The *Examiner* called John 'eldest brother', the *Reporter* 'only surviving brother'. TNA holds John's service record in the [Royal in 1867] Irish Constabulary: '4512, John McNamara [sic], RC, labourer, Clare' recruited January 1841, aged 22, 5'11" tall and recommended by Thomas Blood. He served in Roscommon, Cavan and Cork before his posting to Limerick City, May 1851. No marriage, resignation, pension, or death were recorded, through 'lack of diligence' advises Sgt Paul Maher of the Garda Museum, Dublin. John was 5/6 years younger than Eugene. Thomas Blood, Esq., Roxton House, Corofin, owned property in Kilnaboy (CI) parish, Corofin, and evidently knew John, possibly as the family landlord. Kilnaboy included Bawnkyle townland, where Mary Macnamara lived (Corofin High Street). Both she and Thomas Blood died before *Griffiths Valuation* of the area, 1855,

which recorded the Blood properties, their (CI) church living in Corofin, and several Macnamaras (one, a John) on High Street.

4. *Limerick Reporter*, 16 April, and *Standard*, London, 19 April 1852. Mexican consul in Paris, Guillermo O'Brien, had helped bondholders negotiate with Aberdeen in 1846: *Los Primeros Consulados de México, 1823–72*, (Secretaría de Relaciones Externos; 1974), pp.30, 42.

5. John Hynes, *Diary*, p.332, 8 May 1853, Cork; *Clare Journal*, obituary, 22 August 1853, 'Mrs Macnamara, relict of the late Mr James Macnamara, after a lingering illness'. The *London Gazette*, 5 February 1856, called for claim or forfeit of money advertised in British Guiana,1849 and 1850, £296 owed to William Clancy [d. 19 June 1847] and £126 owed to Eugene Macnamara [d. 19 Jan. 1852]. Dollar and *peso* had parity, at 4 to the £sterling, while the franc hovered around 25 to the pound. £48,000 cash was available. Macnamara's silver mining wealth is credible: Mexican production totalled $30 million in 1850 in a silver, gold and mercury mining boom, through improved techniques, British investment, and exported New Almaden mercury. Consul MacKintosh added the Real del Monte company to five major mine portfolios in 1850, but his failed ventures forced him to sell everything, including his Consulate: B. Tennenbaum, 'Merchants, Money and Mischief', *The Americas*, 35, 3, January 1979, pp.317–339; Rosa M Meyer, 'Los Ingleses en Mexico, Casa Manning y MacKintosh', *Historias* [Mexico], 1986, 13, pp.57–71. He may even have loaned Macnamara money or shares to hide them from creditors, and almost certainly advised him. Kelly Kerbow Hudson of University of Texas at Austin kindly verified that no correspondence with or about Macnamara is indexed in the Manning and MacKintosh archive there. In 1847–8, Frémont and a key witness, John Baldwin, vouched that Macnamara lived at MacKintosh's consulate or at the embassy. At least fifteen UK newspapers reported Macnamara's death and seven carried the *Limerick Examiner's* report of Crown Solicitor Murphy's visit to Paris from Limerick. After Murphy's death, 1873, his son became a law partner with Thomas Kenney. Any copy of the will left with a French notary probably perished in the siege fires of Paris May, 1871; any copy sent to Dublin for Probate, evidently perished with other Irish wills in the Troubles, 1916–23. That it was in Spanish means a notarial copy may still exist in Mexico City.

6. *London Daily News*, 21 October 1852, had the widest coverage.

7. K.A. Miller, *Emigrants and Exiles* (Oxford: OUP, 1985); D.H. Akenson, *The Irish Diaspora, A Primer* (Toronto, 1993); J. Fox, 'Researching The Gold Rush Irish', *California Territorial Quarterly*, 30, 1997, pp.10–11, 52–60; 'Journal of Thomas Kerr', *CHSQ*, 7, 17, September 1928, pp.205–277; J. King, *The Uncounted Irish* (Toronto, 1990); L. Bisceglia, *Irish Identity in the Mother Lode: the Hibernian Benevolence Society, Columbia, Ca.,* (Boston, Mass.: Northeastern University, 1986); P.J. Blessing, *West Among Strangers*, PhD thesis (UCLA, 1977), on the Sacramento and Los Angeles Irish.

8. S.C. Hall, *Ireland* (London: How & Parsons, 1841), Vol. II, pp.239–44, on gold-mining in Wicklow. Hall's father, Col. F. Hall, was a mining engineer. Cemeteries throughout the Sierra Nevada record miners from Wicklow and Tipperary.

9. 'California Letter' collections actually from California: McGiffert (Down) from El Dorado and Sacramento, 1851–3, in private hands; Gamble (Down) from Placer and Calaveras, 1850–55, in private hands; Williamson (Armagh) from Placerville and Monterey, 1850–53, PRO Northern Ireland; Hurley brothers (Cork) from California and Nevada, 1870–1938, Cork Archive. Denis and Michael Hurley of Clonakilty were this writer's great uncles. Professor Kerby Miller, University of Missouri-Colombia, kindly afforded the information.

To these should be added 106 letters at All Hallows missionary college, Dublin, from Bishop Eugene O'Connell of Marysville, California.

10. M.K. Ombaum, *William Clarke's Journal, 1849*, pub. Colusa County Library, California; Colusa County *Deaths and Inquests Book*, 1873.

11. R. and F. Rohrbacher, 'The Fenian Brotherhood in Northern California,1858–75', *California Territorial Quarterly*, 27, Fall, 1996, pp.35–46, and 28, Winter 1996, pp.15–24.

12. Isaac Hartmann, *Brief in Mission Cases* (1852), pp.63–5, Bancroft Pamphlets on New Almaden, Volume 3, 35. Pío Pico was sick, perhaps with a pituitary tumour affecting growth and shape: I. and J. Login, 'Governor Pico, Monster No More', *Pituitary*, 13, 2010, pp.80–86.

13. Letter from Los Angeles, 12 September 1857, Henry D. Burrows to *San Francisco Bulletin*, interviewing Castañares just after the latter's perjury in support of the bogus Limantour claim: Burrows et al., *Memorial and Biographical History of The Coast Counties of Central California* (Chicago: Lewis, 1893), pp.41–44; J. Forster, *Memoir* (1878), Bancroft Mss, 68, 99c, pp.63–5.

14. E. Galindo, *A Puntos para la Historia de California* (1877), Bancroft Mss CD 172.

15. *San José Pioneer*, 17 April 1879, Thomas Lancey (1824–85), remembering 1846.

16. J.R. Browne, *Sketch of the Settlement and Expansion of Lower California* (San Francisco: Bancroft, 1869), p.45; W.M. Gwin, J.C. Frémont, and others, *Memorial of the Senators and Representatives Elect from California Requesting the Admission of California into the Union, 31 Congress, 1st Session, 13 March and 18 March 1850, Senate Misc. Doc 68, House of Representatives Misc. Doc. 44.*

17. N. Botello, *Annales del Sur,* (1875), Bancroft Mss CD 49, 134.

18. A. Coronel, *Cosas de California* (1877), Bancroft Mss CD 61, 69.

19. H. Quigley, *The Irish Race in California* (San Francisco: Roman, 1878), pp.210, 216–19.

20. H.H. Bancroft, *History of California, 1846–8* (San Francisco: The History Company, 1886), Vol.5, pp.215–223.

21. Z. Engelhardt, *Missions and Missionaries of California* (San Francisco: Barry, 1908–1915), Vol.IV, pp.548–50, took from Bancroft that Pico had 'fraudulently backdated'.

22. *The Boston Pilot,* editor John Boyle O'Reilly, Fenian activist, *A Proposed Irish Settlement in California* syndicated, 22 April, 1887, in the *New Zealand Tablet*, XIV, 52, 18 (no connection with *The Tablet* of London and Dublin), edited by Bishop Moran of Dunedin, a voluble Irish controversialist; P.F. Stevens, *The Rogues March and The St Patrick's Battalion* (London: Brassey's, 1999), p.282.

23. J.C. Frémont, *Memoirs of My Life*, Vol.1, (Chicago: Belford Clarke, 1886), pp.545–547, 553–554. (Volume II not published). Volume I and his posthumous account in *The Century*, 41, 6, April 1891, show that he and his wife, Jessie, struggled to the grave to make 1846 palatable and coherent. The secrets of small fish in a large pond, overlapped with those of government. 'Protect the General's memory' Jessie begged *The Century's* editor as she and he collated Frémont's last drafts and notes, her husband's and her father's memory both at stake.

Select Bibliography

ARCHIVES

All Hallows College, Dublin, *John Hynes Correspondence* (*BG: British Guiana*).

All Souls College, Oxford, *Vaughan Papers*, (*Doyle and Bankhead Correspondences*).

Archivo General de La Nacion, Mexico City, (*Gobernacion, Caja 4*, 1845–46, *El Proyecto Macnamara.*)

Archivo Nacional Historico de Chile, Santiago (*Fondo Ministero del Interno*, 78, 4, 3–5, October 1848).

Bancroft Library, University of California, Berkeley, (*Bandini Mss; Vallejo Papers; Legislative Record Vol.4; Moreno Papers*).

British Library, Add Mss 43170 and 43064, *Lord Aberdeen Correspondence.*

Clare County Library and Local Studies Centre, Ennis, Ireland.

Georgetown RC Cathedral Archive, Guyana.

Irish College (former), Paris, Archive Online, (*Registers*).

Irish College, Rome, Archive Online, (*Cullen Papers, British Guiana Supplement*).

The National Archive (TNA), London, (Foreign Office) FO 5; FO 16; FO 203; FO 204; FO 207; FO 331; FO 415; (Colonial Office) CO 111; CO 112; (Admiralty) ADM 52; ADM 53; (Deaths Abroad) RG 35/11.

Santa Bárbara Mission Archive, California.

US State Department, (Microcopy 97 Roll 13), *Despatches from Special Ministers to Secretary of State 1843–47* (Parrott, Mexico, to Buchanan, Washington, complete four despatches August 1845, otherwise edited or omitted in W.R. Manning, *Diplomatic Correspondence of The United States*, VIII, Mexico 1831–48, (Washington: Carnegie, 1937).

Warwickshire Record Office, Warwick, UK, *Seymour Papers* (Admiral Seymour, CR 114A).

NEWSPAPER ARCHIVES (INCLUDING DIGITAL RESOURCES)

Illustrated London News (Oxford City Public Library, hard copy), 8 November 1845, 13 February 1847, 15 December 1849.

Latin American Newspapers Part I and Part II, 1805–1922, Mexican and Chilean newspapers.

British Newspapers Online

Limerick Examiner, 14 April 1852; *Limerick Reporter*, 16 April 1852; *Morning Post* (London), 19 April 1852; (London) *Standard*, 19 April 1852; *London Daily News*, 21 October 1852.

Royal Demerara Gazette 1841–44.
The Century, 41, (6), April 1891, Jessie Benton Frémont and John Charles Frémont (deceased), The Conquest of California.
The London Gazette, 5 February 1856.
The Tablet (London) Archive, 1841–44.
The Times (London) Archive (notably 6 August and 24 September 1845).

HISTORY PERIODICALS
Archivium Hibernicum
California History (formerly *California Historical Society Quarterly*)
California Territorial Quarterly
Historias [Mexico]
Irish Historical Studies
Irish Migration Studies in Latin America
Southern California Quarterly
Southwestern Historical Quarterly

OFFICIAL TRANSCRIPTS
B Condon, *Bishop John Hynes' Diary*, (Melbourne Archdiocese Historical Commission, 2002 Not Online)
Hansard, (Parliament), Series 3, 78, 7 March 1845; 88, 24 August 1846.
New Almaden Mine, US vs Castillero, Case 366, Appeal 420, 4 Volumes, (San Francisco, A Peachey, F. Billings *et al.* 1852–61).
US Senate Committee Report 75 (30th Congress, 1st Session), March 1848, Frémont's *California Claims* and Appendix, Macnamara dossier confiscated in California.

SECONDARY SOURCES
Bancroft, H.H., *History of California*, III 1825–40, IV 1840–45, V 1846–48.
Biographical Sketch of William B. Ide (Claremont: Subscribers, 1880).
Boyle, P., *The Irish College, Paris* (Dublin: Gill, 1901).
Chaffin, T., *et al.*, *Correspondence of James K. Polk*, Vols IX–X (Tennessee UP, 1996, 2004).
Connolly, S.J., *Priests and People in Pre-Famine Ireland, 1780–1845* (Dublin: Gill, 1982).
Costeloe, M.J., *Generals Santa Anna and Paredes y Arrillaga in Mexico, 1841–3* (Bristol UP, 1989).
Costeloe, M.J., *Bonds and Bondholders: British Investors in Mexico's Foreign Debt, 1824–88* (Westport CT.: Praeger, 2003).
Costeloe, M.J., *Bubbles and Bonanzas: British Investments in Mexico, 1827-1900* (Lanham, MD.:, Lexington Books, n.d.).
Cushner, N.P., *Why Have you Come Here?: The Jesuits and the Evangelisation of Native America* (OUP USA, 2006).
Forbes, A., *History of Upper and Lower California* (London: Smith and Elder, 1839).
Frémont, J.C., *Memoirs of My Life* (Chicaco: Belford Clarke, 1886).
Hackel, S.W., *Alta California, Peoples in Motion* (Berkeley: CUP, 2010).
Harlow, N., *California Conquered: The Annexation of a Mexican Province, 1846–50* (Berkeley: CUP, 1982).
Karam, M., *Elusive Entrepreneur: Macnamara's California Land Grant* (Dissertation, University of San Francisco, 1967).

Kay, H.A. (ed.), *Journal of Lt Somerville, RN* (Edinburgh: Pentland, 1986).

Lake, A., *Colonial Rosary, The Spanish and Indian Missions of California* (Ohio UP, 2006).

Lord Aberdeen, Texas y California (Archivo General de La Nación, Publicación 15, 1925).

Manning, W.R., *Diplomatic Correspondence of the United States*, Vols V–VIII (Washington: Carnegie, 1935–37): Great Britain, Chile, France and Mexico 1831–48.

Murphy, I., *Diocese of Killaloe in the Eighteenth Century* (Blackrock: Four Courts, 1991).

Murphy, I., *Diocese of Killaloe, 1800–1850* (Blackrock: Four Courts, 1993).

Murphy, I., *Diocese of Killaloe 1850–1904* (Blackrock: Four Courts, 1995).

Murphy, I., *Before the Famine Struck: Life in West Clare 1834–45* (Dublin: Irish Academic Press, 1996).

Murphy, I., *A Starving People: Life and Death in West Clare 1845–51* (Dublin: Irish Academic Press, 1996).

Nelson, E.C., *A Man Who Can Speak of Plants:Thomas Coulter* (Dublin: E.C. Nelson, 1994).

Quaife, M.M., *Diary of James K. Polk, 1845–49*, 4 Vols, (Chicago: McClurg, 1910).

Salomon, C.M., *Pio Pico, Last Mexican Governor of California* (Oklahoma UP, 2010).

Salvucci, R.J., *Politics, Markets and Mexico's 'London Debt' 1823–87* (Cambridge UP, 2009).

Solares, Robles & de La Torre, *Correspondencia de José Maria Mora 1847-8* (Mexico: Inst. Mora, 2001).

Swords, L., *The Irish French Connection, The Irish College, Paris* (Paris: Irish College, 1978).

Zemke, C., *Stephen C. Rowan and The US Navy*, Ph.D. Thesis (Utah UP, 2012).

Index

Map and Plate references in **Bold**